The spatiality and temporality of urban violence

Manchester University Press

The spatiality and temporality of urban violence

Histories, rhythms and ruptures

Edited by

Mara Albrecht and Alke Jenss

MANCHESTER UNIVERSITY PRESS

Published by Manchester University Press
Oxford Road, Manchester M13 9PL

www.manchesteruniversitypress.co.uk

British Library Cataloguing-in-Publication Data
A catalogue record for this book is available from the British
Library

ISBN 978 1 5261 6573 2 hardback
ISBN 978 1 5261 9562 3 paperback

First published 2023
Paperback published 2026

EU authorised representative for GPSR:
Easy Access System Europe – Mustamäe tee 50,
10621 Tallinn, Estonia
gpsr.requests@easproject.com

Typeset by Newgen Publishing UK

In loving memory of Wolfgang Albrecht (1950–2022)
for his everlasting encouragement and support.

Contents

List of figures

Contributors

Mara Albrecht (University of Erfurt)

Jutta Bakonyi (Durham University)

Andreas Bolte (University of Freiburg)

Alke Jenss (Arnold Bergstraesser Institute Freiburg)

Shrey Kapoor (Cornell University)

Christian Laheij (Max Planck Institute for Social Anthropology, Halle)

Christine Mady (Aalto University)

Roberto Mazza (Independent Scholar)

Niall Ó Dochartaigh (University of Galway)

Hannes Warnecke-Berger (University of Kassel)

Klaus Weinhauer (University of Bielefeld)

Foreword

Niall Ó Dochartaigh

The wellspring for this innovative and ambitious volume is a linked pair of interdisciplinary panels on violence and the city at the annual conference of the European Consortium for Political Research (ECPR) in Hamburg in 2018. Organised by the editors of this volume, Mara Albrecht and Alke Jenss, with colleagues Jutta Bakonyi and Kirsti Stuvøy, the two panels were part of a larger section organised by the ECPR standing group on political violence. Those two panels were very much in tune with the spirit of the standing group, characterised as they were by a deeply rooted interdisciplinarity, diverse and innovative methodological approaches and a commitment to locating the study of political violence in broader theoretical debates in the social sciences and humanities. Their focus on theories of space and time resonated too with an earlier book based on contributions to the ECPR conference: *Political Violence in Context: Time, Space and Milieu* (Bosi, Ó Dochartaigh & Pisoiu 2015).

The work begun in those panels was further developed at a workshop at the University of Erfurt in December 2018 on 'Histories and Rhythms of Urban Violence' organised by those four colleagues who had convened the panels at the ECPR. The organisers took the opportunity to draw several more contributors on board and created an energising and stimulating atmosphere. The workshop was a model of its kind and over those two and a half days in Erfurt there was a productive cross-pollination of ideas as the arguments were refined. The theoretical implications of the wide array of case studies were teased out and contributors gained a strong mutual awareness of the nuances of each other's cases and arguments. The value of that workshop is evidenced in the strong thematic continuities between the chapters and in the powerful overarching vision provided by editors Mara Albrecht and Alke Jenss in their introduction.

The volume is marked out above all by the theoretical ambition of the editors whose introduction offers a rich and stimulating reflection on the ways in which theoretical perspectives on space and time can illuminate the specificities of urban violence. It offers a sophisticated analysis of the rhythms and temporalities of urban violence and the spatial configurations of urban violence that enhances theoretical understandings of spatiotemporalities. It is all the more impressive because it synthesises insights that have emerged across such a wide range of disciplines. The book is much more than the sum of its parts, largely because the introduction so effectively draws out the insights from the numerous cases and provides, as the editors put it, both a mapping and a clocking of violence in the city.

One of the reasons those initial panels in Hamburg and the conversations at the workshop in Erfurt were so productive was the diversity of academic backgrounds among the participants, encompassing history, sociology, political science, anthropology, urban design and architecture. The participants brought with them expertise in widely varying cases, across different time periods and examined widely differing forms of political mobilisation and violence; from labour strikes and rioting through gang violence, vigilantism, insurgency and civil war. The focus on time and space provided a powerful analytical lens through which disparate cases were brought into sharp focus, unified by the many common aspects of violence in urban settings. Among the themes that stand out are: the role of past violence in the maintenance of spatial boundaries and in the labelling of districts and streets as safe or dangerous, bad or good; the spatialisation of identities; and the linking of security and safety with the built environment at the smallest scale – in the shelter offered by an entrance, a shop or an alleyway. The historical depth of many of the case studies allows for the excavation of 'temporal layers' and brings out with great clarity the imbrications of the local and global and the spatial dimensions of memory and remembering. It is especially impressive to see the way in which archival sources that offer detailed accounts of urban violence have been so effectively mined for the insights they offer on the rhythms and spatialities of violence.

As the authors point out, violence changes perception of urban space and time. While war is raging time seems to speed up as weeks are packed into hours. And local spaces in times of violent conflict become much more densely packed with meaning even as their most trivial material features take on a new importance and urgency: the blind alley, the unlocked door that offers passage to safety, the high rooftops from which observers can survey and dominate the ground below.

This book makes a major contribution to our understandings of urban space and violence and succeeds magnificently in demonstrating the value of spatiotemporality as an analytical tool for understanding violence in cities. It puts us in the debt of editors Mara Albrecht and Alke Jenss who have drawn together such a diverse but coherent and illuminating collection of essays.

Acknowledgements

The editors would like to thank the Studies for SpatioTemporality Erfurt group for generously financing a workshop on 'Histories and Rhythms of Urban Violence: Global-local Encounters in the Nexus of Space and Time' in December 2018, organised by Dr. Mara Albrecht (Erfurt), Dr. Jutta Bakonyi (Durham), Dr. Alke Jenss (Freiburg) and Dr. Kirsti Stuvøy (Akershus) which this volume is based on. For supporting this workshop, we also thank the Forum for the Study of the Global Condition, founded by the universities of Leipzig, Halle-Wittenberg, Jena and Erfurt in Germany. Finally, we thank the Durham Global Security Institute for support for the workshop and bearing the copy-editing costs. We are very grateful for Penny Krumm's thoughtful copy-editing and for Johanna Unewisse's help with the index.

A part of the editing of this volume was conducted during a fellowship of one of the editors at the Humanities Center for Advanced Studies 'Religion and Urbanity: Reciprocal Formations', funded by the Deutsche Forschungsgemeinschaft (DFG, German Research Foundation) – FOR 2779.

Introduction: Sites of violence, entangled in space and time

Mara Albrecht and Alke Jenss

Urban violence

Historically, violence has been a regular feature of cities, sometimes even becoming part of the everyday. Moreover, the physical and socio-spatial making and remaking of cities are often facilitated through violence. However, violence is not something exogenous that enters the city from 'outside'; cities have their own contradictions and tensions, and thus, urban space intrinsically has a potential for violence (see Pavoni and Tulumello, 2020; Pullan et al., 2013). Violence not only occurs *in* the city, it is *of* the city (Fuccaro, 2016). Specific characteristics of cities – such as their population density, heterogeneity and spatial proximity of different groups as well as divisions along social, ethno-national, or religious lines – produce violence. These divisions are mirrored in the urban space and can become 'urban frontiers' (Pullan, 2011) at which collective violent actors clash with security forces or with each other. Moreover, different forms of violence can be associated with the urban rather than with the rural context. Riots as a consequence of 'contentious politics' (Tilly and Tarrow, 2012), as in the context of Orange parades in Belfast, are one of the most striking examples that occur almost exclusively in larger cities. Moreover, gang violence, collective violence related to 'hooliganism' after large sports events and ethno-national or sectarian violence connected to contested or symbolic spaces are specific to the urban environment. It seems that life in cities has its own spatial dynamics and its own temporal rhythms, which enable and generate violence, often in successive waves.

The intrinsic connection between space, time and violence in cities is the main theme of this book. The volume contributes specifically to literature on the significance of time in, and the temporalities of, violence, including historical approaches, in contrast to much existing literature on urban violence, which focuses on a contemporary imaginary of 'violent cities' alone. The focus on spatialities of violence is more established in geographical research and urban studies, but frequently less visible in studies on violence.

For this volume, it implies attention to spatial and scalar relations, as well as translocal connections. Finally, this book is strongly interdisciplinary. Its approach is not limited to urban geopolitics, urban sociology, the anthropology of violence, or the history of conflicts in cities, but unites these disciplinary perspectives on the space and time of urban violence.

Talking about urban violence means talking about violence that is produced and shaped by urban characteristics and that in turn transforms the urban. *Urban*, however, is a term that is broadly used yet not well defined (Pavoni and Tulumello, 2020: 49–50). We understand it to mean the physical built environment of a city as well as the symbolic meaning inscribed in the city-space, but also the complex relationships of its inhabitants and their 'way of life' or their 'rhythms of life'. This is a processual understanding of the urban, rather than seeing 'the city' simply as the backdrop to or environment of violent practices (see Pavoni and Tulumello, 2020). Additionally, cities have played a crucial role in the histories of empires and in the violent processes of state formation and nation-building (Fuccaro, 2016: 8; Tilly, 2010). This is intimately linked to their frequent presentation as focal points for social, political and cultural developments within a society, for contemporary moves towards the internationalisation of rule, and as centres for economic power. Cities have been understood as hubs of global flows and networks, where modernity's acceleration and 'progress' crystallise most clearly. With their skyscrapers of glass and steel, they epitomise imaginaries of human civilisation and the triumph of technology and capitalism. Conversely, cities are also often seen as the apex of present-day inequality and insecurity (Body-Gendrot, 2012; Davis, 1990; Müller and Feth, 2011), having deprived millions of people of their 'right to the city' (Lefebvre, 2016). We agree that parts of cities have frequently become insecure and difficult to navigate, if not outright violent spaces. Insecurity is highly selective, however, and vulnerability to urban violence is significantly higher for those who experience other vulnerabilities as well, along categories of difference such as class, race, gender or belonging to a religious minority group (cf. Alves, 2018; Amar, 2013; Kern and Mullings, 2013; LeBrón, 2020).

Nevertheless, until a few years ago, urban violence was only a minor subject within the field of urban studies and other academic disciplines focused their studies of violence on other objects, in particular the nation-state. While the state per se is undoubtedly a violent actor on many different levels, state-centred accounts often suppress subaltern and alternative forms of resistance and activism that are generated by the city as a 'social order of parts' (Fuccaro, 2016: 9). By now, urban violence has become a ubiquitous topic in some disciplines, but remains neglected in others (Koonings and Kruijt, 2007; Moncada, 2015). Few dispute that violence is a pressing problem in modern cities and that it has a significant impact on the security and livelihood of urban dwellers. It is a highly relevant topic as such; in fact, international organisations and observers are increasingly anticipating that conflictual urban relations will shape our future (see Felbab-Brown, 2016). Yet there are more reasons why cities themselves have become prominent in studies on conflict and violence, in conjunction with a lesser focus on nation-states as sites of struggle. *Conflict*, it seems, has become urbanised – even if we should not neglect the rural–urban continuities of violence, and the rural sites of conflict that we encounter, for instance, when paying attention to contemporary, often highly violent land-grabbing processes with intricate spatial and territorial effects (see Ballvé, 2012; Way, 2021). In any case, much scholarly work has recently aimed at disentangling and analysing the more concrete causes and effects of violence in cities. Attention in conflict studies, geography, history and the sociology of violence has shifted from states to cities (Agnew, 2003), particularly in the attempt to give the everyday practices of ordinary citizens in contexts of violence a more prominent role in analyses, instead of focusing on the macro-structural questions of conflict.

When we talk about *violence*, we generally consider it as a social practice and a power-based action that purposefully leads to physical injuries of others by individual or collective actors (Popitz, 1986). And while it is the base of institutional power and hence an instrument to create order, it also enables people to bring about political and social change. Violence has a central role in processes of social order formation, (re-)production and transformation. It can also be instrumental for communitarisation and the formation of collective identities. The term 'violence' covers a large number of different phenomena and we are well aware of debates around what constitutes violence and what doesn't, which also changes according to the historical, political and cultural context. The broad definitions of violence that were promoted by prominent scholars in the late twentieth century, particularly 'structural violence' (Galtung, 1975), 'symbolic violence' (Bourdieu, 1977) and 'normative violence' (Butler, 2004) drew attention to serious social problems. In this volume we adopt a definition of violence that primarily refers to social, direct and physical activity, but does not neglect the symbolic and structural dimensions of urban violence in their interconnectedness with space and time (see Penados et al., 2022; Mabin, 2014; Alves, 2018). In this contribution, we concentrate on the forms, modalities and practices of violence utilised by social actors. To this effect, von Trotha (1997: 20–2) suggests applying Geertz's theoretical-methodical concept of 'thick description' to the study of violence to direct attention to how violence is used. We also largely focus on collective and state violence (Tilly, 2003), although we do not exclude the occasional glance towards individual acts of violence within a larger context of collective violence.

As we have already highlighted, violence is something intrinsic to the urban and its spatiotemporal qualities, which enable and shape violence. The messiness of cities, however, does not necessarily result in physical violence. Present-day urbanism may involve selective feelings of fear and insecurity for many, yet privilege for others. This volume mainly focuses on spatiotemporal practices of urban violence, as we believe violence to be a major trigger for spatial and temporal reconfigurations of cities. However, some chapters also look into non-violent forms of protest (e.g. strikes; see the chapters in this volume by Weinhauer and Albrecht) and measures by the state to regulate settlement, movement and security, which are coercive and constitute structural or symbolic violence, but do not always include physical violence (see, for example, the chapters by Kapoor and Jenss). Without doubt, urban space – and time, as we argue – plays a significant role in conflict transformation processes and practices of peaceful coexistence (Megoran and Dalby, 2018). In this regard, Nick Megoran (2011) criticises the lack of engagement with peace in the study of political geography. Nevertheless, we concentrate on (physical) violence here, to highlight its impact on urban space-time transformations, an aspect that has not been researched from an interdisciplinary perspective.

There is no consensus on what constitutes *urban violence*, and our understanding is a broad one, encompassing different forms of violence: civil wars involving conventional armies and/or irregular combatants, violent insurgencies against the state or colonial powers, riots (including violent political demonstrations, sectarian and ethno-national violence, food riots, etc.), gang violence and other forms of violent organised crime. Moreover, we purposefully include urban representations of violence as a category in this volume, with a particular focus on memories of violence. Although the memory of violence is itself not a violent act, its performance in (contested) urban space and at specific times in accordance with a political and/or religious calendar frequently generates renewed violence, often in forms that have themselves become ritualised over time (Albrecht, 2021). From a spatiotemporal perspective, memories of violence have great potential for the study of urban violence, as they are inscribed in urban space, have a transtemporal (and sometimes also translocal) dimension and are connected to the rhythms of a city.

Violence, space and the city

Since the spatial turn in the humanities and social sciences (Bachmann-Medick, 2016: 211–43; Massey, 1991; Massey and Allen, 1994b), various disciplines have produced a growing body of literature on violence from a spatial perspective. While in 2015, Bosi et al. (2015; Ó Dochartaigh, 2015) still saw major deficits in the literature linking space and (political) violence, today, this strand of research has grown decisively, although unevenly. Especially in the field of history, the specific interrelation of violence and the city and the particular characteristics of urban violence only became a topic for historical city studies a few years ago (Weinhauer and Ellerbrock, 2013). In contrast, in geography, violence and spatial theory perspectives have long been at the centre of debate (Gregory, 2006; Springer and LeBillon, 2016).

Different disciplines have approached the topic of violence and its connection with space in successive waves, covering dissimilar areas of focus. Many scholars from the social sciences have focused on violence and insecurity in cities, considering urban space as a mesh of social relations that is not defined by administrative boundaries but rather constitutes a specific context and specific social conditions for urban violence (cf. Bosi et al., 2015). Spatial approaches to (urban) violence constitute much more than simply recognising the unevenness of the distribution of violence. They are also about understanding how the homogeneity of an imagined national territory is an illusion whose destruction becomes most visible only when violent conflict takes place (cf. Ballvé, 2021; Elden, 2013; Ó Dochartaigh, 2015).

Quite concretely (re-)shaping or even fundamentally transforming space, violence can produce urban segregations or create frontiers within the urban as physical and representational divisions of space (Pullan, 2011; Alves, 2018). It can dissect city-space through the building of barriers and reshape urban landscapes in ways that make ordinary inner-city movements a matter of careful, fearful planning and coordination (cf. Colombijn, 2018; Jenss, 2020). Recent literature on violence against gendered bodies goes even further in declaring bodies a territory that is targeted in an everyday war (cf. Gago and Cavallero, 2018). Spatiality in urban violence focuses on the relationality of violence itself, recognising and foregrounding the varied agency of actors involved in acts of physical violence. The patterns of reproduction of violence in areas occupied by specific actors involved in prior violence tell us about the spatiality of unequal social relations and about the potential persistence or recurrent use of abusive and harmful practices in spaces of perpetuated violence (see Laó-Montes and Dávila, 2012; Ó Dochartaigh, 2015; Hobsbawm, 1983).

There is also a significant emerging literature on the idea that cities are simultaneously entangled in dynamics and processes from a sometimes far away 'elsewhere' (Robinson, 2016; Ranganathan, 2018), on the wider geographies of violence (Doel, 2017; Springer and LeBillon, 2016), on the role of translocal networks and connections with regard to urban violence (Kaldor and Sassen, 2020; Freitag et al., 2015; Fuccaro, 2016), on local–global tensions (Tsing, 2005), and on the hybridity that emerges when one takes seriously the global condition of the local (Sassen, 2001).

Geopolitics, urban conflict and scale

While cities have always played an important role in war and conflict throughout human history, warfare has become increasingly urbanised and cities have been progressively militarised in recent decades (Graham, 2004; Graham, 2011). This can be seen both in direct relation to violent conflict, and in ways that are more reminiscent of processes of securitisation, disciplining strategies and the so-called war on terror (Alves, 2018; Gregory, 2006). Cities have been more than simply 'places' of conflict; violence has strong repercussions for the urban infrastructures and the whole urban fabric of a city, particularly in the spaces of living, through wartime destruction, the drying up of supplies, or the cutting off of one neighbourhood from another (Anderson, 2010; Bauman, 2015; Huffschmid, 2015; Koonings and Kruijt, 2007). Beyond numerous studies on the spatiality of urban violence in conflict, a growing literature of urban geopolitics has turned towards scrutinising actual everyday urban practices in contexts of violence rather than focusing only on militaristic undertakings and the effects of urban warfare as such, promoting an understanding of urban geopolitics that 'accounts for the postcolonial, ordinary, domestic, embodied and vertical dimensions in order to better comprehend recent global shifts and their urban challenges' (Rokem et al., 2017: 1). This focus on the domestic, on the micro-practices within long-term contexts of violence, not just during military onslaught, is exemplified in Sara Fregonese's (2020) work on Beirut. She highlights the renegotiation of geopolitical meanings about sovereignty, territory and the nation-state during close-quarter urban warfare and how these meanings have been re-inscribed in urban space. Fregonese simultaneously connects the everyday to the large-scale geopolitics of war in the Middle East and international diplomacy during the Cold War.

This book includes work on cities in both the so-called Global North and Global South, with several chapters explicitly focusing on everyday life in urban conflicts – an important analytical dimension that will be further explored in the individual case studies. With cities as focal points in geopolitical struggles, global politics and everyday urban practices are thus closely enmeshed with one another (cf. Graham, 2004; Ren, 2022). In particular, collective violent actors in cities are connected to global movements, transnational diasporas and translocal networks. Cities, with their population density and heterogeneity, are an ideal physical and social space for politics that strengthen group identities, allow for recruitment, especially among young males, and drive mobilisation for a cause while at the same time fostering processes of othering and segregation (Kaldor and Sassen, 2020: 7–9). In the individual contributions in this book, we particularly focus on global–local entanglements as well as transregional and translocal perspectives, while also exploring similar spatiotemporal micro-practices of urban violence, but these always connect various scales of action. Our interest in scale stems in part from the particular relationship between the spatiality of violence in cities with broader national, regional and global geopolitical processes – conflict at a larger scale, so to speak – and partly from earlier work on the multi-scalar character of political processes (see Jenss, 2019; Tulumello, 2017b). The city provides a unique research perspective on violence, being situated on the meso-level, but also intricately entangled with global politics and translocal networks on a macro-level, while at the same time allowing for an analysis of practices of violence on the micro-level. Spatially, the city can be regarded at different scales, all of them socially constructed and subject to political instrumentalisation (Massey, 1991: 277). It can be seen as a whole, with its centre and its outskirts, on the level of quarters, of neighbourhoods, of streets, squares, individual buildings, or even just parts of buildings including liminal spaces such as attics, basements, rooftops or backyards that can become strategically important during urban conflicts. Cities may grow not only at the periphery, and urban frontiers may also be found within a city centre (Pullan, 2011). Violence tends to be employed in different forms at different scales, and translocal networks and global dynamics may link it to a faraway 'elsewhere'. The scales of action of parties in conflict are contested and shift over time; and violence plays a major role in shaping this scalar reach.

Violence and temporality

Although studies on urban violence from a spatial perspective are in the majority, there is also an emerging body of literature that explores the connection between violence and time, with a particular focus on the ways violence possesses its own rhythm. Physical violence is often attributed with a suddenness, captured in naturalising metaphors: like forces of nature, violence seems to 'erupt' or to 'break out'. This is of course misleading, as violence is a social action and can always be attributed to specific individual and collective actors. However, direct violence is an extreme and sudden social and bodily act that injures and destroys with the inherent aim of eliminating or reducing the options for action of the other(s) at that precise moment in time (see also epilogue by Bakonyi). Despite its suddenness for all involved actors, a violent act is never chaotic but follows sequential patterns (Collins, 2009). When applying this insight to the level of the city, collective forms of violence such as riots do not occur suddenly either, but involve a certain level of coordination among the violent actors (Tilly, 2003: 3). This implies a consideration of the timing of violence with regard to the *when* as well as to the chronological sequence, at least on a minimal level. Furthermore, violence affects and is subject to mobility and movement in (urban) space (Monroe, 2016; Rokem et al., 2018; Villarreal, 2015). Thus, it has a fundamental effect on the temporalities of the everyday. It may trigger accelerations of movement and simultaneously slow down daily rhythms of life, causing immobility or even incarceration (Colombijn, 2018; Jenss, 2020; Lubkeman, 2008). Violence may also appear as a slow process (Kern, 2016; Nixon, 2011; Penados et al., 2022), eventually leading to long-term developments of residential segregation, forced displacements and radical transformations of livelihoods (Auyero et al., 2015).

Violence can be synchronised with the daily, weekly and yearly rhythms of life in a city, being strongly influenced by cycles of day and night, seasonal changes, or even high and low tide in port cities. It can be subject to daily work cycles, triggered by weekly days of prayer when large numbers of people assemble and listen to incendiary sermons, or concentrated on particular dates of the year such as elections, religious holidays or political commemorations. Violence affects and transforms everyday practices (Jenss, 2020; Scheper-Hughes, 1993; Walker, 2010) and can also lead to ruptures of rhythms of daily life. Moreover, it imposes new time regimes on communities in cities – directly, by official and self-imposed curfews, and indirectly, by barriers, boundaries and checkpoints created by armed actors that serve to direct and slow down people's movement (Madariaga, 2006). However, people usually cope with the enforced new time regimes by normalising and integrating these temporal patterns into their daily routines. They not only learn to navigate a city spatially, but also temporally, by accumulating knowledge of *when* it is safe to be *where*.

Another aspect of temporality that is of particular importance for the urban context is memories of violence. These foster social (re-)construction, strengthen community ties and shape the meaning inscribed in places (Makdisi and Silverstein, 2006; Schindel and Colombo, 2014). They are either communicated actively within a society, through commemoration rituals and performative practices, or, especially in the case of trauma, more or less unconsciously in the form of 'postmemory' through (family) stories, images and behaviour – including not talking about the past and avoiding specific places (Hirsch, 2012). Public memories of violence are generally politicised and often re-enacted with militaristic elements, such as parades in military formation and with uniforms. They create a spatial and temporal continuity between the violence of the past and of the present and also project it into the future. Processions, parades and other commemoration rituals in public, especially in contested space, are charged with symbolic meaning and potentially trigger renewed violence (Albrecht, 2021; Björkdahl and Buckley-Zistel, 2016). With their transtemporal dimension – connecting past, present and future – memories of violence can also change the perception of time by contextualising present violence within an imagined or even mythical past or by generating eschatological meaning.

There is a significant body of literature on memories of violence and urban space, especially with regard to deeply divided post-conflict societies. Some studies focus on state-sponsored memorial projects such as museums and memorial centres, which often further reinforce societal rifts (see Baillie, 2012 on Vukovar; Papadakis, 1994 on Nicosia). Others concentrate on alternative grassroot initiatives that challenge official or sectarian narratives and that can be led by different actors including civil society organisations, trade unions or LGBTQ+ movements (see Carabelli, 2018; Carabelli, 2021 on Mostar; Nagle, 2018 on Beirut and Belfast). Other authors in turn tackle memory projects by semi-state or sectarian actors, such as political parties, which promote exclusive narratives of the past through public commemoration rituals and visual memory practices. These include, for example, political posters or graffiti in order to strengthen in-group solidarity and territorial claims to particular areas of a city, often engaging in memory-wars with each other (see Albrecht, 2020; Albrecht and Akar, 2016; Haugbolle, 2012 on Beirut; Rolston, 2003 with regard to political murals in Belfast). Of particular interest are works that study the commemorative landscape of a city, looking at both the top-down interventions and the bottom-up initiatives as they tend to be inscribed on different scales of a city. Elly Harrowell (2015) has studied Osh, Kyrgyzstan, after the ethnic riots of 2010 in this way, juxtaposing the official ideologies concretised in urban space through monuments erected by the municipal government with the non-elite narratives expressed at street-level by the different communities living in the city. She highlights 'that popular memory can resist the hegemonic discourses of memory' (Harrowell, 2015: 207) and that memory is always diverse and complex, consisting not of one unitary narrative but of a plethora of memories and sub-narratives.

Many works particularly focus on how youths in urban post-conflict contexts handle (post-)memories of war and violence in their everyday practices while encountering them inscribed in urban space when traversing the city (Larkin, 2010; Mady, 2018). Pilar Riaño-Alcalá (2006), for example, has highlighted in her study on Medellin, Colombia, how youths make sense of past and present violence by shifting between practices of memory and forgetting, thus developing strategies for daily survival in violent neighbourhoods. Azra Hromadžić (2015) elucidates in her study on Mostar how Croat and Bosnian high school students attend school together but remain divided both physically, by a spatial organisation of the school that limits mingling of the student bodies, and mentally, through different curricula that confer contesting interpretations of the past. Youths' perceptions of violent memories offer insights into how narratives of the past are socially reconstructed and adapted to present circumstances, by following generations who may be born after the violent events but who nevertheless live in city-spaces that function as repositories of past violence.

Other studies concentrate on the interconnectedness of politicised cultural heritage, contested memories and urban space. In the case of Jerusalem, for instance, the recent archaeological excavations of the 'City of David' in the Palestinian neighbourhood of Silwan have been turned into a major Israeli national monument and tourist attraction. With the aim of (re)creating an historical landscape in which a very selective and particular version of the past is inscribed (Yas, 2000), the excavations have become a source of violent conflict between the government-supported settler movement and Palestinian inhabitants. Thus, the very recently developed concept of the 'City of David' as a 'hegemonic ideological and territorial project' (Pullan and Gwiazda, 2009: 36) leads to the spatial and temporal reconfiguration of an entire neighbourhood, which is now connected to a somewhat imaginary distant past and charged with political meaning in the conflict over the status of Jerusalem.

Memory studies discuss the inherent temporal aspect of memories of violence but they seldom analyse them within an explicit urban space-and-time perspective that sufficiently connects both aspects and fully appreciates their transtemporal and often also translocal dimension, such as when connecting diasporas to a faraway, perhaps even imaginary, homeland.

The development of spatiotemporality as a concept and approach

Time and space are basic principles that structure our everyday lives and we generally think of them as absolute, as being independent from the observer, objects and events. Albert Einstein and Hermann Minkowski discovered at the beginning of the twentieth century that this is far from their true nature. Space and time are relative, subject to the position and the movement of observers, who may experience the distance and timing of an event quite differently. The reasoning behind this is that space and time are intrinsically linked with each other: Minkowski termed this 'space-time' in 1908. This means that space and time are actually the same basic 'thing' on a fundamental level, like two sides of one coin. Newer quantum gravitational approaches even go a step further and suggest that space-time does not exist fundamentally but rather emerges from a non-spatiotemporal fundamental structure (Greene, 2004).

Although these insights do not impact the experience of space and time in our everyday lives, the development of the concept of space-time in the natural sciences revolutionised our understanding of reality and has had its impact on philosophy and, to a certain degree, also on social and cultural sciences. With regard to space, Lucien Febvre and Fernand Braudel criticised the idea of a 'container space' as early as the 1920s (Dorsch, 2013) and especially Henri Lefebvre (1991) changed our understanding of space from deterministic to relational, to something that is socially constructed (Rau, 2013). This view was also used with regard to time in 1937 by Pitirim Sorokin and Robert Merton, who introduced the notion of a 'social time', which was taken up again in the early 1990s (Adam, 1990; Adam 1995; Davies, 1990). Time is usually described as a linear, non-reversable flow (although many theoretical physicists argue that while there may be an 'arrow' of the direction of time, its actual 'flow' may well be an illusion created by our consciousness). Our everyday life, however, is normally dominated by daily repetitions and routines, making us experience a rather cyclical form of time, which is also the case for 'ritual times', whether they are religious, personal or commercial (Crang, 2005). Already in the 1970s, German historian Reinhard Koselleck developed his approach of 'time layers', which is concerned with the complexity of time and its perception. He proposes a layering of historical structures since the eighteenth century and assumes an interconnectedness of three principal time qualities: singularities, repetitions and long continuities in which both singular events and repeating structures are embedded (Koselleck, 2000: 19–26). Edward Hall also identifies eight different types of time: sacred, profane, micro scale, synchronised, personal, biological, physical and metaphysical (Hall, 1983: 17). However, a concept of a 'time-practice' or an approach to the 'production of time', analogous to a 'space-practice' or the 'production of space', has not yet been developed (Dorsch, 2013). Massey (1992) strongly criticised the 'binary opposition' of space and time and emphasised the need to overcome this dichotomy and to recognise 'that space and time are inextricably interwoven' (Massey, 1994a: 260–1).

There have only been a few attempts that explicitly aim to bring space and time together as an analytical tool in the social and cultural sciences (see Koch, 2022). Russian philosopher and literary scholar Mikhail Bakhtin (2008) developed the concept of the 'chronotope' (literally: time-place) in 1937 in order to analyse places and times in narrations and how they are interconnected symbolically. Bakhtin showed that each literary genre operates with different configurations of time and space, thereby creating different forms of narration. Although his interest is focused on fiction rather than reality, literature is nevertheless a reflection of contemporary worldviews and human images (Dorsch et al., 2012). Moreover, Lefebvre attempted to complement his own theory of space with time in his late work on rhythmanalysis (2004), which focuses on the rhythms of everyday life in cities but remains conceptually and methodologically vague. Yet he himself wrote in his *Production of Space* that time 'cannot be constructed, but is consumed and exhausted, and that is all. It leaves no traces. It is concealed in space' (Lefebvre, 1991: 95). We believe that there is more to time than just a passive experience and argue that it is indeed constructed, imagined, performed and actively shaped, especially when it is considered together with space.

Geographers Jon May and Nigel Thrift have likewise pointed out that 'time is irrecoverably bound up with the spatial constitution of society (and vice versa)' (May and Thrift, 2001: 3) and propose a balanced time-space analysis of processes of everyday existence and globalisation as well as of notions such as gender, race and ethnicity. Their conceptual approach to the analysis of 'TimeSpace' is based on four assumptions: our sense of time is shaped by natural timetables and rhythms, although some societies are bound up in these rhythms to a lesser degree than others, especially with the advancement of technology; secular or religious systems of social discipline shape and enact our sense of time (e.g. in the monastery, the factory, the office or at home); our sense of time emerges and is altered through time-measuring instruments and technological devices; various texts that provide particular understandings of time shape and regulate our sense of time, e.g. the medieval book of hours (May and Thrift, 2001: 3–5). We consider May and Thrift's contribution as ground-breaking and valuable, particularly since the broad collection of different topics covered in their edited volume shows the applicability and advantages of a spatiotemporal approach.

The wide range of applicability of spatiotemporal research is also demonstrated by the German interdisciplinary research group 'Studies for SpatioTemporality Erfurt' (Bauer and Fischer, 2019; Dorsch and Vinzent, 2018; Gauthiez, 2020; Meyer et al., 2017; Schmolinsky et al., 2019). They acknowledge the difficulty in bringing space and time together in actual research and suggest that only by bringing in a *tertium comparationis* on the methodological level can the supposed 'binary opposition' of space and time be bridged: 'This *tertium* is the agents and practices by which it produces spatiality and temporality, or spatio-temporality' (Dorsch, 2013: 14). In other words, spatiotemporality is always subject to the thinking and acting of (individual and collective) agents, their perceptions, imaginations and habitualisations, bound up in asymmetrical power relations (Dorsch et al., 2012; Mabin, 2014). We expand on these ideas of spatiotemporality by focusing particularly on a specific subject, urban violence. Violence is an actor-based social practice situated in the nexus of space and time and very much shaped by the agent's cultural contexts, worldviews and social position.

Rethinking urban violence through space and time

In our understanding, spatiotemporality is much more of an approach than a defined theoretical concept. We argue that *space-time*, which we use here as a term to express the combined space-and-time perspective, can help us analyse violence in ways that make prominent the intertwinement of spatial and temporal aspects in the urban context. There is a range of characteristics of urban violence that beg for an analysis from a space-time perspective: (1) Over time, spaces are continuously produced and changed by (historical) actors, and violence with its destructive but also generative potential has a strong catalyst effect on the transformation of urban space over the course of long-lasting conflicts; (2) Urban violence is location- and time-dependent and occurs in particular areas of a city and at specific times (e.g. gang violence in defined territories and often at night); (3) The particular urban space-time configuration shapes the concrete practices of violence (e.g. when using backstreets and courtyards for attacks and retreats, when using loose paving stones as weapons, or when timing a protest with potential for riot to the end of a work shift, when large groups of workers are on their way home); (4) Violence changes the rhythms of cities by enforcing new space and time regimes on the population (e.g. through barriers or curfews); (5) Violence possesses its own rhythms that synchronise with, disrupt or transform the rhythms of a city; (6) Different forms of violence are used on different scales of a city and accordingly have different sequential patterns; (7) Violence remains physically and symbolically inscribed in a city on different scales and in different temporal layers even after the end of conflicts (through visual remains, memory practices, etc.).

Thinking about urban violence in the nexus of space and time is of great advantage when studying practices of violence. This perspective fosters a linking of specific forms and practices of urban violence to the spatial configuration, built environment and particular spatio-social organisation of a city. At the same time, it encourages connecting the timing of violence to the rhythms of a city, its everyday life and its patterns of mobility. The space-time perspective makes us pose once again questions that have been asked before, but often separately from each other: How do violent practices influence and how are they themselves influenced by spatial aspects such as specific urban topographies and architectures, open spaces and public places? How are they at the same time interrelated to temporal characteristics of the city, e.g. everyday rhythms of mobility, shifting perceptions of time due to changing economies, specific time periods with their own (accelerated) tempi such as revolution, war or rapid transformation, as well as multiple temporal layers of contested histories and memories of violence inscribed into the city-space? And lastly, to what extent are space and time actants endowed by human actors with the potential to effect urban violence or reshape violent dynamics?

This raises questions about the concrete but not only situational relationship between violence, space and time. The city is associated with particular spatial and social arrangements, such as linearity and density, specific rhythms, e.g. of movement (Lefebvre, 2004; Reid-Musson, 2017), heterogeneous lifestyles and agglomeration effects (Blokland et al., 2015; Choplin and Ciavolella, 2017; Dinzey, 2017; Jaffe and Koning, 2015). Everyday associations of 'modern city' rhythms – vibrancy, fluidity, speed, rapid transformations – are confronted with a solid built environment (Gayer, 2016; Mulíček, Osman and Seidenglanz, 2016), and a multiplicity of urban forms, which imply much greater heterogeneity of social, political and even infrastructural configurations than is usually acknowledged (Lawhon et al., 2017; Simone, 2010). Linear and dense urban spaces, for instance, support the mobilisation and directional movement of large groups of people. They enable forms of violence commonly practiced during riots, such as the destruction of houses or cars. The spatial configurations and rhythms of cities also facilitate specific modes of policing and counterinsurgency measures inherent in urban planning, for example, mass arrests or house searches, or the use of specific technologies, such as water cannons or tear gas, surveillance technologies or profiling (Graham, 2011; Tulumello, 2017a). These policing practices temporally connect practices of colonial rule by difference with contemporary efforts to 'improve' and 'pacify' cities (cf. Ranganathan, 2018).

The heterogeneity of social groups in cities likely results in different perceptions of both space and time, which can lead to contestation over space, violent conflict and even 'urbicide' in attempts to 'restructure' urban space and deliberately decimate or eliminate a city's heterogeneity (Coward, 2009). Violence begs for an analysis through social power relations (Gago, 2015; Menjívar and Walsh, 2017; Laó-Montes and Dávila, 2012) and greatly benefits from an intersectional perspective (Reid-Musson, 2017). Bosi et al. (2015) have made a strong case for studying political violence in context and argue that time, space and milieu influence the patterns and pace of violence. In our view, this includes its historical, cultural as well as spatiotemporal context, because violence is always subject to contemporary worldviews and norms, cultural coding and the particular (urban) space-time in which it is utilised, whether to maintain order or to bring about political or social change. We aim to build on this important work by not only studying violence in the context of space, time or milieu, but from a combined spatiotemporal perspective.

The purpose of this volume is to apply the space-time perspective on urban violence since there is, as of yet, very little work that brings explicit spatiotemporal conceptualisations to bear on phenomena of urban violence, and even less research based on past and present cases from different regions of the world (Latin America, Middle East, North America, South and Southeast Asia, Western Europe), as is the case here. By advancing existing theories of space as well as of time with regard to urban violence, we aim to demonstrate through case studies from different disciplines the various ways in which spatiotemporality can be used as an analytical tool to study violence in cities. We advocate a combined analysis of the spatial and temporal characteristics of urban violence and propose not only a detailed *mapping*, but similarly a *clocking* of violence in the city, in order to ascertain how rhythms of violence are synchronised with other rhythms and how violence disrupts or transforms these rhythms. Moreover, the analysis of practices of remembering violence in urban space allows for insights into the *translocality* and *transtemporality* of memories of violence. We propose to analyse not only the *scales* on which memories are inscribed in urban space but also the *temporal layers*, thereby moving beyond only the past–present–future trisection towards a more complex and multidimensional understanding of time in conjunction with urban space.

A rhythmanalytical approach to urban violence (see the chapters by Jenss and Albrecht) is one way of linking spatial and temporal aspects, as it not only renders visible the frequency and recurrence of violence (sometimes in different forms and shapes) but also facilitates the carving out of spatial rhythms, of the ways in which time relates to the social production of space (Lefebvre, 2004). Again, rhythmanalysis is a methodological (yet also conceptual) tool, one that invites researchers to grasp sensory elements of social transformations (which may be violent) beyond the structural ones (Chen, 2016), and that focuses on how specific, unequal social relations shape the dynamics of everyday practices in the city, linking them to 'the temporalities in which these activities unfold' (Lefebvre, 2004: 88). The researcher, then, is ' "listening out," but he does not only hear words, discourses, noises and sounds; he is capable of listening to a house, a street, a town as one listens to a symphony, an opera. Of course, he seeks to know how this music is composed, who plays it and for whom' (Lefebvre, 2004: 87). Rhythmanalysis is, however, only one possible way to assume a space-time approach.

In this book, we bring together various interdisciplinary attempts at doing this, which integrate different methodological approaches. Weinhauer combines social and cultural historical perspectives with sociological and anthropological research in his analysis on (violent) collective action and social movements in revolutionary contexts and introduces the concept of space- and time-regimes. Mazza uses a micro-history perspective to examine the transformation of space and time through colonial regulations and measures of urban planning and their effects on escalating violence. Kapoor's multi-sited ethnography draws on scholarship in the fields of urban history, geography, anthropology and sociology, while using the concept of space-time to investigate the production of hegemony and dispossession in the context of postcolonial state formation. Warnecke-Berger's comparative analysis of spatial and temporal dynamics of violence is based on political science and sociological approaches and highlights that the mobilisation and organisation of different forms of violence require manipulations of space and time. Building on architecture and urban planning perspectives, Mady applies a combined mapping and temporal layering of violent events in a city over time while using the concept of a palimpsest as an analytical lens. Bolte combines elements from historiography and the sociology of time in his comparative analysis of memories of violence, which he structures along the three temporal dimensions of past, present and future. Laheij's ethnographic contribution explores how a remapping of socio-spatial and temporal configurations is attempted by religious actors in neighbourhoods characterised by violence, thereby re-inscribing the urban landscape with novel spatiotemporal meaning.

Contributions to recent historical debates

This volume includes contributions about manifestations of urban violence in the present and across different phases of history. The historical studies mainly focus on the 1910s to 1930s and partially also on the mid to late nineteenth century. The rationale behind this is the relevance of these time periods for the transformation of urban societies of the Global North and South in the heydays of imperialism, colonialism and nationalism. Consequently, the perceptions and configurations of space and time in cities changed rapidly, especially in the context of social upheaval and organised forms of urban violence.

The late nineteenth and early twentieth centuries were the era of high imperialism and nationalism. The proliferation of empires on a global scale profoundly transformed the dominated territories and especially their larger cities, in which the imperial presence was most dominant. This included measures of urban development, the introduction of new imperial time regimes and spatial and temporal divisions between ethnic and religious groups. Both space and time are categories that feature heavily in recent works of historians of empire but are mostly treated separately (on time see Nanni, 2012; Cazzola et al., 2020; a noteworthy exception is Meyer et al., 2017). A key factor that has been largely neglected thus far is the imposition of new space and time regimes by the imperial powers, reflecting a Northwest-European (especially a British Protestant) time- and work-discipline (Thompson, 1967) combined with Orientalist and paternalist perceptions of 'colonial subjects' (Said, 1981; Doyle, 2016). This colonial attitude was based on the assumption that the European imperial powers represented modernity while the colonised societies were backward and traditional. Although there certainly is not one but 'multiple modernities' (Eisenstadt, 2000), the imperial powers enforced their views and ways in the territories they ruled, particularly concerning bureaucratic procedures, capitalist production and world market-oriented economies, thus imposing their own dominant modernity, including their spatiotemporal imaginations and practices. These found expression first and foremost in cities through intrusive measures of urban planning and changed urban rhythms (see the chapters by Mazza and Albrecht).

In the field of new imperial history, there is a general lack of studies on a meso-level such as cities (von Hirschhausen and Leonhard, 2011). Studies focusing on violence mostly look at wars and measures of counterinsurgency from an imperial macro-perspective. An exception is the work by John Darwin (2009; 2013) as he highlights the interplay of diverse global, geopolitical and local, anti-imperial forces and how they culminated in violent uprisings in India, Ireland and South Africa. While Darwin neglects the deadly implications of colonial rule, other works from the field of postcolonial studies focus on the resistance of local actors and their differentiated impact on colonial rule (see Gopal, 2019; Gott, 2011; Newsinger, 2010). In any case, the majority of studies on imperial violence and anti-colonial uprisings do not examine the violence itself but concentrate on its causes and consequences. A remarkable exception is Kim Wagner's outstanding study on the Amritsar massacre (2019), which meticulously analyses the practices of violence of both sides during the uprising as well as during the preceding riots and the forms of retribution afterwards. While Wagner describes the segregation between Indians and British in the city in detail, he does not fully account for the specific urban dimension of violence. Our volume explicitly pays attention to the spatiotemporal particularities of urban violence, especially in their larger historical contexts. This may offer new impulses for research on violence in modern history, which has thus far mainly regarded cities as a 'stage' on which violence 'happens' (Weinhauer and Ellerbrock, 2013).

Nationalism is an important factor in the violence discussed in some of the case studies in this volume (see the chapters by Kapoor, Bolte, Mazza and Albrecht). Nationalising tendencies of empires led to segmentation processes and conflicts in multi-ethnic societies (von Hirschhausen and Leonhard, 2011: 396). Moreover, in most European-ruled territories, conflicts with the imperial powers developed because nationalist movements were per se also anti-colonial movements and resisted imperial rule in various forms of uprisings and insurgencies. Particularly in the peripheries of empires, rival nationalist movements emerged, based on ethno-religious categories that had been strengthened and politicised by the imperial powers due to their perceptions of the 'other' and policies of divide-and-rule (Anderson, 2008). Communal violence gradually transformed into nationalist and anti-colonial violence and manifested in cities as symbolic centrepoints of contention. The mobilisation of ethnic nationalisms led to the foundation of new nation-states and also contributed to the fall of empires during the upheavals of World War I (Roshwald, 2001).

The global Great War and its aftermath also figures prominently in some of the historical chapters, as it triggered the production of new forms of (urban) violence and intensified transnational and transregional connections, for example through labour union networks. A main consequence of the war was the disintegration of the great European land empires, but it also triggered decolonisation movements and fuelled wars and nationalist uprisings in the territories of the victorious empires. In some larger cities in Europe it led to the formation of revolutionary as well as reactionary social movements, mass strikes and violent riots (see the chapter by Weinhauer). The discussion of violence in postwar societies has long been taken beyond the 'brutalization thesis' (Mosse, 1990) of soldiers affected by battlefield violence, and focuses on the transition period after the war, particularly the ability of the state to uphold the monopoly of violence, pre-existing conflict lines along ethnic groups or social classes, the success of reintegration of veterans in society and the threat of Bolshevik revolution (Edele and Gerwarth, 2015: 5–7). It also has to be considered in a 'longer (temporally) and wider (spatially)' framework of imperial conflict (Gerwarth and Manela, 2014: 787).

In newer research on the First World War, studies from the French 'Annales' school, with their attention to the history of mentalities, and the German 'Alltagsgeschichte' (history of everyday life) shifted the focus towards the individual experiences of the war by soldiers and workers on the home front (Winter and Prost, 2005). This was complemented by works revolving around questions from cultural history and particularly the field of history of memory (e.g. Winter, 2017; Julien, 2010; Verhey, 2000; King, 1998; Winter, 1995; see also the chapter by Bolte). Moreover, there are studies that explicitly use spatial history approaches (e.g. Nübel, 2014) and numerous works on the experiences of the war in individual cities (e.g. Chickering, 2007; Healy, 2004). Recent historical works on World War I are based on various methodological approaches (Cornelissen and Weinrich, 2021: 7) and focus on different world regions, including internationally comparative research and a global history of the war (see Streets-Salter, 2017; Rinke, 2017; Xu Guoqi, 2017; Winter, 2014; Kramer, 2008; for a historiographical overview, see Kramer, 2014). Central to many of these works are transnational and translocal perspectives that highlight the transfer of ideas, knowledge, goods and people, which had an important impact on the formations of violence in the postwar period. However, while there are recent studies on World War I from the perspective of urban history and an increased focus on violence in postwar societies, there is still a lack of works concentrating on spatial (and especially spatiotemporal) practices and memories of explicitly urban violence in colonial and European postwar cities.

The lack of historical studies on practices of urban violence in global and imperial history as well as the history of World War I and its aftermath point to a general problem in historical research. On the one hand, comprehensive works often do not focus on violence at all or mainly look at wars from a macro perspective. Urban violence is also a relatively new topic in historical research on violence, which mostly fails to address its specific urban character. In the field of urban history, on the other hand, the focus is on social and economic history and on urban planning rather than on practices of physical violence and their contextual embeddedness in urban space. The spatial turn in history has led to a proliferation of works that focus on the study of spatial orders over temporal ones, ignoring 'temporal aspects such as succession, sequentiality, diachrony, procedurality, or acceleration … . Space, namely, cannot be understood at all in its complexity if we do not include the factor of time and multiple temporalities' (Rau, 2021: 61). A combined spatiotemporal approach has great potential to provide new impulses for different fields of history as it offers novel perspectives on the study of violence and its connection to the urban character, spatial qualities and rhythms of cities.

Transregional, translocal, transtemporal and comparative perspectives

The contributions in this volume ask how the city, with its specific urban spatiotemporal features, produces and shapes practices and memories of violence and in what ways different forms and acts of violence transform and reshape urban space-time. We specifically apply our analysis to the reciprocal relationship between the global and the local. Processes of city formation, or social and political urban change, in which violence has taken centre stage, may be shaped globally and locally at the same time. We understand globalisation as a historical process that set in long before the actual word 'globalisation' became prominent in the late twentieth century. Globalisation *avant la lettre* already includes the empires of the early modern period, with their close cultural, religious and economic ties (e.g. between the Safavid, Ottoman and Mughal empires), the trade empires of the era of European colonialism and particularly the period of high imperialism in the late nineteenth and early twentieth centuries, with their intra- and trans-imperial interconnectedness and cultural mobility.

The contributions to this volume focus on a variety of contemporary as well as historical cases situated in different world regions, including the Global South and Global North. Cities of the Global South may well be where 'New Urban Worlds' are most clearly observed today (Simone and Pieterse, 2017) as well as where past entanglements are most visible. The volume as a whole thus provides a comparative and cross-regional perspective on cases that have, thus far, not been brought into relation with each other (see Simone, 2010). What common features does a port city like Buenaventura, Colombia, share with Jerusalem in Mandatory Palestine with regard to rhythms of urban violence? In what wider global or imperial frameworks can these rhythms of violence be contextualised? What role does the memory of violence embedded in urban space play in post-civil war Beirut and how does it compare to commemorations that triggered violence in Singapore in the 1920s? How are these memories connected to a distant or imagined past or to a far-away homeland or diaspora?

It is this perspective, which foregrounds comparative and spatiotemporal entanglement aspects, that interested us when editing the book. The idea is to 'think cities from elsewhere' (Robinson, 2016) instead of conflating violence with a specific subset of cities, historical conjunctures or spatial set-ups. Urban violence, for instance, does not only play a role in so-called Southern Cities or in Southern Urbanism. Informality and slums have become a major trope in postcolonial studies that demand to go beyond binary concepts of violent informality/civil formality (Goldstein, 2016; Roy and AlSayyad, 2004; Varley, 2013). The book's treatment of these topics from a space-and-time theoretical perspective differentiates such binaries and may even change the ways in which we think about future cities. New efforts at recognising the 'interconnected and related processes' (Robinson 2016: 18) between different urban contexts, which we find when studying urban violence collectively in a range of different settings, have produced literature 'from the South' (Mabin, 2014; Villarreal, 2021) without exoticising one or the other research site.

Urban studies have long grappled with questions of particularity v. universality, and the calls for 'a methodological strategy for exploring the zone between planetary and particular urbanisms' (Peck, 2015: 169) have become louder. Postcolonial urban studies has not only demanded that research give a 'greater profile to lesser-known cities' (Parnell and Oldfield, 2014: 2; Robinson, 2005), but simultaneously challenged the ideas of where urban innovation takes place, and whether these are specific places opposed to those that suffer more violence and strife. Smart, green cities located in the so-called North and cities plagued by irrational, violent eruptions, located in the South – such simple binaries seem to be largely in the past of urban studies. Critiques of earlier urban theory saw 'the field of urban studies [as] geographically "segmented"' (Peck, 2015: 165) and asked comparative studies to stop assuming universalisms of Northern cities' developments to which Southern cities should aspire. The cases we chose for this volume aim to contribute to complicating such binary and reductionist identifications of places of urban violence and try to stretch across the Global North–South divide (Robinson, 2011; Robinson, 2005) as well as the divide between past and present.

By no means does this book intend to provide a systematic comparison between cities that are each unique in their own way. The different case studies serve as examples for the various ways the space-time approach can be applied in circumstances with very different historical, cultural and political contexts. In so doing, a comparative perspective makes it possible to highlight similarities across time and space, thereby breaking up the supposed opposition of Global North v. South as well as countering arguments that 'new wars' and conflicts are fundamentally different from past violence (Kaldor, 2012; Kaldor and Sassen, 2020; Münkler, 2002). Our historical chapters show that violence is not essentially 'different' now from the past, and the 'new' wars only seem new from a narrow perspective on Europe and North America during the twentieth century. At the same time, the volume offers insights into which specific spatiotemporal configurations produce particular forms of violence or exceptional memory practices that significantly differ from other contexts. Rokem et al. (2017) have emphasised that urban geopolitics are mostly studied by comparing similar cases from the Global North without appropriate attention to local contexts. They argue for a rethinking of 'current theoretical "categories" and "labels" attributed to cities, based on empirical research in a wide range of urban areas representing radically different visions and division patterns' (Rokem et al., 2017: 13). McFarlane has also emphasised the advantages of comparative thinking as 'a strategy firstly for revealing the assumptions, limits and distinctiveness of particular theoretical or empirical claims, and secondly for formulating new lines of inquiry and more situated accounts' (McFarlane, 2010: 726). This reflection on established theoretical claims, empirical categories and general labels used in urban research is an important point we aim to achieve with the contributions in this book as well, adding also an historical-anthropological self-reflection of the researcher's own cultural and historical background, which severely limits one's abilities to think outside conventional parameters.

What is more, when dealing with violence and death, we as researchers must reflect on how to represent this violence in our studies without analytically rehearsing or reprising it. How do we define, categorise and label it and what gives us any authority to do so? What is our responsibility in writing about violence? Katherine McKittrick (2014) has emphasised this problem in the context of writing about anti-Black violence, especially when working with archival records that provide us only with numbers about dead bodies. This easily leads to a reproduction of 'knowledge about black subjects that renders them less than human. It is a descriptive analytics of violence'(McKittrick, 2014: 18). McKittrick therefore calls for a 'commitment to acknowledging violence and undoing its persistent frame, rather than simply analytically reprising violence'.

A comment on the multi- and interdisciplinarity of this volume

In order to thoroughly study the interconnectedness of space, time and violence in the city, we strongly believe that a detailed, multi- and interdisciplinary analysis of different past and present cases of urban violence in various world regions is indispensable. Space-time in its conjunction must be employed as an analytical instrument in order to investigate the particular characteristics of urban violence. The spatiotemporal approach proposed in this volume is applicable in different disciplines and with regard to past and present cities in the Global South and North. To fully explore the potential of this tool, it has to be applied in studies with diverse perspectives on urban violence from above, below and beyond, focusing on various themes, actors and scales, and operate with different methods, such as participant observation, archival source analysis or qualitative interviews.

Doreen Massey early on urged social scientists to bring different disciplines into a true dialogue with each other, confirming that 'the spatial is integral to the production of history [...] just as the temporal is to geography' (1994a: 296). By bringing together both early-career and senior scholars working in the disciplines of history, sociology, political sciences, urban anthropology, urban planning and architecture, who are based at universities and research institutes across Europe, Latin America, the Levant and the United States and have conducted their research in a wide range of countries, we profit from a truly interdisciplinary and international debate. By including different perspectives offered by disciplines from the social sciences as well as from the humanities, which is seldom done, we are able to explore the conceptual and methodological potential of studying urban violence through a spatiotemporal lens to its full extent.

Furthermore, our multifaceted approach has the potential to trigger dynamics within the interdisciplinary field of urban violence research, which will feed new theoretical-methodological insights into the individual disciplines. While the approaches and situated perspectives that contributors bring to this volume are greatly diverse, the contributions were all developed within a mutual framework, preserving a common thread and addressing the same overarching research questions: How does the city, with its particular spatial and temporal characteristics, produce and shape violence, both in terms of conditions of the built environment, and by providing particular 'urban' social relations in space and time? In what ways do different forms of violence and their commemorations in the city transform and reorganise urban space-time and how do spatialities and temporalities of a city shape memories and potentially trigger renewed violence? How can space-time be employed as an analytical instrument to study urban violence?

While discussing the current theoretical and empirical literature on urban space, time and violence from an interdisciplinary perspective in the inspiring workshop and conference panels that led up to this book, we reflected on the different ways in which urban space-time produces and shapes violent practices, and also considered the generative capacities of violence and how it reconfigures urban space-time. The individual chapters discuss different examples of how this can unfold and of how to analyse it. This also means that a variety of data is used. Some chapters are based on ethnographic work, others on archival sources, some on both. The idea is to explore how, in a multiplicity of ways, space-time can be used as an analytical tool in different disciplines and to highlight differences, commonalities and advantages of multi- and interdisciplinary approaches to the study of urban violence.

Structure of the book

This book is divided into three parts. In some chapters, the focus is on the impact of urban space-time in shaping practices and representations of violence; in others, the transforming effect of violent practices and memories on the space-time of the cities takes centre stage.

In the first part, 'Space-time regimes and regulations', three chapters discuss *changing forms of urban violence* in the context of significant urban transformations. The case studies highlight how new forms of order in cities change spatial and temporal perceptions and regulations, which in turn produce and transform violence. The practices of violence are adapted to novel space- and time-regimes that are either imposed by hegemonic actors or created as forms of protest by revolutionary, subaltern or marginalised groups. The transformation of spatiotemporal practices through violence often seems to gain tempo with the growing number of collective actors involved, and specific collective actions can be seen as ruptures to prior spatiotemporal regimes.

Klaus Weinhauer introduces us to the specific space-time of the port cities of Seattle and Hamburg in the volatile post-World War I era that was characterised by massive strikes and street violence. His chapter investigates the effects of specific forms of collective actions employed by new social movements and uniformed state organisations in public spaces. By focusing on the huge general strike in Seattle in early 1919, and revolutionary actions and street violence in Hamburg in 1918/19, he examines the formation of new space-time regimes in both cities and investigates the different spatial and temporal practices of protest and violence in revolutionary and non-revolutionary settings. Roberto Mazza, in turn, shows how British urban planning and the re-definition of space and time transformed urban violence in Jerusalem in the 1920s. Under the Mandate, Jerusalem became a city where religious affiliation defined space and time, initiating a process of spatial and temporal segregation. By focusing on the Nabi Musa riots in 1920 and the massacres of 1929, he examines how particular spatiotemporal characteristics of Jerusalem generated different forms of violence and highlights how the perception of time, its regulation and the systematic spread of news became an essential part of the conflict between the communities. Shrey Kapoor analyses how past violent evictions of lower caste Hindu and Muslim labourers from the heart of the city of Ahmedabad have served as an instrument in the construction of a spatiotemporally coded, unified and exclusionary Hindu identity that strengthens the Hindu nationalist Bharatiya Janata Party's (BJP) long-term hegemonic project in India. The segregated resettlement sites at the city's margins spatially and temporally extend the violence of dispossession while remaining invisible to Ahmedabad's middle-class public.

In the book's second part, 'Rhythms and spatiotemporal dynamics' we explore *the structuring effects of space and time on violence* and vice versa. The chapters focus on cities in diverse world regions and highlight that different forms of violence are linked to different forms of social organisation and therefore possess different rhythms. These patterns can change during their course, in linkage with the spatial configuration that can speed up, slow down, channel and change the rhythms of violent actions. Contemporary and historical cases show how various forms of violence have their own (changing) rhythms and how these are synchronised with urban rhythms and intertwined with configurations of urban space. In turn, violence also disrupts urban rhythms, reconfigures urban space and continuously transforms the space-time of cities.

Hannes Warnecke-Berger, in focusing on urban gang violence in El Salvador and Jamaica, explores different forms of violence and their temporal dynamics. He highlights how mobilising and organising violence in San Salvador and Kingston requires the violent actors to manipulate urban space and time. In developing a novel concept of forms of violence that focuses on violent interactions that social actors entertain and maintain with regard to (urban) space and time, Warnecke-Berger develops a relational perspective on violence. Alke Jenss explores how Buenaventura, Colombia's largest port city on the Pacific, has been transformed both by the growth in container turnover and through recurring, spatial and temporal practices of violence in the early twenty-first century. She argues that while recurring violence provides urban rhythm itself, social movements may employ the temporal instrument of disruption as a means both of political articulation and transformation within the logics of accelerated accumulation and in a context marked by violent rhythms and forced mobility. Finally, Mara Albrecht, examining the major riots in Belfast in the late nineteenth and early twentieth century and in Jerusalem during the Mandate era, shows how spatiotemporal (re-)configurations produced and shaped practices of violence. She investigates the ways in which violence became synchronised with or disrupted daily, weekly and annual rhythms, and highlights the importance of spatiotemporal imaginations and memories of violence. Albrecht argues that these factors led to the formation of spatiotemporal patterns of violence over time, thereby introducing a 'pulse' to which the historical actors 'clock' their violent actions. Both Albrecht and Jenss draw on Lefebvre's rhythmanalysis and show the diverse possibilities of working with his conceptualisation.

The third part, 'Memory and (religious) imaginations', focuses on spatiotemporal *representations of urban violence*, particularly the space-time dimension of memories of physical violence. Urban violence is intertwined not only with places and topographies, specific sites that later bear memory of it, but simultaneously with different temporal layers of a city, e.g. with an imagined ancient history, or memories of past conflicts, or even aspirations for the future. The chapters show that memories of violence are selectively mobilised when victories, defeats, heroes or martyrs are celebrated at particular dates and places in the city. Collective actors who commemorate violence or create alternative spatiotemporal imaginations are simultaneously performing (or 'doing') space and time through everyday practices and formal rituals.

Beirut's city-space is marked by past violence in its tangible and intangible forms. Christine Mady uses the notion of the palimpsest as an investigative tool to reveal the spatiotemporal intertwining of emerging and disappearing traces of violence embedded in Beirut's city-space. She explores the layers of memory that give significance to specific places and that refer to a non-linear time. The urban fabric becomes a register of past traces, which are experienced today, sometimes surfacing to awaken memories for those who lived that violent past. This makes it possible to appreciate the impact of mnemonic spaces and violence with their markers at various scales, from the wider metropolitan region to the level of streets and buildings, as well as their echoes in the narratives of different socio-political groups. Andreas Bolte analyses the violent commemoration of national 'Humiliation Days', which the Chinese government created in the 1920s, dedicated to the remembrance of imperialist violence in China. He investigates how the large Chinese diaspora in the cities of British Malaya and the Dutch East Indies practiced the memory of violence in urban environments temporally and spatially removed from the original events. Bolte shows how the 'Humiliation Days' conjured up new acts of violence and led the British and Dutch colonial governments to expect renewed violence in the multinational cities. In this way, the commemorations tended to occupy all three temporal dimensions of past, present and future at once. Using an ethnographic case study of a Catholic base community in the periphery of Rio de Janeiro, Christian Laheij explores a completely different instantiation of space-time. Challenging static ideas of city-space, he analyses how religious actors work to challenge established topographies of violence by furnishing alternative spatiotemporal imaginaries that initiate socio-spatial and temporal reconfigurations. Laheij thereby also calls into question the idea that decades of urban violence in Brazil have fixed the space and time of cities in a binary between affluent elites in quiet neighbourhoods and urban poor confined to overpopulated, violent slums.

Bibliography

Adam, B. (1995). *Timewatch: The Social Analysis of Time* (Cambridge, MA: Polity Press).
Adam, B. (1990). *Time and Social Theory* (Cambridge, MA: Polity Press).
Agnew, J. (2003). *Geopolitics: Re-visioning World Politics* (2nd ed.) (London/New York: Routledge).
Albrecht, M. (2021). 'Ritual Performances and Collective Violence in Divided Cities – The Riots in Belfast (1886) and Jerusalem (1929)', *Political Geography*, 86. https://doi.org/10.1016/j.polgeo.2021.102341
Albrecht, M. (2020). 'Clash of Memories: Commemorating the Civil War in Lebanon', *Public History Weekly*, 8:6. https://doi.org/10.1515/phw-2020-16551
Albrecht, M. and Akar, B. (2016). *The Power of Remembrance: Political Parties, Memory and Learning about the Past in Lebanon* (Zouk Mosbeh, Lebanon: CARE, Notre Dame University Press).
Alves, J. A. (2018). *The Anti-Black City: Police Terror and Black Urban Life in Brazil* (Minneapolis: University of Minnesota Press).
Amar, P. (2013). *Security Archipelago: Human-security States, Sexuality Politics, and the End of Neoliberalism* (Durham: Duke University Press).
Anderson, J. (2010). *Democracy, Territoriality and Ethno-national Conflict: A Framework for Studying Ethno-nationally Divided Cities*. Working paper no. 18. https://api.semanticscholar.org/CorpusID:155024940

Anderson, J. (2008). *From Empires to Ethno-National Conflicts. A Framework for Studying 'Divided Cities' in 'Contested States'*, Part I, Divided Cities/Contested States. Working paper no.1. https://tinyurl.com/bdfxavtt

Auyero, J., Bourgois, P. I., and Scheper-Hughes, N. (eds) (2015). *Violence at the Urban Margins* (Oxford: Oxford University Press).

Bachmann-Medick, D. (2016). *Cultural Turns: New Orientations in the Study of Culture* (Berlin/Boston: De Gruyter).

Baillie, B. (2012). *Vukovar's Divided Memory: The Reification of Ethnicity through Memorialisation*. Working paper no. 25. https://conflictincities.org

Bakhtin, M. (2008). *Chronotopos* (Frankfurt am Main: Suhrkamp).

Ballvé, T. (2012). 'Everyday State Formation: Territory, Decentralization, and the Narco Landgrab in Colombia', *Environment and Planning D: Society and Space*, 30:4, 603–22. https://doi.org/10.1068/d4611

Banks, N., Lombard, M., and Mitlin, D. (2019). 'Urban Informality as a Site of Critical Analysis', *The Journal of Development Studies*, 56:2, 1–16. https://doi.org/10.1080/00220388.2019.1577384

Bauer, J. and Fischer, R. (2019). *Perspectives on Henri Lefebvre: Theory, Practices and (Re)Readings* (Berlin/Boston: De Gruyter Oldenbourg).

Baumann, H. (2015). 'Enclaves, Borders, and Everyday Movements: Palestinian Marginal Mobility in East Jerusalem', *Cities*, 59, 173–82.

Björkdahl, A. and Buckley-Zistel, S. (eds) (2016). *Spatializing Peace and Conflict: Mapping the Production of Places, Sites and Scales of Violence* (Basingstoke: Palgrave Macmillan).

Blokland, T., Hentschel, C., Holm A., Lubuhn, H., and Margalit, T. (2015). 'Urban Citizenship and Right to the City: The Fragmentation of Claims', *International Journal of Urban and Regional Research*, 39:4, 655–65. https://doi.org/10.1111/1468-2427.12259

Body-Gendrot, S. (2012). *Globalization, Fear, and Insecurity: The Challenges for Cities North and South* (New York: Palgrave Macmillan).

Bosi, L., Ó Dochartaigh, N., and Pisoiu, D. (eds) (2015). *Political Violence in Context: Time, Space and Milieu* (Colchester: ECPR Press).

Bourdieu, P. (1977). *Outline of a Theory of Practice* (Cambridge: Cambridge University Press).

Felbab-Brown, V. (2016). *Safe in the City: Urban Spaces are the New Frontier for International Security*. Brookings Institution, www.brookings.edu/blog/order-from-chaos/2016/02/18/safe-in-the-city-urban-spaces-are-the-new-frontier-for-international-security/.

Butler, J. (2004). *Undoing Gender* (London/New York: Routledge).

Carabelli, G. (2021). 'Love, Activism, and the Possibility of Radical Social Change in Mostar', in Carabelli, G. et al. (eds) *Challenging the Representation of Ethnically Divided Cities: Perspectives from Mostar* (London/New York: Routledge), 67–81.

Carabelli, G. (2018). *The Divided City and the Grassroots. The (Un)making of Ethnic Divisions in Mostar* (Singapore: Palgrave Macmillan).

Cazzola, M., Corredera, E., Iannuzzi, G., and Beduschi, G. (2020). 'Introduction. Imperial Times: Towards a History of Imperial Uses of Time', *Storia della Storiografia*, 77, 11–26. https:// doi.org/10.19272/202011501001

Chen, Y. (2016). *Practising Rhythmanalysis: Theories and Methodologies* (London/New York: Rowman & Littlefield).

Chickering, R. (2007). *The Great War and Urban Life in Germany: Freiburg, 1914–1918* (Cambridge: Cambridge University Press).

Choplin, A. and Ciavolella, R. (2017). 'Gramsci and the African Città Futura: Urban Subaltern Politics from the Margins of Nouakchott, Mauritania', *Antipode*, 49:2, 314–34. https://doi.org/10.1111/anti.12268

Collins, R. (2009). *Violence. A Micro-sociological Theory* (Princeton: Princeton University Press).

Colombijn, F. (2018). 'The Production of Urban Space by Violence and its Aftermath in Jakarta and Kota Ambon, Indonesia', *Ethnos*, 83:1, 58–79.

Cornelissen, C. and Weinrich, A. (2021). 'German Historiography on World War I, 1914–2019', in Cornelissen, C. and Weinrich, A. (eds) *Writing the Great War: The Historiography of World War I from 1918 to the Present* (New York: Berghahn Books), 148–91.

Coward, M. (2009). *Urbicide: The Politics of Urban Destruction* (London/New York: Routledge).

Crang, M. (2005). 'Time:Space', in Cloke, P. and Johnston, R. (eds) *Spaces of Geographical Thought: Deconstructing Human Geography's Binaries* (London: Sage), 199–220.

Darwin, J. (2013). *Unfinished Empire: The Global Expansion of Britain* (London: Penguin Books).

Darwin, J. (2009). *The Empire Project: The Rise and Fall of the British World-System 1830–1970* (New York: Cambridge).

Davis, M. (1990). *City of Quartz: Excavating the Future in Los Angeles* (London: Verso).

Degen, M. (2016). 'Consuming Urban Rhythms: Let's Ravalejar', in Edensor, T. (ed.) *Geographies of Rhythm* (London/New York: Routledge), 21–32. https://doi.org/10.4324/9781315584430

Dinzey-Flores, Z. Z. (2017). 'Spatially Polarized Landscapes and a New Approach to Urban Inequality', *Latin American Research Review*, 52:2, 241–52. https://doi.org/10.25222/larr.89

Doel, M. (2017). *Geographies of Violence: Killing Space, Killing Time* (Los Angeles: Sage).

Dorsch, S. (2013). 'Space/Time Practices and the Production of Space and Time. An Introduction', *Historical Social Research*, 28:3, 7–21.

Dorsch, S. et al. (2012). *Rahmenpapier: Erfurter RaumZeit-Forschung* (21 February 2012). https://uni-erfurt.de/en/philosophische-fakultaet/forschung/forschungsgruppen/studies-for-spatiotemporality-erfurt/research-profile

Dorsch, S. and Vinzent, J. (eds) (2018). *SpatioTemporalities on the Line: Representations-Practices-Dynamics* (Berlin/Boston: De Gruyter Oldenbourg).

Doyle, M. (2016). *Communal Violence in the British Empire: Disturbing the Pax* (London: Bloomsbury).

Edele, M. and Gerwarth, R. (2015). 'The Limits of Demobilization: Global Perspectives on the Aftermath of the Great War', *Journal of Contemporary History*, 50:1, 3–14.

Edensor, T. (ed.) (2016). *Geographies of Rhythm: Nature, Place, Mobilities and Bodies* (London/New York: Routledge).

Eisenstadt, S. N. (2000). *Die Vielfalt der Moderne* (Weilerswist: Velbrück).

Elden, S. (2004). 'Rhythmanalysis: An Introduction', in Lefebvre, H. (ed.) *Rhythmanalysis: Space, Time, and Everyday Life* (London/New York: Continuum), vii–xv.

Elden, S. (2013). *The Birth of Territory* (Chicago: University of Chicago Press).

Fregonese, S. (2020). *War and the City: Urban Geopolitics in Lebanon* (London: I.B. Tauris).

Fregonese, S. (2012). 'Urban Geopolitics 8 Years on. Hybrid Sovereignties, the Everyday, and Geographies of Peace', *Geography Compass*, 6:5, 290–303.

Freitag, U., Fuccaro, N., Ghrawi, C., and Lafi, N. (eds). (2015). *Urban Violence in the Middle East: Changing Cityscapes in the Transition from Empire to Nation State* (New York/Oxford: Berghahn).

Fuccaro, N. (ed.) (2016). *Violence and the City in the Modern Middle East* (Stanford: Stanford University Press).

Gago, V. (2015). *La razón neoliberal. Economías barrocas y pragmática popular* (Barcelona: traficantes de sueños).

Gago, V. and Cavallero, L. (2018). 'The Writing on the Bodies of Women', Verso blog. https://versobooks.com/blogs/4038-the-writing-on-the-bodies-of-women

Galtung, J. (1975). *Strukturelle Gewalt. Beiträge zur Friedens- und Konfliktforschung* (Reinbek bei Hamburg: Rowohlt).

Gauthiez, B. (2020). *The Production of Urban Space, Temporality, and Spatiality: Lyons, 1500–1900* (Berlin/Boston: De Gruyter Oldenbourg).

Gayer, L. (2016). 'The Need for Speed: Traffic Regulation and the Violent Fabric of Karachi', *Theory, Culture & Society*, 33:7–8, 137–58. https://doi.org/10.1177/0263276416666934

Gerwarth, R. and Manela, E. (2014). 'The Great War as a Global War', *Diplomatic History*, 38:4, 786–800.

Gobal, P. (2020): *Insurgent Empire: Anticolonial Resistance and British Dissent* (London: Verso).

Goldstein, D. M. (2016). *Owners of the Sidewalk: Security and Survival in the Informal City* (Durham, NC: Duke University Press).

Gott, R. (2011). *Britain's Empire: Resistance, Repression and Revolt* (London: Verso).

Graham, S. (2011). *Cities Under Siege* (London: Verso).

Graham, S. (2004). 'Introduction: Cities, Warfare, and States of Emergency', in Graham, S. (ed.) *Cities, War and Terrorism: Towards an Urban Geopolitics* (Malden: Blackwell Publishing), 1–30.

Greene, B. (2004). *The Fabric of the Cosmos: Space, Time, and the Texture of Reality* (New York: Knopf).

Gregory, D. (ed.) (2006). *Violent Geographies: Fear, Terror, and Political Violence* (London/New York: Routledge).

Hall, E. (1983). *The Dance of Life: The Other Dimension of Time* (New York: Doubleday).

Harrowell, E. (2015). 'From Monuments to Mahallas: Contrasting Memories in the Urban Landscape of Osh, Kyrgyzstan', *Social & Cultural Geography*, 16:2, 203–25.

Haugbolle, S. (2012). 'Spatial Representation of Sectarian National Identity in Residential Beirut', in Cinar, A., Roy, S., and Yahya, M. (eds) *Visualizing Secularism and Religion: Egypt, Lebanon, Turkey, India* (Ann Arbor: University of Michigan Press), 308–33.

Healy, M. (2004). *Vienna and the Fall of the Habsburg Empire: Total War and Everyday Life in World War I* (Cambridge: Cambridge University Press).

Hirsch, M. (2012). *The Generation of Postmemory: Writing and Visual Culture After the Holocaust* (New York: Columbia University Press).

Hobsbawm, E. (1983). 'La anatomía de la violencia en Colombia', in E. Hobsbawm (ed.) *Rebeldes Primitivos. Estudio sobre las formas arcaicas de los movimientos sociales en los siglos XIX y XX* (Bogotá: Editorial Ariel), 263–73.

Hromadžić, A. (2015). *Citizens of an Empty Nation: Youth and State-making in Postwar Bosnia and Herzegovina* (Philadelphia: University of Pennsylvania Press).

Huffschmid, A. (2015). *Risse im Raum: Erinnerung, Gewalt und städtisches Leben in Lateinamerika* (Wiesbaden: Springer VS).

Jaffe, R. and Koning, A. D. (2015). *Introducing Urban Anthropology* (London/ New York: Routledge).

Jenss, A. (2020). 'Global Flows and Everyday Violence in Urban Space: The Port-City of Buenaventura, Colombia', *Political Geography*, 77, 102–13.

Jenss, A. (2019). 'Authoritarian Neoliberal Rescaling in Latin America: Urban In/ security and Austerity in Oaxaca', *Globalizations*, 16:3, 304–19. https://doi.org/ 10.1080/14747731.2018.1502493

Julien, E. (2010). *Paris, Berlin, la mémoire de la guerre 1914–1933* (Rennes: Presses universitaires de Rennes).

Kaldor, M. (2012). *New and Old Wars* (Cambridge/Malden: Polity).

Kaldor, M. and Sassen, S. (eds) (2020). *Cities at War: Global Insecurity and Urban Resistance* (New York: Columbia University Press).

Kern, L. (2016). 'Rhythms of Gentrification: Eventfulness and Slow Violence in a Happening Neighbourhood', *Cultural Geographies*, 23:3, 441–57. https://doi. org/10.1177/1474474015591489

Kern, L. and Mullings, B. (2013). 'Urban Neoliberalism, Urban Insecurity and Urban Violence: The Gender Dimensions', in L. Peake and M. Rieker (eds) *Rethinking Feminist Interventions Into the Urban* (London/New York: Routledge), 23–40.

King, A. (1998). *Memorials of the Great War in Britain: The Symbolism and Politics of Remembrance, The Legacy of the Great War* (Oxford: Berg).

Koch, N. (2022). Authoritarian space-time. *Political Geography*, 95, 102628. https:// doi.org/10.1016/j.polgeo.2022.102628

Koonings, K., and Kruijt, D. (2007). *Fractured Cities: Social Exclusion, Urban Violence and Contested Spaces in Latin America* (London: Zed Books).

Koselleck, R. (2000). *Zeitschichten. Studien zur Historik* (Frankfurt am Main: Suhrkamp).

Kramer, A. (2014). 'Recent Historiography of the First World War (Part I)', *Journal of Modern European History*, 12:1, 5–28.

Kramer, A. (2008). *Dynamics of Destruction: Culture and Mass Killing in the First World War* (Oxford: Oxford University Press).

Laó-Montes, A. and Dávila, A. (2012). *Mambo Montage: The Latinization of New York City* (New York: Columbia University Press).

Larkin, C. (2010). 'Beyond the War? The Lebanese Postmemory Experience', *International Journal of Middle East Studies*, 42:4, 615–35.

Lawhon, M., Nilsson, D., Silver, J., Ernston, H., and Lwasa, S. (2017). 'Thinking through Heterogeneous Infrastructure Configurations', *Urban Studies*, 55:4, 720–32. https://doi.org/10.1177/0042098017720149

LeBrón, M. (2020). 'They Don't Care if We Die: The Violence of Urban Policing in Puerto Rico', *Journal of Urban History*, 46:5, 1066–84. https://doi.org/10.1177/ 0096144217705485

Lefebvre, H. (2016). *Das Recht auf Stadt* (Hamburg: Nautilus).

Lefebvre, H. (2004). *Rhythmanalysis: Space, Time, and Everyday Life* (London/New York: Continuum).

Lefebvre, H. (1991). *The Production of Space* (Oxford: Blackwell).

Löw, M. (2010). *Soziologie der Städte* (Frankfurt am Main: Suhrkamp).

Lubkemann, S. (2008). 'Involuntary Immobility: On a Theoretical Invisibility in Forced Migration Studies', *Journal of Refugee Studies,* 21:4, 454–75.

Mabin, A. (2014). 'Grounding Southern City in Time and Place' in *Routledge Handbook on Cities of the Global South* (London/New York: Routledge), 21–36.

Madariaga, P. (2006). 'Región, actores, y conflicto: los episodios', in Archila, N. M. et al. (eds) *Conflictos, poderes e identidades en el magdalena medio, 1990–2001* (Bogotá: Colciencias/Cinep), 37–84.

Mady, C. (2018). 'Public Space Activism in Unstable Contexts: Emancipation from Beirut's Postmemory', in Knierbein, S. and Viderman, T. (eds) *Public Space Unbound: Urban Emancipation and the Post-Political Condition* (London/New York: Routledge), 189–206.

Makdisi, U. and Silverstein, P. (2006). 'Introduction', in Makdisi, U. and Silverstein, P. (eds) *Memory and Violence in the Middle East and North Africa* (Bloomington: Indiana University Press), 1–24.

Massey, D. (1994a). *Space, Place and Gender* (Cambridge, MA: Polity Press).

Massey, D. and Allen, J. (eds) (1994b). *Geography Matters! A Reader* (Cambridge: Cambridge University Press).

Massey, D. (1992). 'Politics and Space/Time', *New Left Review,* 196, 65–84.

Massey, D. (1991). 'A global sense of place', *Marxism Today,* 38, 24–9.

May, J. and Thrift, N. (2001). *TimeSpace: Geographies of Temporality* (London/New York: Routledge).

McFarlane, C. (2010). 'The Comparative City: Knowledge, Learning, Urbanism', *International Journal of Urban and Regional Research,* 34:4, 725–42.

McKittrick, K. (2014). 'Mathematics Black Life', *The Black Scholar,* 44:2, 16–28.

Megoran, N. (2011). 'War and Peace? An Agenda for Peace Research and Practice in Geography', *Political Geography,* 30, 178–89.

Megoran, N. and Dalby, S. (2018). 'Geopolitics and Peace: A Century of Change in the Discipline of Geography', *Geopolitics,* 23:2, 251–76.

Menjívar, C. and Walsh, S. D. (2017). 'The Architecture of Feminicide: The State, Inequalities, and Everyday Gender Violence in Honduras', *Latin American Research Review,* 52:2, 221–40. https://doi.org/10.25222/larr.73

Meyer, H. et al. (eds) (2017). *SpaceTime of the Imperial* (Berlin/Boston: De Gruyter Oldenbourg).

Moncada, E. (2015). *Cities, Business, and the Politics of Urban Violence in Latin America* (Stanford: Stanford University Press).

Monroe, K. (2016). *The Insecure City: Space, Power and Mobility in Beirut* (New Brunswick: Rutgers University Press).

Mosse, G. (1990). *Fallen Soldiers. Reshaping the Memory of the World Wars* (New York and Oxford: Oxford University Press).

Münkler, H. (2002). *Die neuen Kriege* (Reinbek bei Hamburg: Rowohlt).

Müller, M.-M. and Feth, A. (2011). 'Dossier: Spaces of Insecurity, Security Governance in Latin America Revisited: Introduction', *Iberoamericana,* 11:41, 79–82.

Mulíček, O., Osman, R., and Seidenglanz, D. (2016). 'Time–Space Rhythms of the City – The Industrial and Postindustrial Brno', *Environment and Planning A: Economy and Space,* 48:1, 115–31. https://doi.org/10.1177/0308518X15594809

Mara Albrecht and Alke Jenss

Nagle, J. (2018). 'Defying State Amnesia and Memorywars: Non-sectarian Memory Activism in Beirut and Belfast City Centres', *Social and Cultural Geography*, 21:3, 380–401.

Nanni, G. (2012). *The Colonisation of Time: Ritual, Routine, and Resistance in the British Empire* (Manchester: Manchester University Press).

Newsinger, J. (2010). *The Blood Never Died: A People's History of the British Empire* (London: Bookmarks).

Nixon, R. (2011). *Slow Violence and the Environmentalism of the Poor* (Cambridge, MA: Harvard University Press).

Nübel, C. (2014). *Durchhalten und Überleben an der Westfront. Raum und Körper im Ersten Weltkrieg* (Paderborn: Schöningh).

Ó Dochartaigh, N. (2015). 'Spatial Contexts for Political Violence', in L. Bosi, N. Ó Dochartaigh, and D. Pisoiu (eds) *Political Violence in Context: Time, Space and Milieu* (Colchester: ECPR Press), 133–43.

Papadakis, Y. (1994). 'The National Struggle Museums of a Divided City', *Ethnic and Racial Studies*, 17:3, 400–19.

Parnell, S. and Oldfield, S. (eds) (2014). *The Routledge Handbook on Cities of the Global South* (London/New York: Routledge).

Pavoni, A. and Tulumello, S. (2020). 'What is Urban Violence?', *Progress in Human Geography*, 44:1, 49–76. https://doi.org/10.1177/0309132518810432

Peck, J. (2015). 'Cities Beyond Compare?', *Regional Studies*, 49:1, 160–82.

Penados, F., Gahman, L., and Smith, S. (2022). 'Land, race, and (slow) violence: Indigenous resistance to racial capitalism and the coloniality of development in the Caribbean.' *Geoforum* (online first). https://doi.org/10.1016/j.geoforum.2022.07.004

Popitz, H. (1986). *Phänomene der Macht. Autorität – Herrschaft – Gewalt – Technik* (Tübingen: Mohr).

Pullan, W. (2011). 'Frontier Urbanism: The Periphery at the Centre of Contested Cities', *The Journal of Architecture*, 16:1, 15–35. https://doi.org/10.1080/13602365.2011.546999

Pullan, W., Baillie, B., and Kyriacou, L. (eds) (2013). *Locating Urban Conflicts: Ethnicity, Nationalism and the Everyday* (Basingstoke: Palgrave Macmillan).

Pullan, W. and Gwiazda, M. (2009). ' "City of David": Urban Design and Frontier Heritage', *Jerusalem Quarterly*, 39, 29–38.

Ranganathan, M. (2018). 'Rule by Difference: Empire, Liberalism, and the Legacies of Urban "Improvement"', *Environment and Planning A: Economy and Space* 50, 1386–1406.

Rau, S. (2021). 'Spatiotemporal Entanglements: Insights from History', in Million, A. et al. (eds), *Spatial Transformations: Kaleidoscopic Perspectives on the Refiguration of Spaces* (London: Routledge), 60–71.

Rau, S. (2013). *Räume: Konzepte, Wahrnehmungen, Nutzungen* (Frankfurt am Main: Campus).

Reid-Musson, E. (2017). 'Intersectional Rhythmanalysis: Power, Rhythm, and Everyday Life', *Progress in Human Geography*, 42:6, 881–97. https://doi.org/10.1177/0309132517725069

Ren, J. (2022). 'A More Global Urban Studies, besides Empirical Variation.' *Urban Studies*, 59:8, 1741–1748. https://doi.org/10.1177/00420980221085113

Riaño-Alcalá, P. (2006). *Dwellers of Memory: Youth and Violence in Medellín, Colombia* (New Brunswick: Transaction).

Rinke, S. (2017). *Latin America and the First World War* (Cambridge: Cambridge University Press).

Robinson, J. (2016). 'Thinking Cities through Elsewhere', *Progress in Human Geography* 40:1, 3–29. https://doi.org/10.1177/0309132515598025

Robinson, J. (2011). 'Cities in a World of Cities: The Comparative Gesture', *International Journal of Urban and Regional Research*, 35:1, 1–23.

Robinson, J. (2005). *Ordinary Cities. Between Modernity and Development* (London/New York: Routledge).

Rokem, J., Weiss, C., and Miodownik, D. (2018). 'Geographies of Violence in Jerusalem. The Spatial Logic of Urban Intergroup Conflict', *Political Geography*, 66, 88–97. https://doi.org/10.1016/j.polgeo.2018.08.008

Rokem, J. et al. (2017). 'Interventions in Urban Geopolitics', *Political Geography*, 61, 253–62. https://doi.org/10.1016/j.polgeo.2017.04.004

Rolston, B. (2003). 'Changing the Political Landscape: Murals and Transition in Northern Ireland', *Irish Studies Review*, 11:1, 3–16.

Roshwald, A. (2001). *Ethnic Nationalism and the Fall of Empires: Central Europe, Russia, and the Middle East, 1914–1923* (London: Routledge).

Roy, A. and AlSayyad, N. (2004). *Urban Informality: Transnational Perspectives from the Middle East, Latin America, and South Asia* (Lanham, MD: Lexington Books).

Said, E. (1981). *Orientalismus* (Frankfurt/Main: Ullstein).

Sassen, S. (2001). *The Global City: New York, London, Tokyo* (Revised ed.) (Princeton: Princeton University Press).

Scheper-Hughes, N. (1993). *Death Without Weeping: The Violence of Everyday Life in Brazil* (Berkeley: University of California Press).

Schindel, E. and Colombo, P. (eds) (2014). *Space and the Memories of Violence. Landscapes of Erasure, Disappearance and Exception* (Basingstoke: Palgrave Macmillan).

Schmolinsky, S., Hitzke, D., and Stahl, H. (2019). *Taktungen und Rhythmen. Raumzeitliche Perspektiven interdisziplinär* (Berlin/Boston: De Gruyter Oldenbourg).

Simone, A. (2010). *City Life from Jakarta to Dakar: Movements at the Crossroads* (London/New York: Routledge). https://doi.org/10.4324/9780203892497

Simone, A., and Pieterse, E. (2017). *New Urban Worlds: Inhabiting Dissonant Times* (Cambridge/Medford: Polity).

Springer, S. and Le Billon, P. (2016). 'Violence and Space: An Introduction to the Geographies of Violence', *Political Geography*, 52, 1–3. https://doi.org/10.1016/j.polgeo.2016.03.003

Soja, E. W. (2010). 'Cities and States in Geohistory', *Theory and Society*, 39:3–4, 361–76.

Streets-Salter, H. (2017). *World War One in Southeast Asia. Colonialism and Anticolonialism in an Era of Global Conflict* (Cambridge: Cambridge University Press).

Thompson, E. P. (1967). 'Time, Work-discipline and Industrial Capitalism', *Past & Present*, 38:1, 56–97.

Tilly, C. (2010). 'Cities, States, and Trust Networks: Chapter 1 of Cities and States in World History', *Theory and Society*, 39:3–4, 265–80.

Tilly, C. (2003). *The Politics of Collective Violence* (Cambridge: Cambridge University Press).

Tilly C. and Tarrow, S. (2012). *Contentious Politics* (Oxford: Oxford University Press).

Tsing, A. (2005). *Friction: An Ethnography of Global Connection* (Princeton, NJ: Princeton University Press).

Tulumello, S. (2017a). *Fear, Space and Urban Planning: A Critical Perspective* (Cham: Springer).

Tulumello, S. (2017b). 'The Multiscalar Nature of Urban Security and Public Safety: Crime Prevention from Local Policy to Policing in Lisbon (Portugal) and Memphis (the United States)', *Urban Affairs Review*, 54:6, 1134–69. https://doi.org/10.1177/1078087417699532

Varley, A. (2013). 'Postcolonialising Informality?', *Society and Space*, 31:1, 4–22.

Verhey, J. (2000). *The Spirit of 1914. Militarism, Myth, and Mobilization in Germany* (Cambridge: Cambridge University Press).

Villarreal, A. (2021). 'Reconceptualizing Urban Violence from the Global South', *City & Community*, *OnlineFirst*. https://doi.org/10.1111/cico.12506

Villareal, A. (2015). 'Fear and Spectacular Drug Violence in Monterrey' in Auyero, J., Bourgois, P. I., and Scheper-Hughes, N. (eds) *Violence at the Urban Margins* (Oxford: Oxford University Press), 136–61.

von Hirschhausen, U. and Leonhard, J. (2011). 'Zwischen Historisierung und Globalisierung: Titel, Themen und Trends der neueren Empire-Forschung', *Neue Politische Literatur*, 11:3, 389–404.

von Trotha, T. (1997). 'Zur Soziologie der Gewalt' in T. von Trotha (ed.) *Soziologie der Gewalt* (Opladen, Wiesbaden: Westdeutscher Verlag), 9–58.

Wagner, K. A. (2019). *Amritsar 1919: An Empire of Fear and the Making of a Massacre* (New Haven and London: Yale University Press).

Walker, R. (2010). 'Violence, the Everyday and the Question of the Ordinary', *Contemporary South Asia*, 18:1, 9–24.

Way, J. T. (2021). 'Agrotropolis. Youth, Street, and Nation in the New Urban Guatemala', in Way, J. T. (ed.) *Agrotropolis* (Berkeley: University of California Press), 1–26.

Weinhauer, K. and Ellerbrock, D. (2013). 'Perspektiven auf Gewalt in europäischen Städten seit dem 19. Jahrhundert', *IMS*, 13:2, 5–20.

Winter, J. (2017). *War Beyond Words. Languages of Remembrance From the Great War to the Present* (Cambridge: Cambridge University Press).

Winter, J. (ed.) (2014). *Global War* (Cambridge: Cambridge University Press).

Winter, J. (1995). *Sites of Memory, Sites of Mourning. The Great War in European Cultural History* (Cambridge: Cambridge University Press).

Winter, J. and Prost, A. (2005). *The Great War in History: Debates and Controversies, 1914 to the Present* (Cambridge: Cambridge University Press).

Xu, G. (2017). *Asia and the Great War. A Shared History* (Oxford: Oxford University Press).

Yas, J. (2000). '(Re)designing the City of David: Landscape, Narrative and Archaeology in Silwan', *Jerusalem Quarterly*, 7, 17–23.

Part I

Space-time regimes and regulations:

Changing forms of urban violence

1

Revolution lost and found: Collective actions, fears and violently contested space-time regimes in Hamburg and Seattle (c. 1916–20)

Klaus Weinhauer

The centennial of World War I and of the turbulent post-war years gained a great deal of attention, both in historiography and in public remembrance. These years belonged to what global historian John Darwin calls the 'great phase of upheaval', which had roots well before 1914 (Darwin, 2008: 402). In the post-war years some countries even saw revolutions; others were hit by general strikes or had massively violent street confrontations, especially in 1919. Revolutions and strikes of these years mostly took place in big cities. While there is a wealth of social science studies on urban violence, historical analyses of explicitly urban perspectives on the sometimes violent collective actions of this time period are relatively rare (see Glass, Seyboldt and Williams, 2022; Pavoni and Tulomello, 2018; Body-Gendrot, 2012; Rotker, 2002). Overall, research on these years remains dominated by political historical perspectives (see as an exception Wagner, 2019) or by a focus on labour organisations and their leaders. Moreover, there are only very few comparative studies (Carsten, 1976; Bertrand, 1977; Cronin and Sirianni, 1983; Konrad and Schmidlechner, 1991; Wrigley, 1993; Rinke and Wildt, 2017) and only recently have there been publications that focus on post-World War I civil wars (Gerwarth and Horne, 2012; Baberowski et al., 2015; Gerwarth, 2017; Ziemann, 2003).

This strong focus on political or organisational aspects also holds true for studies that explicitly focus on revolutions, a field which is mostly researched by social scientists, whose approaches are shaped by structure-oriented patterns of thinking dominant in the 1970s (see as overviews Lawson, 2019; Goldstone, 2001; Foran, 1993). The main foci of analysis are structures and/or clear-cut entities such as the political systems, state or relevant organisations. This is mirrored in recent definitions of revolution. The latter is characterised by three elements: a transformation of the political system, mass mobilisations and non-institutionalised actions (mass protests, strikes) (Goldstone, 2001: 142). In this analytical setting, regime change is the key component, brought forward by collective actions, some of them rooted in non-institutionalised settings. An important question is how crucial it is to use violence in order to reach the respective aims. Interestingly, we still have nearly no studies that focus on explicit urban aspects of revolutions. Moreover, there are only very few culturally sensitive historical case studies that analyse how all these factors interact to turn collective action into a system change that is labelled a revolution.

Since the late 1990s, prompted by the end of the Cold War and triggered by the growing importance of cultural aspects, the research setting began to change. On the one hand, topics such as narratives, stories, symbols or emotions were integrated into the study of revolutions and collective actions. On the other hand, sociologists began to question the absence of war and also of violence from the great narratives that explained the history of social sciences as well as the history of modern societies. As Sinisa Malesevic underlines, rather than 'being seen as a regular and structurally intrinsic feature of social life, war and violence were largely perceived as irrational, atavistic facets of the primeval era that were bound to disappear with the arrival and spread of modernity' (Malesevic, 2010: 17; see also Joas and Knöbl, 2008).

Thirdly, beginning in the mid-1990s, violence itself was reconceptualised, often inspired by Randall Collins, who opted for a close reading of violent actions and who also stressed that it was not easy to overcome the confrontational tension/fear barrier in order to act violently (Collins, 2008). In German-language sociology there were also impulses to pay much more attention to the practices of physical violence and also to carefully study the situations in which violence was employed (von Trotha, 1998; Koloma Beck, 2017; Knöbl and Hoebel, 2019). Inspired by all these debates my approach sees physical violence as not merely a destructive or irrational action. Violence is a pattern of communication and also an element of social order. Violent activities do not erupt naturally like a volcano; they are always related to social contexts and to cultural interpretations (Weinhauer and Ellerbrock, 2013). In times of radical turmoil, the question of which organisation can legitimately claim a monopoly on physical violence becomes a highly contested issue.

Despite these innovative research tendencies, only a few studies look at temporal or spatial aspects of social upheaval (Newburn, 2021: 65). In such settings space and time regimes are at the centre of sometimes violent collective confrontations. Such patterns of violence happen in a triadic setting involving not only victim and perpetrator but also bystanders, whether 'ordinary' citizens or media representatives. As criminological studies have repeatedly argued since the late 1960s, fears and urban spaces are often closely related (Hale, 1996; Ceccato, 2012). Fear can also be a key element communicated in media reports about violence. Moreover, collective actions can trigger fear, often articulated through the media by persons or social groups who do not actively participate in or believe themselves to be the targets of such actions.

In my chapter I will try to integrate cultural historical perspectives on urban violence and on related social fears (Bourke, 2003) into the space-time approach developed in this book. My understanding of the space-time approach is inspired by Henri Lefebvre, Martina Löw and Aleida Assmann (Lefebvre, 1991; Löw, 2001; Assmann, 2013). With the triadic conception of space as perceived, conceived and lived, my work follows Lefebvre. I also start from his assumption that the urban is shaped by social conflicts. As he puts it, 'there is nothing harmonious about the urban ... as it also incorporates conflict'; it is a place 'where conflicts are expressed' (Lefebvre, 2003: 175). The state is very active in regulating the use of public spaces (through policing, infrastructure). This is closely related to Martina Löw's idea that it is important to check who has the power of spacing, of moving and directing people in space.

In all these settings and activities time matters. In order to integrate aspects of time I use the term 'time regime'. In a pragmatical understanding a time regime is a set of decentred sociocultural perceptions, expectations, norms and values about time (Assmann, 2013: 19). In some places, for example in factories and on the shop-floor, time is tightly controlled. Outside these settings time regimes may not be that explicitly controlled or enforced (see Geyer, 1998 on changes in perception of time). Phases of a thorough change in a political system, especially when this transformation is labelled a revolution, might provide massive impulses for looking back at the past and also for questioning what the future might bring. In such processes time regimes become more visible and thus more disputed. As mentioned earlier, state actions, in this case the activities of armed forces such as the police, are the key player in enforcing public space and time regimes. Such space-time regimes become visible when the police, for example, try to implement a curfew or, as will be discussed later, erect checkpoints and other street barriers.

After a broad review of the state of research, the question remains: What do we gain if we study the explicitly urban aspects of violence (and revolution)? Too often violence as well as revolutions seem to happen in a social nowhere and to come from somewhere outside the urban setting. The understanding of violence as a pattern of communication, as elaborated above, helps to reveal that the density of both personally-based and media-based communication networks are important factors in urban settings. As recent research has stressed, in urban settings the fears of violence are relevant factors that characterise the urban dimension of violence. Violence is not external to society and it is also not external to urban settings. This chapter is a very first step to study what can be gained when we try to integrate some of

these new facets of violence (element of social order, pattern of communication, the role of fears and of space-time regimes) into the study of collective
actions in urban settings.

The turbulent time phase around World War I, which is under scrutiny
here, makes it worthwhile to take a closer look at collective actions and
social movements, at social fears, at perceptions of the state and at practices
and perceptions of its monopoly of physical force. First it will be asked
whether any differences can be discerned between, on the one hand, sometimes violent collective actions that took place in urban settings during a
revolution (which brought a regime change) and, on the other hand, urban
collective actions in non-revolutionary settings. In answering this question,
I try to demonstrate how deeply a revolution affected and was also the product of spatial and temporal practices that shaped new space-time regimes
on public streets and places as well as on the shop floor. My focus is on
social movements and how they interacted with uniformed state organisations. A second question will be how fears mattered in such phases of
urban-based turbulent upheaval. Specifically, I will ask which transnational
political fears, such as of Bolshevism and/or revolution, were present in the
respective urban setting. The Russian Revolution of 1917 prompted strong
emotions across the globe: not only hopes and expectations that a revolution would finally come, but also fears of the spread of a vaguely defined
Bolshevism or communism. These fears we find among middle class and
economic elites but also among members of the established social democratic labour movement. Third, the study of collective actions and social
fears needs to be framed by an analysis of the actions and perceptions of the
state and its armed forces. During the First World War the state and its institutions were not only involved in warfare but also faced severe challenges
on the home front, where under war conditions the availability of decent
food had to be secured. The problems regarding warfare, war production
and the home front could, as happened in Germany, have negative effects
on the perception of the state. Such a perspective draws our attention to a
critical analysis of the state's monopoly on physical force, at least in those
regions where such a monopoly existed at the time. Considering the title
of this book part 'Space-time regimes and regulations: Changing forms of
urban violence', a consequence of this set of questions is that this chapter is
more a micro study of specific collective actions than an analysis of change
over a longer time span.

The three questions outlined above will be employed in a study of two
seaport cities that were renowned for their history of working-class radicalism. Hamburg, the leading German seaport, will be the first case study. It
is not only by far the largest German seaport, but has also had, since the
nineteenth century, a well-established social democratic labour movement

(Grüttner, 1984; Weinhauer, 1994; Weinhauer, 1997; Weinhauer, 2000). In Germany, a revolution took shape in late October/early November 1918. The historiography of this German Revolution saw its heyday in the 1960s and 1970s, meaning that certain aspects of its history remained unexamined: neither history of the everyday, gender history, nor any other form of cultural historical approaches left any traces in the field. It was only in the early 2010s that there was a renewed interest, open to new approaches, in this revolution. Meanwhile many studies agree to subdivide the key events of the German Revolution into three phases. As a consequence, they also let the revolution end in 1920 and not in 1919 (Kluge, 1985). After the first phase – which lasted until late 1918/early 1919 – had brought change to the political system and elections of the National Assembly, the revolution was not yet over. In a second phase of the revolution, strong mass mobilisations could be seen, especially in the urban and industrial centres until April/May 1919. The third phase, the March Revolution, lasted roughly from mid-March to May 1920 and culminated in violent workers' uprisings initiated by the nationalist Kapp Putsch in March 1920. While the first phase of the revolution was relatively peaceful, from spring 1919 onwards there were many violent clashes. In Hamburg, a series of street confrontations reached their peak in June 1919 (on Germany, see Jones, 2016; on Hamburg, see Weinhauer, 2018).

The second seaport city studied in this chapter is Seattle, situated in the Pacific Northwest of the United States. The US did not go through a revolution after World War I. The immediate post-war years, however, saw an interaction of massive fears fuelled by a seemingly omnipresent threat of radicalism of all sorts, as well as by numerous strikes, riots and other social upheavals. Thus, these years have been labelled as a phase of 'Red Scare', culminating in the 'Red Summer' of 1919 with racially coded street violence, attempted killings of politicians (by letter bombs) and governmental countermeasures such as the infamous Palmer Raids in November 1919 (Flores, 2015; McWhirter, 2012; Franz, 2021). When it comes to the study of collective violence, US cities provide fine case examples, as strikes were often extremely violent, with rifles, guns and sometimes even machine guns being used, and violent intimidations of strikers and strike breakers quite common (Graham and Gurr, 1979; Mann, 2012: 635). It is worth posing the question: Was the general strike in Seattle of 1919 shaped by these patterns of violence?

From the early twentieth century, Seattle had established a reputation as a stronghold of workers' radicalism, culminating in the famous general strike in February 1919 (Friedheim, 2018; Winslow, 2020). Until today this strike is mainly studied with a strong focus on the labour movement and its leading elites. Even the reprinted reference study (Friedheim, 2018) still argues against an older interpretation in which the strike is labelled as a 'revolution' (O'Connor, 1964). There are, however, publications that address relevant issues of local consumer politics, which also include the actions of women (Frank, 1994). As with the case of Hamburg, cultural historical perspectives (including space- or/and time-related studies on violent practices) and micro-interactions are still massively understudied (for new perspectives on the US during wartime, see Capozzola, 2008; Zeiler et al., 2017).

Revolution in Hamburg 1918–20: Urban social movement and contested space-time

In November/December 1918, Germany experienced a social and political revolution. The collective actions of a movement of soldiers and workers' councils put an end to the Kaiserreich, a democratic interim government was installed, and women's suffrage, recognition of trade unions and the eight-hour workday were granted. A new democratic government, the Weimar Coalition (Social Democrats, the liberal German Democratic Party and the Catholic Centre Party), was elected in January 1919 and the constitution came into force in mid-August 1919. Thus, in early 1919 order should have been restored in Germany. As we will see, however, there still were massive mobilisations of social movements and violent confrontations. In order to take a closer look at these actions I will focus on two events in Hamburg: one in April 1919 and one in June 1919 (for details, see Weinhauer, 2018). My main attention is on social movements and how they appropriated public space, which time regimes became visible during these activities, which patterns of violence occurred and which fears were articulated. This perspective implies the study of the activities of armed organisations that either claim to execute a state-related monopoly of physical violence or try to locally restore law and order. In both cases space-time regimes become contested. This is especially true when these armed organisations are confronted with social movements that claim to establish their own space-time regimes. Taking Hamburg as an example, I will try to show how socially and culturally far-reaching the changes were that led to and were provoked by the revolution of 1918/20. These changes in the appropriation of and symbolic use of space and time did not end with the election of the Weimar National Assembly or the Hamburg city Parliament (the Bürgerschaft) in early 1919 (see as overviews Ullrich, 1976; Büttner, 1985).

In Germany there was a war-induced erosion of trust towards the state. Governmental politics had not only been unable to ensure the quality of food but also failed to find adequate solutions for an equal distribution of food and other goods (Leonhard, 2018). Especially in the context of political traditions in Germany, this lack of trust in the state was an important factor that motivated citizens to turn to self-help, whether individually or collectively. As the social democratic labour movement and its elite had been deeply involved in war-related governmental activities, including the highly contested supply and distribution of decent food, workers often took a critical stance towards these social democratic officials and towards the social democratic labour movement as a whole. In Hamburg this impulse intensified as the leading officials of the local social democratic labour movement became relatively removed from the everyday needs of the rank and file due to their long time working within the labour movement organisations. Particularly significant, especially when seen against the erosion of trust in the state and in view of the massive presence of weapons, was the lack of a legitimated and accepted monopoly of physical force until late 1920. This setting, also in relation to the German traditions of policing, is an extremely important issue to keep in mind. In the late Kaiserreich, police forces were reformed in order to consolidate their monopoly on physical violence. In this process policing was shaped by an (although slow) emancipation of the police from its military origins, by a professionalisation of policemen and of riot control. The handling of strikes and other collective actions increasingly became a domain of police forces and less the task of military units and their confrontative tactics. After the regime change of November 1918 the uniformed police had (not only in Hamburg but also in Prussian cities) nearly completely disappeared from public streets and places (see Bericht Nr. 78). Re-establishing an accepted monopoly of physical violence was one of the key issues for the early Weimar Republic.

As the cohesion of military units had eroded and the soldiers had demobilised themselves by leaving their units and going home, police tasks were left to the newly established security organisations of the soldiers and workers' councils. These workers' militias (known as *Volkswehr* or *Sicherheitswehr*) patrolled the streets throughout the entire city. It cannot come as a surprise that Hamburg middle classes and economic elites worked hard to recruit clandestine volunteer forces from their own ranks, and also from former soldiers, and from students. Last but not least were the infamous paramilitary free corps units that were set up with governmental support in late 1918. Thus, in spring 1919 roughly five uniformed organisations – police forces, worker militias, free corps and military units, middle-class volunteers and citizen guards (*Einwohnerwehren*) – claimed to represent the monopoly on physical violence. Compared with late imperial Germany, where street policing was the domain of police forces that, when it came to severe confrontations, were supported by military units, this was an extremely unique situation. The history of the early Weimar republic cannot be fully understood if this context is not taken into consideration.

The lack of trust in the police was common among workers and added to the erosion of trust in the state. Moreover, the massive presence of weapons not only intensified this double challenge but was, when related to the aforementioned German traditions of policing, an extremely important factor (Jessen, 1991; Johansen, 2004; Leßmann-Faust, 2012). Although in pre-1914 Germany the private ownership and use of small arms was widespread (Ellerbrock, 2016), this massive presence of weapons marks a significant difference to earlier and later years. Demobilised soldiers had taken home their arms, and military ammunition depots had been left unguarded. Thus, not only pistols, revolvers and rifles but also hand grenades were very present in everyday life. Sometimes a machine gun escorted by groups of roving young males could be seen, especially in the working-class districts close to the harbour.

In early 1919 in Hamburg, as everywhere in Germany, political and social tensions had begun to grow alongside eroded trust in the state (as well as in labour-movement elites), a contested monopoly of physical force, and a massive availability of weapons. After the murder of Karl Liebknecht and Rosa Luxemburg in January 1919 and after paramilitary free corps units had been sent out with governmental approval to crush the council republic in the neighbouring city of Bremen in early February, criticism against governmental security politics was voiced, especially in working-class neighbourhoods. This criticism was directed against the social democratic party as well (Büttner, 1985: 35–40). At the same time, the allied sea blockade had intensified the problems of insufficient nutrition and food supply. Since early 1919 this criticism of the state had become more than individual complaints. Rather, in these months a diffuse social movement, which had originated in the food crisis of 1916, made its presence felt. It is difficult to track its activities and to find leading figures. It was more a diffuse set of ad hoc micro-mobilisations, organising efforts and temporary network hubs that shaped these collective actions. Thus, these activities were more than individual actions that were completely disconnected. Rather, as a working hypothesis I consider these activities to be elements of a social movement.

This social movement had developed outside the organisational channels of the established labour movement. As indicated before, since officials of the established social democratic labour movement were deemed to have cooperated too closely with the government in organising the war effort, they were also blamed for the severe problems in the distribution of food and other necessities, as well as for the deterioration in working conditions. Under war conditions, hungry and/or malnourished workers had to work longer hours and the pressure was high to increase output and productivity. The political parties and trade unions in Hamburg realised that they had only loose ties to the burgeoning social movement. Key players were ad hoc committees and also the revolutionary shop stewards (Revolutionäre Obleute). The working-class neighbourhoods where this movement was primarily active later became strongholds of the Independent Social Democratic Party (USPD), which had split from the SPD in April 1917.

The actions of this social movement were shaped by a mood of collective self-help (see Weinhauer, 2018). This involved collective actions in working-class neighbourhoods close to the harbour, as well as shop floor actions such as informal work stoppages, street protests and strikes. The central aim of this urban social movement was, first, to reclaim public space from its established use, which focused on moving from one destination to another. In the micro contexts of urban streets and public places these activists aimed at establishing a public democracy (Versammlungsdemokratie). Key organisational features were gatherings of informal discussion groups on public streets and places in working-class precincts, but also close to the political and economic centres, as well as inside or in front of important nodes of urban mobility (central rail station, underground stations). Second, the immediate objective of these discussion clubs was to gain and defend their right to the streets. This was understood as the right to follow an independent regime of unrestricted and uninhibited mobility at any time – day or night – on public streets and places, to have the right to discuss in such meetings all topics of their own choice and to organise public street protests to this end. Third, the small groups-based urban social movement and its space- and time-oriented public democracy influenced, and was influenced by, the workers themselves. On the one hand, the movement gained important impulses from shop floor-based actions, which mainly took place in the shipyards but also integrated the collective actions of dock workers. On the other hand, the shipyard workers from the companies Blohm and Voss and Vulcan, as well as dock workers, enforced their newly gained understanding of public democracy also on the shop floor, where they practised their own time regime characterised by a balanced mix of work and leisure. Discussion groups met inside the factories, and workers played cards and walked around in order to organise goods they needed for consumption or to trade them for food, coal or firewood (Staatsarchiv der Freien und Hansestadt Hamburg, Kriegsakten des Senat Z III z, Report Dezember 1919). The shipyards, which as war industries had boomed during the war, had attracted many younger workers who only had loose ties to the social democratic labour movement and its traditions (Ullrich, 1985: 47; Ullrich,

1993: 151). These highly mobile workers lacked a close relationship to their job or to their employer, concerned more about the opportunity to earn high wages in the shipyards. Moreover, among these workers the turnover rate was fairly high, as they had not yet fully incorporated the industrial time regime and its related codes of discipline and output orientation.

Fourth, this social movement of urban workers and consumers aimed to establish through collective action a local order, understood as a practical measure but also as an ideal method for organising the neighbourhood and the shop floor. This locally based order was less about abstract nation-wide social transformations and much more about transforming the micro spaces of their everyday surroundings, although these local changes could indirectly lead to wider social changes. The unique localised understanding of politics articulated by this movement was different from that of the SPD leaders and of the ruling elites and their homogeneity-oriented, nation-state-based centralised understanding of politics. Such a local order was also not a haven of peace and social harmony: during protests anti-Semitic sentiments were voiced, non-local residents were harassed and stigmatised and women were returned to their work at home.

Fifth, and of tremendous importance for this chapter, this social movement that took shape from late 1918 was an explicitly urban social movement, as it integrated demands that, in urban settings, addressed political, consumption, time, shop-floor and city-related issues (Castells, 1983). What turned the actions of this urban social movement into a revolutionary challenge for established space-time regimes was the fact that the space-time regime of this movement was deeply rooted in all elements of the triadic understanding of space: the activists contested the existing space-time regime with their lived everyday activities, whether on public streets or on the shop floor; they conceived these activities as starting points for social and cultural change; and they perceived their neighbourhood and the workplace as physical locations where these changes could locally be put into practice.

Around Easter 1919 the social tensions and the actions of the urban social movement intensified in Hamburg. At that time the unemployed had started to organise themselves and thus became connected to the urban social movement. The jobless demanded higher unemployment benefits and organised numerous protest meetings and street protests. At the same time, in the working-class neighbourhoods close to the harbour, collective actions arose that focused on three issues: criticism of patterns of consumption and wealth that were deemed to be insultingly displayed in public; criticism of governmental security and military policies; and protests against the moral and political denigration of the urban social movement voiced by politicians and the press in Hamburg (Philipski, 2002: 51; Schulte-Varendorff, 2010: 38; *Generalanzeiger* 96, 25 April 1919). From mid-April

1919, activists from the urban social movements began to publicly demand respect for their locally rooted moral codes. They publicly harassed and assaulted wealthy-looking passers-by, appropriating their watches and elegant coats, demanding money and sometimes, also on public streets and places, slapping them in the face. At first the *Volkswehr*, the workers' militia, was called to end all this. As these units were not able (or willing) to stop these activities completely, uniformed middle-class volunteers were sent to St. Pauli (*Hamburger Echo* 184, 22 April 1919; *Hamburger Nachrichten* 204, 22 April 1919). Together with the Volkswehr they tried to clear the streets. These countermeasures led to three days of unrest. Guns and rifles were fired, hand grenades were thrown and machine guns were fired. After three days of explosions and intense shooting, between eight and eighteen people had been killed (Philipski, 2002: 51; Schulte-Varendorff, 2010: 38; *Generalanzeiger* 96, 25 April 1919, *Neue Hamburger Zeitung* 211, 25 April 1919).

The shift from a neighbourhood-based campaign for respect and the mainly symbolic presence of weapons to the use of massively deadly force came in summer 1919. The main actors were the urban social movement on the one side, and the working class Volkswehr units supplemented by uniformed bourgeois volunteers and free corps units on the other side. These latter units were hated by the workers, as many of those volunteers were full of violent enthusiasm to smash the Bolshevists and 'Red' workers (see *Kommunistische Arbeiterzeitung* 46, 25 June 1919 and Nr 47, 26 June 1919; *Hamburger Fremdenblatt* 319, 26 June 1919; *Hamburger Nachrichten* 319, 26 June 1919; Schulte-Varendorff, 2010: 90f; *Generalanzeiger* 146, 26 June 1919). In June 1919, after a scandal about rotten food and meat, new skirmishes took place. This time the fighting was mainly located in those physical spaces of the city where the town hall and the stock exchange were situated. These locations were seen to be the political and economic centres of Hamburg. When violent confrontations occurred here, they were interpreted against this background and thus labelled as much more threatening than clashes confined to working-class precincts. When, in these politically and economically labelled physical spaces, rifles were used and hand grenades were thrown, they were employed not merely against opponents but those who were perceived to be true enemies. In a three-day period in June 1919 some 80 people were killed and 100 injured (Schulte-Varendorff, 2010: 105f.). In comparison to the April events, this high death toll marks a watershed in the quality of violence. In April, worker had stood against worker. The violence they employed in a triadic setting (perpetrator–victim–bystander) also had a strong symbolic component that aimed at communicating messages to the local urban community. Weapons were often only shown but seldom used with the intent of killing the opponent. Moreover, the fighting space was confined to working-class neighbourhoods. In June, the fighting developed into a temporary although localised civil war. It raged in the political and economic centre of Hamburg and contributed to fears of a second revolution (for a critical reflection on the origins of the upheaval of June 1919, see Schulte-Varendorff, 2010: 202–6).

It was also in June 1919 that a series of work stoppages of dock workers demonstrated that workplace and consumption issues still interacted. In the semi-public open space of the free port, dock workers unloaded the US ships that had transported food to be distributed in Germany and also in Hamburg. These workers wanted to work according to their time regime, which combined a mix of work and leisure. Uniformed bourgeois student volunteers (*Bahrenfelder Zeitfreiwillige*) were sent in to stop this work culture, which was rooted in the tradition of pilfering that was widespread among dock workers (Grüttner, 1982; Cooke Johnson, 2000). These paramilitaries tightly controlled and bodily searched not only those dockers who worked the quayside food cargo but also those workers who left the free-port area through the checkpoints (*Generalanzeiger* 141, 20 June 1919). These checks sparked a strike as well as a series of protest marches and open gatherings in central meeting places in Hamburg. The conflicts were also about codes of honour and respect, as the workers felt insulted by these body searches. In the end, the hated units of uniformed volunteers had to be withdrawn and the checks were carried out by customs officials.

After these events of June 1919, the urban social movement was crushed in late July that year. Some 10,000 uniformed soldiers and free corps men, led by the veteran of the East African colonial war Lettow Vorbeck, marched into Hamburg (Schulte-Varendorff, 2010: 105). The main aim of these units was to re-establish law and order, by reorganising the monopoly of physical force. Closely related to this were efforts to reclaim public space from the urban social movement and to re-establish the politically and economically dominant time regime, thus terminating the revolution. These troops erected numerous checkpoints and barbed wire barriers aimed at channelling the movement, in time and space – this movement of the inhabitants of the working-class precincts like St. Pauli and Neustadt, which were deemed to be the breeding grounds of everyday disobedience, political opposition and revolutionary aspirations. For the inhabitants of these working-class precincts the enforcement of this space-time regime had far-reaching consequences: public life was de-accelerated and restructured by these checkpoints and barbed wires. The inhabitants had to queue individually before they could pass the checkpoints and were also searched (either by policemen or by members of the hated paramilitary units). At least for those workers who saw themselves living in a time phase when social change was not a matter of a distant future but of some weeks or months, such a space-time regime enforced by uniformed forces could serve either to deal a fatal blow to any hope of revolutionary change or to contribute to workers' political radicalisation. Moreover, even in 'normal' times such control procedures, which also criminalised and degraded workers, would not have strengthened trust in the new republic and its armed forces. It took more than a year until, in spring 1920, after massive interventions of the Interallied Military Control Commission, a more democratic police force became established and by and large the social acceptance of the monopoly of physical force began to grow (Leßmann-Faust, 2012; Weinhauer, 2018). As the two episodes of April and June 1919 have demonstrated, urban violence is not merely violence that is acted out in cities. Rather, it matters in which urban settings violence is employed and how these violent acts are labelled and perceived. Is this violence confined to certain neighbourhoods like working-class precincts or does it occur near politically or economically relevant buildings? Moreover, it is important how these acts of violence are labelled by the media – in this case the press, politicians and the armed forces. Third, this analysis of collective violence in April and June 1919 has demonstrated that there is no somewhat 'natural' tendency of violence to always escalate. Again, the urban setting, labelling processes and role of social fears are important factors that have to be carefully analysed.

Seattle General Strike of February 1919: A 'revolution'?

Until the last third of the nineteenth century, Seattle remained a city at the fringes of public attention in the United States. This changed some decades later when Seattle became connected to the national railway network. As a consequence, the city's population grew from c. 240,000 (1910) to some 315,000 inhabitants in 1920. World War I gave another economic impulse. During that war, Seattle's shipbuilding industry produced 20 percent of the nation's wartime ship tonnage. Thus, the numbers of shipyard workers steadily grew. By 1919 about 75 percent of the manufacturing workforce had connections to shipbuilding. Before 1910 this proportion had averaged about 6 percent (Berner and Dorpat, 2006: 9). After the war, in early 1919, Seattle's shipyard workers went on strike to maintain their high wartime wages. This event was an important impulse for the general strike of 6–11 February 1919. Among contemporaries this strike fuelled massive fears about radicals and socialists and helped establish Seattle's reputation as a hotbed of political radicalism.

Seattle was well connected to the international newspaper networks. The middle-class newspapers of the city were full of reports about the

Russian Revolution and civil war, as well as about the revolution and other uprisings in Germany's urban and industrial areas. The *Seattle Star* was certain to report that 'anarchy reigns as reds seize Teuton capital' or as the newspaper declared some days later, 'the Spartacan revolution is spreading to all parts of Germany' (*Seattle Star*, 7 and 9 January 1919). Seattle's labour press, *Union Record*, kept its readers informed about the striking workers in Glasgow, commonly known as Red Clydeside (Winslow, 2020: 191) and also reported about the short-lived council republic that was established in Bremen in February 1919 (Union Record, 4 February 1919). Unlike in Germany, where there had been a political revolution (which brought a regime change), in the United States there was no such clear-cut political caesura. In Germany, although there still were racialised fears about Jewish Bolshevism, the political revolution and regime change had made it much easier to name those who seemed responsible for ending the Kaiserreich (social democrats, Spartacists). In the US, the lack of such certainties fuelled a complex imaginary[1] of nearly omnipresent fears focused on innumerable vaguely defined threats: radicals, Bolshevists, migrants, strangers and political aliens of all sorts. These imaginaries of threat were intensified by the widely shared understanding of cities, especially quickly urbanising cities, as hotbeds of radicalism and moral decline.

As we shall see, in Seattle the established channels of collective bargaining and of communication between the social groups involved in the strike remained intact and were used during the strike. In January 1919 the Seattle Central Labor Council, as the umbrella organisation of the more than 100 trade unions of the city, adopted a resolution that was initiated by the Metal Trades Council to call a general strike if this call was supported by a referendum of Seattle's unions. This referendum was organised by a General Strike Committee with representatives from Seattle's labour movement. After the vote the delegates of the committee set the start of the strike for Thursday, 6 February at 10 a.m. The general strike was not about taking over the means of production by the workers. Rather, it was a sympathy strike for the shipyard workers in order to support their wage claims. The start of the strike went like this:

> At ten o'clock on the morning of February 6, 1919, the city of Seattle was ominously quiet. Some sixty thousand organized workingmen had failed to report to work. Buses and trolleys remained in their barns. No smoke poured from the chimneys of factories, workshops, or foundries in the ordinarily bustling industrial portions of the city and its waterfront. On that Thursday morning even the public schools of the Northwest's Queen City were closed. The downtown streets were virtually deserted. (Friedheim, 2018: 3)

While business districts may have been quiet, other neighbourhoods were massively alive, organising the strike and the supply of food, meals and milk for schoolchildren. Electric power and telephones were working, hospitals, butcher shops and food markets remained open. The strike committee had organised a system of essential services: 'Relying on their own skills and commitment, thousands of volunteers took on the strike's tasks, including running the kitchens ..., organizing milk distribution, and policing the city' (Winslow, 2020: 208).

The strike lacked a cogent objective and a clear enemy. Moreover, there were hardly any acts of physical violence committed, which was quite surprising, given the history of massively violent labour conflicts in the United States. Nonetheless, the strike fuelled massive fears about radicals and socialists. Seattle business elites, the press and Mayor Ole Hanson claimed to know that the strike was heading towards a revolution (Friedheim, 2018: 111). Hanson emphasised that the city was 'prepared for a state of siege' (Friedheim, 2018: 113). In his view, put forward on 9 February 1919 in the *New York Times*, the strike was a 'sympathetic revolution': 'Let us clean up the United States of America. Let all men stand up and be counted .... We refuse to treat with these revolutionists. Unconditional surrender are our only terms' ('Anarchists tried revolution in Seattle, but never got to first base', *New York Times*, 9 February 1919). For Hanson and his supporters, a Bolshevist revolution was best fought with patriotic Americanism. As the *Seattle Star*, the leading voice focusing on Americanism (*Seattle Star*, 8 February 1919; Friedheim, 2018: 146), claimed: 'Seattle must be an American city. It must be made free of Bolsheviks and Bolshevism' (*Seattle Star*, 10 February 1919). As the paper put it, the strike is 'an acid test of American citizenship – and an acid test of all those principles for which our soldiers have fought and died' (*Seattle Star*, 6 February 1919). The imaginary of fear that I have outlined above made it quite easy to verbally turn the general strike into a revolution.

Behind the scenes, Mayor Hanson was trying to gain support for his radical anti-strike policy among the local business elites. As a recent research article notes, in these months an 'alarmist, bombastic, reactionary, armed-force wielding Ole Hanson [was] catapulted to fame as the era's most heroic anti-red mayor' (Hodges, 2019: 84). In the end it became obvious that his propagandistic efforts were aimed at guarding the city against violent outbreaks that never happened. Against these efforts the military made it clear that only they had the power to declare martial law – not the mayor (Friedheim, 2018: 129).

As Christopher Capozzola has brilliantly outlined in his study of the influence World War I had on US society, in the United States there was no state that claimed a legitimate monopoly of physical force (Capozzola, 2008: 13).

The army and local police followed their own agendas. Troops were sent in, although they kept a low profile when patrolling on the streets. Labour was left in an 'uneasy uncertainty about the army's possible actions' (Friedheim, 2018: 135). Ole Hanson as mayor of Seattle mobilised some 600 additional policemen and more than 2,000 auxiliary deputies to be prepared to keep order in the city (Friedheim, 2018: 136). Although the police and army were criticised by the strike committee, the authority of the uniformed forces remained uncontested. There was also massive symbolic communication in the public space, since security forces placed machine guns at strategic locations (see photos *Town Crier*, 15 February 1919; Winslow, 2020: 189).

On the part of the labour movement, the hidden agenda of this general strike was to avoid any activities that could fire up imaginaries that a real revolution was approaching. Although many workers had joined the strike, most of them stayed home or visited the strike bureau in the central Labour Temple. They did not try to march collectively through the city streets in large numbers and did not try to collectively reclaim public streets and places. In order to enforce the strike-related time regime, the strike committee declared the end of the strike on Tuesday, 11 February 1919, at 12 o'clock noon. As with fixing the start of the strike, this declaration indicated that the strike committee was keen to specify a precise time to start and to end the strike. This gesture confirmed that it was the workers who still had the power to clearly define when the strike was over. This power did not lie in the hands of business or city officials. Trying to keep public order undisturbed, the labour movement organised three hundred men of the War Veteran Guard, which patrolled the city and helped to keep it peaceful during the strike, although they had no legal authority (Friedheim, 2018: 131). Even the otherwise militant Industrial Workers of the World (IWW) joined this disciplined strike pattern (Friedheim, 2018: 124). No shots were fired from any side at any time. As mentioned above, this absence of physical violence was very remarkable.

At the workplace and on the labour market since 1916 there had been sectoral efforts to challenge time regimes, as the labour market organisation among Seattle longshoremen demonstrates. The labour market for dock labour was the most contested field. Employers using a hiring hall tried to select workers according to their physical fitness, job qualifications, willingness to work overtime and willingness to obey orders. Alternative models were, for example, rotational hiring systems where the work opportunities in dock work were distributed evenly among all registered dock workers. Such a system was often coupled with a closed shop open only to unionised workers. While in Hamburg dock workers until late 1920 had established patterns of rotational hiring and thus enforced a time regime of their choice on employers, in Seattle such systems only existed for brief periods and in some small sections of the port (Weinhauer, 1997; Magden, 1991). Their fellow workers in Hamburg had self-consciously transformed the impulses they both gave to and received from the urban social movement into longer lasting results that were also supported by the social political gains of the revolution, among them union-based collective bargaining and shorter working hours.

Looking at the end of the Seattle strike there are still two interpretations. One states that the strike 'was more than a failure – it was a disaster' (Friedheim, 2018: 146), as it led to internal tensions and to a crushing of labour organisations and accelerated the open-shop drive of employers, in which union membership was not mandatory. The other position states 'the men went back, feeling that they had won the strike …. They went back proud of themselves for the way they had come out; proud of themselves for the way they had kept order under provocation' (Strong, n.d.: 63).

In late 1918/early 1919, the US government withdrew from the regulation of industrial relations. In summer 1919 when government orders for shipbuilding were cancelled, thousands of shipyard workers lost their jobs. In early 1920 the largest shipbuilding company in Seattle, Skinner & Eddy, only employed some 800 men working for reduced wages; during the last phase of the war it had employed 6,000 to 8,000. The post-war depression hit Seattle just as hard as other US cities. By 1921 Seattle had 'become an industrial ghost town' (Friedheim, 2018: 171); it had 'retrogressed almost to the point of its pre-war economic position'. With regard to urban violence, this brief study of the Seattle General Strike has generated two insights. First, in Seattle the channels of communication between the involved parties were kept intact. Second, massive fears of an uncontrollable revolution melted into powerful imaginaries of threat, which led to disciplined actions on the part of the armed forces as well as of the striking workers. Both sides seemed to have realised that if this strike got out of hand, no one would know what the future would bring.

Conclusion

The study of the history of urban-based, sometimes violent, collective actions, and of the fears, practices and perceptions of state actions around World War I benefits intellectually from a space-time approach. In this social and cultural historical chapter, I put forward an understanding of urban violence that sees physical violence as a pattern of communication in triadic settings where violence is a crucial element of (urban) social order, not an anomic anomaly. I also examined how social fears could influence this space-time setting.

The analysis of the second phase of the revolution in Hamburg, which took place in the first half of 1919, demonstrated that a revolution was simultaneously shaped by and could also trigger socially and culturally far-reaching changes of highly contested space-time regimes. An urban social movement acted as a driving force in this contestation. First, this movement tried to establish a space-time regime organised around public democracy, rooted in the working-class neighbourhoods close to the harbour as well as on the shop floor in dock work and in the shipyards. Respect for the locally rooted moral codes was enforced by publicly employed acts of physical violence. These violent acts were not only shaped by the interaction between perpetrators and victims but at the same served to communicate elements of the newly established space-time regime to the local urban public.

Second, in late 1918/early 1919 the middle classes in Hamburg, like those in Seattle, were shaken by a plethora of fears ignited by the Russian Revolution of 1917. There were, however, major differences in the scope and in the social consequences of these fears. In Germany, although there still were racialised fears about Jewish Bolshevism, the political revolution and consequent regime change had made it much easier to name those deemed responsible for ending the Kaiserreich (social democrats, Spartacists). In the United States, the set of diffuse social fears constructed a complex imaginary of nearly omnipresent fear focused on innumerable vaguely defined threats. Thus, the feeling of social vulnerability was much more diffuse and also more dramatic and widespread than was the case in Germany. In the US this imaginary of threat shaped the impression that a revolution, especially in urban settings, could be triggered by any event which was defined as not 'normal' – as un-American. This imaginary contributed strongly to the dramatisation of the Seattle General Strike and its contemporary interpretation as a 'revolution'.

This socially deep-rooted fear-driven dramatisation, however, had a pacifying consequence: the Seattle General Strike clearly showed that even in the United States there is no inbuilt tendency for strikes in urban settings to always escalate into violent confrontations. The massive fears of an uncontrollable revolution led all parties involved in the strike to act very cautiously. This tendency was supported by the fact that there existed functioning channels of communication between the involved parties and of mutual respect between the armed forces and the striking workers, both of which prevented this strike from following the violence-laden patterns of US strike history.

Third, through their collective actions the activists of the urban social movement in Hamburg challenged the legitimacy of the newly established uniformed security forces. Re-establishing an accepted monopoly of physical violence was one of the key problems for the early Weimar Republic. The focus of workers' distrust lay on the uniformed middle-class (student) volunteers and their claims of anti-Bolshevist and anti-worker spacing. In June 1919 these double (and interrelated) contests about control over urban space-time and spacing turned into a localised civil war, fuelled also by the contested monopoly of physical force. As these violent confrontations reached the political and economic centres of Hamburg, which had not occurred in April, the spiral of violence was difficult to stop. This escalation was driven by two interacting factors. The involved parties communicated (if at all) only in a very biased way with each other and mutual distrust and lack of respect became the rule, which reinforced the tendency to employ violence against each other.

When looking at the definition of a revolution given at the start of this article it becomes obvious that the Seattle General Strike of February 1919 was by no means a revolution. There was no regime change, and during the strike the local time regime and urban spatial order remained structurally uncontested. Moreover, there were no newly emerging urban social movements that tried to position themselves against established labour organisations. Additionally, the forces of order remained intact; their actions were not challenged nor was law and order questioned at any time. This underlines the fact that the space and time-related transformative potential of a general strike is much weaker than that of a revolution.

Like other US cities, Seattle saw an upswing of labour activities and rank-and-file organising beginning in the early 1930s, which culminated in the famous West Coast Waterfront Strike that began on 9 May 1934 and lasted more than eighty days. This strike was much more confrontational than the general strike of February 1919. In the end, thanks to state arbitration, the striking longshoremen gained control over the strongly contested hiring process, rendering the ports a stronghold of union power (Nelson, 1988; Kimeldorf, 1988; Johnson, 2000). In Hamburg the rise of national-socialism in the late 1920s/early 1930s was the next phase during which the space-time regimes in public space and on the shop-floor were strongly contested (Forschungsstelle, 2005). In the end the labour movement was destroyed, many of its members incarcerated, tortured or even killed, and the path to racist mass murder had begun.

Note

1 Imaginaries of fear are more than individual feelings, being more stable and including a set of often interrelated fears.

Bibliography

Assmann, A. (2013). *Ist die Zeit aus den Fugen? Aufstieg und Fall des Zeitregimes der Moderne* (München: Hanser).

Baberowski, J. et al. (eds) (2015). 'Special Issue: The Crisis of Empire after 1918', *Journal of Modern European History*, 13:2.

Berner, R. C. and Dorpat, P. (2006) *Seattle 1900–1920. From Boomtown, Through Urban Turbulence, to Restoration* (Seattle: Charles Press).

Bericht [Nr. 78] des von der Bürgerschaft am 4. Juli 1919 zur Prüfung des Antrags des Senats [Nr. 143 von 1919], niedergesetzten Ausschusses zur Untersuchung der Unruhen vom 24. und 25. Juni 1919, Dezember 1920 [MS].

Bertrand, C. L. (1977). *Revolutionary Situations in Europe 1917–1922: Germany, Italy, Austria-Hungary* (Montréal: Interuniversity Centre for European Studies).

Body-Gendrot. S. (2012). *Globalization, Fear, and Insecurity. The Challenges for Cities North and South* (Houndmills, Basingstoke: Palgrave McMillan).

Bourke, J. (2003). 'Fear and Anxiety: Writing about Emotion in Modern History', *History Workshop Journal*, 55:1, 111–33.

Büttner, U. (1985). *Politische Gerechtigkeit und sozialer Geist. Hamburg zur Zeit der Weimarer Republik* (Hamburg: Christian).

Capozzola, C. (2008). *Uncle Sam Wants You. World War I and the Making of the Modern American Citizen* (Oxford: Oxford University Press).

Carsten, F. L. (1976). *Revolution in Central Europe, 1918–1919* (Berkeley: University of California Press).

Castells, M. (1983). *The City and the Grassroots: A Cross-cultural Theory of Urban Social Movements* (London; Caulfield: Arnold, Edward).

Ceccato, V. (ed.) (2012). *The Urban Fabric of Crime and Fear* (Dordrecht: Springer).

Collins, R. (2008). *Violence: A Micro-sociological Theory* (Princeton: Princeton University Press).

Cooke Johnson, L. (2000). 'Criminality on the Docks', in Davies, S. et al. (eds) *Dock Workers: International Explorations in Comparative Labour History, 1790–1970* (Aldershot: Ashgate), 721–45.

Cronin, J. E. and Sirianni, C. (eds) (1983). *Work, Community, and Power: The Experience of Labor in Europe and America, 1900–1925* (Philadelphia: Temple University Press).

Darwin, J. (2008). *After Tamerlane: The Rise and Fall of Global Empires, 1400–2000* (London: Penguin).

Ellerbrock, D. (2016). 'Kriegsausbruch und private Schusswaffen – Regulierungseffekte des Ersten Weltkriegs auf die zivile deutsche Waffenkultur', in Cornelißen, C., Löffelbein, N., and Fehlemann, S. (eds) *Europa 1914. Wege ins Unbekannte* (Paderborn: Schöningh), 67–80.

Flores, N. L. (2015). 'Fear of Revolution. Germany 1918/19 and the US-Palmer Raids', in Weinhauer, K., McElligott, A., and Heinsohn, K. (eds) *Germany 1916–23: A Revolution in Context* (Bielefeld: Transcript Verlag), 127–49.

Foran, J. (1993). 'Theories of Revolution Revisited: Toward a Fourth Generation?', *Sociological Theory*, 11:1, 1–20.

Forschungsstelle für Zeitgeschichte (ed.) (2005). *Hamburg im Dritten Reich* (Göttingen: Wallstein Verlag).

Frank, D. (1994). *Purchasing Power: Consumer Organizing, Gender, and the Seattle Labor Movement, 1919–1929* (Cambridge; New York: Cambridge University Press).

Franz, M. (2021). *'Fight for Americanism'. Preparedness-Bewegung und zivile Mobilisierung in den USA 1914–1920* (Bielefeld: Transcript Verlag).

Friedheim, R. L. ([1964] 2018). *The Seattle General Strike* (Centennial edition) (Seattle: University of Washington Press).

Generalanzeiger 96, 25 April 1919.

Generalanzeiger 141, 20 June 1919.

Generalanzeiger 146, 26 June 1919.

Gerwarth, R. and Horne, J. (eds) (2012). *War in Peace: Paramilitary Violence in Europe After the Great War* (Oxford: Oxford University Press).

Gerwarth, R. (2017). *The Vanquished. Why the First World War Failed to End, 1917–1923* (London: Penguin Books).

Geyer, M. H. (1998). *Verkehrte Welt. Revolution, Inflation und Moderne, München 1914–1924* (Göttingen: Vandenhoeck und Ruprecht).

Glass, M. R., Seyboldt, T., and Williams, P. (eds) (2022). *Urban Violence, Resilience and Security. Governance Responses in the Global South* (Cheltenham: Edward Elgar Publishing).

Goldstone, J. A. (1982). 'The Comparative and Historical Study of Revolutions'. *Annual Review of Sociology*, 8:1, 187–207.

Goldstone, J. A. (2001). 'Toward a Fourth Generation of Revolutionary Theory', *Annual Review of Political Science*, 4:1, 139–87.

Graham, H. D. and Gurr, T. R. (eds) (1979). *Violence in America. Historical and Comparative Perspectives* (Beverley Hills, CA: Sage).

Grüttner, M. (1982). 'Working-class Crime and the Labour Movement. Pilfering in the Hamburg Docks 1888–1923', in Evans, R. J. (ed.) *The German Working Class 1888–1933* (London: Croom Helm), 54–79.

Grüttner, M. (1984). *Arbeitswelt an der Wasserkante: Sozialgeschichte der Hamburger Hafenarbeiter 1886- 1914* (Göttingen: Vandenhoeck & Ruprecht).

Hale, C. (1996). 'Fear of Crime. A Review of the Literature', *International Review of Victimology*, 4, 79–150.

Hamburger Echo 184, 22 April 1919.

Hamburger Fremdenblatt 319, 26 June 1919.

Hamburger Nachrichten 204, 22 April 1919.

Hamburger Nachrichten 319, 26 June 1919.

Hodges, A. J. (2019). 'Understanding a National and Global Red Scare/Red Summer Through the Local Invention of Solidarities', *The Journal of the Gilded Age and Progressive Era*, 18:1, 81–98.

Jessen, R. (1991). *Polizei im Industrierevier Modernisierung und Herrschaftspraxis im westfälischen Ruhrgebiet 1848–1914* (Göttingen: Vandenhoek & Ruprecht).

Joas, H. and Knöbl, W. (2008). *Kriegsverdrängung. Ein Problem in der Geschichte der Sozialtheorie* (Frankfurt am Main: Suhrkamp).

Johansen, A. (2004). *Soldiers as Police. The French und Prussian Armies and the Policing of Popular Protest* (Aldershot: Ashgate).

Johnson, V. (2000). 'The Cultural Foundation of Resources, the Resource Foundation of Political Cultures: An Explanation for the Outcomes of Two General Strikes', *Politics and Society*, 28:3, 331–65.

Jones, M. (2016). *Founding Weimar. Violence and the German Revolution of 1918–1919* (Cambridge: Cambridge University Press).

Kimeldorf, H. (1988). *Reds or Rackets: The Making of Radical and Conservative Unions on the Waterfront* (Berkeley: University of California Press).

Kluge, U. (1985). *Die deutsche Revolution 1918/19. Staat, Politik und Gesellschaft zwischen Weltkrieg und Kapp-Putsch* (Frankfurt/M.: Suhrkamp).

Knöbl, W. and Hoebel, T. (2019). *Gewalt erklären. Plädoyer für eine entdeckende Prozesssoziologie* (Hamburg: Hamburger Edition).

Koloma Beck, T. (2017). 'Gewalt als leibliche Erfahrung', *Mittelweg 36*, 26:3, 52–73.

Kommunistische Arbeiterzeitung 46, 25 June 1919 and Nr 47, 26 June 1919.

Konrad, H. and Schmidlechner, K. M. (1991). *Revolutionäres Potential in Europa am Ende des Ersten Weltkrieges: die Rolle von Strukturen, Konjunkturen und Massenbewegungen* (Vienna: Böhlau).

Lawson, G. (2019). *Anatomies of Revolution* (Cambridge: Cambridge University Press).

Lefebvre, H. (1991). *The Production of Space* (Malden, Ma; Oxford: Blackwell).

Lefebvre, H. (2003 [1970]). *The Urban Revolution* (Minneapolis; London: University of Minnesota Press).

Leonhard, J. (2018). *Pandora's Box. A History of the First World War* (Cambridge: Harvard University Press).

Leßmann-Faust, P. (2012). *Die preußische Schutzpolizei in der Weimarer Republik: Streifendienst und Straßenkampf* (Frankfurt/Main: Verlag für Polizeiwissenschaft).

Löw, M. (2001). *Raumsoziologie* (Frankfurt/Main: Suhrkamp).

Magden, R. E. (1991). *A History of Seattle Waterfront Workers, 1884–1934* (Seattle: ILWU Local 19).

Malesevic, S. (2010). *The Sociology of War and Violence* (Cambridge: Cambridge University Press).

Mann, M. (2012). *The Sources of Social Power. Volume 2: The Rise of Classes and Nation-States, 1760–1914* (Cambridge: Cambridge University Press).

McWhirter, C. (2012). *Red Summer. The Summer of 1919 and the Awakening of Black America* (New York: Henry Holt).

Nelson, B. (1988). *Workers on the Waterfront, Seamen, Longshoremen and Unionism in the 1930s* (Urbana: University of Illinois Press).

Neue Hamburger Zeitung 211, 25 April 1919.

New York Times, 9 February 1919.

Newburn, T. (2021). 'The Causes and Consequences of Urban Riot and Unrest', *Annual Review of Criminology*, 4:1, 53–73.

O'Connor, H. (1964). *Revolution in Seattle: A Memoir* (New York: Monthly Review Press).

Pavoni, A. and Tulumello, S. (2018). 'What is urban violence', *Progress in Human Geography*, 44:1, 49–76.

Philipski, S. (2002). *Ernährungsnot und sozialer Protest: Die Hamburger Sülzeunruhen 1919* (Hamburg: Hamburg University).

Rinke, S. H. and Wildt, M. (2017). *Revolutions and Counter-revolutions: 1917 and its Aftermath From a Global Perspective* (Frankfurt/Main: Campus Verlag).

Rotker, S. (ed.) (2002). *Citizens of Fear. Urban Violence in Latin America* (New Brunswick: Rutgers University Press).

Schulte-Varendorff, U. (2010). *Die Hungerunruhen in Hamburg im Juni 1919 – eine zweite Revolution?* (Hamburg: Hamburg University Press).

Seattle Star, 7 and 9 January 1919.

Seattle Star, 6 February 1919.

Seattle Star, 8 February 1919.

Seattle Star, 10 February 1919.

Staatsarchiv der Freien und Hansestadt Hamburg, Kriegsakten des Senat Z III z, Report Dezember 1919.

Strong, A. L. (n.d.) *Seattle General Strike* (Seattle: Union Record Publishing).

Town Crier, 15 February 1919.

Ullrich, V. (1976). *Die Hamburger Arbeiterbewegung vom Vorabend des Ersten Weltkrieges bis zur Revolution 1918/19* (Hamburg: Lüdke).

Ullrich, V. (1985). 'Der Januarstreik 1918 in Hamburg, Kiel und Bremen. Eine vergleichende Studie zur Geschichte der Streikbewegung im Ersten Weltkrieg', *Zeitschrift des Vereins für Hamburgische Geschichte*, 71, 45–75.

Ullrich, V. (1993). 'Die USPD in Hamburg und im Bezirk Wasserkante 1917/18', *Zeitschrift des Vereins für Hamburgische Geschichte*, 79, 133–62.

von Trotha, T. (ed.) (1998). *Soziologie der Gewalt* (Wiesbaden: VS Verlag für Sozialwissenschaften).

Wagner, K. A. (2019). *Amritsar 1919. An Empire of Fear and the Making of a Massacre.* (New Haven: Yale University Press).

Weinhauer, K. (1994). *Alltag und Arbeitskampf im Hamburger Hafen. Sozialgeschichte der Hamburger Hafenarbeiter 1914–1933* (Paderborn: Schoeningh).

Weinhauer, K. (1997). 'Labour Market, Work Mentality and Syndicalism: Dock Labour in the United States and Hamburg' 1900–1950s', *International Review of Social History*, 42:2, 219–52.

Weinhauer, K. (2000). 'Power and Control on the Waterfront: Casual Labour and Decasualisation', in Davies, S., Davis, C. J., de Vries, D., and van Voss, L. H. (eds) *Dock Workers: International Explorations in Comparative Labour History, 1790–1970* (Aldershot: Ashgate), 580–603.

Weinhauer, K. and Ellerbrock, D. (2013). 'Perspektiven auf Gewalt in europäischen Städten seit dem 19. Jahrhundert', *Informationen zur modernen Stadtgeschichte*, 2, 5–20.

Weinhauer, K., McElligott, A., and Heinsohn, K. (2015). 'Introduction. In search of the German Revolution', in Weinhauer, K., McElligott, A., and Heinsohn, K. (eds) *Germany 1916–23: A revolution in context* (Bielefeld: Transcript Verlag), 7–35.

Weinhauer, K., McElligott, A., and Heinsohn, K. (eds) (2015). *Germany 1916–23. A Revolution in Context* (Bielefeld: Transcript).

Weinhauer, K. (2018). 'Bewaffnete Ordnungskonflikte zwischen Staatsgewalt und urbanen sozialen Bewegungen in Hamburg 1916–1923', in Czech, H.-J., Matthes, O., and Pelc, O. (eds) *Revolution! Revolution? Hamburg 1918/19* (Hamburg: Wachholtz, Murmann Publishers), 272–97.

Winslow, C. (2020). *Radical Seattle: The General Strike of 1919* (New York: Monthly Review Press).

Wrigley, C. (ed.) (1993). *Challenges of Labour: Central and Western Europe, 1917–1920* (London; New York: Routledge).

Zeiler, T. W., Ekbladh, D. K., and Montoya, B. C. (eds) (2017). *Beyond 1917: The United States and the Global Legacies of the Great War* (New York: Oxford University Press).

Ziemann, B. (2003). 'Germany After the First World War – A Violent Society? Results and Implications of Recent Research on Weimar Germany', *Journal of Modern European History*, 1:1, 80–95.

2

From riots to massacres: How space and time changed urban violence in Jerusalem, 1920–29

Roberto Mazza

On 2 September 1929, *The Palestine Bulletin* reported: 'After an intermission of eight years, Palestine again became the scene of massacre and savagery. Horror gripped the country a whole week. The Arab attacks began in Jerusalem and spread all over the country.' (*Palestine Bulletin*, 2 September 1929). As noted in the newspaper, the last serious incidents in Palestine had occurred in 1921 with the Jaffa riots and one year earlier with the Nabi Musa riots in Jerusalem. How do we explain the recurrence of violence after such a relatively long time? How did urban violence change through the late Ottoman period and through the 1920s? Was urban violence becoming a recurrent event in the city, a liturgy to follow? There are certainly many questions that can be asked in order to grasp the development of a phenomenon that dramatically affected – and still affects – the life of ordinary Jerusalemites.

This chapter will strive to show how urban planning, the re-definition of space and time beginning with the British arrival in 1917, influenced the development of urban violence, causing its transformation. The massacres of 1929 reveal how urban violence changed from the time of the incidents of 1920 and 1921. During this period British urban planning of the city developed in two aspects: making Jerusalem – the Old City – an open air museum and sectarianising the new emerging neighbourhoods. Socio-economic transformations also changed the perception of time, which then became standardised as Palestine was included in the global British Empire. It is important to clarify from the very beginning that I choose to use the word 'massacres' instead of 'riots' – as used by the British and many publications – as I believe the word riot denotes a spontaneous eruption of violence, while the events of 1929 show the emergence of a clear pattern that included the premeditated use of violence in order to hurt and kill the enemy. I will later rely on the definition of massacres provided by Jacques Semelin, however it is important here to stress the different nature of the two. Riots and massacres always have a negative connotation, yet behind this vocabulary there is more than just violence, and one of the purposes of this chapter is to understand the acts of collective violence and contextualise them in the city rather than judge them.

While briefly discussing some of the most important urban plans, I will show how the distribution of the population – i.e. its segregation – had a negative impact on the development of intercommunal relations. From a city where space and time were shared, Jerusalem was transformed into a city where space and time had to be defined by national-religious affiliation. I would argue that this process was a reversal from Ottoman times, with their diversity, since the British understood modern identity as something that had to be experienced and developed in a homogeneous environment, whereby each group should have owned its own space and time. A similar argument has been made by Mara Albrecht in this volume in her discussion of both Jerusalem and Belfast as sites where violence developed alongside the transformation of local identity. In the second part of the chapter, I will explore how particular qualities of urban space – in the case of Jerusalem I will refer particularly to sacred space – generated different forms of violence as experienced in the events of 1929. Similarly, I will try to look at the peculiarities of this space with regard to violence; in other words, I will investigate how religious cycles and imagination influenced the outbreak of urban violence in Jerusalem in 1929. In conclusion, through a historical review of the Nabi Musa Riots that occurred in 1920 and the massacres that unfolded in Jerusalem in 1929 as part of a larger period of violence, this chapter will show how the specific spatiotemporal characteristics of Jerusalem shaped different forms of violence in accordance with the evolving historical context. In other words, it will be demonstrated that the semantics of inter- and intra-communal violence developed and experienced before 1920 was rewritten to include space and time as major elements. It will also show how sacred space was mobilised by nationalist groups and made part of a secular liturgy of politics and violence. In her chapter, Mara Albrecht adds a further dimension in her analyses, discussing the question of the synchronisation of religious calendars with the outbreak of violence; while I do not delve into this question, it is quite clear that the religious calendars – as numerous as the religious denominations – became intrinsically connected with the organisation of violence and its ritualisation.

This chapter acknowledges and is certainly indebted to the previous work of scholars who have worked on Jerusalem looking at urban transformations and their impact on the local population, such as the article by Michelle Campos 'Mapping Urban "Mixing" and Intercommunal Relations in Late Ottoman Jerusalem' (Campos, 2021) and the book by Yair Wallach *A City in Fragments* (Wallach, 2020) as well as the work of Noah Rubin Hysler on Patrick Geddes, an important figure for understanding the agency of British urban planners in Jerusalem (Rubin Hysler, 2011). These works and others have provided the methodological framework within which violence is understood in relation to urban planning in Jerusalem. As well, this chapter is also based on the understanding of time as discussed by Avner Wishnitzer in *Reading Clocks, Alla Turca* (Wishnitzer, 2015).

Violence from the Ottoman era to the Nabi Musa riots

In late Ottoman Jerusalem, violence was common, but milder than in other areas of the Ottoman Empire and, more importantly, it was not yet the expression of organised forces. Violence can be briefly defined and associated with the destruction of life, the material world and meaning. The concept of violence, particularly to the Western mind, strongly connotes a behaviour that is in some sense illegitimate or unacceptable. While the act of violence is performed through the infliction of physical or material damage, in different terms violence is a social practice that leads to social change. As mentioned in the introduction of this volume, violence is a physical, social and indeed direct phenomenon which, I argue, in Jerusalem was not an arbitrary expression of uncontrollable anger. It was rather used as a means of socio-political advancement. As argued by Heinrich Popitz, violence is an order-creating experience, one that can redesign relations between people, but also the spatial geography of a city (Popitz, 2017: 25–51). Nelida Fuccaro argues that we should look at violence also as a struggle between those who want to hold power and those who resist (Fuccaro, 2016: 4). David Nirenberg suggests that 'violence [is] a central and systematic aspect of coexistence of majority and minorities'; in other words, he suggests that violence and the threat of it is the guarantee of coexistence, which in Jerusalem was more than that, as evidenced by many accounts and sources that will be discussed later in this chapter (Nirenberg, 1996: 9). It can be safely argued that in the end there is a general consensus on the definition of the instrumental nature of violence; however, its interpretation is certainly open to large and often bitter debates. In this context it is also important to highlight that violence is not the by-product of some sort of innate violent and primordial sectarian hatred, but on the contrary, violence, and more specifically urban violence, has to be understood in its historical context and time (Makdisi, 2019). In the case study under review in this chapter, up until 1920 religion identified people in Jerusalem, yet did not constitute a major cause for the occurrence of violence; in other words when episodes of urban violence broke out in the city, conflicts did not follow straight religious identities – Christians v. Muslims or Muslims v. Jews – but groups were blurred and alliances were the results of personal and family interests. The Ottoman order based on the millet system produced a society based on religious identity, yet space was not segregated. Rather, it was shared, and coexistence was more than just the ability to live side by side avoiding the outbreak of major inter- and intra-community conflict, as demonstrated by the diaries and memoirs of some residents. For instance, Wasif Jawhariyyeh, a famous local musician, left us a great description of the religious festivals in Jerusalem and how they were celebrated by the local people (Tamari and Nassar, 2014: 42–62). Perhaps his memoirs suffer from some sense of nostalgia of a time long gone, as they were written after the tragic events of 1948 known as the Nakba, yet we cannot underestimate the vivid account of a locale that radically changed after 1917. The 'Yahudia Picnic', for instance, gives us a picture of a shared time and space: 'Everyone spent the entire day singing songs and uhzujas. The Christian and Muslim Arabs of Jerusalem celebrated with the Jews, and families went along to take part in what is known to the Arabs as the Judea Festival' (Tamari and Nassar, 2014: 61).

In 1917, the arrival of the British not only marked the end of Ottoman rule, but initiated or facilitated a number of processes including the sectarianisation and segregation of the urban environment and the transformation of space, time and later forms of urban violence. While the British Mandate was taking form in 1919 to be implemented later in 1920, the British were already altering the local environment in many ways. The most important change occurred with the support given to Zionism, which materialised with the immigration of European Jews to Palestine and more importantly with the establishment of a parallel Zionist local government. Despite a limited number of options, Palestinians reacted in different ways to what they perceived as an illegitimate decision from an external power. Until the Spring of 1920, opposition to the British and to Zionism was confined to debates, newspaper articles, creations of societies and parties, official petitions and occasional demonstrations: violence in an organised form was not yet an available option. Interestingly, on the Zionist side a small but vociferous group emerged, led by Vladimir Jabotinsky, that mobilised men and weapons for two reasons: to respond to possible Palestinian attacks, but more importantly to accelerate the establishment of a Jewish state as promised by the British in the Balfour Declaration. By April 1920, however, violence increasingly began to be used but not an inevitable one as some may argue. During the Nabi Musa celebrations, an Islamic festival shared by the inhabitants of Jerusalem and nearby towns, which took place around the same period as Orthodox Easter and the Jewish Passover, Arab nationalists and Zionists confronted each other in what I call the first example of organised national struggle in Palestine.[1] The festival became one of those ritualised parades that served the purpose of stretching and defining the borders of one's 'territory', in a manner of speaking. The Nabi Musa festival was essentially meant to threaten the secureness of the other religious groups in the city (Albrecht, 2021). Though riots started as a result of choices made by few individuals, violence was facilitated by the conjunction of space (new forms of segregation), time (regulated since the establishment of a clock tower under the Ottomans, which was later demolished by the British) and religion (as part of the expression of individual and group identity). Grounding violence in the urban space helps to shift the focus from the macro-level to the intimate knowledge of the local environment that is connected with the public regulation of time and was essential to regulating the presence of crowds in a single space at a given time. Treating violence as contingent on the rhythms of urban life, dictated by space, time and religion, allows us to offer a multi-layered interpretation of the events, avoiding those narratives that solely describe the events or seek victims and perpetrators with the purpose of proving culpability.

The first day of the Nabi Musa festival, Friday 2 April 1920, passed without incident and the local police force successfully controlled the procession. However, on Sunday 4 April, the day of the main pilgrimage from the shrine of the Prophet Moses near Jericho to Jerusalem, things took a different turn. Spatially speaking the processions followed a strict ritual: pilgrims arriving in Jerusalem would have walked briefly on Jaffa Road and from there they would have reached Damascus Gate. Upon entering the Old City, pilgrims would have then walked towards the Haram al-Sharif/Temple Mount, the religious centre of Islamic life in Jerusalem and earlier the site of the last Jewish Temple, passing along streets crowded by mainly Muslim shopkeepers. The ritualisation of this route was meant to highlight the Islamic character of the city at a time when it was simultaneously experiencing a large influx of Christian and Jewish pilgrims for the Easter and Passover celebrations. However, the timing of the Islamic festival should not be understood in juxtaposition with the other religious events, but as a competitive event and to a certain extent also as a shared experience. In 1920 this ritual changed its liturgy, and the procession did not go to the northern Damascus Gate but stopped just outside the western entrance to the Old City, at Jaffa Gate. Changing the route meant changing the nature of the procession from religious, with an established set of behaviours and rituals, to political, including the stop at Jaffa Gate as a non-religious hub. This location represented the most important access point to the city, not affiliated with any specific religious group, and it was a symbol of modernity, with its Ottoman clock tower built on top of the gate. Jaffa Gate, or Bab al-Khalil (Hebron Gate in Arabic), was the city's gateway to the west and south, close to the newly built municipality and its gardens. Jaffa Gate was also meant to be the terminal of the tram lines that had been planned by the Ottomans before the First World War. This centre embodied the modernisation of Jerusalem and the Empire. By 1920 Jaffa Gate had become a contested site where anti-Zionist signs often appeared in public (Wallach, 2020: 54).

Figure 2.1: Rare photo of Jaffa Gate in Jerusalem with the clock tower above and the Turkish customs office (with tiled roof) beside it, during the Ottoman era.

As local notable and religious leaders gathered, they delivered inflam-
matory speeches, contrary to the usual protocol (The National Archives,
London [hereafter TNA], WO 32/9614, 1920). From a nearby balcony
the mayor of Jerusalem – later dismissed by the British – Musa Kazim al-
Husayni[2] spoke against the Zionists and at the end of his speech the crowd
roared 'Palestine is our land, the Jews are our dogs!' A young al-Hajj Amin,
later to become the British-appointed Mufti of Jerusalem, shouted aloud
'O Arabs! This is your King!' while pictures of Faisal were displayed and
acclaimed as King of Syria and Palestine. The famous journalist and historian Aref al-Aref declared 'if we don't use force against the Jews, we will
never be rid of them' (Segev, 2001: 128; TNA, WO/9614, 1920; Porath,
1974: 96–100). The situation was polarised and avenues for an open conflict had been opened, yet they were not inevitable.

At the same time, some Zionist activists were listening to the speeches
being given and likely some of them belonged to the self-defence force organised by Vladimir Jabotinsky (Wasserstein, 1991: 63; Lauren, 1999: 509).[3]
It is not clear what action triggered the beginning of the violence between
the two groups; some evidence suggests that the Zionist spectators were
quite aggressive and one of them pushed an Arab carrying a national flag;
others suggested that a Jew spat on a Nabi Musa banner (TNA, WO 32/
9614, 1920). The Commission of Enquiry established by the British after
the incident tried to ascertain who had started the riots, yet it seems that
neither group was interested in such details and time and timing was not
a real issue for them. As we will see later, after the massacres of 1929
the necessity to establish who used violence first became paramount and
time was an essential component of the investigation as well as of the self-
definition of victims. Given that both sides were preparing some sort of
action, the definition of 'victim' is quite irrelevant here; more interesting in
the context of this chapter is the kind of violence perpetrated, which mostly
targeted individuals who clearly belonged to one group or the other. This
was still a pre-nation-state kind of violence rooted in the Ottoman context,
when the semantics of violence relating to a national struggle was in its
infancy. The riots developed through the Old City, where mostly Jewish
shops were looted and a number of spectators were beaten with sticks
and rocks. Some Zionists actually carried guns – a relatively new feature
for Jerusalemites – and two, while shooting from a house overlooking the
procession route, were shot by the British-Indian police deployed by the
governor of Jerusalem, Ronald Storrs. The incidents started at around 10
a.m. and were over by midday (TNA, WO 32/9614, 1920). By the end of
the week the situation was mostly under control, though a few episodes
of violence occurred around the Old City, leaving a total of 251 casualties, including five Jews and four Arabs who were killed in the riots (TNA,

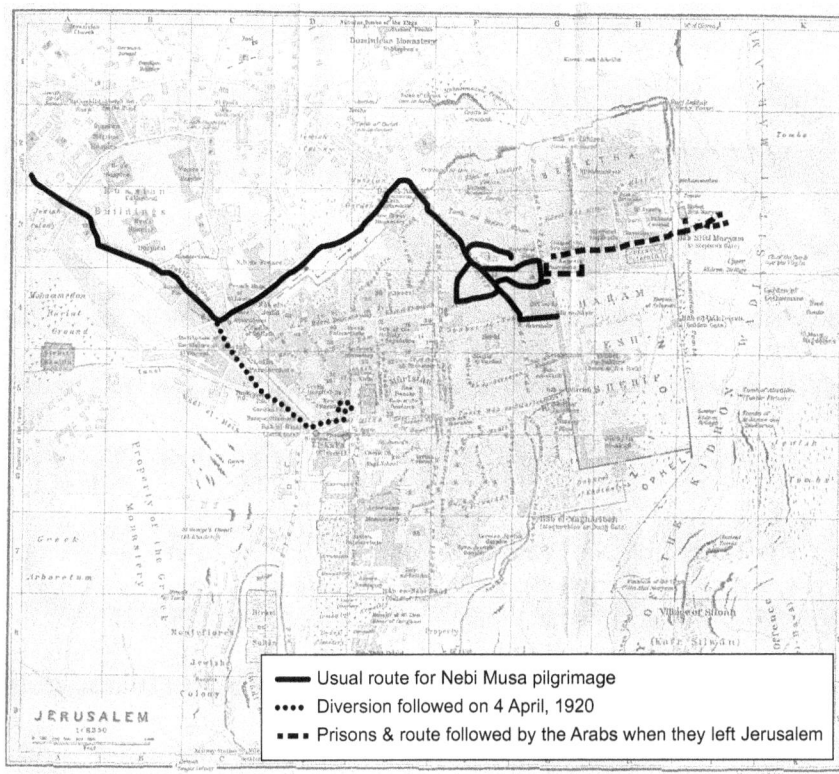

Figure 2.2: Map of Jerusalem with route of Nabi Musa procession 1920. The solid line shows the usual road taken by pilgrims; the dotted line, the road taken in 1920; the dashes indicate the road taken by pilgrims after the riots were over.

WO 32/9614, 1920; Mazza, 2009: 165–78). This count includes a young girl, a Palestinian, who was killed by a bullet to the head and then fell from a window under the eyes of Edward Keith-Roach close to the Church of the Holy Sepulchre (TNA, WO 32/9614, 1920; Keith-Roach, 1994: 71).

Planning Jerusalem

I have argued elsewhere (Mazza, 2018) that in order to understand the Nabi Musa riots we need to look at the broader context, including urban planning and perceptions of urban violence, not to mention the development of strong nationalist feelings. I would suggest here that the renegotiation of the urban environment following the British capture of Jerusalem and the establishment of civil rule was instrumental in the creation of a space intended to actively foster segregation along religious-nationalist lines. Hillel Cohen, in his seminal work *Year Zero of the Arab-Israeli Conflict 1929*, is right to suggest that nationalist feelings and religious sentiments merged and the result became apparent with the massacres of 1929, yet I believe we need to consider urban planning as a crucial factor in this development. Rasmus Christian Elling suggests that the historical transformation of cities presents historians with the need to interpret violence in relation to spatial changes and vice versa (Elling, 2016: 35). Urban and demographic changes transformed the sites of sociability and of violence, traditional meeting places were replaced by others, for instance while Jaffa Gate remained a hub in the city by 1929 the socio-political centres had shifted towards newly developed and more segregated neighbourhoods. As mentioned earlier, considering riots and massacres to be *of* the city takes us to a micro-level that can help us to understand the city not as a stage or container for violence, but as a flexible space that can change according the contingency of the time. In other words, the massacres would have certainly happened anyway, but the changes in the configuration of the city, its neighbourhoods and the growing ghettoisation of local communities led to a transformation of the local environment that significantly influenced the unfolding on the 1929 events in Jerusalem. The British, through the agency of Ronald Storrs, the Pro-Jerusalem Society and the Town Planning Commission, set in motion a process that aimed at the division and homogenisation of the Old City and the city outside the walls according to religious affiliation and fixed ideas about national collective identity: essentially, they contributed to the confessionalisation and segregation of the city. In a recent groundbreaking article, Michelle Campos, using GIS technology, has demonstrated that segregation was normalised under British rule not just in Jerusalem but throughout the British Empire as well. Her work shows that a level of segregation had previously existed in Jerusalem at a street/building level, but not in terms of neighbourhoods, which remained largely mixed in the late Ottoman era (Campos, 2021: 133–69). Paradoxically, Storrs promoted the idea of sectarian harmony based on the misconception that communities in Jerusalem were divided and in fact already in conflict with each other (Mazza, 2018: 403–22; Roberts, 2013: 7–26; Barakat, 2016: 22–34). The residential segregation of communities and the separation of the Old City from the New City encouraged the 'unmixing' of the population and brought centuries of relatively peaceful coexistence and active cohabitation to an end. The shared space described in the writings of Wasif Jawhariyyeh and of Gad Frumkin – a local Jewish resident who became one of the most important judges during the British Mandate – was rapidly disappearing (Tamari and Nassar, 2014; Frumkin, 1954). The Old City, which was the main focus of the Pro-Jerusalem Society, was meant to become an 'open air museum'; Ronald Storrs and Charles Ashbee – the famous British urban planner – envisioned old Jerusalem as a space to be protected and isolated from the New City, which was meant to become the locus of everyday life for Jerusalemites (Pro-Jerusalem Society, 1921). The New City was meant to accommodate the needs of the Zionist immigrants and indeed the local Palestinian population, and though the Pro-Jerusalem Society was responsible for the establishment of some libraries and music centres, the main bulk of the planning was left with the more politicised Town Planning Commission.[4] In this section, I want to discuss two specific interventions that I believe denied residents the possibility to create common and shared spaces throughout the city and in the second case created homogenised neighbourhoods preventing any meaningful interactions between Jerusalemites.

With the establishment of the British military administration in Jerusalem in 1917, Ronald Storrs had to make important decisions in relation to concessions that were granted to individuals or companies before the First World War. One of them was a concession to establish a street-car line – a tram – to Bethlehem and the Mount of Olives (Dimitriadis, 2018: 475–89). Storrs reportedly said: 'the first rail section would have to be laid over the dead body of the military governor.' (*New York Times*, 21 July 1921). His decision was in line with the idea of preserving and safeguarding the status of Jerusalem as a 'celestial' city. There were multiple repercussions following this decision; we can safely say that this was a poor economic decision, as there was an expanding market asking for better local transportation. Secondly, and from our perspective more importantly, the lack of internal transportation acted as a catalyser to construct and enforce new segregating communal boundaries. Storrs and his fellow British administrators de facto denied the possibility to create a shared space, a locus for potential encounters. The second urban intervention under scrutiny is the homogenisation of neighbourhoods. In order to appreciate this policy, I would suggest looking at the '1944 Survey Distribution of Population' map (Kendall, 1948: 34). Unfortunately, a similar map does not exist for an earlier period; nevertheless while the distribution of the population was only mapped in 1944, the same distribution had been visible for decades, as the process began under the Ottomans and largely continued under the British.

This map shows clearly how communal boundaries were renegotiated after the arrival of the British through urban planning, zoning and the remapping of administrative boundaries; not surprisingly some of the most heinous killings and beatings that occurred in 1929 took place in small religious enclaves and alongside the new religiously demarcated communal boundaries where there had been none before (Winder, 2012: 6–23). The semantics of spatial violence was redefined according to the new boundaries. While the city was indeed producing creative spaces for cultural production

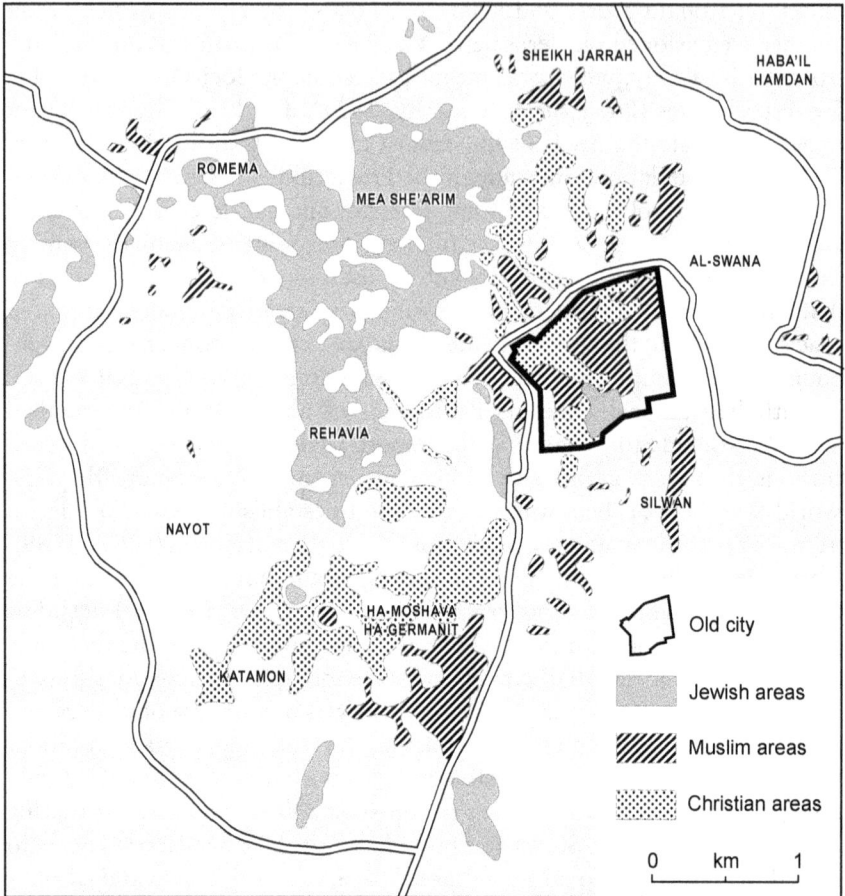

Figure 2.3: Map based on Henry Kendall's '1944 Survey: Distribution of the Population', showing regions of Jewish, Christian and Muslim population.

and enjoyment, the destructive forces produced by ethno-religious national-ism obscured the positive features only to highlight conflict. Obviously, this is a larger question about the narrative of violence, which tends to demon-ise the sides involved so as to justify or vilify violence. While asymmetry between parts can exist, these asymmetries must be understood in different terms including race, ethnicity, religion and opportunities. One of the most enduring legacies of British rule in Palestine is certainly linked to the trans-formation of violence and its semantics. For instance, while religious places were the source of inter- and intra-communal strife, they did not yet rep-resent a national identity nor a symbol of national struggle. As mentioned earlier, Hillel Cohen is correct in pointing out that 1929 is the end of what Nora Lafi has called the Ottoman Pax Urbana (Lafi, 2016: 96).

The Western Wall – Al Buraq

The massacres of 1929 have been defined as the 'Wailing Wall Riots' in light of the fact that according to the British Commission of Enquiry (Shaw Commission) one of the reasons for the outbreak of violence was the desire to define and control that holy site. *HaKotel HaMa'aravi* (the Western Wall), in Arabic *al-Mabkā* (the place of weeping) or *Ḥā'iṭ al-Burāq*, or in many languages the equivalent of 'wailing wall', is today largely recognised as the most sacred place for the Jews. The official history of the Western Wall commissioned by the Israeli Ministry of Defence suggests that as early as the fourth century some sources reported Jews visiting the Wall once a year (Ben Dov, Naor, and Aner, 1983). The Memorandum on the Western Wall prepared by the Special Commission of the League of Nations on behalf of the Jewish Agency in the aftermath of the 1929 Wailing Wall Riots even collected sources dating back to the third century. However, the report effectively fails to show any sign of consistent reverence and pilgrimage towards the Western Wall until the modern era (Adler, 1930). The same official history by the Ministry of Defence of the Western Wall adds that: '[...] it should be pointed out that for hundreds of years, during nearly the whole of the Middle Ages, there is hardly any reference to the Wall' (Ben Dov, Naor, and Aner, 1983: 65). A major shift occurred at the beginning of the nineteenth century with the rediscovery of the Holy Land by European travellers and with internal changes within the Jewish diaspora (Kamel, 2015). Slowly the Wall turned into a spiritual symbol, and as worshippers at the Wall grew in number, services and prayers were also designed to fit the renewed interest in the Wall. Yet, to many Jews around the world the Wall was a symbol of destruction and degradation, a site that reminded them of the suffering of the Jews in contrast to the development of modern societies throughout the nineteenth century. Yair Wallach reminds us that the Wall was full of graffiti left by pilgrims who visited the holy site. Nevertheless, Zionists had begun to transform the Wall into a monument of national revival and after the massacres of 1929 the graffiti were understood as a way to claim Jewish ownership of the Western Wall. Eventually a special commission established by the League of Nations after the massacres decided to remove the graffiti as a danger to peace and order in Jerusalem and Palestine. Quite interestingly, all parties agreed with this decision (Wallach, 2020: 171–86). Numerous sources show the religious growth of the Wall as a Jewish site of prayer and the increasing number of requests by local and foreign Jews for better access to the area. For instance, in 1840, Jews asked to pave the area adjacent to the Wall; the request was rejected by the Ottoman authorities as the area bordered with the Haram al-Sharif and it belonged to the Waqf – religious endowment – of Abu Madyan (Ben Arieh, 1984: 309).

During the nineteenth century, the Wall became the most evocative space for the Jews in Jerusalem. More and more people began to pray around the Wall and more travellers paid a visit to the area. The Wall, in other words, had, by the end of the century, become a *lieu de memoir*, a symbolic element of the cultural heritage of the Jewish community (Nora and Kritzman, 1996: 1–20). The growth of the Jewish presence around the Wall elicited a response from the Muslims as it was transformed from a symbolic to a real issue. However, as Abraham Moses Luncz – a local chronicler – reported, 'Muslims never showed intolerance towards those who worshipped the One God in whom they believed too' (Luncz, 1914: 1–58).[5] The situation would change as a number of attempts were made by Zionist leaders to purchase the Wall or sections of the Maghrebi quarter in front of the Wall with the purpose of increasing the area available for Jewish believers and visitors (Mazza, 2021: 696–711). Despite the failure of these attempts, they further raised awareness of Zionism and its goals: to increase the Jewish presence in Palestine and possibly establish a Jewish commonwealth of some sort amongst the local Arabs. It would be wrong, however, to suggest that local Muslims and Christians wished to deny religious rights to the Jews, particularly the right to pray at the Wall. Jewish expansion in the city was perceived as a challenge but also as an opportunity, considering that newly arrived Jews from Europe were often equipped with capital that was invested locally, especially for the purchase of real estate. The complexities of the relationship between local communities cannot be summarised in a few lines, but suffice it to say that the communities were not estranged from each other in the late Ottoman era. And although signs of an impending struggle were showing before the beginning of the First World War, nothing was predetermined and possibilities were still open to all parties involved (Campos, 2011; Gribetz, 2014; Jacobson and Naor, 2016; Klein, 2014; Lemire, 2017). Jewish interest in the Wall, however, had a direct impact on how Muslims looked at the same site and prompted the development of a counter-narrative celebrating the sanctity of al-Buraq, the tethering place of the Prophet's stallion during his Night Journey to Jerusalem (Ricca, 2010: 172).

Islamic reverence of Jerusalem is often associated with two episodes related to the life of the Prophet Muhammad: the first is the Night Journey to Jerusalem – *isra'* – and Ascension to Heaven – *mi'raj* – and the second is the temporary adoption of Jerusalem as the first direction of prayer – *qibla* (Mourad, 2008: 87). During the Night Journey, the Prophet was transported on a sort of magic stallion named al-Buraq; the site where the stallion was tethered became, over time, a revered spot, yet not sacred. Early Islamic scholars disagreed on the story even though in time it became can-onised; nonetheless, some disagreement seems to have remained, until more recently, as to the exact site of the tethering. A small mosque, Jami al'Buraq, was erected to mark the alleged spot where the magic stallion was teth-ered by the Prophet inside the precinct of the Haram al-Sharif (Elad, 1995; Berkowitz, 2001). By the beginning of the twenty-first century, the location of the Buraq had shifted to correspond with the Western Wall, but the trans-ferral was slow and did not originally include the Islamic sacralisation of the Wall (Ricca, 2010: 173). For instance, the famous Palestinian historian and nationalist Aref al-Aref in his work *The Detailed History of Jerusalem* included the Wall in a list of Jewish holy places (al-Aref, 1961: 544).

In 1928, on the eve of Yom Kippur, a separation screen was put in place to divide men and women worshipping at the Wall, which prompted a strong reaction from the local Arab leaders (Segev, 2001: 295–309).[6] This led to violent demonstrations and, from the Arab side, a strike and a series of official proclamations and letters to various authorities. In time, ten-sions diminished, yet isolated incidents occurred. Claims over the Wall were becoming stronger and more politicised. As in 1920, religious symbols were mobilised and transformed to serve political purposes. In terms of urban studies, as argued earlier, the intimate knowledge of the built environment became a tool in the hands of both parties, once again rendering the occur-rence of violence contingent to time and place. Yet, in 1929, space changed its dimension, as from the micro, violence was perpetrated at a macro level, given that other cities became involved. As we will see later, the introduction of a standardised time throughout Palestine acted as a crucial element in the organisation and transformation of violence.

The massacres of 1929 – Jerusalem

By August 1929 the lull that had lasted nearly a decade was over. A series of small incidents involving single individuals occurred on the Ninth of Av (14 August) – a day of fasting for the Jews in remembrance of the destruction of the Temple – and two days later, on the day of the Prophet Muhammad's birthday (Cohen, 2015: 95, 96, and 102). The foundations had been laid for a major struggle. This does not mean that violence was inevitable, yet I believe it was considered by many as the only available choice to change the status quo and have claims recognised and satisfied. As highlighted by Mara Albrecht in this volume, the religious calendars had, by now, become fully mobilised in the struggle between Zionists and Arabs, making violence almost predictable. Tom Segev and Hillel Cohen, as well as Rana Barakat, have described the events of 1929 with great detail, relying on numerous sources. In contrast, this chapter aims to analyse these events through the lenses of urban planning and the relationship between time and space. While building on existing literature, this chapter offers the possibility to understand how urban violence changed in Jerusalem and was understood at the micro-level, without attempting to discuss the events from a chronological or political perspective. In other words, the chapter will not avoid the question of responsibility or of who started first: each side claimed that the other did. Furthermore, this chapter does not aim to offer a teleological discussion of the 1929 massacres, as while events were unfolding no one could have anticipated the outcomes nor the interactions with the larger historical context.

On 23 August 1929, as thousands of Arabs – armed with sticks and knives – gathered for prayer at Haram al-Sharif in the early hours of Friday, Jewish merchants in the Old City, sensing the potential for conflict, were rapidly closing their shops. By the time the prayer was over and Arabs were exiting Jaffa Gate, the sources describe that violence spread quickly throughout the city, yet I would argue that violence followed the urban structure as designed by the British in its segregated nature. The urban fabric was not just a prerogative of surveyors, bureaucrats and police, but also the rioters, who quickly adapted to the new layout of the city and also re-adjusted the threat of violence according to it. The kind of violence perpetrated was not much different from that of 1920, yet the numbers involved and more importantly their willingness to strike were certainly different. Those who died did not necessarily simply succumb to their injuries but were deliberately killed or lynched. A number of worshippers exited from Nablus Gate instead Damascus Gate and at 12:30 p.m. a '[...] mob of huge proportions stormed the neighbourhood [the Gurji courtyard – a small area inhabited by Georgian Jews]. They broke into houses and began to kill, rob and burn' (Amikan, 1929: 21). More or less at the same time, in the ultra-orthodox Jewish neighbourhood Mea She'arim, two Arabs were attacked: Dahudi al-Dajani was killed, while Khamis Salem al-Sayyed was rescued by a local Jewish family (Cohen, 2015: 107–8). In the isolated Jewish neighbourhoods of Bayit VeGan, southwest of Jerusalem, three Jews were killed by a small group of Arab attackers. In Zikhron Moshe, a central Jewish neighbourhood, a mosque – Nabi 'Ukkasha – was attacked by a Jewish mob that destroyed books and curtains (Cohen, 2015: 114–17).

The spatiality of these incidents is not coincidental. Attacks took place in homogeneous areas; unlike during the events of 1920, shared spaces were not the target of the attackers. Jews attacked Arabs in Jewish neighbourhoods, either claiming to protect their properties or to push the Arabs out; Arabs on the other hand attacked Jewish neighbourhoods as a way to materialise their claims over land ownership. Though I am not questioning here the nature of the violence perpetrated in 1929, it is quite obvious that urban planning had a major role in redefining how and where violence was performed in the city. The coerced segregation acted as a catalyser and gave attackers clear objectives; as communal areas had been largely reduced, the possibility to channel violence through different avenues was removed.

As mentioned earlier, the study of 'massacres' is quite problematic due to a rather elusive definition. Jacques Semelin argues that a massacre is the murder of the defenceless in a distinct time and place when the killers are not in danger. In Jerusalem all sides were heavily armed, and it is clear that attackers followed this pattern of attacking those who were relatively defenceless at a particular time or place (Semelin, 2007: 1–8; Semelin, 2002: 435). There are indeed exceptions to this, but overall, the unfolding events seem to fall into this model. For instance, young Jews reportedly set fire to Arab houses and attacked Arabs at the border between Lifta and the Bukharian quarter, knowing that they were stronger in terms of weapons and organisation. Similarly, the killing of two Jewish brothers at Jaffa Gate occurred when a large crowd of Palestinians was emerging from the gate and the two found themselves isolated (Cohen, 2015: 91 and 96). In Talpiot, a mostly Jewish neighbourhood cut off from the rest of the Jewish areas, a concerted series of attacks took place; similarly, the small enclave of the Gurji (Georgian) quarter in what nowadays is East Jerusalem, was the target of Arab attacks, as mentioned earlier. The desecration of the Nabi 'Ukkasha Mosque was indeed an easy target given that it was the only Muslim site in the heart of an entire Jewish area in central Jerusalem. If we take the definition of massacres by Semelin as valid, it becomes obvious that from 1920 to 1929 we can see a full transition from riots to massacres, from non-organised to organised violence. Ever since 1929, the unfolding of urban violence in Jerusalem has been clearly marked by the boundaries of the neighbourhoods created by British urban planning, as proven by the tragic events of 1948. By then also time had become essential, as the synchronicity of violence was fully mediated by the diffusion of information. Yet it is important to remember, as Salim Tamari has shown, that these neighbourhoods, while homogeneous, were not fully separated and daily contacts were shaped by shared economic interdependence, calendars and social coexistence, all of which made the violence of 1948 even more devastating (Tamari, 1999: 3).

Space, however, is not the only major contributor to the ways in which violence changed through the 1920s. As noted by Mara Albrecht, by 1929 the modern culture of violence in Jerusalem has become associated with sacred space; however, here I would argue that another striking factor that emerged from the proceedings of the Shaw Commission is the significance of time (Albrecht, 2021). For the British, as well as for the

Jews and Arabs in the aftermath of the massacres, it became paramount
to establish the time when the first victim was killed. For the British, this
was part of their understanding of justice and of how violence should
be understood. More importantly for the Jews and Arabs, establishing
who was killed first meant the possibility to claim the title of 'victim'
rather than perpetrator. However, the question of whether the first fatal-
ity was a Jew or an Arab was a propaganda issue, as rightly argued by
Hillel Cohen. In fact, the killings did not trigger each other, as we should
remember that despite the fact that news could travel faster than in the
past, the various mobs had no, or very little, real-time knowledge of the
various events unfolding in the city (Cohen, 2015: 95–6). Violence developed synchronously throughout the city, involving groups belonging to
different neighbourhoods, yet this was not mediated by real-time information. From a temporal perspective the 1929 massacres fall into a limbo
where violence was not necessarily the outcome of information; rather,
its occurrence, which lasted for days, was the by-product of a slow relationship between the unfolding of events and knowledge about them. For
Arabs and Zionists, time was not the essence in this round of massacres,
yet time played a major role in the aftermath of these events, adding a
new layer to the development of urban violence. The report of the Shaw
Commission investigating the massacres is plagued with constant references to the time at which events occurred and virtually all witnesses
were asked to recall when violence happened. In 1920, even though people may have worn watches and public time was dictated by the clock
tower and the religious call for prayers, time was of very little relevance
for the performance and understanding of violence. By 1929, however,
time had become an essential component of violence and its performance.
Not only did it serve to determine the status of victim or perpetrator
but, more importantly, time developed its own agency in relation to the
performance of violence. The questions of 'when' and 'where' paralleled
'who' and were becoming an essential part of how violence was to be
practiced. In other words, violence was transformed into a fully organised set of events that had to follow a specific chronology when it was
examined in retrospect. The addition of time to the theory of urban violence developed in Jerusalem thus far included the possibility of planning
for violence. Both the 1920 riots and 1929 massacres developed in the
context of political and communal tensions; nevertheless, I would argue
that from 1929 onwards violence was not just dictated by these elements,
but crucially also by the time and place. As both Arabs and Jews became
more militant and prone to violence, when and where to perform this act
became a crucial question.

I believe that the introduction of a new construction of time in the understanding of violence had also the effect of compartmentalising time itself, as at any given time only one group could perform their rituals. Temporal culture that is the creation of a system of time-related practices that defines social practices, filling them with meaning, was already being developed under the Ottomans. As demonstrated by Avner Wishnitzer, the religious cycles that dictated time in Ottoman cities were then flanked, in the late nineteenth century, by the secular clock (Wishnitzer, 2015). With the arrival of the British, secular time fully overtook the mix of religious and secular time culture, making the clock a necessary companion of daily life. Yet by 1929 the shift was gradually taking place. It was understood that the temporal coincidence of events such as festivals, processions and public demonstrations, regardless of their nature, could potentially lead to violence; therefore the events had to be planned at different times, so as to reduce the possibility of encounters to a minimum. In 1929 the adolescent experimentation with violence, as the riots of 1920 can be characterised, was finally transformed into a pragmatic shape defined by space and time – violence had reached maturity.

Notes

1 Details of the festival can be found in Eddie Halabi's dissertation (2007) and in his recently published book (Halabi, 2023).

2 Muza Kazim Husayni was a member of one of the elites of Jerusalem and served as mayor of Jerusalem from 1918 to 1920. Mohammed Amin al-Husseini belonged to the same family and was appointed Grand Mufti of Jerusalem from 1921 to 1937.

3 Henry Laurens argues that Jabotinsky's force was composed of 200 men, while other sources argue he had enlisted up to 600 men.

4 The Pro-Jerusalem Society was a society for the 'preservation and advancement of the interests of Jerusalem', including its amenities, antiquities, cultural institutions and education. Established by Ronald Storrs, the Pro-Jerusalem Society engaged in various projects including urban planning. An official town planning commission was appointed in 1921, and its primary task was to prepare a development scheme for Jerusalem, which culminated with the plans of 1922, 1929 and 1930. Other plans were prepared later in the aftermath of the 1929 massacres.

5 Luncz (1854–1918) moved to Jerusalem from Russia when he was 14. He owned a small printing press from which he published several works on Palestine.

6 Muslims were afraid that Jews would transform the Wall into a synagogue, effectively changing the status quo of the Holy Places.

Bibliography

Adler, C. (1930). *Memorandum on the Western Wall Prepared for the Special Commission of the League of Nations on behalf of the Jewish Agency for Palestine* (Philadelphia: Publisher Unknown).

Albrecht, M. (2021). 'Ritual Performances and Collective Violence in Divided Cities. The Riots in Belfast (1886) and Jerusalem (1929)' *Political Geography* 86, 1–13.

al-Aref, A. (1961). *Al-Muffassal fi tarikh al-Quds* [*The Detailed History of Jerusalem*] (Amman: Publisher Unknown) [Arabic].

Amikam, Y. (1929). *HaHatkafah 'al ha Yishuv ha Yehudi bEretz Yisrael beTaRPaT* (Haifa: Defus Omanut) [Hebrew].

Barakat, R. (2016). 'Urban Planning, Colonialism and the Pro-Jerusalem Society' *Jerusalem Quarterly*, 65, 22–34.

Ben Arieh, Y. (1984). *Jerusalem in the 19th Century: The Old City* (New York: St. Martin's Press).

Ben Dov, M., Naor, M. and Aner, Z. (eds) (1983). *The Western Wall* (Tel Aviv: Ministry of Defense Publishing House).

Berkowitz, S. (2001). *The Temple Mount and the Western Wall in Israeli Law* (Jerusalem: The Teddy Kollek Center for Jerusalem Studies).

Campos, M. (2021). 'Mapping Urban "Mixing" and Intercommunal Relations in Late Ottoman Jerusalem: A Neighborhood Study', *Comparative Study of Society and History*, 63:1, 133–69.

Campos, M. (2011). *Ottoman Brothers. Muslims, Christians, and Jews in Early Twentieth-Century Palestine* (Stanford: Stanford University Press).

Cohen, H. (2015). *Year Zero of the Arab-Israeli Conflict 1929* (Boston: Brandeis University Press).

The Council of the Pro-Jerusalem Society (1921). *Jerusalem 1918–1920. Being the Records of the Pro-Jerusalem Council during the period of the British Military Administration* (London: J. Murray).

Dimitriadis, S. (2018). 'The Tramway Concession of Jerusalem, 1908–1914: Elite Citizenship, Urban Infrastructure, and the Abortive Modernization of a Late Ottoman City' in Dalachanis, A. and Lemire, V. (eds) *Ordinary Jerusalem 1840–1940 Opening New Archives, Revisiting a Global City* (Leiden: Brill), 475–89.

Elad, A. (1995). *Medieval Jerusalem and Islamic Worship* (Leiden: Brill).

Elling, R.C. (2016). 'The Semantics of Violence and Space' in Nelida Fuccaro (ed.) *Violence and the City in the Modern Middle East* (Stanford: Stanford University Press), 23–36.

Frumkin, G. (1954). *Derekh Shofet bi-Yerushalaim* [*The Path of a Judge in Jerusalem*] (Tel Aviv: Dvir) [Hebrew].

Fuccaro, N. (2016). 'Urban Life and Questions of Violence', in Fuccaro, N. (ed.) *Violence and the City in the Modern Middle East* (Stanford: Stanford University Press), 3–22.

Gribetz, J. (2014). *Defining Neighbors. Religion, Race and the Early Zionist-Arab Encounter* (Princeton: Princeton University Press).

Halabi, A. (2023). *Palestinian Rituals of Identity. The Prophet Moses Festival in Jerusalem, 1850–1948* (Austin: University of Texas Press).

Halabi, E. (2007). 'The Transformation of the Prophet Moses Festival in Jerusalem 1917–1937: From Local and Islamic to Modern and Nationalist Celebrations', PhD. Dissertation (Toronto: University of Toronto).

Henry, H. (1948). *Jerusalem. The City Plan. Preservation and Development During the British Mandate 1918–1948* (London: H.M.S.O).

Hylser-Rubin, N. (2011). *Patrick Geddes and Town Planning. A Critical View* (London: Routledge).

Jacobson, A. and Naor, M. (2016). *Oriental Neighbors. Middle Eastern Jews and Arabs in Mandatory Palestine* (Waltham, MA: Brandeis University Press).

Kamel, L. (2015). *Imperial Perceptions of Palestine: British Influence and Power in Late Ottoman Times* (London: I.B. Tauris).

Keith-Roach, E. (1994). *Pasha of Jerusalem* (London: Radcliffe Press).

Klein, M. (2014). *Lives in Common* (Oxford: Oxford University Press).

Lafi, N. (2016). 'Challenging the Ottoman *Pax Urbana*: Intercommunal Clashes in 1857 Tunis', in Fuccaro, N. (ed.) *Violence and the City in the Modern Middle East* (Stanford: Stanford University Press), 95–108.

Laurens, H. (1999). *La Question de Palestine*, Vol. 1 (Paris: Fayard).

Lemire, V. (2017). *Jerusalem 1900. The Holy City in the Age of Possibilities* (Chicago: University of Chicago Press).

Luncz, A.M. (1914). *[Jerusalem Yearbook]*, Vol. X, 1–58 [Hebrew].

Makdisi, U. (2019). *Age of Coexistence. The Ecumenical Frame and the Making of the Modern Arab World* (Oakland: University of California Press).

Mazza, R. (2009). *Jerusalem from the Ottomans to the British* (London: IB Tauris).

Mazza, R. (2018). ' "The Preservation and Safeguarding of the Amenities of the Holy City without Favour of Prejudice to Race or Creed": The Pro-Jerusalem Society and Ronald Storrs, 1917–1926', in Lemire, V. and Dalachanis, A. (eds) *Ordinary Jerusalem 1840–1940. Opening New Archives, Revisiting a Global City* (Leiden: Brill), 403–22.

Mazza, R. (2021). 'The deal of the century? The Attempted sale of the Western Wall by Cemal Pasha in 1916' *Middle Eastern Studies*, 57:5 (2021), 696–711.

Mourad, S. (2008). 'The Symbolism of Jerusalem in Early Islam', in Mayer, T. and Ali Mourad, S. (eds) *Jerusalem Idea and Reality* (New York: Routledge), 86–102.

The National Archives (TNA), London, WO 32/9614, Report of the Court of Enquiry into the Riots in Jerusalem during Last April, Jerusalem, 1920.

The New York Times (21 July 1921).

Nirenberg, D. (1996). *Communities of Violence: Persecution of Minorities in the Middle Ages* (Princeton: Princeton University Press).

Nora, P. and Kritzman, L. (eds) (1996). *Realms of Memory: Rethinking the French Past. Vol. 1: conflicts and divisions* (New York: Columbia University Press).

The Palestine Bulletin (2 September 1929).

Popitz, H. (2017). *Phenomena of Power* (New York: Columbia University Press).

Porath, Y. (1974). *Emergence of the Palestinian-Arab National Movement 1918–1929* (London: Frank Cass).

Ricca, S. (2010). 'Heritage, Nationalism and the Shifting Symbolism of the Wailing Wall' in *Archives de Sciences Sociales des Religions*, 55:151 (July–September), 169–88.

Roberts, N.E. (2013). 'Dividing Jerusalem: British Urban Planning in the Holy City' *Journal of Palestine Studies*, 42:4, 7–26.

Segev, T. (2001). *One Palestine Complete* (New York: Henry Holt).

Semelin, J. (2007). *Purify and Destroy. The Political Use of Massacre and Genocide* (New York: Columbia University Press).

Semelin, J. (2002). 'From Massacre to the Genocidal 'Process', *International Social Science Journal*, 54:174, 433–42.

Tamari, S. (1999). *Jerusalem 1948: The Arab Neighbourhoods and their Fate in the War* (Ramallah: Institute for Palestine Studies).

Tamari, S. and Nassar, I. (eds) (2014). *The Storyteller of Jerusalem. The Life and Times of Wasif Jawhariyyeh, 1904–1948* (Northampton: Olive Branch Press).

Wallach, Y. (2020). *A City in Fragments Urban Text in Modern Jerusalem* (Stanford: Stanford University Press).

Wasserstein, B. (1991). *The British in Palestine* (Oxford: Blackwell).

Winder, A. (2012). 'Religious Boundaries and the 1929 Communal Violence in Palestine: Jerusalem, Hebron and Safad' *Journal of Palestine Studies*, 165:1, 6–23.

Wishnitzer, A. (2015). '"At Approximately Eleven, Just Before Nightfall": An Introduction to Ottoman Temporal Culture' in Dror, Z. and Toledano, E. R. (eds) *Society, Law, and Culture in the Middle East: Modernities in the Making* (De Gruyter Open Poland), 121–34.

Wishnitzer, A. (2015). *Reading Clocks, Alla Turca* (Chicago: University of Chicago Press).

3

Resisting a hegemonic spatiotemporal order: Hindu nationalist violence and subterranean agency in Ahmedabad

Shrey Kapoor

Introduction

Violence has shaped the city of Ahmedabad like no other urban centre in India. Beginning in the 1960s, the Hindu Right made the economic and de facto political capital of Gujarat the epicentre of repeated Hindu–Muslim riots. By strategically targeting all manifestations of Hindu–Muslim copresence, this riot violence birthed a segregated social order in Ahmedabad and imparted it with the dubious honour of India's most 'ghettoized' city (Susewind, 2017). As a result, the Sabarmati River that traverses Ahmedabad has come to act as a material dividing line between prosperous Hindu areas to its west and downtrodden Muslim areas in the east. It was then-chief minister Narendra Modi who oversaw the most recent and virulent return to this 'institutionalized riot system'. With the 2002 Gujarat pogrom, his BJP (*Bharatiya Janata Party*) state government orchestrated Independent India's single most damaging episode of Hindu–Muslim violence to date (Dhattiwala and Biggs, 2012).

The conspicuous absence of large-scale riots in Gujarat since 2002 belies the Hindu Right's continued exertion of strategic violence throughout Modi's 13-year tenure as chief minister. Before the blood and dust of the pogrom's violence could settle, the Modi government forcefully asserted control over the Sabarmati Riverfront Project. This 'world-class' infrastructure and beautification project became the centrepiece of an aggressive post-2002 urban development agenda that precipitated the violent transformation of Ahmedabad's morphology. The Riverfront's construction provoked a decade-long struggle over resettlement and rehabilitation that culminated in the exceedingly violent eviction of over 40,000 lower-caste Hindu and Muslim day laborers from the heart of the city. Many have since been left with no choice but to make life and livelihoods in segregated and underserved enclosures at the margins, marked by equally potent forms of ongoing violence.

The pragmatism, efficiency and decisiveness Modi displayed in enforcing the Riverfront Project and others of its kind, however, convinced high-profile liberal voices in India that he had forsaken violence in favour of development (Donthi, 2019). It was this distancing from past violence and the promise of elevating Gujarat's aspirational 'model of development' to all of India that ultimately paved the way for Modi's rise to the country's highest office in 2014 (see Jaffrelot, 2015).

The manicured parks and promenades at the Riverfront, moreover, seem to have erased the violence of their own making from space and time. Not only have the hutments that once lined the river been razed to the ground; the memories of their inhabitants' lifelong political struggles have been drowned out in the process. As one of countless TripAdvisor 'reviews' of the Riverfront suggests, all that remains is a peaceful and modern Hindu utopia directly credited to Modi himself, undisturbed at last by the faceless 'encroachers' it replaced.

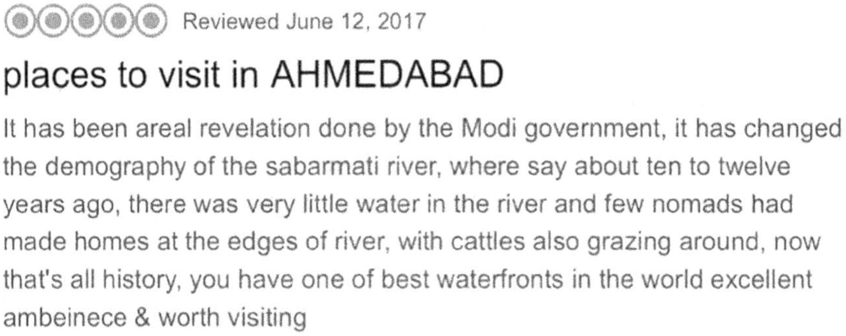

⊚⊚⊚⊚⊚ Reviewed June 12, 2017

places to visit in AHMEDABAD

It has been areal revelation done by the Modi government, it has changed the demography of the sabarmati river, where say about ten to twelve years ago, there was very little water in the river and few nomads had made homes at the edges of river, with cattles also grazing around, now that's all history, you have one of best waterfronts in the world excellent ambeinece & worth visiting

Figure 3.1: TripAdvisor review of the Sabarmati Riverfront posted online on June 12, 2017.

I contend that the separation of 'political' riot violence and the 'economico-juridical' violence of dispossession that permeates the discourse on the Riverfront Project has tacitly facilitated Modi and the Hindu Right's evasion of collective reprisals against their use of violence. Above all, I argue that this static view of violence has prevented a deeper engagement with the political agency of the groups that have become its targets. Critical scholarship has analysed the Riverfront Project's planning, implementation and resettlement in great detail (Chatterjee, 2014; Renu Desai, 2014; Mathur, 2012; Kamna Patel, 2016; Sejal Patel, Sliuzas, and Mathur, 2015; Salmi, 2019). Yet much like the literature on development-induced dispossession in other parts of the world (see Ince, 2018), writings have paid scant attention to the Riverfront Project's violence beyond its relation to neoliberal governance. In most accounts, the Hindu Right's riot violence and attending transformations of Ahmedabad's morphology have functioned as spatiotemporally isolated background conditions to the Riverfront's violence of dispossession. Although many of the same groups that were entangled in the 2002 pogrom subsequently became subjects of dispossession, scholars have yet to examine how these forms of violence and the reactions to them might be connected.

This chapter addresses these limitations by stretching the analytical scope of the Riverfront Project's politics through space and time. I home in on the lives and movements of the Sabarmati's inhabitants from the 1920s to the present. I thereby reveal how the unruly practices of these inhabitants consistently brought them into the crosshairs of the very forms of spatiotemporal violence that fuelled the production of Ahmedabad's segregated social order. By highlighting their historical and ongoing responses to these cascading forms of violence, I expose the hidden spatiotemporal mechanisms that have animated the Hindu Right's hegemonic project in Gujarat. In so doing, I aim to uncover unexpected articulations of agency that could undermine this hegemonic project as Modi and the BJP continue to extend Gujarat's violent spatiotemporal relations across India at large.

My arguments are based on a multi-sited ethnography I conducted between 2016 and 2021. During my research, I 'followed' the production of violence and hegemony in Ahmedabad backwards through space and time from the Riverfront Project's resettlement sites. I interweave my insights with writings that examine Ahmedabad's history from the perspective of its Gandhian legacy and shifting political power structures (Spodek, 2010; 2011) (de)industrialisation and labour (Breman, 2004), Hindu–Muslim riots (Dhattiwala and Biggs, 2012; Ornit Shani, 2007) and ghettoisation (Jaffrelot and Thomas, 2012; Mahadevia, 2007; Rajagopal, 2010).

Coercive spatiotemporal relations in twentieth-century Ahmedabad

In order to adequately explore the broader political valence of the riverbed's inhabitants, it is important to understand the broader coercive relations within and against which they operated. This section thus takes on a birds-eye view to outline how modes of violence at distinct spatiotemporal scales coalesced in twentieth-century Ahmedabad to establish a segregated social order in the city.

When M.K. Gandhi first opened the gates to his ashram on the banks of the Sabarmati in 1915, Ahmedabad looked to become a key site for progressive challenges to capitalist and colonial oppression. Gandhi's hunger strike in 1918 provided critical support to the wage demands of Ahmedabad's rapidly growing population of lower-caste Hindu and Muslim textile workers and laid the groundwork for the formation of the Textile Labour Association (TLA) in 1920. The Independence movement's non-cooperation and civil disobedience campaigns, in turn, heavily relied on mobilising TLA volunteers who were trained in camps at the riverbed (Combating the Campaign of Civil Disobedience, 1930).

Yet in the decades that followed, Ahmedabad's subordinated groups increasingly found themselves in the grip of coercive spatiotemporal relations that variously curtailed their engagement in radical politics and forms of sociality.

Until the eventual disintegration of the textile industry in the mid-1980s, Gujarat's ruling Congress government used its influence over the TLA to rally the political support of Ahmedabad's working-class population. It did so by upholding a clientelistic patronage system that delivered piecemeal improvements to the labourers' working conditions in exchange for their loyalty at the voting booth (Jaffrelot and Thomas, 2012: 48). Participating in this patronage system, however, came at a far greater cost than political loyalty. Both the TLA and Congress leadership in Gujarat largely remained in the hands of Hindu elites whose concessions to the labourers belied their active repression of radical politics that could threaten their place at the apex of Gujarat's religious, economic and political hierarchy (see Breman, 2004).

Gandhi's own ethos of nonviolence and 'trusteeship' legitimated this protection of entrenched power, pressuring Ahmedabad's lower-caste and lower-class Hindus and Muslims to conform to the predetermined roles conferred to them within the 'organicist social system' he had envisaged (Jaffrelot, 2017: 252). As Guha (1997: 110) reveals, Gandhi and the nationalist Congress elite often replicated the British Raj's coercive tactics in their pursuit to mobilise the 'masses' for the Independence movement, meting out physical punishment and caste sanctions against those who dared to break with the dharmic moral practices that animated the movement's disciplinary order.

In Ahmedabad, the rigidity of Gujarat's hierarchical social structure was further compounded by the city's traditional division into *pols*, a dense system of housing clusters that was established by its Muslim founders in the fifteenth century. What is now known as the 'Old City' was enclosed by defensive walls arranged in a half-circle towards the east, while the Sabarmati River acted as Ahmedabad's western border (Mahadevia, 2007). The guarded gateways and narrow lanes leading into the pols emphasise the logic of fortification against outside invaders that guided their construction. Their segregation by caste, religion and occupation, moreover, suggests that the pols also served to protect the city's residents from each other. Ahmedabad's rigid housing arrangements were not contained to the pols of the Old City. By the 1920s, the rapid growth of the textile industry compelled mill owners to accommodate rural migrant workers in rowed tenement housing known as *chawls*. In the process, they extended the city beyond its eastern walls, and replicated existing forms of segregation by assigning separate housing rows to Schedule Caste, Dalit and Muslim workers (Jaffrelot and Thomas, 2012: 46; Ornit Shani, 2007). Yet the pol system of segregation was more 'promiscuous' than it seemed: Dalit, Vanya, Brahmin and Muslim pols were often located beside one another, erecting mosques and temples in the same locality. The pols and the chawls thus represented a 'relative form of segregation' that gave the city a 'mosaic-like structure' (Jaffrelot and Thomas, 2012: 45, 50).

The second half of the twentieth century, however, brought an end to these relations of tessellated coexistence found in the pols and chawls. This process began with a state-sponsored shift of capital and power that bifurcated the city into eastern and western halves along caste and class lines.

The steady decline in the profitability of Ahmedabad's textile industry since the 1960s precipitated a downward trajectory in the already cramped living conditions of the pols and chawls. Eager to assert its political authority over the newly formed state of Gujarat after its split from Bombay, the Congress government empowered a bureaucratic-political class of urban planners within the AMC (Ahmedabad Municipal Corporation). Ahmedabad's upper- and middle-class Hindu elites, aided by the AMC, established gated housing cooperatives in previously unoccupied areas beyond the western banks of the Sabarmati. By strategically selling plots in the cooperatives to fellow Hindus with similar caste and class backgrounds, these elite groups effectively made 'the western side of the city […] an upper-caste Hindu enclave, albeit without walls' (Rajagopal, 2010: 541).

This process eventually siphoned commercial activity and capital investment out of the Old City to expand the financial tertiary sector and construct 'state-of-the-art' public and private infrastructure in western Ahmedabad. Prosperity and political influence in Ahmedabad consequently fell upon the Hindu elites in the west, leaving behind the city's lower-caste Hindus and Muslims in the east in relative economic deprivation. A smaller number of wealthy Muslims, however, also crossed the river from the Old City to settle in Muslim housing cooperatives in the western areas of Paldi and Navrangpura (Jaffrelot and Thomas, 2012: 67). Spatial bifurcation reached its coda when industrialists disinvested from Ahmedabad's composite mills and redirected their capital to more profitable locations and sectors in the mid-1980s. The resulting mill closures led to a loss of roughly 100,000 jobs in eastern Ahmedabad. Following decades of strain, the TLA all but dissolved, irrevocably rupturing the patronage ties between the Congress and Ahmedabad's (former) industrial working class (Breman, 2004).

The loss of these political ties would not go unpunished. It spelled opportunity for the Hindu Right's own violent incursions into the city, which eventually superimposed a system of religious segregation onto Ahmedabad's ongoing caste and class-based bifurcation.

The Hindu Right can be traced to a militant cadre force by the name of *Rashtriya Swayamsevak Sangh* (RSS). Since its establishment in 1925, its estimated membership has swelled to six million across the country, making the RSS 'the largest civil society organisation in the world' (Giorgio Shani, 2021: 276). Not unlike the Congress, RSS leaders in Gujarat primarily sought to ensure their claim to power by advancing the entrenchment of upper-caste Hindu orthodoxy. From the outset, the RSS' political project of re-establishing a mythical Hindu *rashtra* (Hindu nation) has hinged on assimilating minorities and supposed foreigners into a cohesive and strictly hierarchical 'social body' that predetermines one's place in society along the yardstick of Brahminical cultural and racial traits (Jaffrelot, 1996).

In contrast to Gandhi and the nationalist Congress elite, however, RSS leaders understood that violence could be much more than a mere instrument of coercion. Their repeated orchestration of riots in eastern Ahmedabad's industrial areas allowed them to exploit resentments among immiserated lower-caste Hindu labourers that had once fuelled their struggles against capitalist and colonial oppression, and redirect them into attacks against their Muslim counterparts. The experience of Hindu superiority that comes with participating in collective violence against the Muslim Other fostered cohesion around a unified Hindu national identity. It thus bound lower-caste Hindus to the Hindu Right's political agenda while glossing over its efforts to preserve upper-caste dominance.

The 1969 and 1984–85 Hindu–Muslim riots demonstrate the political calculus and consequences of violence at the hands of the RSS and its extended 'family' of affiliated organisations[1]. Both the scholarship and numerous independent reports on these and subsequent riots have established that they were indeed meticulously orchestrated and not merely spontaneous expressions of inter-community strife. In both instances, the Hindu Right deliberately incited violence in mixed Hindu–Muslim areas where it faced high levels of electoral competition. Furthermore, its members encouraged Hindu participation in anti-Muslim violence by orchestrating riots in colonies where Hindus were involved in property disputes with Muslims or competed against Muslim businesses (Ornit Shani, 2007). The Hindu Right's strategic orchestration of riots thus compelled a large number of Muslims to abandon their once mixed communities in eastern Ahmedabad out of fear of further violence at the hands of their Hindu neighbours. By 1985, then, the Hindu Right's riot violence had increasingly relegated Muslim minorities to underserved ghettoes at the margins of the city, birthing a segregated and hegemonic social order that perpetually reinforced Hindu superiority and legitimated further anti-Muslim violence.

Alternative politics at the river

Ahmedabad's coercive spatiotemporal relations, however, were far from uncontested. Turning our attention to the Sabarmati suggests that the riverbed provided an often-overlooked stage for exchanges of agency and violence that exploded the limitations placed on the city's subordinated groups.

This is most explicitly demonstrated by the frequent uprisings that have taken place at the riverbed since the early twentieth century. When the 1919 flour mill riot erupted after rumours of Gandhi's arrest by the colonial government had spread among Ahmedabad's millworkers, the *Times of India* expressed great awe at the 'monster procession' taking place at the Sabarmati, while one of the trial judges struggled to conceal his fears over this savage mob's destructive potential (Ahmedabad Trials, 1919). Elsewhere, reports regularly exaggerated the violence and savagery among those who participated in political gatherings at the riverbed, ostensibly to justify the colonial administration's brutal attempts to subdue them:

> A meeting was held on the banks of the Sabarmati River this evening. Through the police asked the members to disperse, they refused to do so, and a *light* lathi [baton] charge followed. As some of the crowd continued to be defiant, the mounted police rode through the crowd. About fifty persons are alleged to have been injured, and thirty women were arrested. *It is stated that the crowd hurled sand in the faces of the policemen during the melee* [emphasis added]. (Melee at Ahmedabad, 1932)

Uprisings of this kind upended colonial narratives of native docility and drew attention to the illegitimacy of British rule. Yet they also represented challenges to Gandhi's own maxims of nonviolence, calling into question the disciplinary control the Congress party in Gujarat exerted over the masses.

Crucially, historical accounts also seem to disregard the subterranean agentic politics of the migrant groups that had begun setting up improvised shelter by the Sabarmati in the early 1920s (Chatterjee, 2014: 73). Even though their arrival in Ahmedabad coincided with that of other groups expelled from the colonial agrarian economy, the city's growing textile industry only partially absorbed the migrants at the river. While some gained short-term employment in the mills performing menial labour, they were not granted accommodation in the chawls, and travelled daily to the mills on the other side of the city in search of steady work. Placed outside Ahmedabad's tightly regimented housing arrangements and the ranks of the industrial working class, their very exteriority turned the settlers at the river into a permanent threat to the incumbent Congress leadership and the emergent Hindu Right.

The lives of the riverbed's settlers never quite conformed to the entrenched hierarchies and relative forms of segregation that had been etched into Ahmedabad's morphology. They used the location outside the city's western margins to expand their makeshift homes into horizontal clusters that could accommodate their growing families and the arrivals of kin. While localities at the riverbed evolved around familiar regional, caste and religious groupings, it was not unusual to find Muslim households that shared a wall or corrugated roof with their Hindu neighbours. The riverbed's former inhabitants would often tell me about how common it was for them to have chai with their Hindu or Muslim neighbours, help organise each other's weddings and form lasting business relationships. Coupled with the absence of a disciplinary planning authority or architectural tradition, the riverbed thus allowed for more fluid and promiscuous articulations of sociality than those of the pols and chawls in eastern Ahmedabad.

However, the settlers' emplacement at the riverbed did require them to adapt to the rhythms of the Sabarmati, which typically used to run dry, only to erupt into floods during monsoon season (*Stupendous Destruction of Houses*, 1927). The entanglement of illicit market relations with these temperamental flows contributed to the emergence of highly asymmetrical power relations in the riverbed's localities. The scarcity of legally inhabitable and investible land in eastern Ahmedabad spurred these processes of social differentiation during the period of peak industrialisation in the 1960s. Local mafias, incentivised by this shortage and the 'tacit consent of local politicians', established a parallel market for state-owned and officially unsalable public land to extract rent from rural migrants who lacked the means to settle anywhere else in the city (Bobbio, 2018: 116–19).

By placing vulnerable migrants in a position of spatial and social subordination vis-à-vis those who had been given the 'privilege' of time to adapt to the whims of the Sabarmati, these illicit market forces produced hierarchical relations that materially aligned with the slope of the riverbed. Earlier arrivals at the Sabarmati had developed strong kinship and community ties that helped them keep the land mafia at a distance. They also accrued sufficient financial means and predictive knowledge to build semi-permanent dwellings in elevated areas at the outer edges of the riverbed that could withstand the monsoon floods. The far greater number of migrants that came to the riverbed's lower-lying areas after the 1960s, however, found themselves in a near-constant state of liminality, trapped within exploitative tenancy systems.

At the surface, these hierarchies conformed with those in the rest of the city. A closer look, however, reveals that the parallel land market also created openings for highly unusual concentrations of power among the riverbed's Muslim inhabitants, which posed a lasting threat to Ahmedabad's congealed hierarchical relations. Historically 'account[ing] for the lowest strata of [Ahmedabad's] informal working class' (Chatterjee, 2014: 62), Muslims had even fewer chances than the lower-caste Hindus who lined up alongside them in front of cotton mills and construction sites for daily wage work. Many Muslims born in and around the riverbed recount that this chronic lack of opportunity drove their families to construct livelihoods around what they refer to as *do number ke dhande* ('number two-type business activities'). Buoyed by the promiscuous social relations that provided a diverse and sizeable client base, partaking in these activities soon earned them a reputation as 'fixers'. They became known for their ability to procure almost anything of interest for their communities, from stolen or scavenged scrap metal for hutments, replacement parts for bicycle rickshaws, to bootleg liquor. Muslim fixers eventually leveraged their resourcefulness and exhaustive networks to become intermediaries on the parallel land market, pocketing considerable fees for manipulating 'official' land records and brokering 'vacant' lots and across localities at the river.

Besides monetary benefits, their position as intermediaries earned them the title of *agyavaans*, a local term designating political leaders that defend their communities' rights and interests. It was an open secret that the Muslim agyavaans protected incoming settlers from state authorities and particularly overzealous debt collectors as part of a delicate balancing act to preserve their financial assets. On the one hand, they supported the migrants in maintaining adequately stable livelihoods to ensure the steady flow of rent payments at the riverbed. On the other, they kept the settlers from passing a threshold of vulnerability that would allow them to leave the riverbed's lowlands behind for more secure tenure. This delicate balance, then, was not only grounded in coercive relations, but also required the agyavaans to nurture a certain degree of trust among the riverbed's settlers.

It was this intimate hold on the ever-growing migrant population that established the Muslim agyavaans as primary gatekeepers for votes at the riverbed. Local politicians would offer monetary payoffs to the agyavaans in return for mobilising the riverbed's settlers on election day. Muslim agyavaans thus came to perform a critical hinge function within an alternative patronage system at the Sabarmati. As opposed to the patronage system that had formed around the TLA, the system at the riverbed was neither beholden to the Congress party, nor restricted to those who constituted Ahmedabad's industrial working class. Both the Congress and the Hindu Right's elected municipal corporators rarely managed to foster lasting political allegiances among riverbed constituents. Aware of their own dependence on its inhabitants' growing numbers, however, local corporators could not afford to turn their back on the riverbed.

The riverbed's patronage system unsurprisingly clashed with the spatial shift of the city's economic and political centre of gravity to its emergent business districts in western Ahmedabad. The clandestine nature of the riverbed's parallel land market stood at odds with the expansion of private property relations required for the frictionless movement of capital from east to west. The growth of the settlements into a byzantine and ever-shifting maze, moreover, frustrated the AMC's attempts to impose fixity onto the riverbed's relations through practices of mapping and calculation.

Their incompatibility with the imperatives of state-sponsored urbanisation often exposed the riverbed's settlers to the threat of 'slum clearances' at the hands of AMC officials. These threats most notably emerged in the form of early endeavours by illustrious architects in 1961 and 1976 to redevelop the riverbanks into recreational spaces for the city's western elites (Renu Desai, 2012). Yet these efforts never advanced beyond the planning stages, in part due to the Muslim agyavaans who reminded local officials to resist state endeavours that could turn the over 40,000[2] active voters at the riverbed against them.

Juhapura: Extending violence through space and time

The riverbed's patronage system acted as a reliable bulwark against the Congress government's coercive state power. However, it was unable to fend off a consortium of progressive civil society organisations that demanded the AMC's support for the relocation of thousands of settlers whose dwellings had been destroyed by a particularly virulent flood in 1973 (Bobbio, 2018: 139). As this resettlement project was constrained by a limited budget and the lack of available land in Ahmedabad proper, those who had been affected by the floods had little choice but to accept their resettlement to a remote area outside Ahmedabad's administrative boundaries. This resettlement site, Sankalit Nagar, was located in the larger area of Juhapura, which, at that point, was a semi-rural village more than nine kilometres southwest outside of the city (Jaffrelot and Thomas, 2012: 69).

At that time, none of the parties involved could have anticipated that the resettlement to Juhapura would expose its subjects to an essential cycle of spatiotemporal violence that would come back to haunt the riverbed at the turn of the twenty-first century.

The Juhapura relocation project looked to have all the right intentions and ingredients to become a model for participatory and inclusive urban planning. The residents of the 2,248 resettlement households – with Hindus and Muslims in almost equal number – were 'provided special programmes for teaching new economic skills of cottage industries [and] allowed ... to modify and expand their housing to suit individual conditions' (Spodek, 1983: 1582). The groups were also given the choice to be resettled in mixed caste and religious communities that mirrored the promiscuous relations at the riverbed. The consortium overlooking resettlement, moreover, promised to furnish the new sites with the basic infrastructures and civic amenities the displaced groups had limited access to at the banks of the river (Jaffrelot and Thomas, 2012: 69).

Soon after the displaced settlers moved into their new homes, however, they were confronted with the complete lack of livelihood opportunities in this remote area and the near-insurmountable distance to their previous sources of income. Relocation had severed their connections to the river-bed's agyavaans, which significantly diminished their power to make claims towards local authorities. The living conditions in Sankalit Nagar, then, were decidedly poorer than those they were forced to leave behind at the riverbed (Bobbio, 2018: 140; Jaffrelot and Thomas, 2012: 69).

Crucially, resettlement disrupted the social balance the riverbed's inhabit-ants had maintained back 'home'. Even though they had chosen to replicate their mixed settlement patterns in Sankalit Nagar, they were not resettled with the same people. In the absence of the complex relations of depend-ence and trust of the agyavaans' patronage system, religious frictions that had swelled in the city since the 1969 riots also began to spread among the resettled groups. Despite attaining legal tenure, abjection and the threat of Hindu–Muslim violence led more than half of the resettled population to sell or rent out their dwellings in Sankalit Nagar and return to their locali-ties at the Sabarmati by 1983 (Bobbio, 2018: 140; Jaffrelot and Thomas, 2012: 69).

The vacated homes in Sankalit Nagar found occupants in the growing number of former mill workers and other precarianised members of eastern Ahmedabad's working class. The above-average ratio of Muslims among the relocated groups from the riverbed made Sankalit Nagar a particularly favourable destination for Muslim newcomers who increasingly feared for their safety in the mixed pols and chawls. The mill closures and resurgence of Hindu–Muslim riots in the mid-1980s intensified this trend, as Muslim arrivals established new dwellings around Sankalit Nagar's original resettle-ment colony (Bobbio, 2018: 141–2).

While the riot violence in 1985–86 did not directly target Juhapura, the growth and changing composition of its population rekindled the very same religious tensions that had prompted the relocated groups from the Sabarmati to leave the area during the preceding decade. The simmering conflicts spurred a process of self-segregation in and around Juhapura. Large parts of its Hindu minority moved to the Dalit-dominated area of

Vasna on its western side, while some established their own communities in Vejalpur towards the north. This process emphasised the reverberations of the Hindu Right's violence across space and time to create conflict and division in areas that had not (yet) been physically targeted by this violence.

The early 1990s witnessed a significant escalation in the scope and intensity of Hindu–Muslim violence in the city. This third phase of riots targeted instantiations of Hindu–Muslim copresence outside the Old City for the first time, including the few higher-income Muslim localities in western Ahmedabad, and most notably, the wider Juhapura area beyond the western margins of the city.

The violence in Juhapura drew on and intensified existing tensions and imbued the ongoing process of self-segregation in the area with a sense of irrevocable finality. A small number of Hindus had remained in Juhapura's Muslim-majority localities around Sankalit Nagar, just as some Muslims had still lived in its Hindu areas until the 1990s. These riots, however, established strict divisions between the neighbourhoods, which in one case, materialised in the erection of a literal border wall (Renu Desai, 2010: 112).

The sequestration of Muslims in Juhapura, provoked by the threatened and ultimately realised spatiotemporal expansion of riot violence, created a ripple effect throughout the city. Not knowing where violence would strike next, Muslims from across Ahmedabad began to relocate to Juhapura. Its borders became a gravitational field that represented one of the few safe havens where Muslims could evade the threat of being murdered by their Hindu neighbours. While over 200,000 Muslims had moved to Juhapura by the mid-1990s, violent transformations of the city since then have increased this number to over 750,000, making it the largest Muslim ghetto in contemporary India (Laliwala et al., 2020: 103).

With the violent 'creation' of Juhapura, the Hindu Right made massive strides towards imposing a hegemonic social order onto Ahmedabad's already segregated morphology. Restricting Muslim presence to the Old City and Juhapura allowed the Hindu Right to further disenfranchise Muslims by actively restricting access to public services in these very areas. Besides bodily harm, violence impacted Muslim livelihoods, which, in turn, increased the likelihood of domestic violence and encounters with law enforcement more generally. Separating Muslims from the daily lives of the Hindu elites living in western Ahmedabad, moreover, facilitated the construction of a Muslim Other with an innate propensity for violence. As Hindus living in western Ahmedabad could now 'spend extended periods of time without ever seeing a Muslim', the Hindu Right's narratives of Muslim violence and inferiority were increasingly allowed to spread unchecked (Rajagopal, 2010: 544).

The case of Juhapura, however, also suggests that the Hindu Right's violence in Ahmedabad did not aim to erase the Muslim Other from the organic body of the nation altogether. Spatially, its hegemonic social order hinges on a fluid network of internal frontiers in the minds of its subjects that manifest as external frontiers in the form of physical borders between Hindus and Muslims. These frontiers segregate and simultaneously act as zones of violent engagement, as displays of communal hostility perpetually reinforce Hindu–Muslim irreconcilability (Renu Desai, 2010: 115).

Conjoining riot violence with the violence of dispossession

The riot violence of the early 1990s translated in an 'immediate electoral bonus' for the BJP in Gujarat, which wrested state power from the Congress for the first time in 1995 (Radhika Desai, 2011). The segregated social order in Ahmedabad that both fuelled and reflected the Hindu Right's claim to hegemony, however, remained conspicuously incomplete. Much like in Juhapura, violence and the state-sponsored ruination of eastern Ahmedabad had further increased the riverbed's population. This strengthened the river-bed's patronage system, especially as it had become one of the few remaining avenues for local Congress politicians to mobilise Ahmedabad's informal-ised workers following the disintegration of the TLA.

Arguably the greatest threat to the Hindu Right, however, was that Ahmedabad's westward expansion had effectively transported the river-bed from what once were its western margins to the heart of the city. The dependence of Ahmedabad's Hindu elites on cheap labour both produced and necessitated an intimate proximity between their gated properties and the riverbed. Its settlers provided them with fruits and vegetables, washed their clothes, looked after their children, cleaned their homes, took them to work on their rickshaws and unclogged their latrines. In contrast to the distant and enclosed 'moral pollution' of Juhapura and the Old City (Rajagopal, 2010: 533), Ahmedabad's western inhabitants could not simply avert their eyes from the promiscuous relations at the Sabarmati. The very groups supposed to embody the common-sense notion of Hindu identity at the core of the Hindu Right's hegemonic social order were permanently confronted with forms of life that destabilised this common sense: Muslim agyavaans continued to wield power and dominate the social hierarchies in the mixed localities at the heart of the city, despite decades of riot violence designed to segregate and subordinate.

The agyavaans put this power on display to thwart yet another attempt at Riverfront redevelopment in 1997. For this Project, Surendra Patel, chair-man of the AMC's steering committee and BJP state treasurer, received the prominent backing of incumbent BJP chief minister Keshubhai Patel. They enlisted Berkeley-educated architect and urban planner Bimal Patel to devise a Riverfront redevelopment plan, based on discourses tailor-made to weaken the fragile relations between the riverbed's settlers and Ahmedabad's western elites. Bimal Patel's proposal did just that, displaying an eerily prescient instinct for emergent juridico-aesthetic discourses that would be deployed across India's major cities to elicit middle-class support for anti-poor urban renewal projects after the mid-2000s.

The development plan proposed to 'reclaim' 162 hectares of riverbed land on both sides of the Sabarmati to build 'an expansive network of parks, waterside promenades, markets, cultural institutions, ... and commercial developments' that could rival waterfronts in Paris, London and New York and, thus, 'create a new forward-looking identity for Ahmedabad' (Bimal Patel and Kansal, 2011: 1). In Bimal Patel's view, this would mitigate pressing environmental and social concerns in the city, arguing that the Sabarmati's occupation by 'illegal encroachers' who had 'neglected' and 'abused' the river for decades had contaminated its water and rendered its banks inaccessible to Ahmedabad's citizens (Bimal Patel and Kansal, 2011: 4). In the same breath, Patel emphasised 'social upliftment' as one of the Project's key dimensions, promising that affected 'slum dwellers' would receive alternative housing on the reclaimed land itself. Perhaps most importantly, Patel proposed to make the Riverfront 'pay for itself' by auctioning 20 percent of the reclaimed land to private property developers, which would both please fiscally conservative taxpayers and isolate its implementation from the 'cumbersome' politics of municipal budgeting (Bimal Patel and Kansal, 2011: 11). Gujarat's state government accepted Patel's proposal in 1998 and established the Sabarmati Riverfront Development Corporation (SRFDC, a public–private arm of the AMC).

The SRFDC's troubles began in 1999, when it tasked external contractors to conduct a comprehensive household survey of the settlements to render their complex property relations legible for intervention. In a bid to retain control, the agyavaans soon organised the riverbed's inhabitants against these household surveys. Given the experience of the 1973 resettlement to Juhapura, the settlers were more than willing to assert themselves against what they saw as agents of the state, by engaging in aggressive altercations, or by simply feeding false and contradictory information to the surveyors. These practices significantly slowed progress on the surveys. Critical voices within the city government soon questioned the Riverfront's political viability, and it appeared that the project would suffer a similar fate as its predecessors in the 1960s and 1970s.

The BJP in Gujarat similarly faced an uphill battle at the time. Modi replaced Keshubhai Patel in October 2001 after the BJP had lost control over the Ahmedabad Municipal Corporation (AMC) and suffered defeats in the State Assembly and parliamentary by-elections. The BJP's fortunes did not change after Modi took charge, losing two Assembly seats in three by-elections in February 2002. This exacerbated the ongoing turmoil within the Hindu Right in Gujarat and threatened to leave Modi politically isolated in the face of looming state elections in 2002 (Basu, 2015: 181–2; Dhattiwala and Biggs, 2012: 489).

The spatiotemporal logics of the 2002 anti-Muslim pogrom reveal how the Riverfront Project and riot violence coalesced in Modi's hands to advance the Hindu Right's hegemonic project in Gujarat.

Over the course of twelve months after the initial violence on 27 February, concerted attacks by Hindus across caste and class lines killed 984 predominantly Muslim people and left thousands injured and homeless across Gujarat (Dhattiwala and Biggs 2012: 284–5, 493). Spatially, the likelihood of violence increased in constituencies with a higher proportion of Muslims where the BJP expected the greatest competition in the forthcoming election. It decreased in those it already controlled. This logic seemed to pay off once again: the BJP's vote share increased in the very districts that had experienced the most intense violence (Dhattiwala and Biggs, 2012: 499–502). Regaining this electoral support empowered Modi to quell dissent among the Hindu Right, staff his cabinet with loyalists and curtail the Legislative Assembly's decision-making power, thereby furnishing him with an unprecedented degree of control over Gujarat's state apparatus (Basu, 2015: 164, 182).

Temporally echoing its prior spatial expansion to Juhapura, moreover, the 2002 violence finally made its way to to the banks of the Sabarmati, one of the last remaining holdouts of allied Hindu–Muslim copresence in the city. The incursion of riot violence into the riverbed's localities had come unexpectedly to many of their inhabitants who thought they have escaped the riot-prone areas by settling closer to the western part of the city. Most of all, it surprised the agyavaans themselves. Whereas their interdependent relations with local Hindu politicians and power brokers had previously allowed them to quell emergent religious conflict, this time, the agyavaans were suddenly attacked by those very allies. The pogrom, then, had compelled many of the Muslim agyavaans and settlers in mixed localities to escape from the violence at the riverbed. Hindus found shelter in nearby Hindu-majority areas arranged by the Sangh Parivar's welfare wing. Most Muslims, in turn, were provided with safe housing in Muslim-majority areas such as Juhapura by Islamist reform movements like the Jamaat-e-Islami and their own welfare wing, the Islamic Relief Committee (Jasani, 2008).

For some time, it had looked as though the Hindu Right's riot violence under Modi succeeded to remove the threat of the unruly settlements at the river from the heart of the city and incorporate them into the spatio-social locations that accorded to the construction of its hegemonic social order. However, most settlers made their way back to the localities at the river-banks by the end of 2002, defying the Hindu Right's social order yet again.

Modi and the BJP's broader political ambitions were further imperilled by the fact that the 2002 pogrom was the first and only time large-scale Hindu–Muslim violence had taken place under a ruling BJP government. It was now possible to hold the ruling BJP government liable for the violence. The resulting backlash against Modi included legal inquiries at home and visa bans from the United States and other foreign governments (Kaul, 2017). The attribution of violence with the state also endangered Modi's relationship with business elites and middle-class constituents, whose support critically rested on the government's ability to attract capital investment to Gujarat's urban centres (see Desai, 2010).

Faced with these threats, Modi proceeded to rebrand himself as Gujarat's own *vikas purush* ('development man'), pivoting away from his and the BJP's public perception as instigators of violence to those capable of meeting the imperatives of neo-liberalisation head-on. One of his first acts of business to underscore this new persona was to breathe new life into the Riverfront Project. During an elaborate inauguration ceremony in mid-2003, Modi positioned himself as the Project's figurehead. He 'urged the [SRFDC] to complete the project in 1000 days', and exerted his newfound control over the state apparatus to staff SRFDC leadership with loyalists who began executing a series of unilateral evictions to meet this expedited timeline (Renu Desai, 2014: 7).

Transforming agyavaans into vectors of hegemonic violence

Initially, it appeared as though coming back together at the river galvanised the settlers to join forces against the SRFDC. Following the Project's post-inauguration evictions, the agyavaans became leaders of the *Sabarmati Nagrik Adhikar Manch* (SNAM, right to the river movement) with the help of the civil society organisations that had been operating at the river since the 2002 riots. The movement's emphasis on the settlers' 'right to the city' that opposed their characterisation as 'illegal encroachers' found broad support among members of Ahmedabad's intelligentsia and brought the Riverfront Project under increased public scrutiny.

As co-petitioners in a Public Interest Litigation (PIL) filed in Gujarat's High Court, the SNAM agyavaans even recorded a widely celebrated victory against the SRFDC. In 2005, a sympathetic judge issued a stay order 'prohibiting various state authorities including AMC and SRFDC from evicting any resident until the courts had seen the rehabilitation plans' (Renu Desai, 2012: 54). This moment of resistance, however, was fleeting. The court's decision effectively limited political opposition to the Riverfront Project to the legal-bureaucratic details of resettlement and rehabilitation.

Months after the court 'victory', Gujarat's inclusion in the national Congress' Jawaharlal Nehru National Urban Renewal Mission (JnNURM) made clear that the SRFDC would not provide alternative housing to the settlers on the Riverfront's rejuvenated areas itself. JnNURM provided municipal corporations with grant funding for urban infrastructure projects conditioned to public–private partnerships. Through its Basic Services for the Urban Poor (BSUP) sub-mission, it incentivised municipal corporations to sell underutilised land to private builders at subsidised rates to construct low-income housing for the 'project-affected families' displaced by said infrastructure projects (Chatterjee, 2014: 69). The JnNURM windfall allowed the SRFDC to draft a resettlement plan that would move the riverbed's inhabitants to four-storey housing units, most of which were built on the grounds of abandoned textile mills in eastern Ahmedabad. Resettlement, then, looked to take the riverbed's settlers back to the very marginal areas of violence and decay many of them had escaped decades ago. In other Indian cities, JnNURM merely intensified capitalist processes of urban accumulation by dispossession. In Modi's Ahmedabad, however, this national policy also potentiated the spatiotemporal extension of the Hindu Right's long-standing riot violence.

The pogrom, moreover, had a significant temporal aftereffect on the riverbed's settlers. The agyavaans recognised that the material basis of the patronage system that sustained them had already been lost. While they continued to live side by side with their Hindu and Muslim neighbours, their basic trust in each other had been significantly weakened. This lack of trust most notably manifested in changes to the 'ethno-spatiality of everyday existence' at the river, as the settlers began to limit meaningful interactions with their extended family units and increasingly avoided contact across religious and caste lines (see Chatterjee, 2014: 104–5). While they had not descended into conflict, relations had begun to echo those in Juhapura that had compelled the resettled migrants to return to the Sabarmati almost thirty years earlier.

At this point, the SRFDC's main goal was to carry out resettlement and the construction of the Riverfront as swiftly as possible, in a manner that underscored Modi's effectiveness in delivering his vision of development to India's urban middle class. Identified by the High Court and local civil society organisations as the only legitimate representatives for the concerns of the riverbed's inhabitants and wielding influence over them, the SRFDC was keenly aware that this endeavour's success critically hinged on the support of the SNAM agyavaans. The latter, in turn, were quick to recognise that their tenuous grip over the land market at the river was inevitably falling into the hands of the SRFDC and corporate investors. However, the agyavaans also realised that collaborating with the SRFDC could potentially allow them to act as intermediaries on the emerging market land market established by the process of resettlement and rehabilitation.

The SRFDC's resettlement strategy significantly compressed the lived temporal experience of the riverbed's inhabitants, which allowed the agyavaans to construct a shadow economy that continues to form the basis of their wealth and political influence over a decade later. Having submitted their resettlement plan to the High Court in 2008, the SRFDC officially resumed Project-related evictions that took place in five phases between mid-2009 and early 2012. As the riverbed's inhabitants had been excluded from the High Court negotiations and clandestine meetings between the SRFDC and SNAM agyavaans, they had only heard about the status of their impending eviction and resettlement through rumours and scattered newspaper reports (Desai, 2014: 7). This lack of information, coupled with the staggered eviction process, left the riverbed's inhabitants with little time or opportunity to stage a collective response to these evictions. Instead, the SRFDC created a frenzied scramble among the inhabitants to gain access to resettlement benefits.

Whereas the 1973 Juhapura resettlement was distinguished by its participatory approach, the SRFDC's resettlement strategy explicitly harkened back to the divisive effects of the Hindu Right's riot violence. The SRFDC determined resettlement eligibility based on the fragmentary household surveys that the 2002 riots had cut short. This failed to reflect subsequent changes to the spatial morphology of the hutment colonies. The SRFDC further raised the bar for eligibility by pressing inhabitants to produce an ever-expanding catalogue of official documents proving their residence at the riverbed that very few possessed or had the means to acquire (Sejal Patel, Sliuzas, and Mathur, 2015: 252). Moreover, the SRFDC did not attempt to relocate inhabitants in groups that reflected pre-existing community formations to sites that were closest to their localities of origin. To avoid charges of discrimination based on caste and religion, SRFDC officials relied on a 'scientifically neutral' lottery system that determined each family's eventual location in one of the eighteen resettlement sites through random allotment draws. Echoing Juhapura once again, this process inevitably resulted in the separation of riverbed communities and meant that Hindus and Muslims from different localities would be resettled together.

Much to the chagrin of the SRFDC, the implementation of this resettlement plan was met by massive resistance. While they had worked hard to maintain a peaceful yet uneasy coexistence with their Hindu and Muslim neighbours at the banks of the river in the aftermath of the 2002 violence, the thought of living with strangers from a different religious community raised existential fears among the riverbed's inhabitants. These fears were exacerbated when Hindus living near one of the proposed resettlement sites took to the streets to protest plans to bring Muslims to their neighbourhood and threw stones at arriving Muslims during the first phase of resettlement (Renu Desai, 2014: 31). With tensions rising, the SRFDC officials brought on the SNAM agyavaans to advise them in redrawing the resettlement map in a way that would mitigate further religious friction. Furthermore, High Court and civil society organisations vested the agyavaans with the task of producing an allotment list that more accurately represented the project-affected people at the river using a new 2007 eligibility cut-off date.

The SNAM agyavaans did not use their increased control over the allotment list and resettlement geography to do either one of these things. In fact, many of them not only colluded with SRFDC officials to extort the riverbed's settlers for exorbitant fees to procure the necessary documents that could get them on the allotment list, but also to secure housing units in the most desirable resettlement sites (i.e. those with the highest potential for increasing land prices) for themselves and their entourages (Renu Desai, 2014: 39). My research further suggests that SNAM agyavaans collaborated with SRFDC staff to instigate rather than mitigate Hindu–Muslim conflict in the riverbed communities, as internal divisions increased the settlers' willingness to pay higher extortion fees. As a result, those who could not or refused to line the pockets of those profiteering from this new shadow economy failed to get their names onto the final allotment list.

Many who had been excluded from resettlement and rehabilitation left the riverbed behind to set up their cots and shacks on the city's open pavements. Others returned to their villages to work as landless agricultural labourers. In 2011, those who continued to fight for their right to the city were removed from the banks of the Sabarmati in exceedingly violent fashion. Some 1,000 AMC officials and 1,500 armed police were deployed to beat down and lock up those who resisted the demolitions by pelting stones at the incoming bulldozers. As Mathur (2012: 72) notes, this series of forced evictions was carried out during both the hottest and coldest months of the year. This left thousands of families without alternative housing in harsh conditions for days or even weeks, causing widespread hunger, disease and the 'deaths of children, infants, [and] pregnant women'. The AMC provided these families and others who had been unable to produce sufficient evidence to prove their eligibility for resettlement with 'chalk-drawn open plots of 10 by 15 feet' to set up 'temporary' encampments in a marshland area 'adjacent to a municipal solid waste dump site' (Mathur, 2012: 66).

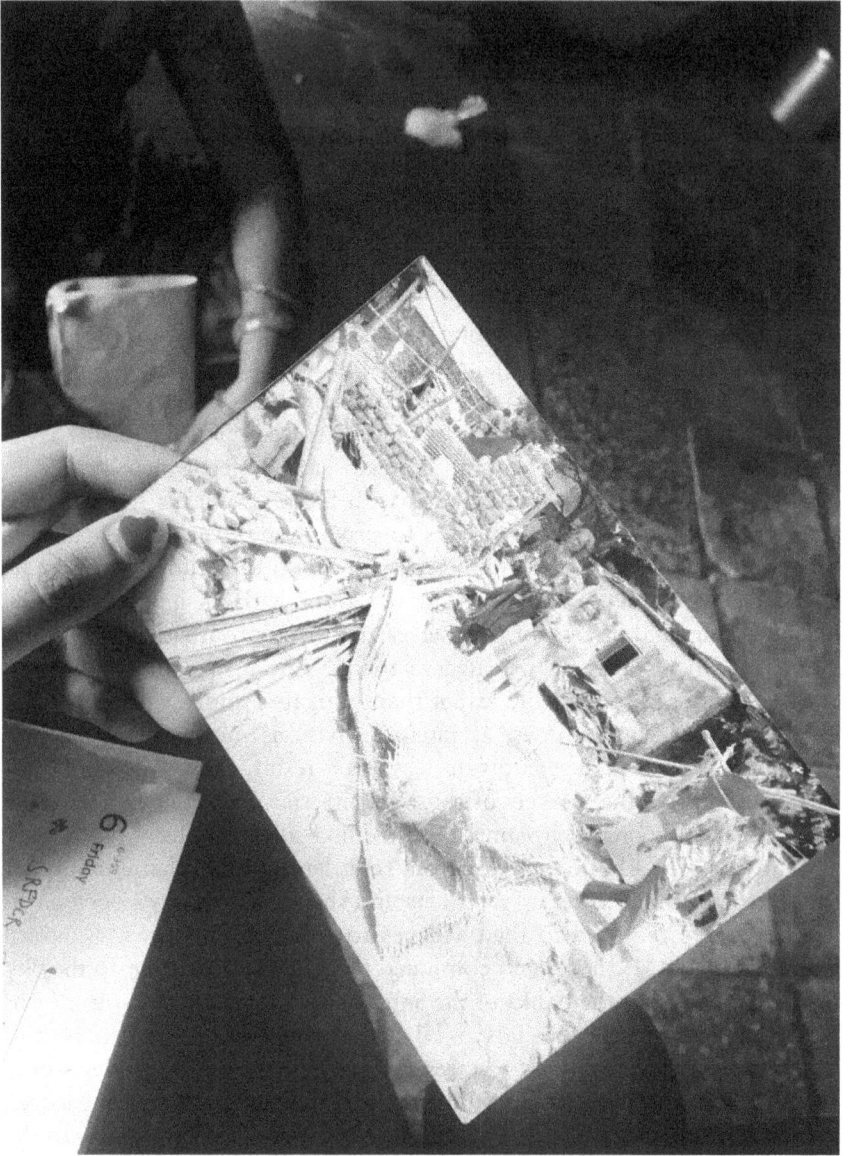

Figure 3.2: A Vaghri woman displaying a photo of the day her family was evicted from the riverbed.

While some of these families were eventually assigned to a home in one of the permanent resettlement sites, more than 1,000 of the riverbed's settlers continue to live in this temporary encampment, with little hope of ever receiving an allotment letter.

Vatva: Cascading violence in resettlement

Narratives surrounding resettlement have since made clear that the Riverfront Project fulfilled its ambitions of social upliftment. While acknowledging that the resettlement process was far from perfect, the likes of Bimal Patel have emphasised that the approximately 14,000 project-affected people who benefited from resettlement were set on a path of property ownership and self-determination, breaking the cycle of poverty and dependence on government largesse (see Patel and Kansal, 2011). As part of the cost-sharing arrangement of the BSUP scheme, the evicted were given a chance to own the flats they were assigned, pending a down payment and ten years of monthly instalments. The BSUP scheme intended for government-appointed NGOs to help provide the beneficiaries with access to bank loans for these house payments. They were also tasked with setting up Resident Welfare Associations (RWAs) that would collect funds from the beneficiaries for basic services and maintenance in the sites without the need for further public assistance.

However, the violent process of dispossession and resettlement, coupled with the infrastructural violence fused into the spatial fabric of the resettlement sites themselves, only exposed the riverbed's former inhabitants to further forms of violence at the hands of local corporators and SNAM agyavaans.

The scholarship on resettlement and rehabilitation has most clearly highlighted this in their examination of the Vatva resettlement site. Vatva is an industrial neighbourhood at the south-eastern periphery of the city, around twelve kilometres from the Riverfront. Not unlike Juhapura, Vatva has gained a degree of infamy among Ahmedabad's urban poor. It is the largest resettlement site in the city, housing 20,000 inhabitants that were evicted by the Bus Rapid Transit System, Kankaria Lakefront, and Riverfront Projects, all of which were implemented by the Modi government. The resettlement process has caused religious and caste-based segregation in its two main blocks, which are informally referred to as 'Hindustan' and 'Pakistan'.

As in many other sites, residents in Vatva refused to cooperate with the NGOs to pay for their homes and maintenance. They were adamant that they were owed 'a house for a house' for their demolished dwellings. Above all, the experience of violent resettlement had irreparably eroded their trust in the government and its agents (Salmi, 2019: 11). Most could not afford to make these payments even if they wanted to, as their new homes were located

Figure 3.3: The 'Pakistan' section of the Vatva resettlement site. Photograph taken by Surabhi Vaya on 24 August 2018.

at an unnecessarily vast distance from their prior livelihood opportunities, adding significant cost to performing already low-paying daily wage work.

Vatva's infrastructure and governance systems appear intentionally designed to keep its inhabitants in a constant state of liminal destitution and conflict that inhibits the formation of kinship and community. The poor standard of basic services has routinely turned the lack of trust among residents into violent confrontations over 'common property issues' such as the accumulation of garbage and 'water pilferage from common tanks' (Sejal Patel, Sliuzas, and Mathur, 2015: 249). The police, moreover, strictly enforce resettlement terms and conditions that prohibit any commercial activity or physical changes to the structures themselves. This has added to the residents' lack of income-generating opportunities while constraining public life and individual expression (Kamna Patel, 2016: 108–9). In stark contrast to the riverbed's hutments that could be adapted to the community and livelihood configurations of the riverbed's inhabitants, the four-storey buildings in the resettlement sites do not allow for any irregularity. Architect Neelkanth Chhaya (who was incidentally involved in the Juhapura resettlement of 1973) notes in an interview that 'the concrete boxes [are] cast in C2, it's impossible to drive a nail into them. ... You cannot do anything to that house unless you have very good tools. You can't even hang a photograph.'

In fact, the resettlement sites display an eerie similarity to South Africa's apartheid-era townships in the 1950s described by von Schnitzler (2016: 14):

> If apartheid infrastructures were often primarily designed to prevent the emergence of a (counter)public, this was most obvious in the mass building of townships from the 1950s as spaces intentionally without important city features. Conceived as mere dormitories for laborers and built far away from the white city centers, the townships had no plazas or public squares, and business operations, if they existed at all, were heavily restricted. Instead of building and supporting a public, infrastructures often followed a security or military logic [...]. The grids of streets were planned such that they could be easily surveilled and closed off.

In the decade following the evictions, SNAM agyavaans have taken on a critical role in maintaining the infrastructural violence that extends across the Riverfront's resettlement sites, by appropriating this violence for their own financial and political gain. Thanks to their control over the resettlement process, SNAM agyavaans compelled many of the riverbed's most vulnerable inhabitants into distress sales of the titles to their officially assigned homes. This has allowed the agyavaans to illegally 'own' and rent out a considerable number of flats in the resettlement sites to 'beggars, illegal migrants, and other marginalised people who did not have the means to access the legal housing market' (Salmi, 2019: 11). The constant influx of new 'strangers' continues to prevent the establishment of stable communities and social norms in the resettlement sites, and as in other spaces marked by anomie, has led their inhabitants to take further recourse in common-sense assumptions 'regarding people's status, reputation and character ... to make sense of their surroundings and demarcate belonging' (Ramakrishnan, 2014: 68). This has most notably articulated itself in the hardening of hierarchies and social divisions between the Hindustan and Pakistan areas in Vatva, but also within these areas themselves, between lower- and lower-middle-caste Hindus and Muslims. After the government-appointed NGOs tasked with forming the RWAs abandoned the resettlement sites, SNAM agyavaans took control of the RWAs. They have become gatekeepers for the funds any outside donors or local corporators pledge for the provision of basic services. While the SNAM agyavaans pocket most of these funds, they strategically distribute them to single-caste and religious groups, which further reinforces divisions and spurs open conflict over these scarce resources.

Elected municipal corporators from both major parties are more than happy to uphold this status quo. They often collaborate with SNAM agyavaans to employ carrot-and-stick tactics against the inhabitants of the resettlement sites to build a perpetually desperate and acquiescent voting base that keeps them in power. For instance, corporators variously allow

'quiet encroachments' by the residents that include turning 'hallways ...
into storage rooms, empty dwelling units into animal sheds, or [painting]
the inner and outer walls of apartments with pastel pinks, greens, and blues,
[...] all in violation of policy guidelines' (Salmi, 2019: 11). They also 'over-
look' the missing housing payments and the illegal rental market in the
sites. At the time of municipal elections, they promise to get the overflow-
ing gutters fixed and to send municipal workers to clear the piles of trash
that have accumulated on every corner. However, they also routinely order
police raids against families for minor transgressions when sensing that
they could rally other residents against the corporator to mount a political
challenge of their own. SNAM agyavaans not only hold a monopoly over
the offering of payment-based protection to the resettlement sites' inhabitants against the corporators' violent intrusions but have also become the
ultimate conflict mediator between the inhabitants themselves. They now
act as intermediaries for a violent mafia system in the resettlement sites that
has spatiotemporally extended the shadow economy they helped construct
at the riverbed.

Figure 3.4: The Sabarmati Riverfront in Ahmedabad.

At the Riverfront itself, the nexus of violence, politics and agency that
continues to envelop the Sabarmati's dangerous classes looks to have been
erased from view. The materiality of the Riverfront intimately mirrors that
of the resettlement sites, severing its connections with the ongoing infrastructural violence it has effected by keeping away those entangled in it.
As it stands, the Riverfront appears relatively barren, lined with few parks
and gardens, waiting for buyers to build hotels and luxury apartments on
its rejuvenated spaces. Fruit vendors and food hawkers are prohibited from
operating on its stark and lifeless promenades, which are flanked by two
four-lane traffic-carrying roads that are closed to auto-rickshaws and buses.
Access to the manicured gardens and parks scattered around the river costs
an entry fee of 20 rupees. A visitor tells me that a 'nominal ticket is required
for entry. This is good so that stray passers do not spoil the garden.' This

entry fee represents yet another aspect of this infrastructure that closes the area off to those who do not, or no longer, belong to the 'public'.

Conclusion

In the hands of the Modi government, the Riverfront Project's violence of dispossession became a spatiotemporal extension of the Hindu Right's hegemonic riot violence. In Vatva, this violence has precipitated the construction of external frontiers between the evicted in the form of material borders that visibly segregate Hindus from Muslims. These external frontiers are mirrored in the construction of internal frontiers among Vatva's residents. The violence they encounter burrows hegemonic meanings of Hindu identity, its Muslim Other, and caste hierarchy ever deeper into the common sense governing their everyday lives. Lower-middle-caste Hindus that have been confined to Vatva's 'Hindustan' now more actively lend their votes to the BJP government that planned and executed this violence.

The Muslim agyavaans have expanded their financial means and political influence through their participation in this violence. This seemingly runs counter to the dominant relations undergirding the Hindu Right's hegemonic project that generally strives to suppress any and all articulations of Muslim power. When observed within the context of Ahmedabad's segregated social order, however, the confinement of their power to the margins ultimately serves to strengthen its coercive spatiotemporal relations by reinforcing Hindu–Muslim separation and antagonism. The extractive nature of the agyavaans' power, moreover, helps uphold stereotypes that paint Muslim spaces as zones of inherent violence, savagery and illegality.

Highlighting the 'afterlife' of eviction in Vatva represents a necessary but insufficient step in exploring the nexus of violence and hegemony that currently characterises Ahmedabad's development-induced resettlement sites. As it stands, the sparse scholarship on this topic has limited its focus to Vatva alone. Most importantly, these debates have homed in on the relations between Hindus and tended to depict Muslims as a monolithic group. Given what we know about the perpetual excess of agency Muslims have displayed in their encounters with this violence, it would be short-sighted to assume that their relations across Ahmedabad's resettlement sites are entirely determined by the imperatives of the Hindu Right's hegemonic project. After all, while the Muslim agyavaans I followed in this chapter might have become vectors for and intermediaries of hegemonic violence at one point, they also continue to be 'real living individuals' who retain the agency to engage in counter-hegemonic practices.

The Riverfront Project erased all traces of the violence of its own making and the counter-hegemonic openings the riverbed once represented.

However, the brief glimpses scholars have provided into the Vatva resettlement site suggest that the nexus of violence and hegemony at the banks of the river has not been extinguished, but merely relocated to the margins of the city. It is here that the mechanisms of violence driving the Hindu Right's hegemonic project can be witnessed at their fullest extent. Taking heed of the considerable divergence in the spatiotemporal trajectories of the resettlement sites that house the dangerous classes from the Sabarmati could serve as portals into how the Hindu Right's violent hegemony can be contested in the current conjuncture. Hence, future research needs to adopt a relational perspective in its engagement with the marginal formations produced by the Hindu Right's spatiotemporal violence in Modi's India.

Notes

1 During the second half of the twentieth century, the RSS came to operate as the cultural wing of the *Sangh Parivar*, a 'family' of Hindu nationalist organisations that also includes the *Vishva Hindu Parishad* (VHP) as its religious wing, and the *Bharatiya Janata Party* (BJP, formerly Jana Sangh), its primary political exponent.
2 Given the settlers' impermeability to household surveys, it is difficult to establish exact estimates of their numbers at the riverbed. Most informants who worked for NGOs at the riverbed since the late 1960s agree that around 35,000–50,000 people lived at the riverbed since that time.

Bibliography

Ahmedabad Trials (1919). 'Ahmedabad Trials: Floor Mill Riots. Court's Judgement', *The Times of India* (26 June 1919), 9, ProQuest Historical Newspapers.
Basu, A. (2015). *Violent Conjunctures in Democratic India* (New York: Cambridge University Press).
Bobbio, T. (2018). *Urbanisation, Citizenship and Conflict in India: Ahmedabad 1900–2000* (London, New York: Routledge).
Breman, J. (2004). *The Making and Unmaking of an Industrial Working Class: Sliding down the Labour Hierarchy in Ahmedabad, India* (Amsterdam: Amsterdam University Press).
Chatterjee, I. (2014). *Displacement, Revolution, and the New Urban Condition: Theories and Case Studies* (Los Angeles: SAGE Publications).
Combating The Campaign of Civil Disobedience (1930). 'Combating The Campaign of Civil Disobedience', *The Times of India* (2 April 1930), 10, ProQuest Historical Newspapers.
Desai, R. (2011). 'Gujarat's Hindutva of Capitalist Development', *South Asia: Journal of South Asian Studies*, 34:3, 354–81. https://doi.org/10.1080/00856401.2011.620551

Desai, R. (2010). 'Producing and contesting the "communalized city": Hindutva politics and urban space in Ahmedabad', in *The Fundamentalist City? Religiosity and the Remaking of Urban Spaces* (New York: Routledge), 99–124.

Desai, R. (2012). 'Governing the Urban Poor: Riverfront Development, Slum Resettlement and the Politics of Inclusion in Ahmedabad', *Economic & Political Weekly*, 47:2, 7.

Desai, R. (2014). 'Municipal Politics, Court Sympathy and Housing Rights: A Post-mortem of Displacement and Resettlement Under the Sabarmati Riverfront Project, Ahmedabad', Centre for Urban Equity (CUE). Working paper no. 23, 1–56.

Dhattiwala, R. and Biggs, M. (2012). 'The Political Logic of Ethnic Violence: The Anti-Muslim Pogrom in Gujarat, 2002', *Politics & Society*, 40:4, 483–516. https://doi.org/10.1177/0032329212461125

Donthi, P. (2019). 'The Liberals who Loved Modi', *The Caravan* (16 May 2019), https://caravanmagazine.in/politics/the-liberals-who-loved-modi (accessed 23 May 2019).

Guha, R. (1997). *Dominance Without Hegemony: History and Power in Colonial India* (Cambridge, MA: Harvard University Press).

Ince, O. U. (2018). 'Between Equal Rights: Primitive Accumulation and Capital's Violence', *Political Theory*, 46:6, 885–914. https://doi.org/10.1177/009059171 7748420

Jaffrelot, C. (1996). *The Hindu Nationalist Movement in India* (New York: Columbia University Press).

Jaffrelot, C. (2015). 'What "Gujarat Model"? – Growth without Development – and with Socio-Political Polarisation', *South Asia: Journal of South Asian Studies*, 38:4, 820–38. https://doi.org/10.1080/00856401.2015.1087456

Jaffrelot, C. (2017). 'The Congress in Gujarat (1917–1969): Conservative Face of a Progressive Party', *Studies in Indian Politics*, 5:2, 248–61. https://doi.org/10.1177/2321023017727982

Jaffrelot, C. and Thomas, C. (2012). 'Facing Ghettoisation in "Riot-City": Old Ahmedabad and Juhapura Between Victimisation and Self-Help', in *Muslims in Indian Cities: Trajectories of Marginalisation* (Columbia University Press), 43–80.

Jasani, R. (2008). 'Violence, Reconstruction and Islamic Reform–Stories from the Muslim "Ghetto"', *Modern Asian Studies*, 42:2–3, 431–56. https://doi.org/10.1017/S0026749X07003150

Kaul, N. (2017). 'Rise of the Political Right in India: Hindutva-Development Mix, Modi Myth, and Dualities', *Journal of Labor and Society*, 20:4, 523–48. https://doi.org/10.1111/wusa.12318

Laliwala, S., Jaffrelot, C., Thakkar, P., and Desai, A. (2020). 'Paradoxes of Ghettoization: Juhapura "in" Ahmedabad', in *India Exclusion Report 2019–2020* (Center for Equity Studies with Three Essays Collective), 103–34.

Mahadevia, D. (2007). 'A City With Many Borders–Beyond Ghettoisation in Ahmedabad', in *Indian Cities in Transition* (Orient Longman Hyderabad), 341–89.

Mathur, N. (2012). 'On the Sabarmati Riverfront: Urban Planning as Totalitarian Governance in Ahmedabad', *Economic and Political Weekly*, 47:47–8, 64–75.

Melee at Ahmedabad (1932). 'Melee at Ahmedabad: Unlawful Meeting Sargeant Injured in Bombay Disturbance', *The Times of India* (13 January 1932), 7, ProQuest Historical Newspapers.

Patel, B. and Kansal, T. (2011). 'Bringing a City Back to Its River: Why the Sabarmati Riverfront Development Project Has Come Thus Far', Unpublished report, 1–28.

Patel, K. (2016). 'Encountering the State Through Legal Tenure Security: Perspectives from a Low Income Resettlement Scheme in Urban India', *Land Use Policy*, 58, 102–13. https://doi.org/10.1016/j.landusepol.2016.07.016

Patel, S., Sliuzas, R., and Mathur, N. (2015). 'The Risk of Impoverishment in Urban Development-induced Displacement and Resettlement in Ahmedabad', *Environment and Urbanization*, 27:1, 231–56. https://doi.org/10.1177/0956247815569128

Rajagopal, A. (2010). 'Special Political Zone: Urban Planning, Spatial Segregation and the Infrastructure of Violence in Ahmedabad', *South Asian History and Culture*, 1:4, 529–56. https://doi.org/10.1080/19472498.2010.507024

Ramakrishnan, K. (2014). 'Cosmopolitan Imaginaries on the Margins: Negotiating Difference and Belonging in a Delhi Resettlement Colony', *Contemporary South Asia*, 22:1, 67–81. https://doi.org/10.1080/09584935.2013.870976

Salmi, J. (2019). 'From Third-Class to World-Class Citizens: Claiming Belonging, Countering Betrayal in the Margins of Ahmedabad', *City & Society*, 31:3, 392–412. https://doi.org/10.1111/ciso.12238

Shani, G. (2021). 'Towards a Hindu Rashtra: Hindutva, Religion, and Nationalism in India', *Religion, State and Society*, 49:3, 264–80. https://doi.org/10.1080/09637494.2021.1947731

Shani, O. (2007). *Communalism, Caste, and Hindu Nationalism: The Violence in Gujarat* (Cambridge; New York: Cambridge University Press).

Spodek, H. (1983). 'Squatter Settlements in Urban India: Self-Help and Government Policies', *Economic and Political Weekly*, 18:36–37, 1575–86.

Spodek, H. (2010). 'From Gandhi to Modi: Ahmedabad, 1915–2017', in E. Simpson and A. Kapadia (eds), *Idea of Gujarat: History, Ethnography and Text* (New Delhi: Orient Blackswan), 136–52.

Spodek, H. (2011). *Ahmedabad: Shock City of Twentieth-Century India* (Bloomington, IN: Indiana University Press).

Stupendous Destruction of Houses (1927). 'Stupendous Destruction of Houses – Sabarmati River Rising', *The Times of India* (2 August 1927), 9–11, ProQuest Historical Newspapers.

Susewind, R. (2017). 'Muslims in Indian cities: Degrees of segregation and the elusive ghetto', *Environment and Planning: A*, 49:6, 1286–307. https://doi.org/10.1177/0308518X17696071

Von Schnitzler, A. (2016). *Democracy's Infrastructure: Techno-Politics and Protest After Apartheid* (Princeton: Princeton University Press).

Part II

Rhythms and spatiotemporal dynamics:

*Structuring effects on and of practices
of urban violence*

4

Temporalities of urban violence: A comparative perspective on El Salvador and Jamaica

Hannes Warnecke-Berger

Introduction

During a discussion with a community leader in a violence-ridden community in San Salvador, where I regularly spent time for interviews, participant
observation and focus group discussions, I asked about the local histories of
violence. In her response, Doña Martha, the community leader, used the bib-
lical metaphor of seven good and seven bad years. Martha was an impressive person. She had lost three of her sons during the civil war, and the other
three were shot in skirmishes between feuding street gangs after the war had
come to an end. She had fled from the mountains to escape the civil war
but always remained loosely connected to the Salvadoran left and worked
as a community organiser for the local branch of the *Frente Farabundo
Martí para la Liberación Nacional* (FMLN), the former guerrilla group that
became a political party. Despite having suffered so much pain and loss, she
continued to work in community affairs, particularly in persuading youth
gang members not to threaten their own families or people living on their
turf. During the time I was there, the community saw a wave of violence,
with several murders per week taking place in a small shanty-town neighbourhood. Local gangs, the so-called *maras*,[1] held the community hostage.
The police were simply not powerful enough to control this situation and
often resorted to violence themselves. In any case, the residents were suspi-
cious of the police and afraid of police raids at night. Yet they feared the
local *maras* even more. This situation was fuelled by fear and anxiety.

The *mara* in the community consisted of about 10 youths armed with
heavy guns and grenades. They controlled the turf and the local drug
market. This gang extorted money from street vendors – the occupation
of many of the inhabitants of the community within the urban informal
sector – but also schoolchildren and students who passed through the gang
turf on their way to school or college. It was only after a particular escalation
of the rivalry between the then two leading gangs, *MS-13* and *barrio 18* –
when some gang members were killed in street battles, others by the police

or by rival gangs, others imprisoned and a few even escaped the bloodshed and began living a 'civilian' life – that the local *mara* was finally defeated, and the community was able to enjoy seven good years until another local branch of the gangs re-emerged.

Violence not only changes over time, but it changes time. This is the starting point of this chapter. Following the idea of Lefebvre (1994 [1971]) and others that not only space but also time is socially constructed and produced dialectically both by materialised social relations and social practices, in this chapter I elaborate on the manipulation of time and space in urban violent encounters in the capital cities of El Salvador and Jamaica. In scrutinising the particular entanglements of space, time and different forms of violence in a comparative perspective throughout San Salvador and Kingston, I emphasise that mobilising and organising violence requires the manipulation of space and time. In this way, I contest the image of violence as an ontological monolith – in other words, the fact that descriptions and analyses of violence usually do not take into account its multiple expressions, particularly in violent interactions. Instead, this chapter elaborates on different forms of violence and their spatial and particularly temporal dynamics. In so doing, it adds a temporal dimension to an ongoing discussion on the spatial foundations of violence, shedding light on different forms of violence. This relates back to the notion of the ontological monolith. In order to understand the spatiotemporal condition of violence, different forms of violence need to be distinguished. I particularly focus on the structure of interactions that people maintain by exerting violence. Elaborating on this relational perspective, I scrutinise how forms of violence and their temporal dynamics can be explained by these interactions. Finally, the chapter states that every form of violence develops its own space-time, and violence then becomes a performative act. Spaces, times and rhythms of violence in urban areas form part of local experiences and everyday lives. Violence, then, is not only the product of space and time, but in turn, violent actors are able to manipulate time and space through violence.

The empirical background of this chapter is Central America and the Caribbean, particularly the urban agglomerations of San Salvador, El Salvador and Kingston, Jamaica.[2] Both societies and in particular their capital cities are regularly at the top of international statistics on crime and violence. Violence, particularly murder, has become an everyday phenomenon in both countries. Everyday life finds a mode of survival, and it is this mode of survival that is deeply entangled with space, time and violence, as the introductory narrative underlines.

However, these narratives frequently clash with the abstract statistics on homicide and murder that brand these societies as violent. Statistics foster the impression that violence takes place always and everywhere. The usual perception of violence is invariant to space and time. Obviously, however, this is not the case. Violence follows its own rhythm, and violence both is shaped by time and space and dialectically shapes space and time, as Lefebvre (2010) prominently accentuated in his *Rhythmanalysis*. Within theoretical discussions in violence research and empirical debates on Central America and the Caribbean, however, the spatiotemporal conditions of violence are rarely the object of more thorough analyses (exceptions include Rodgers, 2004; Gutiérrez Rivera, 2013). This is particularly interesting because the topic of urban violence has received a large audience in recent times (e.g. Pavoni and Tulumello, 2020; Moser and McIlwaine, 2014; Winton 2004).

While social science research discovered space as an object of study some time ago, and the spatial turn contributed to deconstructing different notions of space (see Warf and Arias, 2009, for an overview), time still remains understudied and only loosely connected to the research both on violence as well as on space. Against the empirical background of Central America and the Caribbean, this is somewhat surprising. In many interviews and focus group discussions during my extensive field research, people usually began talking about violence by stating that everything was better before. Events experienced in their 'here and now' seemed disconnected from history. In turn, much of the history of violence is covered by memories and oral histories that displace, exclude and even ignore threatening, disrupting and violent events (Warnecke-Berger and Huhn, 2017). Violence is never constantly present. It occurs in waves in a peculiar rhythm.

The chapter is organised in six sections. The first section gives an overview of the theoretical entanglements of space, time and violence. In the next section, I elaborate on the concept of violence and then continue to concretise the terms and concepts in the third section, primarily to introduce my understanding of forms of violence. The fourth section is the empirical analysis of violence in San Salvador and Kingston. The fifth section relates the two cases to each other in a comparative perspective and interprets the underlying spatial and temporal dynamics in the formation of violence. The chapter ends with a short conclusion.

Space, time and violence

Violence is a peculiar thing. Seemingly, violence is underrepresented in traditional social science research; from its theoretical concepts as well as its methodological approaches. Empirically, it is challenging to document violence, as it is almost impossible to observe violence directly. Social science researchers cannot 'look at' violence like they would look at other research objects. Violence is a slippery and blurry phenomenon, and it is situated between the traditional social science concepts (Stewart and Strathern, 2002). Violence destroys language and discourse, yet at the same time it produces rumours and gossip, thus again producing discourse (Scarry, 1987). Violence is embedded in culture, and at the same time, it transgresses culture. Violence is part of the body, inscribed in somatic experiences and able to produce subjectivities (Das et al., 2000), yet, at the same time, it harms, humiliates, mutilates, is directed against, and even destroys the body. Social theory has mostly ignored violence as a phenomenon in itself and as a particular explanandum (Joas and Knöbl, 2013), and perhaps more importantly, it still fails to distinguish between different forms of violence or to open the discussion on variations of violence, as the recent critique of the term urban violence forcefully shows (Pavoni and Tulumello, 2020). As a consequence, research on the topic still tends to analyse violence as an ontological monolith (for a similar critique from a geographical perspective, see e.g. Tyner and Inwood, 2014).

These fundamental ambivalences include the relation of violence to space and/or time. Since Lefebvre (1991 [1974]) began deconstructing the notion of space as a Newtonian container (see Löw, 2016, for an overview), the study of space has become enormously attractive. Likewise, research on violence has recently explored social spaces in which violence occurs (for an overview, see Koloma Beck, 2016). However, the research on violence remains conceptually vague (Knöbl, 2017) and it still lacks a detailed understanding of how space and violence are intertwined (Springer and Le Billon, 2016). This also applies to the multiple relations between violence and time. Although social theory has rediscovered time in the light of time-space compressions (Harvey, 1989), social acceleration (Rosa, 2013) and spatiotemporal fixes (Jessop, 2006), still, sociological and historical research usually focuses on a chronological understanding of time in which different violent events occur as sequences or as an effect of different historical prerequisites (e.g. Hoebel 2014). In the metaphor of space-time compression, Harvey (1989) indicates that due to innovations in transportation technology, the world is becoming increasingly densely connected and people need less time for their activities. However, the underlying understanding of time remains linear and accordingly a unit of measurement. The anthropological discussion, in contrast, focuses on the experience of time as the violent rupture in the period before and the period after a violent incident (e.g. Sofsky, 1997; Abbink, 2000). Discussing both concepts, the philosophy of time distinguishes two different notions of time: time can be conceptualised as an A-series, hence as different events in chronological order or sequence, or as a B-series, as the experience of before and after (for this distinction, which seems to be commonplace in the philosophy of time, see McTaggart, 1908). However, these rather general approaches have thus far ignored the concept of violence. In short, research on violence ignores time, and research on (space)time has not yet looked at violence. Furthermore, both bodies of literature fail to differentiate different forms of violence and the different socio-spatial and temporal contexts in which varying forms of violence evolve (Warnecke-Berger, 2018b). Research on space and particularly on time, in turn, neglects violence as a phenomenon to be studied.

Structures and processes of violence

The work of Norbert Elias provides a solution. Elias (1992) not only studies violence in detail but has also developed a relational concept of time in his sociology of knowledge. His relational sociology adds to the ongoing debate on (urban) violence in the sense that he offers an inspiring step to a more nuanced conceptualisation of the spatiotemporal dynamics of violence. Elias (1992: XVII) argues that people constitute time through 'putting-into-relation' different events, subjects and objects. Hence, time (as well as violence) is embedded in human interactions and interdependencies. With regard to violence, moreover, his sociology can be read as a plea for a relational understanding of violence that does not *a priori* focus on motivations and hence on the psychological structure of perpetrators of violence, but on the interdependencies and relations in which violent actors, victims and witnesses are caught (see also Riches, 1986). This is also compatible with an analysis of violence that is sensitive to the different forms that violence takes. This perspective examines the structure as well as the dynamics of the social interactions in which the different violent actors engage through their violence.

Concerning the structure of violent interactions, research on violence usually links violence theoretically to domination and authority. Violence then is a vertical relation between 'those above' and 'those below', between elites and the subaltern (see, for instance, the classic approach of Dahrendorf, 1958). Violence in this perspective takes the form of rebellion/revolution or repression. This 'vertical violence' has been among the main interests of violence research from its very beginnings, mainly because violence then links to issues of power and politics.

However, current violence in Central America and the Caribbean, and not only there, seems no longer and not as exclusively to fit into this vertical setting. Some prominent examples are youth gangs, warlords or individual murders. It is no longer the objective to organise masses of people or to mobilise an entire social class. Quite the contrary, violence in these regions, particularly in urban settings, appears to be anomic and diffuse – not located in particular places, not directed against clear enemies, and not politically motivated (Warnecke-Berger, 2020a). This violence is not directed against the state or intended to challenge the social fabric. In short, it is 'horizontal violence' (for this concept, see Warnecke-Berger, 2018b). The sociology of Norbert Elias (1992) serves to grasp this horizontal violence as it places the emphasis on the interdependencies of humans rather than on the motivational structure of either elites or subalterns.

Theoretically, horizontal violence typically involves equally powerful rivals. None of these rivals is able to overpower the other to establish domination. Violence then is inscribed in a social relation between more or less equally powerful actors. Without external inference, horizontal violence leads to a violent equilibrium, and this equilibrium is reinforced because violent actors perceive peaceful strategies as too risky (Helbling, 2006). Since superior authorities, such as a state, remain unable or unwilling to control this type of violence, rituals are highly important in managing escalations. Furthermore, emotions, such as fear, rage and feelings of honour, are crucial within this horizontal setting in both mobilising and controlling violence.

Distinguishing between vertical and horizontal violence has further consequences for the analysis of the spatiotemporal dynamics of violence (Warnecke-Berger, 2018a). While vertical violence is about the unilateral defeat of the opponent, horizontal violence is about a violent equilibrium in which a violent act triggers other violent acts. While rhythms of violence in the first case are rooted in the superiority of a single violent actor, in the second case, rhythms of violence are linked to the relative weakness of every violent actor. In this second case, violence needs to be understood as a reciprocal and sequential relation.

Forms of violence as figurational relations

In order to analyse variations of violence, however, some conceptual work is needed, and therefore I add several definitions. I distinguish violent actors, practices of violence and forms of violence. Violent actors individually or collectively exert violence. Violent actors cannot be reduced to violence itself, since additional features, such as membership, hierarchy or legitimacy, need to be considered for their classification (Schlichte, 2009). Practices of violence, in contrast, are singular events, acts or movements of the body in the course of a larger history. In accordance with recent developments in practice theory and praxeology (e.g. Reckwitz, 2002), they can be defined as activities that make practical use of knowledge to ultimately inflict physical harm on other people.

The notion of form, in contrast to actor and practice, refers to something more durable than the single event (Feldman, 2008). Violent actors might use several forms of violence. It is also possible that these actors specialise in a single form of violence (Tilly, 2003: 35–6). Consequently, I use the definition of form of violence as a 'specific set of violent practices that a social actor routinely uses to make claims on other social actors' (Warnecke-Berger, 2018b: 27). This understanding of forms of violence merges an ideational as well as a material component. Forms are material in the sense that they exist due to acts of violence that actually occur. Forms are at the same time ideational in the sense of signifying systems, repertoires and cultural scripts that link implicit knowledge on practices of violence.

In this regard, forms of violence comprise acts or practices of violence. They link both different and similar acts of violence with each other through rules that govern the exertion of violence. Violent actors employ forms of violence by exerting sets of violent practices. Moreover, violent actors are able to employ different forms of violence. Therefore, forms of violence are not directly related to specific violent actors. While some violent actors may specialise in one well-defined form of violence, others might apply several forms of violence. Finally, a particular form of violence is not the essence of a specific violent actor. Thus, forms of violence are not fixed. They change over time. These forms cannot be described as ideal-types. Instead, they need to be analysed in their 'family resemblance', as Ludwig Wittgenstein (2003: §67) dubbed it.[3]

This perspective on forms of violence focuses on the social relationships that violent actors establish with other social actors by waging violence. It focuses on figurations. Within these figurations (collective) practices of violence need to be mobilised and socially organised in order to take a coherent form. Mobilisation of violence depends on strategic action and power, and it involves manipulating, bargaining, convincing other actors and sometimes even force. Those who are able to give meaning to violent acts then become particularly powerful. This perspective is sensitive to both the magnitude and intensity of violence (scale of social organisation) as well as to the structure of social interaction (vertical/horizontal).

Time deeply shapes the processes through which forms of violence emerge. More than this, time is crucial for understanding how violence is shaped. By mobilising violence, violent actors are able to situate acts of violence in space and time and to create ideational sequences of violence. Within these sequences, different acts of violence that happened at different places and at different times become related to each other. I call this process synchronisation. In the process of mobilising, organising and forming violence, violent actors synchronise violent acts.

Micro-dynamics of violence in El Salvador and Jamaica

Both El Salvador and Jamaica, and especially their capital cities San Salvador and Kingston, are intensively shaped by neoliberal globalisation and structural adjustment policies. However, these global processes have imposed their influence in distinct ways, and these processes ultimately materialise in different social relations and situations (Warnecke-Berger, 2018b). Apart from all historical, cultural, social, political and economic differences, however, the two cases share an exorbitantly high level of violence measured in homicides per 100,000 inhabitants, and both societies are characterised by the presence of similar violent actors and forms of violence. Hence, the comparative perspective on the two cases is instructive, because the cases are so different from each other and contradict the usual explanations for violence.

Jamaica integrated into the capitalist world system as a plantation economy in which sugar was produced by slaves (Bulmer-Thomas, 2012). It soon advanced to become Britain's economic and political powerhouse in the Atlantic. After the Great Depression of the 1930s, constitutional decolonisation led to the emergence of a Westminster-style political system in which the leading political parties competed for power and secured popular support through clientelism, vote buying and electoral fraud (Munroe, 1972). Lower-class sectors in turn received preferential access to housing and employment. This is one reason why by the 1970s, when the ideological cleavages between the two leading parties had deepened, garrison communities developed, in which urban communities in Kingston collectively supported either one or the other party (Stone, 1980; Sives, 2010). Within this setting, community gangs secured social and political cohesion and vertically linked the community to national politicians, political parties and the state. When Jamaica advanced to a global hub in the drug trade between South American cocaine producers and the United States and Europe, these community gangs discovered the comparative advantage of the independent income provided by drug trafficking rather than relying on politicians for support (Harriott, 2008; Gray, 2004). The motivation for violence shifted from the political to the economic, and Jamaica even exported this gang culture to the US, where Jamaican *posses* played a significant role in organising the local drug trade (Headley, 1996; Hazlehurst and Hazlehurst, 1998). At the same time, community identities in Kingston, forged in the experience and suffering of everyday violence, endured (Charles, 2004; Jaffe, 2012).

Quite in contrast to Jamaica, El Salvador was of peripheral importance during the colonial era. The tiny country in the Central American isthmus eventually became an important coffee exporter by the last quarter of the nineteenth century (Lindo-Fuentes, 2002; Lauria-Santiago, 1999). As opposed to Jamaica, where the subaltern integrated into politics through clientelism, the oligarchic nature of politics in El Salvador secured the harsh exclusion of the subaltern. Marginalisation and expulsion from the land was and still is a common theme (Segovia, 2002). The political system therefore proved unable to ameliorate social and political conflicts. By the late 1970s, a bloody civil war had erupted, in which left-wing revolutionary organisations challenged the dominant role of the traditional landholding class. After 12 years of civil war that claimed more than 75,000 lives, the conflict came to an end, and peace accords were signed. This peace was fragile, however, and violence endured. Peace negotiations excluded economic issues, and therefore provided only a political peace, owing to the stalemate between the left and the right (Cardenal and González, 2007). Social cleavages as well as the precarity and impoverishment of a large mass of the population still characterise today's social reality in El Salvador. It was against the background of the injustices and inequalities exacerbated by years of conflict that urban gangs, the so-called *maras*, emerged (Savenije, 2009; Cruz and Portillo, 1998). These gangs have become strong actors controlling local turfs and communities, particularly in San Salvador. However, the discussion on gangs and *maras* still obscures the deeper structure of horizontal violence of everyday violent interactions in the country.

The following three subsections present narratives about particular incidences of violence in both societies. After presenting these events, the comparison will focus on the spatiotemporal dimensions.

Everyday urban cruelties in El Salvador (Case 1)

El Salvador is at the top of the list of the most violent countries in the world. Even after more than a decade of civil war, which ended in 1992 with the signing of peace accords, the level of violence in terms of homicides has remained high. In recent times, it has even increased. Fear of violence is omnipresent. However, violence in general, and particularly horizontal violence, follows a specific logic in El Salvador (Warnecke-Berger, 2017). Historically, honour and revenge have both provoked violence and restrained the escalation of violence. Even though the level of violence has historically remained high, predominant actors and forms of violence have changed over time. The most persistent feature of this violence is that it is ordinary and horizontal.

The following event highlights a typical violent interaction of the sort that all too often results in fatalities. This event, which occurred on an October morning in 2009, was covered for several weeks in Salvadoran national newspapers. It took place in a microbus along route no. 3, which runs from Soyapango, one of San Salvador's 14 *municipios*, to the centre of San Salvador. In the area where Boulevard del Ejército crosses Boulevard

Venezuela, two men and a young woman joined the 20 passengers on their daily commute to work, then forced the driver at knife-point to close the doors and drive on. They demanded that all the passengers place their valuables, mobile phones and wallets into a plastic bag, threatening them with knives. A 32-year-old *vigilante*, a private security guard who worked for one of the countless security companies that 'secure' residential areas, shops, gas stations and commercial malls, was among the passengers. Initially, he followed the order to surrender his mobile phone. When the thieves decided that their plastic bag was still not full enough, they started a second round of extortion, renewing their threats and demanding more loot. The thieves also accosted a 19-year-old girl who was heavily pregnant, and who unwisely attempted to resist, provoking a dispute. One of the thieves shouted at her, slapped and punched her and finally stabbed her in her pregnant belly. Panic erupted, and the thieves immediately attempted to flee the minibus with their stolen goods. The vigilante drew his pistol, which he had managed to conceal during the assault, and fired. The bullets hit two of the thieves, one of them five times, as well as an uninvolved passenger. In an interview after the event, the vigilante stated: 'I was outraged, that's why I got up and shot them' (*La Prensa Gráfica*, 2009). The outrage, disgust and blind rage at the assault led him to shoot, he told the journalists. The two wounded thieves died shortly afterwards in the hospital, and the pregnant girl, severely injured, eventually recovered. The vigilante was ultimately cleared of all charges when it was decided that he had acted in legitimate self-defence.

This particular violent event underlines the characteristics of horizontal violence. The economic objective of the assault and its underlying emotional basis, envy, seem obvious. However, a purely economic explanation falls short: Why should the offender escalate the violence just because of the refusal of several passengers to hand over their valuables? The assailants had initially entered the bus to steal and not to kill. It is possible that the thieves' initial threats were not convincing enough and that is why they felt the need to escalate the violence. In effect, however, the offenders did not have the power to enforce their will. I would argue that this powerlessness needs to be considered as a root cause of violence, instead of power and domination. This is a clear expression of horizontal violence. Violence, in these circumstances, is not nested in a vertical relationship, clear-cut hierarchies, or even authority, but develops within a social relationship that is much more characterised by equality between violent opponents.

Restoring and maintaining this horizontality and the equality between opponents in social interactions is a struggle for social recognition. In these settings, violence is often related to honour, as the historiography has pointed out in detail (e.g. Piccato, 2001). Even ordinary conflicts without any discernible cause, such as disputes among drunkards, easily transform into personal insults and quickly escalate into extremes to 'resolve' these differences (Bejar, 1998). Honour and revenge frequently cause ordinary conflicts between normal citizens to erupt into violence. This can take the shape of family vendettas, wedding parties that turn into stabbings or even shootouts, bloody dramas of jealousy and everyday frustrations that quickly lead to bloodshed (Savenije and Andrade-Eekhoff, 2003: 87).

Horizontal violence is not restricted to honour violence and revenge, however. The reaction of the vigilante illustrates a further issue. Shaken by the offender's attack of the pregnant girl and frustrated because of the thieves' brazenness in harassing the passengers a second time, the vigilante was overcome by rage, which quickly escalated into blind hatred. These emotionally inspired practices of violence are different from violence that follows sober economic calculations. Violence induced by rage usually lacks individual motivation. Rage therefore leads to arbitrary practices of violence and the offender even accepts the risk of being injured (Neckel, 1999: 162).

Revenge and warfare in Jamaica (Case 2)

In Jamaica, in contrast, horizontal violence has historically been fuelled by party identities instead of individual feelings of honour. After the 1930s, horizontal violence was mainly linked to the political arena, namely the conflict between the People's National Party (PNP) and the Jamaica Labour Party (JLP). Unlike in El Salvador, where the need to (re)gain social recognition through the exertion of violence historically remained at the individual level, horizontal violence in Jamaica was densely interwoven with party identities and therefore easily transcended the individual level to the collective defence of honour and respect along party lines. These cleavages fragmented over time, but in essence prevail until today and still influence conflicts between warring communities (Sives, 2012).

An example of these communal conflicts is a particular instance back in the late 1990s in Kingston when a conflict between an area in August Town known as Jungle 12 and its neighbouring community Hermitage turned into a community war leading to several homicides (The Jamaica Gleaner, 2011; Jamaica Observer, 2002). The two warring communities still have opposite political affiliations; Jungle 12 is a PNP community, and Hermitage is JLP affiliated. At one point, Jungle 12 seemed to be winning the war, and so Hermitage sent for help from Tivoli Gardens, another well-known neighbourhood in Kingston. Some Tivoli gunmen, well-trained shooters, came to support their affiliates. One day, there was a particularly violent shootout. Usually, shootouts between corner crews or local street gangs happen at a distance, or as a drive-by shooting if street gang members can afford a car. Moreover, corner crews do have guns, but they are not trained in shooting.

Guns are more about the prestige and power delivered by the image of the gun than the practice of using it. This time, however, after the leader of the Jungle 12 corner crew was shot, a Hermitage-affiliated gunman from Tivoli Gardens walked up to him and pumped bullets into his body.

This incident points to the continued existence of political relations between different neighbourhoods as a trigger for violence. Even though partisan identity had diminished, party identity was still an underlying theme that could prompt communities to engage in violence. Longstanding political conflicts and newly arising ones thus become difficult to distinguish, since they lead to cycles of revenge of which the root cause is often unclear. Secondly, the brutal and expressive killing of the Jungle 12 leader was a criminal act in the perception of the community; an act that did not follow the usual rules. The particular practices of violence exerted in this shootout gave an external meaning to this community conflict, namely the intended annihilation of the enemy. People were not concerned with the fact that the leader was killed, but with the modus operandi of his killing, through which the logic of community conflict somehow became distorted.

Local defence crew violence is based on a clear reciprocal relationship inherent to cycles of revenge (Charles, 2004: 41). Given the historically grown and sometimes forced homogeneity of garrison communities, often based on kinship, street gang violence resembles violence among communities, and street gang members are like a militant defence wing of the community.

Within this context, urban communities tend to interpret single acts of violence in the framework of community cleavages and longstanding political divisions between political parties. Practices of violence thus bear 'notions of collective responsibility and punishment for display of solidarity [...] that [are] linked to the salience of primacy or group identity' (Harriott, 2003: 96). This is why single acts of violence potentially escalate into even larger cycles of revenge and the indiscriminate victimisation of rivals.

The political response to everyday violence: Grassroots vigilantism in El Salvador (Case 3)

A final case leaves the logics of horizontal violence and focuses instead on vertical violence to exemplify the differences between the two. Vertical violence links to a vertical relation that is entangled with domination and more structural forms of power. Violence, in this case, is often used as a tool to repress the population. Given the long history of state-led repression in El Salvador, it is not surprising that death squad violence as well as vigilantism persist (see Warnecke-Berger, 2020c, for a detailed discussion on vertical violence). The two forms of violence share an apparent similarity: victims are killed selectively. For analytical purposes, however, vigilantism can be distinguished from death squad violence. There is a spectrum of vigilante violence that ranges from very fluid, informal and diffuse to highly formal, organised and even institutionalised (Huggins, 1991). Hence, it is possible to distinguish spontaneous forms of vigilante violence from more organised forms. This continuum can be translated into the concept of vertical violence. Vigilantism arises either from within civil society to compensate for a lack of public social control and to locally execute sanctions in order to defend social order, or it arises as an extended arm of the state to control civil society in order to defend a certain image of society. The former refers to grassroots vigilantism and social cleansings and the latter case to death squads.

A well-documented case of social cleansing took place on 1 February 2010 in Suchitoto, El Salvador, where eight adolescents were killed (ContraPunto, 2010; El Diario de Hoy, 2010; La Prensa Gráfica, 2010). To date, Suchitoto is one of the main tourist sites in El Salvador. The small city never experienced high levels of violence and the presence of *maras* was almost unknown to inhabitants. Compared to the densely populated urban communities of San Salvador, Suchitoto is characterised by its calm atmosphere and its community spirit based on the memory of civil war violence, which was particularly severe since Suchitoto was considered a left-wing city. Widespread fear of *mareros* who allegedly wanted to establish a *clika* in the region of Suchitoto preceded the event in February 2010. People were afraid that several *mareros* wanted to recruit youngsters in the area. This alerted the community. The *junta directiva* (local leadership) organised a meeting to discuss how to react to the perceived threat imposed by the potential presence of *maras*. The then director of the PNC stated in an interview that 'several adults warned [the local youth] not to be fooled by gang members'. In the afternoon of the following day, a group of three people from the community, dressed in black, searched for some of the teenagers who they suspected of cooperating with the *mara* and opened fire with semi-automatic weapons including M-16 assault rifles and 9 mm pistols. Eight teenagers were killed. The victims were literally sprayed with bullets. The next day, the bodies of the teenagers were found in a small river near the community. The identification of the victims was complicated by the brutal wounds. In some cases, even the heads were missing. In the newspaper coverage soon after the event, the families and relatives of these teenagers claimed that their children had never been connected to *maras*. Finally, the mayor of Suchitoto offered financial support for the funerals of some of the teenagers killed in the occurrence. Events like this are commonplace in El Salvador even today.

The modus operandi suggests that such spontaneous violence emerges to compensate for instability and in response to widespread fears. Firstly, practices of violence related to social cleansings are often expressive (Kowalewski, 2003). As the example of Suchitoto exemplifies, it is not simply about killing a suspected criminal, but about transmitting a message through violence. These practices of violence aim at cleansing one's own community and threatening and warning future intruders. Social cleansings, as a subtype of vertical violence, follow processes of social closure at a local level (on the role of social closure in violent processes, see e.g. Warnecke-Berger, 2018b). Secondly, perceptions of insecurity and the lack of legal resources enable practices of violence. Thirdly, the community collectively defends itself against threats. Often, these threats rely on perceptions rather than on hard facts, since a large number of victims of social cleansings belong to 'excluded social sectors or are seen as "dangerous" or "undesirable"' (Tutela Legal del Arzobispado de San Salvador, 2008: 40), such as criminalised youths, homosexuals or sex-workers. Social cleansings draw on an established community spirit that can quickly be mobilised in times of increasing fear. As the case of Suchitoto demonstrates, an abrupt intensification in the perception of insecurity is a necessary precondition. Finally, social cleansings are frequently enacted by community leaders and by groups of private interests (Campbell, 2002: 2).

With increasing levels of violence and the state's inability to control violence and crime effectively, state-sponsored death squads have reappeared in El Salvador. As in the case of social cleansings, the main victims are street children and youths who allegedly support or are members of *maras*, as well as sex-workers and homosexuals. The modus operandi of death squads (*grupos de exterminio*) often resembles those practices applied by death squads during the civil war. Many of the victims today are found in plastic bags near the larger highways or in refuse dumps with bound hands and clear signs of torture, killed by multiple shots to the head. Frequently, death squads report about their activities. In a communiqué handed to me in the street during field research, a death squad advised that all *mareros* and common criminals should be prepared (for details, see Warnecke-Berger, 2020c). This group, which referred to itself as 'Brigada General Maximiliano Hernández Martínez', a well-known death squad during the civil war, claimed to be giving criminals the 'medicine that they deserve' and to be forced into action because of the ineffectiveness of the country's security institutions.

Temporalities and forms of violence in comparative perspectives

At first glance, these three case studies in San Salvador and Kingston have little in common. In looking at the scale of the social organisation of violence as well as the structure of social interaction in which the violence is embedded, however, I use the three cases to elucidate the detailed mechanisms through which violence and space-time interact in the formation of violence.

Scale of the social organisation of violence

First, the cases differ in the scale of the social organisation of violence. While in San Salvador (Case 1), violence is exerted individually, in Kingston (Case 2) and San Salvador (Case 3), violence is directed by and against groups. This becomes particularly clear with regard to revenge. In San Salvador, honour and revenge usually remain individual matters, sometimes concerning feuding families, but rarely entire communities. In Jamaica, in contrast, cycles of revenge between communities, historically fuelled by party identities and only recently disconnected from political parties, can last over decades. While in El Salvador single violent offences are most likely to be followed by similar individual acts of retaliation, violent situations in Jamaica are detached from each other. In the latter case, a single act of violence is usually embedded in a series of violent practices, which are ideationally related but situationally and temporally disconnected. They may happen at different times and different places. While in El Salvador, honour as a regulating force within conflicts distant from state authority is individually cultivated and thus leads to individual expressions of horizontal violence, violence in Jamaica follows a group logic. Although in both cases horizontal violence is present, horizontal violence is socially organised on different scales.

Structure of violent interactions

The variances of horizontal violence are furthermore based on varying degrees of reciprocity, as will be shown in the following. First, ordinary horizontal violence, which takes place predominantly on a relatively low scale of social organisation, is the most dominant form of violence in San Salvador. Ordinary horizontal violence occurs between individuals. In Kingston, horizontal violence happens on a higher scale of social organisation, as entire communities are in conflict with each other. Such violence often involves defence crews/street gangs. In San Salvador, the complexity lies in the diffuse appearance of horizontal violence; the complexity of the Jamaican case in Kingston consists in the relevance of horizontal violence within inter-group dynamics. In Kingston, revenge is an essential driver for groups dynamics; cycles of revenge endure for years, and victims seek revenge for offences suffered long ago. Revenge between different conflicting communities maintains and reinforces equality among groups.

Reciprocity evolves out of and requires the equality of actors involved in a violent relationship. This equality can be a subjective perception or it can exist factually. In the case of horizontal violence, perpetrators resort to violence either to claim equality between rivals or to regain equality. The claim in itself, even though it might never lead to the successful (re)establishment of equality, illustrates the deep roots of horizontal violence: actors feel and expect equality among themselves and their rivals. These partly objective and partly subjective dimensions of horizontal violence become particularly evident in sequences of retaliation and revenge. Revenge is only opportune between equals (Boehm, 1984). Revenge does not intend to annihilate the rival, but to re-establish a certain kind of balance and equality among individuals and groups (Paul, 2005: 247). It only emerges if already established rights and obligations have been violated. Violence is consequently used to regain equality (Elwert, 1991: 169). Sequences of violent practices in cycles of revenge often follow rigid and ritualised logics to maintain equality (Schlee and Turner, 2008). As violence is exerted to reproduce equality in this relationship, revenge is the purest form of reciprocity. The importance of revenge in inter-community conflicts indicates the reciprocal nature of violent relationships in Kingston. In San Salvador, the reciprocity of horizontal violence seems to be incomplete, and violent actors are unable to establish reciprocal interactions 'through' their violence. This usually leads to diffuse violence.

Time and mechanisms

In the case of revenge, different violent events that happened in the past are synchronised in order to provoke a response through violence. Case 2 exemplifies this issue. In Kingston, a community reacts to a particular event by waging war against another community. The single event needs to be contextualised in a larger history of atrocities. The link between past events and the present, however, is neither natural nor automatic, but needs to be built or even fabricated. Here strategic action comes in, as it builds these links, and time is manipulated. In this regard, these cycles of revenge are about the *extension of time into the past*. Revenge enlarges the scope of time into the past. Today's violence is a reaction to violent acts that occurred in the past, and the very mobilisers of violence, often the community leaders in the case of Jamaica, produce rhythms of violence. These leaders manipulate time. They synchronise dispersed events in space and time by waging war and violence.

This is quite in contrast to Case 1, where envy violence initially predominates. In the case of envy, synchronisation additionally affects the future since it is supposed to prevent the rival from 'escaping' from equality. Thus, even though envy requires the desire for a state of equality, reciprocity in the face of relative deprivation is incomplete. The situation in San Salvador became violent and rage turned into destructive violence. In this case, the formation of sequences of singular acts is undermined. Violence is a situational outcome and only follows these (random and accidental) circumstances. Time in these situations is extremely constricted and the single violent actor is exclusively tied to the very moment and to the very event. Due to this *constriction of time*, it is more like a situational panic reaction, one that even dissolves (Riekenberg, 2002).

In the Jamaican case, individual incidents are linked to longstanding antagonisms between communities in the perception of group members. A single violent event, thus, is interpreted as part of a larger history of animosities. While in the Salvadoran case, the immediate situational context leads to violence, and time is constricted to the very moment, in Jamaica, strategic action detaches violent events from their particular context and integrates them into an existing antagonism. In the case that took place in Kingston, strategic action is less emotionally driven but builds on the extension of time, since different violent practices occurring at different points of time and possibly in different spaces are brought into a logical sequence of revenge. The mechanism for horizontal violence in Jamaica, thus, is backward synchronisation since different practices of violence are linked retrospectively in order to restore equality.

Finally, Case 2 and Case 3 show further similarities, even though the structure of violence is different. In Case 2 (Jamaica) it is about horizontal violence; in Case 3 (El Salvador) it is about vertical violence. However, in Case 3, the very practices of violence likewise are linked to other acts of violence. Here, it is more about the fear of future retaliation. Violence is exerted to prevent a particular future and the perceived demise of social order. In this regard, time is similarly extended, and events are synchronised. However, this synchronisation is not related to the past but to a possible and imagined future. The *extension of time into the future*, hence, forward synchronisation of violent events, justifies violence by projecting the exertion of violence onto an imaginary future disruptive act. Both mechanisms – the extension of time into the future and the extension of time into the past – produce imagined sequences of violent practices by synchronising meanings, and both fulfil the purpose of maintaining and/or (re)establishing a certain (yet existent) social order. Both mechanisms are based on the extension of time in order to synchronise sequences of violence. Finally, forward panic triggers violence through emotions and stress. Forward panic is based on the constriction of time and demands immediate reactions.

Each of these cases therefore demonstrates that by forming violence, violent actors, or those actors who are able to evoke violence, manipulate time.

Furthermore, in the organisation of violence and the creation of rhythms of violent interactions, time is rebuilt and reordered. Time and violence are then dialectically written into everyday lives and by creating social meaning, violence can be experienced, suffered and resisted.

Conclusion

The concept of violence as an ontological monolith needs to be scrutinised and opened up for detailed analysis. In order to accentuate the micro-dynamics of urban violence and to advance typological and theoretical work, forms of violence need to be examined more closely. In focusing on forms of violence as a specific set of violent practices that a social actor routinely uses to make claims on other social actors, I have developed a relational understanding of violence. Through this relational understanding, the approach is able to grasp details of escalations and de-escalations of violence as well as the (re)production of different forms of violence within these violent confrontations. Time, then, is a key resource for violent actors in structuring the present. Each form of violence, as I demonstrated in the chapter, has its own spatial and temporal logic and follows particular mechanisms. I therefore call for re-shifting the focus in research on violence to sequences and for including the analysis of spatiotemporal mechanisms of violence.

Within this relational approach to forms of violence, space and time are essential both as concepts for analysing the dynamics and rhythms of violence and as strategic resources for violent actors in organising violence. However, some doubts about the excessive use of space and time have accompanied my work in this chapter: The recent debate on space, time and spatiotemporality has the potential tendency to de-materialise space and time: these discussions are either about the disappearance of space or about the multiplication of space (see e.g. Schroer, 2013). In either of these cases, space and time are situated within the cognitive sphere of human experience. However, in the case of violence, these perspectives collide with the pure materiality of killing. If people are killed, they are dead, and the times of suffering violence often withdraw from language. Pain and experiences of violence are difficult to express in language (Scarry, 1987).

The processes of social construction of spaces of violence thus mostly refer to post-violence experiences, in which the actual violence itself, however, no longer seems to play a role as Helmuth Plessner (1982) once argued in his philosophical anthropology. What remains is the construction by others, by witnesses and bystanders, but the very act of violence and its cause are then partially displaced and banished from the analysis.

There is, however, another, and perhaps a more radical approach to the study of violence. This approach goes back to Norbert Elias and his idea of researching violence, time and space. This approach focuses on the interrelations and interdependencies that people maintain, produce and reproduce through their social practices. Through these practices, social figurations are created, produced and reproduced (see Warnecke-Berger, 2020b, for a detailed discussion of Central American violence from the perspective of Elias). These conceptualisations can help research on violence to refine its theoretical as well as methodological strength.

Notes

1 Mareros are members of *maras*. These are Central American (youth) gangs that are long-lived, militant and often hierarchically organised. Locally, *maras* are organised in *clikas*. *Maras* transnationally entangle Central America, the United States and today even South America and Europe. They are usually held responsible for the vast majority of homicides in the region, while their actual contribution to the overall level of violence is widely debated and indeed is a matter for speculation due to the severe lack of sources. For an overview of the topic, see e.g. Wolf (2017) and Zinecker (2014).

2 This chapter is the result of a historical comparative study on forms of violence in Central America and the Caribbean, namely El Salvador, Belize and Jamaica. Empirical data are based on archival records, newspaper analysis, several hundred qualitative interviews with perpetrators and victims of violence, police officers, judges, politicians, members of civil society and academics. Focus group discussions as well as several months of participatory observation have been conducted in particularly violence-ridden marginalised communities in each of the three societies.

3 The analogy to chess illustrates these concepts: violent actors are like chess players. They exert different or similar practices of violence, like the chess player moves the pieces. The concept of violence in general thus encompasses the sum of all possible moves of pieces within all possible chess games. Forms of violence are typical bundles and relations of different moves. In chess language, these forms are chess openings, creative combinations, as well as checkmates.

Bibliography

Abbink, J. (2000). 'Preface: Violation and Violence as Cultural Phenomena', in Aijmer, G. and Abbink, J. (eds), *Meanings of Violence: A Cross Cultural Perspective* (Oxford: Berg), xi–xvii.

Bejar, R. G. (1998). 'El Salvador de posguerra: formas de violencia en la transición', in Programa de las Naciones Unidas para el Desarrollo (ed.), *Violencia en una sociedad en transición* (San Salvador: PNUD), 96–105.

Boehm, C. (1984). *Blood Revenge: The Anthropology of Feuding in Montenegro and Other Tribal Societies* (Philadelphia: University of Pennsylvania Press).

Bulmer-Thomas, V. (2012). *The Economic History of the Caribbean since the Napoleonic Wars* (Cambridge: Cambridge University Press).

Campbell, B. B. (2002). 'Death Squads: Definition, Problems, and Historical Context', in Campbell, B. B. and Brenner, A. D. (eds) *Death Squads in Global Perspective: Murder with Deniability* (New York: Palgrave Macmillan), 1–26.

Cardenal, R., and González, L. A. (eds) (2007). *El Salvador: la transición y sus problemas* (San Salvador: UCA Editores).

Charles, C. A. D. (2004). 'Political Identity and Criminal Violence in Jamaica: The Garrison Community of August Town and the 2002 Election', *Social and Economic Studies*, 53:2, 31–73.

Collins, R. (1990). 'Violent Conflict and Social Organization: Some Theoretical Implications of the Sociology of War', *Amsterdams Sociologisch Tijdschrift*, 16:4, 63–87.

Collins, R. (2008). *Violence: A Micro-Sociological Theory* (Princeton: Princeton University Press).

ContraPunto. (2010). 'A Suchitoto lo sacudió la muerte', *ContraPunto* (3 February 2010), www.archivocp.contrapunto.com.sv/violencia (accessed 25 November 2015).

Cruz, J. M., and Portillo Peña, N. (1998). *Solidaridad y violencia en las pandillas del gran San Salvador. Más allá de la vida loca.* (San Salvador: UCA Editores).

Dahrendorf, R. (1958). 'Toward a Theory of Social Conflict', *Journal of Conflict Resolution*, 2:2, 170–83. https://doi.org/10.1177/002200275800200204

Das, V., Kleinman, A., Ramphele, M., and Reynolds, P. (eds) (2000). *Violence and Subjectivity*. Berkeley (Los Angeles: University of California Press).

El Diario de Hoy. (2010). 'Ultiman a Ocho Pandilleros', *El Diario de Hoy* (2 February 2010), www.elsalvador.com/mwedh/nota/nota_completa.asp?idCat=6358andidArt=4485230 (accessed 25 November 2015).

Elias, N. (1992). *Über die Zeit: Arbeiten zur Wissenssoziologie II.* (Frankfurt a.M.: Suhrkamp).

Elwert, G. (1991). 'Gabe, Reziprozität und Warentausch. Überlegungen zu einigen Ausdrücken und Begriffen', in Berg, E. and Löffler, L. G. (eds) *Ethnologie im Widerstreit. Kontroversen über Macht, Geschäft, Geschlecht in fremden Kulturen* (München: Trickster), 159–77.

Feldman, A. (2008). *Formations of Violence: Narrative of the Body and Political Terror in Northern Ireland* (Chicago: University of Chicago Press).

Gray, O. (2004). *Demeaned but Empowered: The Social Power of the Urban Poor in Jamaica* (Kingston: University of the West Indies Press).

Gutiérrez Rivera, L. (2013). *Territories of Violence: State, Marginal Youth, and Public Security in Honduras* (London, New York: Palgrave Macmillan).

Harriott, A. (2003). 'Social Identities and the Escalation of Homicidal Violence in Jamaica', in Harriott, A. (ed.) *Understanding Crime in Jamaica. New Challenges for Public Policy* (Kingston: University of the West Indies Press), 89–112.

Harriott, A. (2008). *Organized Crime and Politics in Jamaica. Breaking the Nexus* (Kingston: Canoe Press).

Harvey, D. (1989). *The Condition of Postmodernity: An Enquiry into the Origins of Cultural Change* (Malden: Blackwell).

Hazlehurst, C. and Hazlehurst, K. M. (1998). 'Gangs in Cross-Cultural Perspective', in Hazlehurst, K. M. and Hazlehurst, C. (eds) *Gangs and youth subcultures: International explorations* (New Brunswick: Transaction Publishers), 1–34.

Headley, B. D. (1996). *The Jamaican Crime Scene: A Perspective* (Washington, DC: Howard University Press).

Helbling, J. (2006). *Tribale Kriege: Konflikte in Gesellschaften ohne Zentralgewalt* (Frankfurt a.M.: Campus).

Hoebel, T. (2014). 'Organisierte Plötzlichkeit: Eine Prozesssoziologische Erklärung Antisymmetrischer Gewaltsituationen', *Zeitschrift für Soziologie*, 43:6, 441–57.

Huggins, M. K. (1991). 'Introduction: Vigilantism and the State – a Look South and North', in Huggins, M. K. (ed.) *Vigilantism and the State in Modern Latin America: Essays on Extralegal Violence* (New York: Praeger), 1–18.

Huhn, S. and Warnecke-Berger, H. (eds) (2017). *Politics and History of Violence and Crime in Central America* (New York: Palgrave Macmillan).

Inhetveen, K. (2005). 'Gewalt in ihren Deutungen: Anmerkungen zu Kulturalität und Kulturalisierung', *Österreichische Zeitschrift für Soziologie*, 30:3, 28–50.

Jaffe, R. (2012). 'The Popular Culture of Illegality: Crime and the Politics of Aesthetics in Urban Jamaica', *Anthropological Quarterly*, 85:1, 79–102.

Jamaica Observer. (2002). 'Gangs Stage Peace March', *Jamaica Observer* (20 December 2002), www.jamaicaobserver.com/pfversion/36915_Gangs-stage-peace-march (accessed 25 November 2015)

Jessop, B. (2006). 'Spatial Fixes, Temporal Fixes and Spatio-Temporal Fixes', in Castree, N. and Gregory, D. (eds) *David Harvey: A Critical Reader* (Malden: Blackwell), 142–66.

Joas, H. and Knöbl, W. (2013). *War in Social Thought: Hobbes to the Present* (Princeton: Princeton University Press).

Knöbl, W. (2017). 'Perspektiven Der Gewaltforschung', *Mittelweg 36*, 26:3, 4–27.

Koloma Beck, T. (2016). 'Gewalt, Raum: Aktuelle Debatten und deren Beiträge zur raumsensiblen Erweiterung der Gewaltsoziologie', *Soziale Welt*, 67:4, 431–50.

Koonings, K. and Kruijt, D. (eds) (2004). *Armed Actors: Organized Violence and State Failure in Latin America* (London, New York: Zed Books).

Kowalewski, D. (2003). 'Vigilantism' in Heitmeyer, W. and Hagan, J. (eds) *International Handbook of Violence Research* (Dordrecht, Boston: Kluwer Academic Publishers), p. 339.

La Prensa Gráfica. (2009). 'Me Indigné, Por Eso Me Levanté Y Les Dispararé', *La Prensa Gráfica* (23 October 2009), www.laprensagrafica.com/el-salvador/judicial/68264-me-indigne-por-eso-me-levante-y-les-disparare (accessed 25 November 2015).

La Prensa Gráfica. (2010). 'Siete Muertos Y Tres Heridos Tras Tiroteo En Suchitoto', *La Prensa Gráfica* (3 February 2010), www.laprensagrafica.com/el-salvador/judicial/90600-siete-muertos-y-tres-heridos-tras-tiroteo-en-suchitoto.html (accessed 25 November 2015).

Lauria-Santiago, A. A. (1999). *An Agrarian Republic. Commercial Agriculture and the Politics of Peasant Communities in El Salvador, 1823–1914* (Pittsburgh: University of Pittsburgh Press).

Lindo-Fuentes, H. (2002). *La Economía de El Salvador en el Siglo XIX. Biblioteca de Historia Salvadoreña*. (San Salvador: CONCULTURA).

Lefebvre, Henri. (2010). *Rhythmanalysis: Space, Time and Everyday Life* (London: Continuum).

Lefebvre, Henri. ([1974] 1991). *The Production of Space* (Malden, Oxford, Victoria: Blackwell).

Löw, Martina. (2016). *The Sociology of Space: Materiality, Social Structures, and Action* (New York: Palgrave Macmillan).

McTaggart, E. J. (1908). 'The Unreality of Time', *Mind. A Quarterly Review of Psychology and Philosophy*, 17:68, 457–74.

Moser, C. O. N., and McIlwaine, C. (2014). 'New Frontiers in Twenty-first Century Urban Conflict and Violence', *Environment and Urbanization*, 26:2, 331–44. https://doi.org/10.1177/0956247814546283

Munroe, T. (1972). *The Politics of Constitutional Decolonization: Jamaica 1944–62.* (Kingston: Institute of Social and Economic Research, University of the West Indies).

Neckel, S. (1999). 'Blanker Neid, blinde Wut? Sozialstruktur und kollektive Gefühle', *Leviathan*, 27:2, 145–65. www.jstor.org/stable/23984405

Paul, A. T. (2005). 'Die Rache und das Rätsel der Gabe', *Leviathan*, 33:2, 240–56.

Pavoni, A. and Tulumello, S. (2020). 'What Is Urban Violence?', *Progress in Human Geography*, 44:1, 49–76.

Piccato, P. (2001). *City of Suspects: Crime in Mexico City, 1900–1931* (Durham, London: Duke University Press).

Plessner, H. (1982). 'Lachen und Weinen. Eine Untersuchung der Grenzen menschlichen Verhaltens (1941)', in Plessner, H. (ed.) *Ausdruck und menschliche Natur.* Gesammelte Schriften VII (Frankfurt a.M.: Suhrkamp), 201–387.

Reckwitz, A. (2002). 'Toward a Theory of Social Practices: A Development in Culturalist Theorizing', *European Journal of Social Theory*, 5:2, 243–63. https://doi.org/10.1177/13684310222225432

Riches, D. (1986). 'The Phenomenon of Violence', in D. Riches (ed.), *The Anthropology of Violence (Oxford:* Blackwell), 1–27.

Riekenberg, M. (2002). 'Vorläufige Betrachtungen der Ohnmacht am Beispiel Lateinamerikas', in Hettling, M. (ed.) *Figuren und Strukturen: Historische Essays für Hartmut Zwahr zum 65. Geburtstag* (München: Sour), 495–506.

Rodgers, D. (2004). ' "Disembedding" the city: crime, insecurity and spatial organization in Managua, Nicaragua', *Environment and Urbanization*, 16:2, 113–24. https://doi.org/10.1177/095624780401600202

Rosa, H. (2013). *Beschleunigung und Entfremdung: Entwurf einer kritischen Theorie spätmoderner Zeitlichkeit* (Berlin: Suhrkamp).

Savenije, W. and Andrade-Eekhoff, K. (2003). *Conviviendo en la Orilla: Exclusión social y violencia en el Area Metropolitana de San Salvador* (San Salvador, El Salvador: FLACSO).

Savenije, W. (2009). *Maras y Barras: Pandillas y violencia juvenil en los barrios marginales de Centroamérica* (San Salvador: FLACSO).

Scarry, E. (1987). *The Body in Pain: The Making and Unmaking of the World* (New York: Oxford University Press).

Schlee, G. and Turner, B. (2008). 'Wirkungskontexte des Vergeltungsprinzips in der Konfliktregulierung', in Turner, B. and Schlee, G. (eds) *Vergeltung. Eine interdisziplinäre Betrachtung der Rechtfertigung und Regulation von Gewalt* (Frankfurt a.M., New York: Campus), 7–47.

Schlichte, K. (2009). *In the Shadow of Violence: The Politics of Armed Groups* (Frankfurt a.M., New York: Campus).

Schroer, M. (2013). 'Raum, Zeit, Soziale Ordnung', in Ernst, P. and Strohmaier, A. (eds) *Raum: Konzepte in Den Künsten, Kultur- Und Naturwissenschaften* (Baden-Baden: Nomos), 11–23.

Segovia, A. (2002). *Transformación estructural y reforma económica en El Salvador* (Guatemala City: FandG Editores).

Sives, A. (2012). 'A Calculated Assault on the Authority of the State? Crime, Politics and Extradition in 21st Century Jamaica', *Crime, Law and Social Change*, 58:4, 415–35.

Sives, A. (2010). *Elections, Violence, and the Democratic Process in Jamaica, 1944–2007* (Kingston: Ian Randle).

Stone, C. (1980). *Democracy and Clientelism in Jamaica*. (New Brunswick: Transaction Publishers).

Sofsky, W. (1997). 'Gewaltzeit', in von Trotha, T. (ed.) *Soziologie der Gewalt*, KZfSS Sonderheft 37 (Opladen: Westdeutscher Verlag), 102–21.

Springer, S. and Le Billon, P. (2016). 'Violence and Space: An Introduction to the Geographies of Violence', *Political Geography*, 52, 1–3. https://doi.org/10.1016/j.polgeo.2016.03.003

Stewart, P. J. and Strathern, A. (2002). *Violence: Theory and Ethnography* (London: Continuum).

The Jamaica Gleaner. (2011). 'August Town Celebrates Three Years of Peace', June 27, 2011. www.jamaica-gleaner.com/gleaner/20110627/lead/lead91.html (accessed 25 November 2015).

Tilly, C. (2003). *The Politics of Collective Violence* (Cambridge: Cambridge University Press).

Tutela Legal del Arzobispado de San Salvador. (2008). *La violencia homicida y otros patrones de grave afectación a los derechos humanos en El Salvador*. Informe Anual de Tutela Legal del Arzobispado de San Salvador. (San Salvador: Tutela Legal del Arzobispado de San Salvador).

Tyner, J., and Inwood, J. (2014). 'Violence as Fetish', *Progress in Human Geography*, 38:6, 771–84. https://doi.org/10.1177/0309132513516177

Warf, B. and Arias, S. (eds) (2009). *The Spatial Turn: Interdisciplinary Perspectives* (London, New York: Routledge).

Warnecke-Berger, H. (2017). 'Forms of Violence in Past and Present: El Salvador and Belize in Comparative Perspective', in Huhn, S. and Warnecke-Berger, H. (eds) *Politics and History of Violence and Crime in Central America* (New York: Palgrave Macmillan), 241–79.

Warnecke-Berger, H. (2018a). 'La Globalisation De La Rente Et La Montée De La Violence', *Naqd: Revue d'études et de critique sociale*, 36, 171–82.

Warnecke-Berger, H. (2018b). *Politics and Violence in Central America and the Caribbean* (London, New York: Palgrave Macmillan).

Warnecke-Berger, H. (2020a). 'Capitalism, Rents and the Transformation of Violence', *International Studies*, 57:2, 111–31. https://doi.org/10.1177/0020881720912898

Warnecke-Berger, H. (2020b). 'Die Selbstreproduktion der Gewalt? Zentralamerika nach den Bürgerkriegen', in Peters, S. (ed.) *Gewalt und Konfliktbearbeitung in Lateinamerika* (Baden-Baden: Nomos), 33–52.

Warnecke-Berger, H. (2020c). 'Todesschwadrone, Soziale Säuberungen, Polizeigewalt: Gewalt in Zentralamerika und Die Rechtswende in Lateinamerika', in Eser, P. and Witthaus, J.-H. (eds) *Rechtswende in Lateinamerika: Politische*

Pendelbewegungen, Sozioökonomische Umbrüche und kulturelle Imaginarien in Geschichte und Gegenwart (Wien: Mandelbaum), 223–43.

Warnecke-Berger, H. and Huhn, S. (2017). 'The Enigma of Violent Realities in Central America: Towards a Historical Perspective' in Huhn, S. and Warnecke-Berger, H. (eds) *Politics and History of Violence and Crime in Central America* (New York: Palgrave Macmillan), 1–22.

Winton, A. (2004). 'Urban Violence: A Guide to the Literature', *Environment and Urbanization*, 16:2, 165–84.

Wittgenstein, L. (2003). *Philosophische Untersuchungen* (Frankfurt a.M.: Suhrkamp).

Wolf, S. (2017). *Mano Dura: The Politics of Gang Control in El Salvador* (Austin: University of Texas Press).

Zinecker, H. (2014). *Gewalt im Frieden: Formen und Ursachen der Gewaltkriminalität in Zentralamerika* (Baden-Baden: Nomos).

5

Disrupting the rhythms of violence: Anti-port protests in the city of Buenaventura[*]

Alke Jenss

The 2017 strike

In May 2017, 89 grassroots organisations blocked the entrance to the ports of Buenaventura, Colombia's most important Pacific port-city. They declared a 'civic strike' which they upheld for 22 days, demanding a socio-economic investment programme from the Colombian government. Buenaventura is one of the most violent municipalities in Colombia, and one of the poorest in the Cauca region (FEDESARROLLO-CERAC, 2013: 12; Medicina Legal, 2017). Both port businesses and protestors continually framed the protest as a disruption of the global supply chain running through the port (Comité del Paro Cívico, 2017; El Tiempo, 2017). Yet while the former perceived it as a threat and claimed their losses amounted to roughly 10 million US$ in the first five strike days alone (Patrón, 2017), the latter centred its positive impacts on urban social relations in a context of physical violence.

This contribution complements methodological and conceptual elements of rhythmanalysis with an urban political economy of assemblage (Brenner et al., 2011) to reveal the productive spatiotemporal effects of physical violence on urban rhythms. Through rhythmanalysis, I analyse frictions between infrastructural nodes of acceleration, inhabitants' mobility and urban space. Empirically, I ask how both the growth in container turnover, and spatial and temporal, recurring practices of violence have transformed Buenaventura, one of Colombia's largest ports. What role does violence play in the relation between trade-driven acceleration through the port, and the aquatic rhythm that historically shaped the city?

I argue that the global port assemblage, defined by acceleration, disrupted the tidal, aquatic rhythm the city was built on. Economic boom and physical violence resulted in an imposing rhythm of forced disappearances–displacement–port expansion. While recurring violence itself provides and

* This text first appeared as 'Disrupting the Rhythms of Violence: Anti-Port Protests in the City of Buenaventura' in *Global Policy* 12 (S2): 67–77 in 2021.

imposes urban rhythm, social movements can mobilise disruption, a temporal instrument, as a means of political articulation and transformation within the logics of accelerated accumulation and in contexts marked by violent rhythms and forced mobility. For Buenaventura's social movements, the strike disrupted rhythms of violence; it allowed them to underscore their temporal impact on the logics of accelerated accumulation. Through this impact social movements created the possibility to open up a horizon of potential, premised on an emancipatory understanding of urban politics instead of violence. Dockworker mobilisations and civic strike organisers such as Afro-Colombian and indigenous civil society initiatives, complemented each other.

Buenaventura, as both a city of violence and global trade hub is an exemplary case of contrasting rhythms; the port makes it a crucial site of acceleration. Buenaventura belongs to the under-researched intermediate cities over half the world's population now lives in (IADB, 2015; UN Habitat III, 2015). While it represents a great number of intermediate cities facing similar, if less acute, contradictions, Buenaventura illustrates that labour precarity (Neilson, 2019) is only one possible expression of such frictions.

Perpetuated rhythms of urban violence are unlike those of cities at war (Harb, 2017), but the resulting fatalities often exceed the number of fatalities in armed conflicts (Glebbeek and Koonings, 2015). Yet, usual imaginaries of cities of violence refer to megacities such as Rio de Janeiro (Arias, 2006). Uneven patterns of safe and unsafe spaces and experiences of insecurity which impact daily rhythms are interpreted as security bubbles (Hentschel, 2015), security archipelagos (Amar, 2013) or zig-zag patterns of insecure mobility defined by markers of class (Monroe, 2016). Important scholarship has shown how racialised security regimes 'govern through death' (Alves, 2018: 246; see Willis, 2015). This literature does not conceptually include rhythmanalysis, while rhythmanalysis seldom focuses on violence.

This contribution is based on content analysis of two national newspapers' perspectives (*El País, El Espectador*) on the civic strike during May 2017 and the following months. I analysed a sample of 42, respectively 30 articles through iterative coding, particularly attentive to discursive patterns. I complement this with qualitative content analysis of radio, video and print interviews with local actors (political activists, human rights lawyers, business representatives and local officials), sampled according to function and timeframe (2015–2018). The topic of rhythm emerged as a major theme from analysing those interviews. Additionally, I relied on NGO reports for crosschecks and numbers not provided by official sources. Research notes from my prior research project on security sector reform in Colombia and Mexico (2009) provided background knowledge.

A brief theoretical section combines rhythmanalysis with an urban political economy of assemblages, which complement each other in revealing the relational and temporal dimensions of acceleration, repetitive and routine violence, and disruption. The second section contextualises Buenaventura's historical urbanisation in the interplay of the aquatic rhythm and the political economy of the port assemblage. The third section explores the frictions emerging between the port as a node of acceleration, driven by a global assemblage of agents and materialities, inhabitants' mobility and the aquatic rhythm of the city. The fourth section explains the rhythm of disappearance, displacement and expansion that developed. The fifth section posits disruption of global flows as urban protestors' means of opening up political potential against the rhythm of acceleration. A short conclusion summarises the insights a rhythmanalytical perspective provides for understanding the space-time of urban violence.

Rhythm and temporal dimensions of violence

Both urban and postcolonial research explore how temporalities are indeed dynamic, plural and hierarchised across social stratification (Edensor, 2016; Vogelpohl, 2012; Mignolo, 2008). Similar research exists in the field of mobilities (Lombard, 2013; Brand and Dávila, 2011; de Boeck, 2015, Sheller and Urry, 2016). Recent work recognises that, beyond Lefebvre, specific spatiotemporal relations are imbued with asymmetrical power relations along class, race and gender (Reid-Musson, 2017).

This contribution adds another layer, bringing the primarily methodological, but also conceptual aspects of rhythmanalysis (Lefebvre, 2004) and urban political economy of assemblage (Brenner et al., 2011) to bear on research on urban violence. The focus on 'rhythm' integrates a temporal dimension into analysing urban spaces defined by repetitive violence (as opposed to a single outburst or temporally limited war).

I employ rhythmanalysis as a tool for mapping temporal-spatial conditions and relations (Chen, 2016: 4, 6). Temporal-spatial aspects of social relations can be bundled into rhythms; the lens of rhythmanalysis is to render vivid, for instance, the rhythmical effects radical transformations may have on social relations, grasping both sensory and structural elements (Chen, 2016: 3). The researcher not simply observes social action, but 'recognizes [...] the temporalities in which these activities unfold.' (Lefebvre, 2004: 87–8).

To illustrate the rhythmanalytical method, I identify acceleration, violence and disruption, which I explain below. Rhythmanalysis research has analysed the 'slow violence' of structural processes like gentrification rather than physical violence (Degen, 2016; Kern, 2016). In several ways, however, violence and urban rhythm co-constitute each other. This contribution expands Lefebvre's idea of rhythm, stressing the rhythmical qualities physical violence acquires, which accompanies acceleration, beyond transformations of rhythmical social relations through capitalist work rhythms (Lefebvre 2004). Most generally, 'collective rhythm is determined by the forms of alliances that human groups give themselves' (Lefebvre, 2004: 94). Social contradictions can imply highly unequal experiences of rhythm, and the alliances of different groups that form society are driven by power asymmetries which critical scholarship has shown to be violent (see Reid-Musson, 2017). Second, the violence of racialisation often assigns Afro-descendant Colombians both a naturalised feeling for rhythm, and 'traditional', 'slower' rhythms; constructing 'them' as an 'other' to modernity (Laó-Montes and Dávila, 2012; Oslender, 2016).

In this contribution, I focus on a third, specific relation, namely rhythmical qualities of physical violence, its effect on everyday rhythms of spatial practices, and the structuring of urban space through violence, i.e. the destruction of public spaces and other material changes resulting from violent acts. When places are 'usually stabilised by regular patterns of flow that possess particular rhythmic qualities whether steady, intermittent, volatile or surging' (Edensor, 2016: 3), the intensification of violent rhythms can either destabilise these or establish new patterns. Violence as 'the extra-everyday rhythms the everyday and vice versa' (Lefebvre, 2004: 95). Violence itself can imply the disruption and transformation of social interaction. Agents of violence impose social codes and orders; violence results in new behavioural norms (Zeiderman, 2016). This productive character of violence has been lacking from rhythmanalysis.

Acceleration has been defined as a key notion of contemporary lives in general (Rosa, 2015). In this contribution, I use acceleration to exemplify rhythm, in the literal sense of accelerated global trade and capital flows. Deepening logistics' impact on urban space, the logics of accelerated capital accumulation have often radically changed urban rhythms. The need to accelerate trade imposes pressure on procedures, transport and work relations. Acceleration is visible in the homogenisation and rationalisation of urban space, the serial architecture of planned housing and the uniform, ordered urban in planning visions. Lefebvre's (2004: 6) insistence that 'no rhythm' exists 'without repetition' implies that visions of future cities, such as the modern port-city of Buenaventura, set a specific rhythm for urban space. The rhythms of such urban logistics hubs are only comprehensively assessed by recognising the accelerated rhythms of global trade, i.e. container turnover, reduced quay times for ships and faster loading processes through automation.

Social movements literature increasingly stresses the 'disruptive agency' of unions, civil society organisations and grassroots mobilisations (Bailey et al., 2018; Huke et al., 2015; Trommer, 2019) that can unsettle even the vast assemblages of energy trade (Brown and Spiegel, 2017: 103). A central term of global logistics literature, disruption stands for the fundamental role logistics play for capitalism (Cowen, 2014), such as harbours. Workers and others with access to cargo networks possess considerable power, as industrial disputes of this kind affect the whole chain (Cole, 2018) and thus its central product, the service of delivery (Cowen, 2014). As this rhythmic effect is temporary, disruption's transformative power should not be overestimated. However, in logistics, disruption marks an agency-focused counterpoint to the accelerated flows of goods in global economy, so acceleration and disruption need to be conceptualised in conjunction. The power of disruption indeed depends on the need for acceleration.

While recognising the disruptive power of violence and its rhythm-producing qualities, I explore the temporal aspects of disruption as a potentially emancipatory tool for social movements in violent contexts. Social movements produce, modify and contest spatiotemporal conditions. Like the grassroots strikers in Buenaventura in 2017, they can disrupt distribution, depending on their 'network of social relations that … targets the quality of space' (Brenner et al., 2009: 202; see Jaramillo Marín et al., 2022).

Rhythms are illustrations of social relations, with actual agents. While accelerated rhythms are often thought of as a structural imposition, I stress the power of agents that shape such acceleration (similar to disruptions), through the concept of 'political economy of assemblages' (Brenner et al., 2011). The latter, as 'methodological extension of urban political economy' (Brenner et al. 2011: 231), enables me to think of accelerated rhythms, disruption and violence in terms of entangled local and global actors, flows and structures, which all shape the local context. Considering the Pacific's place-bound particularities, 'aquatic urban rhythm' adapts Oslender's (2016: 12) notion of an 'aquatic sense of place' as human/non-human assemblage in a 'landscape characterised by diverse aquatic features'. This understanding of assemblage offers me a sense of place and space beyond urbanites adapting to a new environment – a 'spatial sensitivity' rather than place-less identity-based theorisations of contentious politics (Oslender, 2016: 13–14). Without reproducing the space place-discussion, it provides place-specific context for the enactment of political agency through disruption (Oslender, 2016: 35).

After I describe the historical context, thinking through the rhythmic qualities of acceleration, violence and disruption in the following sections allows me to sketch out spatiotemporal relations of a specific place, recognising the global assemblages implicated in these conditions.

Making space between violent tides, aquatic space and the port assemblage

'little by little, people claimed ground from the sea' (CMH, 2017).

In his rhythmanalysis, Lefebvre contrasts Mediterranean to oceanic towns 'governed by the cosmic rhythms of tides' (Lefebvre, 2004: 91). Tidal movement is essential to understand Buenaventura's history, and instrumental for a slow communal urbanisation process driven by Afro-Colombian fishermen communities. They made Buenaventura city. They won land by continually adding alluvial material to build houses, bridges and the ground they stood on. Neighbours used sea-shells, waste, parts of mangroves and their firewood bark to fill up terrain at the lowest tide line until it formed a solid ground (Estupiñán, 2017: 6). Collectively, they 'made land' (CMH, 2015: 44). The attraction which the small, but dynamic port generated for fishermen resulted in slowly expanding the central Cascajal Island in the twentieth century, which grew not just in terms of population density, but in terms of its surface (CMH, 2015; Estupiñán, 2017; Machado, 2018). Wooden bridges and pathways link 'houses and dwellings back to their distribution in' urban aquatic space (Lefebvre, 2004: 97). Tidal rhythms, due to shallow waters, defined river travel even far upstream.

Contemporary frictions are not new. Local dominant fractions' interest in Buenaventura as a gate to the Pacific date back to the nineteenth century. Violent social relations are integral to Buenaventura's 'history of space' (Lefebvre in Brenner et al., 2009: 229). Urban space evolved in dialectical interaction, between rural–urban communities in dispersed settlements along river shorelines and the Pacific, and the extractive and trade-oriented economic activity of dominant fractions who often lived elsewhere (CMH, 2015: 39–43).

From 1961 onwards, state-owned port operator Colpuertos largely shaped the city's rhythms. Strongly unionised, Colpuertos bound whole segments of Buenaventura's population to the expanding port as workers, contributing to upward social mobility and the emergence of an Afro-Colombian elite in Buenaventura, and in turn to social distancing towards non-unionised, non-port inhabitants in Buenaventura (Centro de Memoria, 2015). Urban settlement patterns continued to resemble rural livelihoods, as families defined themselves according to their ancestors' riverside settlements and spatially reproduced hydrographic formations, but also because a considerable percentage of Buenaventura's inhabitants were forcibly displaced from surrounding departments (Centro de Memoria, 2015: 38). The aquatic space, opposed and prior to violence, defines the rhythms of Afro-Colombian social movements on the Pacific coast in self-definitions (PCN and FUNDEMUJER, 2011; Oslender, 2016), essential to understand violent urban space on the coast.

A real change of pace impacted Buenaventura when the Colombian state privatised Colpuertos during the 1990s' 'economic opening'. Socially, the union partly broke away as an organising principle when it accepted to enter the new Sociedad Portuaria de Buenaventura as a shareholder (Delgado and Martínez, 2012). Changes in labour relations were radical. The majority of workers were laid off, some re-employed on precarious contracts (Fox-Hodess, 2019). While the Work Ministry later imposed sanctions on 30 port operators who had ignored labour laws for years (El País, 2014), automation made port workers partly superfluous, decoupling the port from urban space, local political authority and the hinterland (Findeter, 2015: 90). Spatially, 'the privatization produced dual territorial dynamics which abruptly separated Afro-Colombians and indigenous [...] from the port's profitability' (CMH 2015: 54). New port gates prohibit access to city areas. Major national planning instruments such as Agenda Pacífico XXI described the Pacific region as a raw materials dispense which infrastructure investments would 'develop' into a major logistics hub for accessing Pacific markets (CMH, 2015: 50). Making delivery, distribution and transport the central product, this logistics turn aimed at overcoming the region's boom-and-bust cycles of extractive economies.

Disturbing rhythms of violence during the 1990s seemed to hamper such projects. When peace negotiations between the Colombian government and the FARC guerrilla failed at the end of that decade, this was partly due to surges in (paramilitary) violence in many regions. Critical scholarship interprets this violence as a reaction to the negotiations which paramilitaries saw as detrimental to their interests, fearing potential concessions to guerrillas (Centro de Memoria, 2015). In consequence, paramilitary groups turned the Pacific region, relatively untouched by armed conflict, into a hotspot of forced displacement and violently drove people from community land. Many 'black communities' had only recently acquired collective land titles through article 55 of the progressive 1991 constitution and subsequent Law 70 (PCN and FUNDEMUJER, 2011: 10–18).

While new movements emerged based on territorial protection, Buenaventura then experienced man-made ebbs and flows of violence in 2003, 2006–2007 and 2011 (FEDESARROLLO-CERAC, 2013). In a spike of homicidal violence in 2013 and 2014, attributed to disputes between so-called criminal gangs, 13,000 Afro-Colombians became victims of intra-urban displacement. This repeated many experiences of forced displacement from rural areas of Chocó or Valle del Cauca (HRW, 2014: 35; Humanas, 2016). Government assistance to displaced persons was scarce, allowing waves of mass displacement to happen (HRW, 2014: 30) – one expression of violent rhythms.

This awarded criminal gangs relative power in shaping Buenaventura's everyday rhythms. To grasp the relation which rhythms of violence have with the city, I turn to the transformative, accelerative power of the port assemblage.

Assemblages of conflicting rhythms: acceleration, the port and its other

References to (past) aquatic rhythms (Oslender, 2016) provide emblematic contrast to the rhythms of the port assemblage (that transcend the local scale) and of violence. By combining rhythmanalysis and political economy of assemblage (Brenner et al., 2011) in this section, I turn to the assembled actors, policies and imaginaries that drive acceleration, through Buenaventura's port. Buenaventura port handles 80 percent of exported coffee and 60 percent of all Colombian imports (Cámara de Comercio Buenaventura, 2015). Five ports with multiple terminals fragment regular rhythms of urban movement. The Buenaventuran Port Society holds terminals on central Cascajal Island, as does TCBUEN group, dominated by Catalan Puertos de Barcelona Grup Maritim, which Dutch logistics giant Maersk acquired in 2015 (ASCRI, 2015).

The notion of assemblage helps me theorise actors, infrastructure plans, spatial policies and imaginaries in relation to each other (Brenner et al., 2011). The various ports in Buenaventura form a complex assemblage of agents, processes, materialities and power relations connecting various scales. Ports are characterised by the 'mobilities that course through' them (Edensor, 2016: 5), illustrated by ships coming and going, containers being offloaded, trucks dropping them off or taking them on. There is a regulatory dimension organising this rhythm (Edensor 2016: 5), through customs searches, security measures separating port terminals from a city that lies between the port and the connecting motorway, and trade laws that define the flows of goods through the port.

The quest for competitiveness defines the ports' dominant temporalities. The symbol of the accelerated rhythms of global circulation is the shipping container, shipping making up 90 percent of global trade; intermodal infrastructures increasingly facilitate its accelerated transport across rail, road and sea (Cowen, 2014). Logistics multinationals like Maersk or Evergreen, together with Colombian exporters and transport companies, coordinate the accelerated flows through the port. Yearly, 20 million tons of goods arrive at Buenaventura, and its capacity is of 1.5 million TEUs (TEUs measure container units). Port turnover has grown exponentially with investments in new terminals to export oil and liquid gas. In 2014 alone, container turnover in Buenaventura port grew by 13.2 percent (Cámara de Comercio

Buenaventura, 2015); in 2023, growth still made 3.9 percent frente al tiempo prepandémico (Cámara de Comercio de Cali, 2023: 3).

A host of actors produces this space entangled with the global economy's circuits. While inhabitants live close by, others are involved in its trade rhythms, loading and unloading containers from ships, coordinating their transport or investing in goods flows and construction. Since 2017, Philippine and Singaporean conglomerates PSA and ICTSI operate the giant terminal Aguadulce in cooperation with the Colombian Pacific Businesses Group which unites 200 local shareholders (Findeter, 2015: 27). Two more port projects have not passed the planning stage (El Tiempo, 2016). Financial services, i.e. by Dutch-, US- or UK-based funds, gas stations, or hotels catering to management segments and construction firms, form the assemblage's ramifications. The Buenaventuran Chamber of Commerce represents local businesses. Agencies such as Invest Pacific, which promotes investment and Colombian business on the coast, and the public–private Findeter which finances and plans infrastructure, shape the port-city. Colombian producers' federations exert regular influence over regulatory issues in the port (Delgado and Martínez, 2012: 16). They expect the Pacific Alliance of Trade, which declared Buenaventura its capital in 2013, to bring expanded trade with Perú, Chile and México (El País, 2014).

Particular frictions emerge between accelerated flows and their imposition of difference as a defining trait of socio-spatial ordering (Cowen, 2014). Temporally, the separation of port and work force from the city meant that port rhythms shaped the city less by imposing strict working rhythms on the city's inhabitants, and instead through acoustic and spatial impositions: container ships drone past their houses, up to 3,000 trucks daily (Cifuentes, 2017) rumble by on the one route to port, causing frequent traffic jams, new roads cutting through community space or access restrictions change their movement patterns.

Port growth unsettles and reshapes social arrangements by simultaneous acceleration and exclusion. Urban rhythms shift with local economies' insertion in global economy, and locals see the port assemblage expanding rapidly beyond their control, encroaching on everyday livelihood practices of fishing, river- and sea-related activities and housing on shore (Bedoya, 2017): 'The port is a sacrifice of the Buenaventurans to the rest of Colombia' (Vidal, 2017). The repetitive offloading of heavy containers and heavy vehicles transiting through the immediate proximity cause cracks and fractures in houses and accelerate the rhythm in which owners need to repair these (Estupiñán, 2017: 11–14). Telluric movements caused by artificial, heavy machinery vibrations have become a 'cyclical force that, by being systematic and repetitive, can modify the physical conditions of the ground' (technical report cited in Estupiñán, 2017: 19–20). For instance, TCBUEN terminal replaced the natural swimming pools at La Loma, where neighbours would gather on Sundays for refreshments (Estupiñán, 2017: 8).

The port assemblage imposes serial rhythms and rationalised spaces on the city through planned urban restructuring: The Masterplan 'Buenaventura 2050' aims to restructure urban transport grid and housing. Corresponding laws add institutional layers: In 2013, the Colombian congress declared Buenaventura a Special Industrial, Port, Biodiverse, Ecotourist District through Law 1617, and a large area north of the city an Integral Development Zone with special jurisdiction to accelerate its development into an industrial complex. The National Planning Program Nuevas Ciudades aims for the same (DNP, 2016; Esteyco and Findeter, 2015).

I recognise the Masterplan institutionalises specific spatiotemporal relations, shaped by the port assemblage. It aims to further separate the port from the urban poor, while integrating urban society very selectively. A total of 568 residential units were inaugurated in 2015 for internally displaced persons in Ciudadela San Antonio (Mundubat/JyP 2015: 30–1). Producing a repetitive, uniform space, these 45 m² houses were placed in a rural area south of Buenaventura are 40 minutes from the sea (Taula Catalana, 2016). Planning agencies (Findeter/Esteyco, 2015: 127) later recognised that the location isolated populations, uprooting their daily rhythms defined by living close to the sea. Planners ignored the tropical, humid bioclimatic conditions producing standard, prefabricated houses that lacked ventilation (Mundubat and JyP, 2015: 31). The national government envisioned 4052 serially planned housing units, but developed less clear plans for health centres or schools (Mundubat and JyP, 2015: 31). Urban redevelopment exerts urgency on informal settlements on territory 'claimed from the sea'. Pressure on aquatic rhythm intensifies, as 'you can't fish here anymore, because the tide is contaminated' (CMH, 2017), and housing prices rise. Official numbers confirm the accelerated growth of housing prices in Buenaventura and expect future growth rhythms (IGAC, 2016).

Acceleration and exclusion became ordering principles for urban space. According to protestors, the secure spaces created around different terminals replicate this exclusion through acceleration. Greater parts of Buenaventura's population, with a now astonishing 90.3 percent partly relying on informal income (DNP, 2018: 2), increasingly represented the 'supposedly wasteful rhythms of the long term unemployed' (Edensor 2016: 11). Their rhythm became an 'other' to the port they had shaped as dockworkers or fishermen. The exclusion of certain groups from the benefits of accelerated trade is nothing new. This asymmetrical relation to some extent conjures up imaginaries from Colombian history, when Afro-Colombians were either unfree or hardly allowed to own private property (Safford and Palacios, 2003).

The gradual production of city dwellers as an 'other' to the port has rhythmanalytical dimensions: I interpret the confrontation of logistical acceleration and aquatic rhythm, based on the tide, as conflicting rhythms, as arrhythmia (Lefebvre 2004), and now turn to the resulting, productive role of violent rhythms.

A violent rhythm of disappearances, displacement and expansion

The acceleration of capital flows into Buenaventura and the intensification of violence are intertwined. This section deals with the conflicting and contrasting rhythms of the port assemblage and city dwellers, and the violent frictions that emerge from trade acceleration, which a focus on rhythm can foreground. I ask how people navigate through space-time while patterns of order and violence both imposed rhythms of violence on everyday life and shaped interactions.

The port expansion has not led to more security or to more predictable, serial rhythms for city dwellers. Local organisations claim the opposite (Castillo, 2018; Celeita, 2018; Estupiñán, 2017). The city's greater attractiveness for global investment simultaneously signalled an intensification of violence, a rhythm defined by torture houses and curfews imposed by re-emerging paramilitary or, so-called 'criminal' groups.

I argue that accelerated investment interests and state planning themselves led to or at least contributed to a rhythm of disappearances – displacement – port expansion. Local activists claim that an intensification of violent rhythms took place every time a new harbour project was planned (Machado, 2018). Political activists and inhabitants state that patterns of homicidal violence changed from selective murder and massacres in the early 2000s to torture and forced disappearances in the 2010s; frequently, dismembered bodies are found in the mangroves; '[...] there was an intensification, because they started with normal murder.... I think they never thought that after this situation people would stay in the territory, they don't comprehend how after such atrocity, such damage [...], people still live here.' (Centro de Memoria Histórica, 2015: 336). A new wave of violence came in 2017, but forced disappearance made it less visible (El Espectador, 2017a).

The nature of the actual relation between perpetrators, the state and inhabitants is disputed. The Defence Ministry defines the perpetrators in Buenaventura as 'criminal gangs' that in some instances meet criteria for Organised Armed Groups (Refworld UNHCR, 2017). International organisations describe dynamic alliances and confrontations, particularly during 2013 and 2014 (Refworld UNHCR, 2018). Nongovernmental organisations define them as 'narcoparamilitary structures' which reproduce traits of former paramilitary groups and have established links to some officials (INDEPAZ, 2017). For instance, six Colombian marines were detained for links to the group Los Rastrojos in November 2017 (UNHCR, 2017).

The intensification of violence has transformed 'rhythmically apprehended routines' (Edensor, 2016: 8) in the city, making urban navigation a precarious endeavour, particularly for the lower social strata. According to available data (CMH, 2015; El Espectador, 2017b), they visit public spaces less, impose strict schedules on family members and avoid certain areas, lengthening what might have been a short distance to cross, or shortening appearances in public (Machado, 2018). Spatiotemporal practices, such as regular movement, are fractured and limited, having changed in differentiated ways for different social segments (see Graham and Marvin, 2001; Monroe, 2016).

Inhabitants are caught between what Ritterbusch (2016) calls 'mobilities at gunpoint', as violence displaced thousands of inhabitants towards other neighbourhoods at different moments in time (FEDESARROLLO-CERAC, 2013) and containment, as 'criminal gangs' frequently prohibited inhabitants from crossing into other neighbourhoods or imposed curfews (FIP, 2014). Other inhabitants choose not to move through the city anymore for fear of being disappeared or tortured (Obispo Epalza, 2015). This absence of movement, or its forced version, defined daily rhythms.

Violence disrupted social relations. Not just an individual experience, such violence within the very own neighbourhood upset the experience of community, a notion regularly mobilised by Pacific social movements referring to the existing urban social net of Buenaventura (PCN and FUNDEMUJER, 2011: 20). If 'collective rhythm is determined by the forms of alliances that human groups give themselves' (Lefebvre, 2004: 94), violence now determines this collective rhythm, inflicted by 'criminal gangs' who recruit soldiers from among the inhabitants themselves (Rentería, 2017).

The former habitability of space, in which river and sea (an aquatic rhythm) were instrumental in defining work and livelihood practices and family ties, related to an 'aquatic sense of place' (Oslender, 2016: 135–6; CMH, 2015: 343), transformed through violence, the absence of the disappeared and the impacts of global port activity. Practices such as having neighbours with a quasi-family status watch the children while doing household chores disappeared (CMH, 2015: 343). In the partly matrifocal society of Buenaventura (CMH 2015: 344), forced disappearances of women, who act as the base for household and community, increased. Armed actors have both co-opted and fractured rivershore social spaces, where people would gather to have a chat, take a walk or have dinner together (see Oslender, 2016). Now, acuafosas (water graves) mark the sea (CMH, 2015: 179; 278; Machado, 2018). Fishermen testify that in the estuary of La Loma, the former bathing outlet, they regularly find human remains (Estupiñán, 2017: 10). Inhabitants started to avoid such places which used to form part of their daily rhythms.

Inhabitants themselves name the rhythms of violence both in media interviews and testimonies for human rights reports. They argue that disappearances, dismemberments or torture would surge when and where a new port project was underway (Castillo, 2018), as part of struggles for appropriation (Lefebvre, 2004: 96). Violence would pave the way for these projects by introducing fear and causing people to flee, and thus facilitate port acceleration (Bedoya, 2017; Celeita, 2018; Mundubat and JyP, 2015). For instance, in La Immaculada neighbourhood, 'there was no violence, nothing like that, but when we heard they would build this new terminal, strange people started appearing and this became hell' (testimony in Estupiñán, 2017: 8).

Rhythms play a major role in navigating violent urban space, appreciable, for instance, in activists' strategies to protect themselves from violence by not disclosing their timeframes (as the activist who arrives hours later to conceal his patterns of movement, Machado, 2018). This goes far beyond port infrastructure destroying places of encounter.

Buenaventura's rhythms of violence are hardly understood without taking into account capitalist expansion and acceleration which combine legal and illegal trade (see Nordstrom, 2007: 115–27). 'Criminal gangs' or narcoparamilitary structures form an integral part of the port assemblage, as they are involved in transporting illegal goods. 'The blurring of lines between the state and the non-state' (Monroe, 2016) is particularly salient in the co-presence of state forces (military, navy), private port security and illegal armed actors. Access to the port is central for the transit economy and a step in the value chain for cocaine brokers. What scholars term graduated sovereignty (Ong, 2000), or changing unofficial networks (Grajales, 2016), had tangible results in Buenaventura. The state's infrequent intervention allowed criminal gangs to order material and social space, yet violence never truly affected projects of economic expansion.

Violence lets us understand the Buenaventura Masterplan as a spatiotemporal project, coercive towards deviant populations. Communities on Cascajal Island claim coercion and urgency to be characteristics of state-led relocation (CMH, 2015: 75). Pressures talk of hurrying up to make way for future prosperity. 'They say that if we don't leave now we will be left with nothing, because they will get us out here anyhow [...] other more honest officials told us they need this to construct buildings with balcony, hotels, houses for the rich' (San José inhabitant, cited in El Espectador, 2013). Masterplan temporalities thus continually clashed with inhabitants' hopes not to move.

In the above paragraphs, I have illustrated how rhythms of violence intertwine with capitalist acceleration. Not only did violence acquire rhythmical qualities, but agents located in the port assemblage produced violent rhythms, transforming urban spatiotemporal practices.

A disruptive moment: Blocking the port, halting violent rhythms

In mid-May 2017, 89 grassroots organisations, among them the well-known Afro-Colombian organisation Proceso de Comunidades Negras (PCN), the National Afro-Colombian Council on Peace (Conpaz) and the Association of Terrains Won from the Sea (Asociación Terrenos Ganados Al Mar) declared a peaceful strike. Their 'civic strike', a mass protest of diverse social groups with overlapping political aims, as Kane/Celeita (2019) defined it, was an organised mobilisation rather than spontaneous collective upheaval. This section explores the strike as a deliberate disruption of global flows of goods, but also of rhythms of violence. The organisations explicitly demanded social, health and educational policy solutions (instead of selective military operations shown to fail) to the structural conditions of violence, and directed part of their actions towards the port assemblage, blocking access to port gates completely for 22 days (Vidal, 2017). They 'paralyzed' the rhythm of the port and its daily commercial movements, blocking principal roads and closing down trade and public transport in town (El Espectador, 2017b; El País, 2017a). Barricades inhibited the movement of vehicles. Heavy truck after truck was stuck for weeks on the outskirts of Buenaventura, the drivers immobilised for fear of losing their vehicles (El Espectador, 2017c). Protestors' means were limited given the context, but they temporarily modified city space. They declared 11 strike meeting points where they met every day to coordinate community care (Kane/Celeita, 2019), and established working groups which oversaw the free transit of food, the administration of Buenaventura's water services schedule and intra-urban transport (Comité del Paro Cívico, 2017; Riascos, 2017).

The mobilisation is a prime example of the political nature of rhythm. I argue that this disruption not only affected the global flows of the port, defying their imposing linear space-time. Instead, the political mobilisation disrupted the rhythms of violence. It gave activists a platform to claim that dispossession close to port terminals was systematic and that disappearances–displacement–port expansion formed an integral rhythm (CMH, 2017). A city shaped by forced mobility and even its outright inhibition turned the disruption of goods mobility into its primary resource of mobilisation, to flesh out the spatiotemporal effects of violence.

More than simply providing 'alternative modes of spending time' (Edensor, 2016: 16), these grassroots organisations converted disruption into a means of political articulation. They achieved precisely what global economic agents perceived as the principal threat (Cowen 2014), the disruption of the supply chain, which potentially 'cascades' into distant sites. The effectiveness of disruption was possible due to the Buenaventura city road network, often described as a bottleneck, the lack of multiple lanes making it vulnerable to such mobilisations (El País, 2014). Protests disrupted the logics of the port assemblage, based on acceleration, reduced turnover time and just-in-time networks of production and distribution. The reliance on speed in transport denotes a dominant rhythm. Cowen (2014) describes how international port spaces are dominated by the quest for 'seamlessness'; the circulation of goods is supposed to function 'as frictionless as possible'. Indeed, during the first five days of the strike, Colombian businesses alone claimed losses of 3.8 million pesos in export products such as coffee; the port economy reportedly lost 25 million pesos (Patrón, 2017). The local chamber of commerce representative, Micolta (2017), urged the government to rapidly reach a negotiation, but the protestors held up the strike for 22 days until both sides signed an agreement. Strikers themselves demanded 'immediate' but lasting measures to relieve the city's social emergency. 'Government can take immediate decisions' (Vidal, 2017). While both statements transport urgency, the contradictions between a logic of accelerated accumulation and the city as a social space are apparent.

Blockages such as closing port access are clearly seen as threats; labour mobilisation generates short-term costs some corporations have likened to the effects of terror attacks (Cowen, 2014). This perception of disruption as threat partly explains why access to the port terminals in Buenaventura is so highly selective, a selectivity that dramatically changed the rhythms of the aquatic space. We can see it replicated in Colombian media focusing their reports on the strike on lootings and chaos supposedly caused by protestors. These reports securitised the strike's peaceful spatial strategies of rhythmic intervention as threat. Anti-riot police forces and the military once again made their appearance in the city (El País, 2017a, 2017b), and paradoxically, an official curfew after 6 pm 'inhibited people from mobilizing, while riot police then accompanies lorries to the ports to leave their cargo' (Ruiz, 2017) in 'caravans of 15 trucks' (Cifuentes, 2017). Protestors themselves claimed at least 10 people suffered bullet wounds by police during anti-strike operations (Ruiz, 2017), denied any participation in lootings, and condemned the quick repressive state response (Riascos, 2017) and threats by reorganised paramilitary groups (Bedoya, 2017; Comité del Paro Cívico, 2017; El Espectador, 2017b).

In a context where public space could no longer 'spontaneously become a place for walks and encounters, ... deals and negotiations' (Lefebvre, 2004: 96) because of the imminent threat of violence, the civic strike mobilisation in 2017 implied a 'use of time' through which 'the citizen resists the state'. Protestors mobilised disruption, a temporal instrument, as a means of political articulation within the logics of accelerated accumulation. Torture and disappearance don't disrupt container shipments as much as a blockage of this kind. A strike spokesperson explained this: 'if they keep killing, but it doesn't affect port activities, nobody cares, so we had to block the port to be heard.' (Vidal, 2017).

The strikers succeeded in disrupting, temporarily halting, rhythms of violence and opened up a horizon of potential, not premised anymore on violence and precariousness, but on an emancipatory understanding of urban politics. Its effects, organisers hoped (Vidal, 2017), would be public services such as water provision from the nine river basins and a functioning hospital based on the funds Buenaventura contributes to the state via the port. An NGO activist called it 'a victory because the people saw that they could hold the city for that long and that the streets were not just for capital. ... before only big trucks passed by, these became public spaces. And so even if in the end those victories are not complied with, it's a victory.' (Celeita, 2018).

Afro-Colombian and indigenous civil society initiatives organised this biggest strike in the port's history, not dockworkers, but dockworker mobilisations and civic strike did not contradict each other. These are not separate groups, but one heterogeneous urban society. 'We all got together, women's and youth organizations, traders, transporters, unions' (Riascos, 2017). The strike gave dockworkers the potential to call on the effects of their own precarious conditions (Fox-Hodess, 2019), and those dockworkers that are dwellers also suffered the violent urban rhythm. The strike is a deliberate intervention into rhythmic regularity. For the movements, instead of instability and anomie (Edensor, 2016: 16), it uprooted rhythms imposed on them. The potential of disrupting the rhythms of accumulation (Edensor, 2016: 12) give those that control access to crucial nodes such as Buenaventura's terminals considerable power, not only the dockworkers.

Historically, and during the strike, social movements' mobilisation of disruption referenced tidal rhythm. Activists speak of the mangroves, estuaries, the river delta and the sea as integral to the city (Bedoya, 2017), illustrating their protest narratives are spatially and materially embedded in aquatic rhythms (CMH, 2017; El Espectador, 2017c; Oslender, 2016). It is telling that fishermen supported the strike (Bedoya, 2017). The reference to aquatic rhythm allowed for solidarity from other port-cities. The economic networks wrought by global flows brought disparate groups into relation (Celeita, 2018). Civil society organisations in other places accompanied the strike. These references imply that beyond temporalities (Tilly and Tarrow, 2007: 183) or place (Escobar, 2008) in their own right, it is the temporalities of place that contribute to social movements' contentious politics. They represent a 'quest for a counter-space' (Oslender, 2016: 129; see Lombard et al., 2021).

The strike did have long-term rhythmical effects, illustrating how, despite violent rhythms, Lefebvre (2004) reminds us that emancipatory horizons are integral to everyday life in capitalism, and his understanding of moments of surprise, the appearance of difference in regularity and self-awareness implies that these events cannot be commodified (see Edensor, 2016: 14). Government and strike committee reached an agreement after 22 days, agreeing on future participatory spatial transformation with funds of 408 million euros destined to sanitation, a hospital and health centres, additional teachers and electricity supply (Alcaldía Buenaventura and Comité Paro Cívico, 2017). Rhythms of violence and accelerated port logistics persist, disruption was temporary and unidentified actors have exercised violence against strike organisers (Celeita, 2018; Riascos, 2017). However, Buenaventurans elected a mayor from among the strike organisers for the term starting in January 2020, who repeatedly stressed the necessity to change the 'historical, structural problems of abandonment and inequality' as his motivation for protest (Vidal, 2017).

This section explored the rhythmanalytical qualities of disruption, such as moments of awareness and surprise (Lefebvre 2004), understood as opening up potential for transforming the violent everyday. This simultaneously grasps how disruption serves as a temporal tool for social movements, making a rhythmanalytical contribution to social movement studies.

Conclusion

This contribution argued that the lenses of rhythmanalysis and political economy of assemblage complement each other to reveal the productive spatiotemporal effects of physical violence on urban rhythms, in the case of the port-city of Buenaventura.

Three sections explored the rhythmical qualities of logistical acceleration, of violence and of disruption. First, during the last decades, the ever-accelerating logic of accumulation transformed Buenaventura's urban rhythm. The acceleration of global flows and the subsequent restructuring of urban space according to the envisioned modern port-city, produces particular frictions, arrhythmia, in Lefebvre's (2004) terms, with historic rhythms defined by the tide.

Second, the contribution expanded Lefebvrian ideas of arrhythmia by carving out how physical violence, in conjunction with acceleration, acquired rhythmical qualities and impacted everyday urban rhythm. The repetitive flows that characterise the movement of shipping containers, goods and trucks through Buenaventura and repetitive waves of homicides and forced displacement had, over years, formed an integral rhythm which included disappearances –displacement–port expansion. The political economy of assemblage allows me to depict the local and global actors, flows and structures as agents that shape such spatiotemporal relations.

Third, I argued that in the context of violently imposed urban rhythms and the logics of accelerated accumulation, social movements in Buenaventura's civic strike in 2017 used disruption to underscore their temporal impact, and enhance their political articulation, in fact opening up a horizon of positive incremental change. An entire city shaped by forced mobility and containment, turned the disruption of goods flows into its prime means of mobilisation to flesh out the spatiotemporal effects of violence.

This chapter contributes a rhythmanalytical perspective on disruption, and brings spatiotemporal urban analysis into social movement studies in global supply chains. The power of disruption to ripple through the whole supply chain, rhythms of distribution and production at distant localities, draws attention not only to logistics unions, but to cities as sites of logistics struggles.

Bibliography

Alcaldía Buenaventura, and Comité Paro Cívico (2017). *Gobierno Nacional y Comité Ejecutivo Del Paro Cívico Firmaron Acuerdo Para Levantar El Paro* (Buenaventura: Alcaldía, 6 June), www.buenaventura.gov.co/articulos/gobierno-nacional-y-comite-ejecutivo-del-paro-civico-firmaron-acuerdo-para-levantar-el-paro (accessed 6 June 2017).

Alves, J. A. (2018). *The Anti-Black City: Police Terror and Black Urban Life in Brazil* (1st ed.) (Minneapolis: University of Minnesota Press).

Amar, P. (2013). *Security Archipelago: Human-Security States, Sexuality Politics, and the End of Neoliberalism* (Durham: Duke University Press).

Arias, E. D. (2006). *Drugs and Democracy in Rio de Janeiro: Trafficking, Social Networks, and Public Security* (Chapel Hill: University of North Carolina Press).

ASCRI (2015). *El Grupo Maersk Aterriza En El Puerto de Barcelona Con La Compra de TCB* – (Barcelona: Asociación Espanola de Capital, Crecimiento e Inversión), https://ascri.org/el-grupo-maersk-aterriza-en-el-puerto-de-barcelona-con-la-compra-de-tcb/ (accessed 20 May 2017).

Bailey, D. J., Clua-Losada, M., Huke, N., Ribera-Almandoz, O., and Rogers, K. (2018). 'Challenging the age of austerity: Disruptive agency after the global economic crisis', *Comparative European Politics*, 16:1, 9–31. https://doi.org/10.1057/s41295-016-0072-8

Bedoya, M. (2017). 'Interview', *Contagio Radio* (Buenaventura, 19 May 2017), www.contagioradio.com/pescadores-de-buenaventura-son-amenazados-por-paramilitares/ (accessed 22 September 2018).

de Boeck, F. (2015). ' "Poverty" and the Politics of Syncopation. Urban Examples from Kinshasa (DR Congo)', *Current Anthropology*, 56:11, 146–58. https://doi.org/10.1086/682392

Brand, P. and Dávila, J. D. (2011). 'Mobility innovation at the urban margins', *City*, 15:6, 647–61. https://doi.org/10.1080/13604813.2011.609007

Brenner, N., Elden, S., and Lefebvre, H. (2009). *State, Space, World: Selected Essays* (Minneapolis: University of Minnesota Press).

Brenner, N., Madden, D. J., and Wachsmuth, D. (2011). 'Assemblage urbanism and the challenges of critical urban theory', *City*, 15:2, 225–40. https://doi.org/10.1080/13604813.2011.568717

Brown, B. and Spiegel, S. J. (2017). 'Resisting coal: Hydrocarbon politics and assemblages of protest in the UK and Indonesia', *Geoforum*, 85, 101–11. https://doi.org/10.1016/j.geoforum.2017.07.015

Cámara de Comercio Buenaventura (2015). 'Puerto de Buenaventura, con mayor crecimiento en salida de contenedores de la Comunidad Andina', La República (15 April 2015), https://ccbun.org/noticias/1/1/1332/puerto-de-buenaventura-con-mayor-crecimiento-en-salida-de-contenedores-de-la-comunidad-andina (accessed 20 May 2017).

Cámara de Comercio de Cali (2023). Enfoque Competitivo, www.ccc.org.co/inc/uploads/2023/06/Enfoque-Buenaventura-VF.pdf

Castillo, O. (2018). 'Interview', *Verdad Abierta* (Bogotá, 3 February 2018), https://verdadabierta.com/si-me-quitan-el-esquema-de-seguridad-sere-asesinado-en-cualquier-momento/ (accessed 9 October 2018).

Celeita, B. (2018). 'Interview', *Canadian Union of Public Employees* (Toronto, 19 November 2018), https://cupe.ca/colombian-leader-berenice-celeita-full-interview (accessed 21 November 2018).

Centro de Memoria Histórica (2015). *Buenaventura – Un Puerto Sin Comunidad* (Bogotá/Buenaventura: Centro de Memoria Histórica).

Chen, Y. (2016). *Practising Rhythmanalysis: Theories and Methodologies*. (Lanham: Rowman & Littlefield).

Cifuentes, I. (2017). Isaías Cifuentes, Colombian activist, confronts Minister of the Interior about violent repression of Buenaventura's civil strike (5 June 2017), https://vimeo.com/220336225 (accessed 31 August 2018).

CMH (2017). *Puerto Sin Comunidad* (Buenaventura, 2 February 2017), https://youtube.com/watch?v=bEkNlY2hc0A (accessed 23 May 2017).

Cole, P. (2018). *Dockworker Power. Race and Activism in Durban and the San Francisco Bay Area* (Illinois: University of Illinois Press).

Comité del Paro Cívico (2017). *Comunicados Del Paro* (Buenaventura: Comité del Paro Cívico para vivir con Dignidad y en Paz en el Territorio).

Cowen, D. (2014). *The Deadly Life of Logistics: Mapping Violence in Global Trade* (Minneapolis: University of Minnesota Press).

Degen, M. (2016). 'Consuming Urban Rhythms: Let's Ravalejar', in Edensor, T. (ed.) *Geographies of Rhythm: Nature, Place, Mobilities and Bodies* (London: Routledge), 21–32.

Delgado Moreno, W., and Martínez Sander, Á. M. (2012). 'La privatización portuaria en Colombia: los modos de gestión y las relaciones de poder entre lo público y lo privado. Los casos de las Sociedades Portuarias Regionales de Cartagena y Buenaventura' (presented at the CLAD Reforma del Estado y de la Administración Pública, Cartagena: Universidad del Valle).

DNP (2016). *Buenaventura, Tumaco y Necoclí Liderarán Programa de Las Nuevas Ciudades En Colombia: DNP* (Bogotá: Departamento Nacional de Planeación (DNP).

DNP (2018). *Complejo de Actividades Económicas de Buenaventura* (Bogotá: Departamento Nacional de Planeación/Gerencia del CAEB), www.buenaventurapuertosyconectividad.com/wp-content/uploads/2018/10/13A.-Didier-Sinisterra-CAEB.pdf (accessed 30 October 2018).

Edensor, T. (2016). *Geographies of Rhythm: Nature, Place, Mobilities and Bodies* (London: Routledge).

El Espectador (2013). 'La guerra por los terrenos del área urbana', *El Espectador* (Bogotá, 24 February 2013), https://elespectador.com/noticias/nacional/guerra-los-terrenos-del-area-urbana-articulo-406663 (accessed 6 June 2017).

El Espectador (2017a). ['¿Qué está pasando en Buenaventura?'], *El Espectador* (Bogotá, 21 December 2017), https://colombia2020.elespectador.com/territorio/que-esta-pasando-en-buenaventura (accessed 22 March 2019).

El Espectador (2017b). ['El clamor de Buenaventura: "Nos tienen que pagar hasta el último alfiler"'], *El Espectador* (Bogotá, 21 May 2017), http://elespectador.com/noticias/nacional/valle/el-clamor-de-buenaventura-nos-tienen-que-pagar-hasta-el-ultimo-alfiler-articulo-694895 (accessed 31 May 2017).

El Espectador (2017c). ['Buenaventura, en rebeldía hasta con Dios'], *El Espectador* (Bogotá, 28 May 2017), https://elespectador.com/noticias/nacional/buenaventura-en-rebeldia-hasta-con-dios-articulo-695991 (accessed 6 June 2017).

El País (2014). ['Puertos de Buenaventura, listos para poner a andar la Alianza del Pacífico'], *EL PAÍS* (Madrid, 24 February 2014), https://elpais.com.co/economia/puertos-de-buenaventura-listos-para-poner-a-andar-la-alianza-del-pacifico.html (accessed 31 October 2017).

El País (2017a). ['Caos en Buenaventura: disparos, saqueos, enfrentamientos y toque de queda'], *EL PAÍS* (Bogotá, 19 May 2017), https//elpais.com.co/judicial/caos-en-buenaventura-disparos-saqueos-enfrentamientos-y-toque-de-queda.html (accessed 31 October 2017).

El País (2017b). ['Aumentarán fuerzas militares en Buenaventura tras desmanes de este viernes'], *El País* (Bogotá, 20 May 2017), https://elpais.com.co/valle/aumentaran-fuerzas-militares-en-buenaventura-tras-desmanes-de-este-viernes.html (accessed 6 November 2017).

El Tiempo (2016). ['Hay visto bueno para tres nuevos puertos en el país',] *El Tiempo* (25 January 2016), https://eltiempo.com/economia/sectores/infraestructura-en-colombia-tres-nuevos-puertos-/16491132 (accessed 31 May 2017).

El Tiempo (2017). ['Mininterior aspiraba a conjurar el paro en Buenaventura'], *El Tiempo* (Bogotá, 3 June 2017), https://eltiempo.com/colombia/cali/buenaventura-en-paro-civico-95088 (accessed 26 July 2018).

Escobar, A. (2008). *Territories of Difference. Place, Movements, Life, Redes* (Durham: Duke University Press).

Esteyco, and Findeter (2015). *La Buenaventura Que Nos Merecemos. Masterplan Buenaventura 2050* (Madrid/Bogotá: Findeter).

Estupiñán Valencia, D. (2017). *Buenaventura: Mas Puertos; Menos Comunidad* (Bogotá), https://slideshare.net/delDespojoCrnicas/buenaventura-mas-puertos-menos-comunidad (accessed 24 July 2018).

FEDESARROLLO-CERAC (2013). *Hacia Un Desarrollo Integral de La Ciudad de Buenaventura y Su Área de Influencia* (Bogotá: FEDESARROLLO-CERAC para Oleoducto al Pacífico).

Findeter (2015). *Plan de Acción 2015* (Bogotá: Findeter).

FFIP (2014). *La Crisis de Buenaventura La Vive Todo El Pacífico* (Bogotá: Fundación Ideas Para la Paz), https://ideaspaz.org/publicaciones/investigaciones-analisis/2014-05/no-70-la-crisis-de-buenaventura-la-vive-todo-el-pacifico (accessed 22 August, 2023).

Fox-Hodess, K. (2019). 'Worker Power, Trade Union Strategy, and International Connections: Dockworker Unionism in Colombia and Chile', *Latin American Politics and Society*, 61:3, 29–54. https://doi.org/10.1017/lap.2019.4

Glebbeek, M.-L., and Koonings, K. (2015). 'Between Morro and Asfalto. Violence, insecurity and socio-spatial segregation in Latin American cities', *Habitat International*, 54:1, 3–9. https://doi.org/10.1016/j.habitatint.2015.08.012

Graham, S., and Marvin, S. (2001). *Splintering Urbanism: Networked Infrastructures, Technological Mobilities and the Urban Condition* (1st ed.) (London/New York: Routledge).

Grajales, J. (2016). 'Violence Entrepreneurs, Law and Authority in Colombia', *Development and Change*, 47:6, 1294–1315. https://doi.org/10.1111/dech.12278

Harb, M. (2017). 'Diversifying Urban Studies' Perspectives on the City at War', *International Journal of Urban and Regional Research*, np. www.ijurr.org/spotlight-on/the-city-at-war-reflections-on-beirut-brussels-and-beyond/diversifying-urban-studies-perspectives-on-the-city-at-war

Hentschel, C. (2015). *Security in the Bubble* (Minneapolis: University of Minnesota Press).

HRW (2014). *La Crisis de Buenaventura. Desapariciones, Desmembramientos y Desplazamiento En El Principal Puerto de Colombia En El Pacífico* (Washington, DC: Human Rights Watch).

Huke, N., Clua-Losada, M., and Bailey, D. J. (2015). 'Disrupting the European Crisis: A Critical Political Economy of Contestation, Subversion and Escape', *New Political Economy*, 20:5, 725–51. https://doi.org/10.1080/13563467.2014.999759

Humanas (2016). *Información Estadística. Contexto Regional Departamento Del Valle Del Cauca* (Bogotá: Corporación Humanas – Centro Regional de Derechos Humanos y Justicia de Género).

IADB (2015). *Actualización Universo de Ciudades Emergentes* (Washington: Interamerican Development Bank/ICES).

IGAC (2016). *$6,5 Billones Cuesta Todo El Municipio de Buenaventura* – (Bogotá: Instituto Agustín Codazzi), http://noticias.igac.gov.co/65-billones-cuesta-todo-el-municipio-de-buenaventura/ (accessed 31 May 2017).

INDEPAZ (2017). *XII Informe Sobre Presencia de Grupos Narcoparamilitares 2016* (Bogotá: Instituto de Estudios para el Desarrollo y la Paz (INDEPAZ)).

Jaramillo Marín, J., Rushton, S., Díaz, J. M., and D. Mosquera Camacho (2022). 'El diálogo social territorial. Contribuciones teórico-prácticas desde la experiencia de Buenaventura, Colombia', *Colombia Internacional*, 109: 59–87.

Kane, P. and Celeyta, B. (2019). No tenemos armas pero tenemos dignidad: learning from the civic strike in Buenaventura, Colombia, in Harley, A. and Scandrett, E. (eds), *Environmental Justice, Popular Struggle, and Community Development* (London: Policy Press), 29–52.

Kern, L. (2016). 'Rhythms of gentrification: eventfulness and slow violence in a happening neighbourhood', *Cultural Geographies*, 23:3, 441–57. https://doi.org/10.1177/1474474015591489

Laó-Montes, A. and Dávila, A. (2012). *Mambo Montage: The Latinization of New York City* (New York: Columbia University Press).

Lefebvre, H. (2004). *Rhythmanalysis* (New York: Continuum).

Lombard, M., Hernández-García, J., and Salgado-Ramírez, I. (2021). 'Beyond Displacement: Territorialization in the Port City of Buenaventura, Colombia', *Territory, Politics, Governance Online First*.

Lombard, M. (2013). 'Struggling, Suffering, Hoping, Waiting: Perceptions of Temporality in Two Informal Neighbourhoods in Mexico', *Environment and Planning D: Society and Space*, 31:5, 813–29. https://doi.org/10.1068/d21610

Machado, T. (2018). ' "Buenaventura es una contradicción": Temístocles Machado', *Verdad Abierta* (Bogotá, 29 January 2018), https://verdadabierta.com/buenavent ura-es-una-contradiccion-temistocles-machado/ (accessed 24 July 2018).

Medicina Legal (2017). *Forensis* (Bogotá: Instituto de Medicina Legal y Ciencias Forenses), http://medicinalegal.gov.co/documents/20143/49526/Forensis+2016.+ Datos+para+la+vida.pdf (accessed 20 February 2018).

Micolta, A. (2017). 'Interview', *La W Radio* (Bogotá, 22 May 2017), https:// youtube.com/watch?v=h0dLeTWrLWQ (accessed 20 August 2018).

Mignolo, W. D. (2008). 'The Geopolitics of Knowledge and the Colonial Difference', in Dussel, E., Moraña, M., and Jáuregui, C. A. (eds) *Coloniality at Large: Latin America and the Postcolonial Debate* (Durham: Duke University Press), 225–59.

Monroe, K. V. (2016). *The Insecure City. Space, Power and Mobility in Beirut* (New Brunswick: Rutgers University Press).

Mundubat, and Justicia y Paz (2015). *El Despojo Para La Competitividad* (Buenaventura: Comisión Intereclesial de Justicia y Paz/ Mundubat).

Neilson, B. (2019). 'Precarious in Piraeus: on the making of labour insecurity in a port concession', *Globalizations*, 16:4, 559–74. https://doi.org/10.1080/14747 731.2018.1463755

Nordstrom, C. (2007). *Global Outlaws* (San Francisco: University of California Press).

Obispo Epalza (2015). 'Interview', *Verdad Abierta* (Bogotá, 8 June 2015), https:// verdadabierta.com/vemos-entrar-y-salir-la-riqueza-solo-como-espectadores- obispo-de-buenaventura/ (accessed 9 April 2018).

Ong, A. (2000). 'Graduated Sovereignty in South-East Asia', *Theory, Culture & Society*, 17:4, 55–75. https://doi.org/10.1177/02632760022051310

Oslender, U. (2016). *The Geographies of Social Movements: Afro-Colombian Mobilization and the Aquatic Space* (Durham: Duke University Press).

Patrón, L. P. (2017). 'Las pérdidas millonarias que deja el paro en Buenaventura', *El Colombiano* (Medellín, 20 May 2017), https//elcolombiano.com/negoc ios/transportadores-y-caficultores-reportaron-afectaciones-del-paro-en- buenaventura-AX6572288 (accessed 31 May 2017).

PCN and FUNDEMUJER (2011). *Propuesta de Reparación Colectiva Para La Comunidad Negra de Buenaventura* (Buenaventura: Proceso de Comunidades Negras PCN/ Fundación para el Desarrollo de la Mujer de Buenaventura y la Costa Pacífica).

Refworld UNHCR (2017). *Colombia: Paramilitary Successor Groups and Criminal Bands (Bandas Criminales, BACRIM), 2016–2017* (Geneva: UNHCR), https// refworld.org/docid/591614014.html (accessed 9 April 2019).

Refworld UNHCR (2018). *Colombia: The Presence and Activities of Los Rastrojos* (Geneva: UNHCR), https//refworld.org/docid/5afadb104.html (accessed 5 January 2020).

Reid-Musson, E. (2017). 'Intersectional rhythmanalysis: Power, rhythm, and every- day life', *Progress in Human Geography*, 42:6, 881–97. https://doi.org/10.1177/ 0309132517725069

Rentería, L. (2017). 'Interview', *Verdad Abierta* (Bogotá, 23 April 2017), https://verdadabierta.com/hacer-memoria-es-entretejer-un-camino-que-nos-permita-construir-reconciliacion/ (accessed 22 September 2018).

Riascos, M. (2017). 'Interview', *Contagio Radio* (Bogotá, 2 June 2017), https://de.ivoox.com/de/miyela-riascos-sobre-ataques-del-esmad-a-poblacion-audios-mp3_rf_19047255_1.html (accessed 30 October 2018).

Ritterbusch, A. (2016). 'Mobilities at Gunpoint: The Geographies of (Im)mobilities of Transgender Sex Workers in Colombia', *Annals of the Association of American Geographers*, 106:2, 422–33.

Rosa, H. (2015). *Social Acceleration: A New Theory of Modernity* (New York: Columbia University Press).

Ruiz, A. (2017). 'Interview', *Contagio Radio* (Bogotá, 2 June 2017), https://de.ivoox.com/de/adriel-ruiz-sobre-situacion-derechos-humanos-audios-mp3_rf_19047175_1.html (accessed 20 June 2017).

Safford, F. and Palacios, M. (2003). *Latin American Histories: Fragmented Land, Divided Society* (Oxford: Oxford University Press).

Sheller, M. and Urry, J. (2016). 'The New Mobilities Paradigm', *Environment and Planning A: Economy and Space*, 38:2, 207–26. https://doi.org/10.1068/a37268

Taula Catalana (2016). *Informe de La Visita de La Delegación Catalana a Buenaventura* (Barcelona: Taula Catalana per la Pau i els Drets Humans a Colòmbia).

Tilly, C. and Tarrow, S. (2007). *Contentious Politics* (Boulder: Paradigm).

Trommer, S. (2019), 'Watering Down Austerity: Scalar Politics and Disruptive Resistance in Ireland', *New Political Economy*, 24:2, 218–34. https://doi.org/10.1080/13563467.2018.1431620

UN Habitat III (2015). *Habitat III Declaration Intermediate Cities (Cuenca)* (Cuenca: UN Habitat) http://habitat3.cuenca.gob.ec/archivos/declaration/HIII-Declaration CuencaES.pdf (accessed 4 January 2017).

UNHCR (2017). *Colombia: Paramilitary Successor Groups and Criminal Bands* (UNHCR Refworld), www.refworld.org/docid/591614014.html (accessed 22 March 2019).

Vidal, V. (2017). 'Interview', *Contagio Radio* (Buenaventura, 17 May 2017), https://contagioradio.com/si-no-cerramos-el-puerto-el-gobierno-no-nos-presta-atencion-habitantes-de-buenaventura-articulo-40641/ (accessed 31 May 2017).

Vogelpohl, A. (2012). 'Alltag – Rhythmus – Stadt: Konzeption und empirischer Aufbau' in Vogelpohl, A. *Urbanes Alltagsleben* (VS Verlag für Sozialwissenschaften), 71–102. https://doi.org/10.1007/978-3-531-19473-8_4

Willis, G. (2015). *The Killing Consensus* (Oakland: University of California Press).

Zeiderman, A. (2016). 'Submergence. Precarious Politics in Colombia's Future Port-City', *Antipode*, 48:3, 809–31. https://doi.org/10.1111/anti.12207

6

The urban pulse of violence: Spatiotemporal patterns in the riots in Belfast and Jerusalem during the era of the British Empire

Mara Albrecht

We beg leave now to direct your Excellency's attention to certain other proceedings on that day, which have excited great attention in Belfast. ... The leading street, separating the two districts, we have stated to be Albert-street; opposite ... stands Christ's Church, in which Dr. Drew officiates. Thus this church ... stands exactly at the point of division between the two districts, infelicitously situated to be selected as the place for a great and unusual celebration of the festival of the 12th of July. ... The festival having fallen on a Sunday, the evening service at Christ's Church was especially for them [the Orangemen, M.A.]. (Report Belfast, 1858: 2)

On Friday, being a Moslem holiday [the Birthday of the Prophet, M.A.], an Arab demonstration was permitted by the Government, although it was known in advance that the objective of the demonstration was the Wailing Wall, a fact that clearly stamped the demonstration as calculated to produce a collision with Jewish worshippers and a breach of the peace. ... Many hundreds of Arabs poured out of the Haram or Mosque area, some of them forcing a way through the recently opened door establishing direct communication from the Haram to the Wailing Wall. (The National Archives, London (hereafter TNA), CO 733/163/4, 1929)

These two quotes strikingly illustrate the interconnectedness of space and time regarding the production of urban violence in Belfast and Jerusalem in the era of the British Empire. Both quotes hint at the important role of religious places, holidays and prayer days for the unfolding of riots. They also point to the substantial effect of the spatial configuration of the cities – or their reconfiguration – in triggering and shaping violence. I claim that the interplay of spatial and temporal factors in the context of rapidly growing and transforming cities is a main precondition for the production of violence. Spatial configurations such as public places at interface areas between neighbourhoods inhabited by different communities, the proximity of sacralised sites, the narrowness of streets, or even the way they are paved, can have a significant impact on how historical actors employ violence.

Similarly, the rhythms of a city have an impact on the timing and pacing of violence. The religious holidays and political commemorations that pervade the annual calendar not only serve as a catalyst for violence, but they also define when, where, by whom and how it is used. Over time, a specific set of violent practices evolves that is shaped in accordance with the particular spatiotemporal features of a city.

The idea that urban space and time shape practices of violence and that those in turn rearrange the spatial and temporal configuration of a city is the main hypothesis of this book. Concerning urban space, a similar claim has also been made in the field of urban geography by Springer and Le Billon, who maintain that '[b]y addressing how violence shapes space, understood in its broad political and processual sense, and how space shapes violence beyond the instrumental way of analysing spatial patterns to help "explain" violence, geographers are bringing greater attention to the constitution of violence through space' (Springer and Le Billon, 2016: 1). In the chapters of this volume, we include time as a main aspect of analysis and look at urban violence from different disciplinary backgrounds – in the case of this chapter from the perspective of history. My aim is to explore how violence in Belfast and Jerusalem was produced and shaped by the spatiotemporal configuration of the cities, meaning the specific characteristics of the urban and its spatial qualities in connection with urban rhythms and changing perceptions of time. A historical perspective not only provides the historical background for current episodes of violence, but also allows us to understand the historical evolution of forms and practices of violence and their spatiotemporal and cultural coding. It also causes us to reflect on the historicity of our own viewpoint, which is often omitted in research on present-day violence.

I suggest that the space-time of Belfast and Jerusalem underwent substantial transformation processes in the time period covered here, which facilitated the development of spatiotemporal patterns of violence. A key factor in this process was British imperial policies, especially the favouring of one group over another, which was reflected in urban planning strategies based on the principle of spatial (and to some extent temporal) separation of different religious communities. The recurring riots in both cities accelerated these spatiotemporal urban reconfigurations, resulting in increased processes of spatiotemporal division, residential segregation and the inscription of urban space-time with symbolic meaning. I further argue that violence became synchronised with the annual calendars and the religious and political urban rhythms in both cities, but that it also changed and disrupted these rhythms. My intention is to reveal how spatiotemporal patterns of violence evolved during the riots in this era, introducing a new urban 'pulse' to which the historical actors 'clocked' their use of violence.

I follow a definition of direct, physical violence as a social practice, (historical) form of action, and pattern of communication, which is always embedded in historical situations and forms of social organisation (Lindenberger and Lüdtke, 1995: 7; Weinhauer and Ellerbrock, 2013: 5). Violence is an instrument of power and an order-creating practice (Popitz, 1986: 61–2) but as part of collective action it can also bring about political or social change. While the decision to use collective violence is in practically all cases to some extent premeditated (Tilly, 2003: 3) and usually has rational objectives, the mobilisation of a large crowd for a riot presupposes the activation of collective emotions. Although 'political violence' by state and non-state actors serves political aims, it can have diffuse motivations and often incorporates other aspects such as venting anger, material gain or forms of (male) assertion in a like-minded peer-group.

The interconnectedness of space and urban violence has been an emerging topic in the social and cultural sciences in the wake of the spatial turn. In history, though, especially that of the nineteenth and twentieth centuries, it occupies only a marginal position, with many studies focusing on crime (statistics), policing and youth delinquency, but rarely paying attention to concrete practices of violence and their interconnectedness with urban space. A notable exception is Weinhauer (2010), who studied the impact of youth delinquency on urban spaces in Germany in the late nineteenth century and in the 1960s and 1970s. Weinhauer and Ellerbrock (2013) have pointed towards this gap in literature, as has Fuccaro (2016), who argues that it is necessary for historians to traverse disciplinary and regional boundaries to study violence in cities, using approaches and concepts from sociology, anthropology and political geography, as well as urban and postcolonial studies (Fuccaro, 2016: 4). Considering the state of research on West Asian and North African cities, she points out that '[p]articularly for the twentieth century, many local histories of violence and of less flamboyant episodes of bloodshed have yet to be written' (Fuccaro, 2016: 16). This chapter endeavours to contribute to the emerging literature on urban violence in modern history from a spatiotemporal perspective. In so doing, it also adds to the body of literature on this topic from urban studies and geography as it highlights the importance of historical transformation processes in cities for the formation of spatiotemporal practices of violence that are still used in today's urban conflicts.

My focus is on the major urban riots in Belfast in 1857, 1864, 1886 and 1920–22 as well as in Jerusalem during the Mandate years, particularly in 1920, 1921, 1929, 1933 and 1936–39. The rationale for choosing these two rather dissimilar cities situated in different world regions is twofold. For one thing, in both contexts the British had installed and supported an external settler group in contrast to the local majority population and distinguished them according to their religious affiliation. In addition, many of the politicians that were concerned with the 'Irish Question' in the late nineteenth and early twentieth centuries were also framing the British policies for Mandate Palestine. The British transferred significant numbers of troops, officers and administrative personnel from Ireland to Palestine after the Irish War of Independence, which implies the transfer of imperial perceptions about violence, spatialities, temporalities and religious identities.

There are only a few historical studies that explicitly deal with one or several of the riots during the late nineteenth and early twentieth centuries in Belfast (Boyd, 1987; Budge and O'Leary, 1973: 73–172; Stewart, 1977; Farrell, 2000; Holmes, 2002; Parkinson, 2004; Parkinson, 2010; McDermott, 2001; Hepburn, 1996: 174–202). While outlining the events in detail, these studies judiciously contextualise the riots in the socioeconomic and political situation of their time but seldom discuss the forms and practices of the violence itself. Although all these works refer to the contested nature of Belfast, their analyses do not consider the relation of violence to urban space (or time). However, two studies particularly highlight the ways in which the historical actors employed violence on the local level. Hirst (2002) studied how the conflict between Protestants and Catholics on the national level played out on the street level in the riots of the nineteenth century by focusing on two working-class areas in Belfast, the Catholic Pound district and the Protestant Sandy Row. While Hirst gives an excellent account of how both areas developed their local political and religious identities over time, she does not explain the spatiality or temporality of violence during the riots. Doyle (2009) wrote a history of Victorian Belfast in which he describes the local riots in the broader context of the British Empire and argues that traditions of violence became rooted in everyday life. Doyle's outstanding work provides new perspectives for the study of violence in nineteenth-century Belfast but does not entirely explain the interconnectedness of violence with the spatial characteristics and urban rhythms of Belfast.

The state of research is similar regarding British Mandate Jerusalem (1920–48). Only a few works focus on the riots and other instances of urban violence in Jerusalem and most of them do not apply a spatial or spatiotemporal perspective (Mazza, 2009: 165–78; Segev, 2002: 127–44, 295–313; Barakat, 2007; Cohen, 2015: 59–121; Wasserstein, 1991: 220–38; Winder, 2012; Nicault, 2000; al-ʿAlamī, 2000; Swedenburg, 1995; Porath, 1977; Hughes, 2010; Kelly, 2015). A remarkable exception is the chapter by Mazza (2015) on the Nabi Musa Riots in Jerusalem in 1920, which are particularly neglected in historical research as it is. Mazza describes the emergence of structured urban violence in Jerusalem and contrasts it to (intra-)communal violence in late Ottoman times. He also analyses how the reconfiguration of urban space through the urban planning strategies of the British led to a radicalisation of local politics and a process of residential segregation along confessional lines.

Recent works from the disciplines of urban studies, geography and conflict sociology deal as well with the interconnectedness of urban violence and space in present-day Belfast and Jerusalem. While they sometimes include a discussion of the 'historical background' of the conflict, consisting of a summary of past violent events, they usually do not consider the historical dimension of the formation of spatial practices of violence that can be traced from the time-period covered in this chapter up until the present day. Concerning Jerusalem, for example, the outstanding study by Rokem, Weiss and Miodownik (2018) provides us with a meticulous mapping of violence in Jerusalem. The authors analyse the impact of mobility, street patterns, street connectivity and other socio-spatial factors on violence, but do not discuss how these factors changed in the long term. As a remarkable exception, the works on Jerusalem by Wendy Pullan (e.g. 2013a; 2013b; Pullan and Gwiazda, 2010) must be pointed out, as they often include a thorough analysis of spatial imaginations and practices of historical actors and the historical transformation of urban space and its impact on violence.

Regarding Belfast, an important study by O'Dowd and McKnight (2013) focuses on the intersection of religion and violence in urban space, mapping institutionalised religion (churches) in the city as well as popular forms of religion such as parades and open-air preaching. While mainly concentrating on present-day Belfast, the authors briefly refer to the development of these places and practices in the past. An equally interesting study by Cunningham and Gregory (2014), a cooperation between a geographer and an historian, highlights the role of segregated space, interface areas and peace lines during the Troubles in Belfast. The authors quantitatively trace political killings within the city-space and conclude that interface areas constitute battlegrounds for the ongoing conflict between the communities, but that the death rates were actually higher within segregated neighbourhoods, deemed as 'sanctuaries' for both the Protestant and Catholic population. However, they do not consider how the processes of segregation and the formation of interface areas as lines of conflicts were already established in the early nineteenth century and evolved further during subsequent riots.

Hence, the interesting findings of such studies should be complemented by additional historical research on the origins of spatial configurations, urban rhythms and associated spatiotemporal practices of violence and their long-term development. This includes aspects such as the shifting manifestations of power-relations in city-spaces, colonial and postcolonial spatial policies and their impact on segregation and mobility, changing forms of spatiotemporal religious practices, as well as the reconfigurations of space and urban rhythms through successive episodes of violence over time. This chapter contributes to filling this gap in research and provides a historical perspective on spatiotemporal studies of violence in Belfast and Jerusalem.

My analysis of the riots is based on reports by British commissions of enquiry that were set up to examine the detailed sequence of events, to analyse the underlying causes, and to provide recommendations for avoiding future episodes of violence. The reports usually include in-depth descriptions of the urban space and the ways in which the rioters made use of it. The commissions convened in the form of a court of law and their reports include appendices with documents presented to the commission as well as minutes of evidence from the examination of witnesses, representing all communities and classes. This offers insights into their viewpoints and their perceptions of the riots, albeit with undeniable limitations due to the intimidating setting and the methods of questioning, such as cross-examinations. Furthermore, I use archival records, historical maps and newspaper articles. Apart from the minutes of evidence and newspapers, most of the sources provide the perspective of the British Empire and their local proxies but not the view of the historical actors who participated in the riots, so they must be interpreted with due caution.

In what follows, I first outline the theoretical concepts and approaches I use for my analysis, particularly Lefebvre's thoughts on rhythmanalysis. On that basis, I work with the historical sources to demonstrate how spatiotemporal (re-)configurations of both cities, also driven by British imperial perceptions of religious communities and related urban planning policies, produced and shaped practices of violence in Belfast and Jerusalem. I then show the ways in which violence became synchronised with emerging annual calendars and religious and mundane urban rhythms but also transformed and disrupted these rhythms. Thereafter, I explain how the successive riots accelerated urban reconfigurations and, by imbuing space with memories of violence, altered imaginations of (sacralised) space and time. In the conclusion, I point out the similarities and differences of the riots in Belfast and Jerusalem and highlight how the successive riots established long-term patterns of violence, which are characterised by the spatiotemporal particularities of the cities. The recurrent riots generated an accelerated 'urban pulse' infused with violence that still beats in both Belfast and Jerusalem to this day.

The spatiotemporality of violence

Henri Lefebvre advocates in his works to think of space (and time) as something 'lived' that is continuously produced, appropriated, transformed and reproduced through social practices of individual and collective actors (Lefebvre, 1991a). He characterises social space as an integral part of the everyday, consisting of 'a relatively dense fabric of network and channels' (Lefebvre, 1991b: 231–2). In this chapter, I draw on his notion of a 'spatial triad', consisting of 'perceived space', meaning actual and concrete space that is produced and appropriated through spatial practices that structure lived reality (Lefebvre, 1991a: 38); 'conceived space', which is conceptualised and abstract space that is objectified and pervaded by ideologies, knowledge and power (Lefebvre, 1991a: 33, 38–9, 42); and 'lived space', which is social space as it is passively experienced in the everyday through symbols and images on a physical, intellectual and emotional level (Lefebvre, 1991a: 39).

These ideas are useful when thinking about urban violence as a spatial practice that utilises, appropriates and reconfigures space on a physical and imaginary level while at the same time being shaped by perceptions of space, which are in turn influenced by imperial, religious or nationalist conceptualisations of space and embedded power hierarchies. Edward Said argued in *Orientalism* that space is charged with imperial inscriptions, constructions of the other and projections of counter-images (Said, 1981). This is true for the British perception not only of Palestine but also of Ireland, to which British officials likewise applied an orientalist and paternalistic perspective (Doyle, 2016: 6, 38–9, 80–2).

Spatial practices of violence are frequently subject to a specific timing and pacing, e.g. during the night or adjusting to the patterns of police patrols. They are influenced by not only spatial but also temporal imaginations and perceptions, for example regarding memories of violence imbued within urban space or regarding sacralised space, with its inherent temporal relation to eternity. Moreover, conceived space is very much informed by temporalities, especially when they are created in imperial contexts, which may assume slower rhythms of life in supposedly backward 'traditional' societies as opposed to purportedly accelerated 'modern' ones.[1] Furthermore, religious and nationalist imaginations connect spaces with a long-distant or imagined past when imbuing them with meaning through myths and rituals. In this way, various imaginings and visions can be associated with a space over time or in the case of contested space, simultaneously. As Merrifield phrases it vis-à-vis the hyper-complexity of Lefebvre's notion of space: the interpenetrations of (and within) spaces, with their different temporalities, 'get superimposed on one another in a *present* space; different layers of time are inscribed in the built landscape' (Merrifield, 2006: 105; italics in original).

Considering urban violence, I think it is rather fitting that Lefebvre describes spaces as alive, using terms of movements, rhythms, flows and waves. Spaces are 'traversed by myriad currents', colliding and interfering with other spaces (Lefebvre, 1991a: 87–8). Thinking of space and time together, as living and in motion with different rhythms and tempi, led me to introduce the term 'urban pulse of violence' as a metaphor here. It expresses the entirety and interplay of the flows of everyday life and religious and political rhythms of a city and their interconnectedness with collective violence, thereby endowing the violence with a kind of regularity. The recurring riots can be described as a pulse that palpitates quickly or slowly in synchronisation with public agitation, even becoming dangerously accelerated during the height of conflict with the potential risk of leading to a collapse. The metaphor of the pulse is particularly suitable for an analysis of violence, as the first is a bodily function and the latter a bodily practice.

The notion of an 'urban pulse' can also be connected to the recent work on 'affective atmospheres' by Sara Fregonese (2017), who focuses on the lived experiences of conflict escalation and de-escalation in Beirut after the armed conflict of May 2008. She applies the concept of 'affective atmospheres' (Anderson, 2009) to urban conflicts, and advocates for a new research approach on atmospheric urban geopolitics. This centres on the importance of built environments 'as shared grounds from which affective atmospheres of conflict (de-)escalation propagate and/or are made to propagate' (Fregonese, 2017: 8) as well as on the intensities of feeling of the (collective) residents of urban spaces. Based on their everyday experiences, in which intangible atmospheres 'feed into spatial knowledges that are situated and embodied', the residents develop and utilise 'a "know-how" of the intangible sides of urban conflict' (Fregonese, 2017: 1–2). This line of thought is quite similar to my notion of an 'urban pulse of violence' in that both refer to the (historical) actors' everyday rhythms and the ways in which they navigate urban space, which can be altered during times of conflict.

Central for the analysis in this chapter is the term 'rhythm', which expresses a specific arrangement of spatial and temporal relations, especially regarding movements. It includes information on a specific order of things, consisting of temporal repetitions, differences and shifts. Rhythms regulate velocities and define the chronological order or succession of people, objects, acts and artefacts in their temporal and spatial frames (Stahl et al., 2018: 1–2). A rhythm has its own temporality, which may or may not harmonise with other rhythms, and is connected to a specific spatiality (a location or movement) (Rau, 2018: 18). Another significant concept for the analysis of rhythms is 'clocking', the measurement of the pace at which something occurs. The clocking of a rhythm supposes a predictable repeatability of specific processes and creates at least the impression of symmetry, regularity and traceability (Stahl et al., 2018: 2–3).

Lefebvre also uses the notions of isorhythmic (similar, homogeneous), polyrhythmic (different, heterogeneous), eurhythmic (different but phased with each other) and arrhythmic (different and not phased with each other) in his writings about rhythms and everyday life (Lefebvre, 2004: 16, 67–8). Cities by their very nature are polyrhythmic, with a plethora of different, even conflicting, rhythms coexisting and forming what I call the pulse of a city. This can but does not have to be a eurhythmic coexistence, with the different rhythms creating a mainly harmonious unity. During periods of violence, however, the urban rhythms are disrupted, and everyday city life becomes arrhythmic. From the perspective of the inhabitants, the regular flow of time in the city breaks down and spatiotemporal patterns of movement have to be adjusted to the violent circumstances, thereby creating a new accelerated pulse.

Considering social time, Lefebvre emphasised the opposition between cyclic and linear processes and time scales and their relativeness. While cyclic time scales are related to natural, cosmic and bodily rhythms, linear time scales can be continuous or discontinuous and are related to social practice and human activity (Lefebvre, 2004: 8). By looking at different periodicities and their relations as well as the relatively fast or slow 'tempo' of each group that 'varies between work and everyday life outside work', he proposes a 'sociological rhythmanalysis' to 'develop a theory of the multiplicity of social time scales' (Lefebvre, 1991b: 231–2). Lefebvre developed rhythmanalysis as a tool to study patterns of movement in urban spaces, thereby combining aspects of temporalities and spatialities. Rhythmanalysis allows for a study of rhythms of public and private spaces as well as the sacral and the mundane spheres and how they are connected and interrelated (Rau, 2018: 10, 18).

I draw on some of the key concepts of Lefebvre's 'rhythmanalysis' and apply them to the context of urban violence in Belfast and Jerusalem. Of particular importance is his notion of repetition and difference of social rhythms – and how the former produces the latter. Although repetition is a defining feature of a rhythm, it does not characterise it fully, as there are always other elements at play (Lefebvre, 2004: 6). This not only applies to everyday life but also to rituals and ceremonies, which are specifically built upon repetition. Lefebvre created more binary oppositions as analytical instruments for rhythmanalysis. Next to the central notions of cyclical and linear as well as repetition and difference, there are the oppositions of mechanical and organic, continuous and discontinuous, as well as quantitative and qualitative rhythms (Lefebvre, 2004: 6, 8–9), which are useful when analysing rhythms of everyday life in cities and how they may be in sync with or disrupted by violence. However, rhythms are often not only one or the other but both at the same time, e.g. they can include repetition and difference simultaneously (Rau, 2018: 15). Measurement is another core term in Lefebvre's rhythmanalysis. When analysing rhythms, we must measure them to be able to tell something about them. He suggests focusing on three aspects of rhythms for measuring: speed, frequency and consistency (Lefebvre, 2004: 10), all of which can successfully be applied to rhythms of urban violence.

The transformation of urban space-time and the production of violence

In Belfast and Jerusalem, the reconfiguration of urban space during the late nineteenth and early twentieth centuries was a result of the rapid growth and changing composition of the population, which was linked to processes of migration, urbanisation and, especially in the case of Belfast, industrialisation. The previously small Protestant port city in the north of Ireland grew extensively in the nineteenth century. It contributed to Britain's rise as a principal imperial naval power with its shipyards, rope-making shops and linen mills. The required workforce facilitated the influx of many Catholics, also because of the rural exodus during the Great Famine. Consequently, the sectarian composition of Belfast's inhabitants dramatically changed within a short time, although Protestants always remained the majority (Boal, 2002; Hepburn, 2004: 163–4). However, the formation of a considerable Catholic minority in Belfast fuelled Orangeism and Anti-Catholicism, which were important factors in the deterioration of communal relations (Farrell, 2000: 129). Conflicts between the communities began early in the nineteenth century and the first riot with fatalities occurred in 1813, sparked by a parade of the Orange Order (Hepburn, 2004: 164–5). After that, a process of residential segregation commenced that intensified with each successive riot and eased slightly during less violent phases. Two distinctively Protestant and Catholic working-class areas emerged, the Sandy Row and the Pound District, respectively, which became the main riot-spaces of the city by the mid-nineteenth century.[2]

The conflicts were also generated by fierce competition for work and a severe scarcity of affordable living space, as the working-class areas in the city did not expand rapidly enough to keep up with the population growth. This led to massive overcrowding, inadequate sanitary conditions and low life expectancy. A contemporary source describes the housing conditions of the working-class areas in 1852:

> Indeed, as regards the tenements of the poor, the tendency to crowd them
> into the smallest space is so great ... . The great majority of the poorer class
> of houses in this town consist of four rooms in two storeys. These are gener-
> ally occupied by two families. ... Such a house is manifestly insufficient to be
> the domicile of ten individuals; but we have known, and not unfrequently, so
> many as eighteen or even twenty persons sleeping within such limited apart-
> ments. (Malcolm, 1973 [1852]: 158)

Consequently, houses of the 'others' within territory primarily claimed by
one community became a main target for violence during the riots. The
Presbyterian minister and Irish Nationalist politician Isaac Nelson stated
about the riots of 1864:

> [F]or these four ... melancholy nights my Protestant neighbours remained up,
> wandering round the houses, playing 'The Protestant Boys' and 'The Boyne
> Water' [...]. I saw that crowd come up to the houses of four poor members
> of the Latin Church. ... I saw the furniture broken to pieces on the floor, and
> I saw the houses, as you express it, gutted. [...] The mobs in my neighbour-
> hood not only hunted poor Roman Catholic neighbours out of their houses,
> but I had to go and beseech them to grant so many hours to these poor people
> to take their furniture out of the places. I had also to go and get horses and
> carts to remove the furniture, and I had a great deal to do to repress the vio-
> lence of the mob. (Minutes of Evidence, Belfast Commission, 1865: 271, par.
> 10836–7)

The attacks on houses included their inhabitants, who were often pelted
with stones by several hundred assailants while having to escape their home
perilously, such as the family of Catholic publican John Riordan during the
riots of 1886. They 'had to get out through a sky-light, and they suffered
very severely, having been attacked with stones on the roofs of the houses'
(Report Belfast, Minutes of Evidence, 1887: 496, par. 14048). The wrecking of houses served the purpose of further homogenising and sectarianising
territory and resulted from the rapid changes in the spatiotemporal configuration of the city in the nineteenth century. It was a consistently used
practice of violence, conducted rapidly and very frequently; Riordan's house
was attacked five times in 1886. It became closely linked to riots in Belfast,
especially in the early 1920s[3] and during the Troubles.

Although Jerusalem did not undergo a process of industrialisation like
Belfast, it also grew rapidly in the second half of the nineteenth century,
expanding beyond its city walls. The New City consisted of mixed and
exclusively Jewish neighbourhoods, in which immigrants from Europe
of the Zionist Aliyoth (immigration of Jews from the diaspora to Eretz
Israel) settled (Campos, 2011: 16–17; Naïli, 2018: 10). After the defeat of
the Ottoman Empire in World War I and the occupation of Jerusalem by

General Edmund Allenby in December 1917, the British implemented radical changes in urban planning. In the 'Western' imagination, Jerusalem's Old City was divided into four religious quarters as depicted on numerous maps from the 1860s on. These maps were representations of places rather than of people and did not describe the demographic reality of a more heterogeneous population and a division into seven administrative neighbourhoods (Lemire, 2013: 26–30; al-ʿAref, 1951). Nonetheless, the maps corresponded with the British policy of dividing the population along religious lines while ignoring other dominant identity frames, such as social class, Ottoman citizenship or shared Arab urban culture (Campos, 2011: 5–11; Tamari, 2000: 23–4). Sir Ronald Storrs, the first British governor of Jerusalem (1918–26) and an ardent Christian Zionist, strove to preserve and restore the 'holy character' of the Old City, which allegedly had been diluted by Ottoman urban modernisations and the structural developments of a living city. Pursuing a 'sanctification' of Jerusalem, he founded the Pro-Jerusalem Society as an instrument for realising his romanticised vision of the city and weakening secular institutions such as the municipal council established in late Ottoman times (Mazza, 2018: 409; Naïli, 2018: 10–11; for more details on the urban planning initiatives of Storrs and the British Mandate authorities see the chapter by Mazza in this volume).

The British designated the New City as the 'modern', productive centre of Jerusalem while the Old City was intended to have a timeless and tranquil atmosphere, discounting the bustling rhythms of everyday life in its mixed residential and commercial neighbourhoods. The reshaping of the notion of urban space (Mazza, 2009: 163–5) was accompanied by the imposition of orientalist-infused imaginations of time that promoted further divisions between the communities, such as in this disparaging description of Palestinian peasants by the military officers of the commission of enquiry in 1920: 'The fellah is extremely backward in his methods and apathetic and slow in his intelligence: a reasonable inoculation with the vigorous mental force of the Jew would be invaluable in the development of the country and the people' (TNA, WO 32/9614, 1920: 15). By stylising the Palestinians as retrograde and subjugated to the supposedly slow rhythms of oriental life, the British constructed the Zionist immigrants as a counter-image, bringing with them capitalist modes of production and the acceleration of modernity. While this construction of opposing others falls in the category of orientalist stereotypes, the British also changed the rhythms of Jerusalem by implementing their dominant modernity through new bureaucratic procedures and security routines. As Lefebvre would have put it (2004: 14), they actually did imprint a new rhythm on this era.

Changes in the spatiotemporal configuration also shaped violent practices over time. The Haram al-Sharif/Temple Mount area is an instructive example in this regard. One has to keep in mind that the current spatial arrangement is very different from the Mandate era. Today, the area in front of the Wall is a huge town square of 20,000 m², the Western Wall Plaza, built directly after Israel's victory in the Six-Day War of 1967, when the Wall became accessible to Jews for the first time in 19 years.[4] In Ottoman and Mandate times, the space available for Jewish worshippers in front of the Wall was only a narrow street 3.35 m wide, measuring in total about 100 m². Directly behind the worshippers were houses of the Mughrabi Quarter and the small street was in daily use by their residents (Report Palestine, 1930: 27–8, 31). The narrowness of the contested space presented opportunities for daily provocations such as the throwing of garbage at the Wall from the houses. Harry Sacher, a prominent Zionist leader, describes the commotion of daily life in front of the Wall and uses it as evidence against the claim of the Muslims that the Wall – revered as the place where Muhammad had tethered up his horse Buraq before his celestial Night Journey – was also of importance as a sacralised space for them: 'So little sanctity do the Moslems attach to this area that ... they are in the habit of driving donkey carts laden with dung across the pavement immediately in front of the Wall where the Jews pray' (TNA, CO 733/160/19, 1929; for the importance of the wall in Jewish and Muslim religious thought see the chapter by Mazza in this volume).

From the mid-1920s, the conflict over ownership of and access to sacralised places in Jerusalem increased continuously as both groups transformed sacralised space into the object of nationalist aspirations. Hajj Amin al-Husseini, Grand Mufti of Jerusalem, enhanced his reputation in the Islamic world by pursuing the restoration and decoration of the Haram compound (Krämer, 2002: 261). Several building projects near the Wall led to a spatiotemporal reconfiguration of the area, especially the opening of a passage and the construction of a flight of stone steps leading from the Haram compound to the pavement in front of the Wall. This effectively transformed the cul-de-sac into a thoroughfare, changing the rhythms of daily life in this place of Jewish prayer. Moreover, the transformation of a building in the street into a *zāwiyah*, from where a muezzin called to prayer, and of another directly above in the Haram area, where the ceremony of *dikr* was held while music was played repeatedly, was regarded as a provocation by Jewish organisations (Report Palestine, 1930: 32–3, 39). These religious rituals constitute a spatiotemporal practice that symbolically appropriates space and time by creating a soundscape with a significant radius within a religiously contested space, thereby disturbing Jewish worship at the Wall.

The British recognised the complaints by the Zionist organisations and stipulated:

> If the erection of the new building results in the observance of Moslem rites in the presence of Jewish worshippers or in an invasion by Moslems during the customary times of Jewish worship as to cause genuine annoyance or disturbance, this would amount to an interference with existing rights. ... In accordance with this opinion, His Excellency has informed the President of the Supreme Muslim Council that the work on the building, which has been suspended, may be resumed on the conditions that the wall in the lane leading to the Bab El Mughrabi of the Haram area is built up to its former height, and that no annoyance or disturbance is caused to Jewish worshipers during the customary times of their prayer. ... [W]hile there is no objection to an opening being made in that wall which will give access from the lane to the building, there must be no incursion of Moslems into the pavement during the customary times of Jewish worship, and no other act calculated to cause annoyance. (Palestine Commission, Evidence Vol. 1, 1930: 281, par. 7486)

This quote offers insights into the British policy of dividing not only urban space but also time among the religious communities. Careful consideration is made to adhere to the status quo in safeguarding the religious rights of each group while trying to avoid conflicts between them. Muslims as well as Jews are preferably to remain in separate spaces, especially avoiding disturbances during precisely assigned time periods. This increased the spatial and temporal separation of the communities in the city.

The synchronisation of violence with the annual calendar and urban rhythms

The industrialisation of Belfast in the Victorian era not only reconfigured the urban space but also initiated a profound transformation of temporalities by introducing a new time-discipline characterised by capitalist modes of production (Thompson, 1967). This led to a more precise and small-scale time measurement, subjugating the rhythms of daily life to the pacing set by the work shifts in the factories and docksides. The speed of the urban rhythms was significantly increased, and their frequencies and consistencies aligned with the requirements of industrialised production. The 'mechanic' rhythms of the linen mills altered the everyday rhythms of the city's inhabitants and superimposed themselves on the needs of the 'organic' rhythms of the body. This new urban pulse also influenced the rhythms of violence during periods of unrest. A common trait of all the riots of that time is their general correspondence with the cycle of day and night, in accordance with the work shifts. It is noteworthy that in the working-class areas, adolescents had the same daily cycles as adults, as they started working in the mills and shipyards at a very early age. Violence usually commenced in the evening hours when the workers returned in groups from the port and the mills and traversed through working-class areas of the city inhabited by the other group. Often, the violence continued until the early hours of the next morning, culminating in attacks on workers who were back on their way to their workplaces. This reveals a spatiotemporal pattern of violence in sync with the work shifts and also linked to the spatial configuration of the city. For example, in the report about the riots in 1864, the commissioners state:

> Within an hour after the Mayor left [around 8 p.m.], Belfast was in violent commotion. Rioting of a serious character took place in Durham-street, where the opposing mobs again came into collision. [...] Not only there, but in many of the surrounding streets, rioting was going on actively, and continued for hours, the constabulary doing their best to check it, and making several arrests, in effecting which they were badly assaulted. The millworkers, Protestant and Roman Catholic, proceeding to their several mills at 5.30, A.M., were attacked as they passed respectively through the Pound or Sandy-row district, both by their own and of the other sex. Houses of both Protestants and Roman Catholics, in several parts of the town, were wrecked. (Report Belfast, 1865: 9–10)

Another way in which violence was synchronised with daily work rhythms was the IRA bombings of clearly labelled shipyard trams, bringing Protestant workers to and from their workplaces, and the retaliation shootings of Catholic workers in trams by Loyalist gunmen (Parkinson, 2004: 181). This disruption of the daily rhythms of commuting, one of the central practices of violence during the period of civil unrest in Belfast in 1920–22, was again extensively used during the Troubles and is still a form of political violence in the city today, when Translink buses are hijacked and burned with petrol-bombs.

Violence also synchronises with daily and weekly religious rhythms when huge crowds of people gather for services and prayers, which are sometimes used for incendiary sermons and laments. In Jerusalem, riots often commenced after noon prayer (*ṣalāt aẓ-ẓuhr*) or Friday prayer (*ṣalāt al-jumuʿah*) at the Al-Aqsa Mosque (Report Palestine, 1930: 51, 54–5; Report Palestine, 1934: 91, 102–3). In Belfast, the spatiotemporal practice of open-air preaching on Sundays by firebrand Protestant preachers had a huge impact on the riots (Albrecht, 2022). The commission report of the riots in Belfast of 1857 points out:

> In Belfast, for many years, open-air preaching has been practised by the Presbyterian clergy and Wesleyan Methodists. This practice hitherto was never regarded as a matter of offence by any party; and it is regretted ... that the practice of open-air preaching became almost necessarily in the public mind

connected with the celebration of the last 12th of July festival, and as a new means for its further celebration. [...] This year, for the first time, a new and unusual step was taken by the clergy of the Established Church. During the riots in July ... a series of open-air sermons were to be preached at the Custom-house situate[d] at one of the greatest thoroughfares in Belfast, on each suc-ceeding Sunday; and the first clergyman named as preacher was the Rev. Mr. M'Ilwaine ... well known in Belfast as [a] controversial preacher. [...] [T]he matter became mixed up as part of the celebration of the 12th of July festival; and its effect was to shift the scene of rioting from its peculiar districts, and to involve in riot and outrage the best parts of town, which before that time were peaceable and orderly. (Report Belfast, 1858: 11–12)

The quote underlines that by exploiting the spatiotemporal makeup of the city, open-air preaching was intended to be done at public places at a time of the day when many of the inhabitants of the city were passing by, with the purpose of reaching a wider audience including Catholics, who could be offended with the anti-Papalist content of the sermon. The preachers instrumentalised the weekly rhythm of religious service for political purposes and thereby marked a weekly pulse to which the violence was synchronised. The British Government was well aware of the effect street-preaching had on triggering unrest in Belfast and intended to prohibit the practice (National Archive of Ireland, CSORP/1857/6165, 1857). However, the infamous Rev. Hugh 'Roaring' Hanna opposed the initiative and repeatedly used this and other provocative religious practices during later times of unrest, e.g. politicised Sunday School excursions in 1886 (Belfast Riots Commission, 1887: 10–12, 16).

Although violence synchronises with urban rhythms, it also changes and disrupts them. Collective violence in modern history is frequently connected with social movements, e.g. labour movements and collective social action such as strikes, boycotts and demonstrations. General strikes are of par-ticular interest, as they completely suspend rhythms of everyday urban life. They were repeatedly used as a form of protest in Mandatory Palestine and also after the founding of the state of Israel. In 1933, a strike and a rally of six to seven thousand Arab Palestinians turned into a riot, which triggered further violence in other cities as well as Jerusalem itself. The report on the riots highlights the total standstill of public life: 'On the 8th October, 1933, the Palestine Arab Executive Committee decided that a "general strike", which in Palestine implies the cessation of business, the closing of shops and the stoppage of public transport, should be held on the 13th October and that on that day a large demonstration should be made in Jerusalem' (Report Palestine, 1934: 90).

Of even greater significance was the general strike in Palestine between April and October 1936, which totally disrupted and changed daily rhythms in Jerusalem for about six months and gradually led to the 1936–39 Arab

Revolt. The 'Palestine Royal Commission Report' points out that striking as an 'economic weapon' had been used before but compared to the earlier riots, 'the outbreak of 1936 overshadowed all its predecessors', especially with regard to the scope and duration of the strike (Palestine Report, 1937: 103–4). A member of the Second Battalion of the Lincolnshire Regiment who served in Palestine in 1936 describes the resurgence of public life in Jerusalem after the end of the strike:

> In Jerusalem the dramatic change since yesterday was evident from the moment of awakening this morning. The city, silent as a town of the dead for the past six months, had suddenly resumed its normal busy, noisy life. The air was filled with the cries of street hawkers, mingled with the sound of cranking motors. For the first time since April Jewish buses were running without escort, maintaining regular services to all parts of the city. ... In the old city the transformation was even more striking. I entered it just after special prayers had ended in the Mosque of Akhsa [sic]. It was quite pleasant, after so long an absence of these features, to be jostled by donkeys, nearly knocked over by goats, importuned by peddlers, and drenched by water sellers as one descended David-street. (The Lincolnshire Regiment, 1935–36)

Violence was also synchronised to the annual calendar, with its political and religious holidays. Since the early nineteenth century, riots in Belfast have been a regular occurrence on the festival of the 'Twelfth', the annual celebration of the victory of the Protestant King William of Orange over the Catholic King James II in the Battle of the Boyne in 1690. Up to the present day, the festival is a provocative demonstration of Protestant territorial dominance, with tens of thousands participating in parades that traverse through the entire city of Belfast, including contested and Catholic neighbourhoods. In the report on the riots of 1857, the commissioners described how the spatial separation between both groups intensified even in advance:

> The feeling which leads to the separation of these districts in July is merely a class feeling – it is a feeling of dominancy and insult on the one side, and of opposition to its display on the other; and the separation of these two districts into exclusive encampments appears to us to be little more than the preparation for the festivals of July, and the clearing out of the supposed supporters of the opposite classes to prepare the respective districts for the scenes which follow the celebration of these festivals. The state of these districts – the separation of them into classes, Orange and Catholic, has now existed for years; the 12th of July has always brought with it its Orange gatherings, its party displays, its consequent riots. (Report Belfast, 1858: 2)

This quote also reveals the establishment of a yearly pattern of violence in particular areas of Belfast well before 1857. It is important to add that while the linear repetition of the social practices of this annual celebration is a continuous rhythm that always produces heightened tensions, it does not necessarily generate large-scale riots, which appear to have a rather discontinuous rhythm. This can be explained by the production of difference through repetition. Certain new and unusual spatiotemporal elements have to be added to the regular procedure in order to trigger riots, e.g. the sermon by Dr Drew in Christ's Church to which the quote at the beginning of this chapter relates, or the coincidence with other conflictive events such as election days or Home Rule campaigns, which lead to gatherings of opposed groups in public spaces.

Likewise, there was a strong correlation between annual festivities and riots in Jerusalem as well. Tamir Sorek (2013) has highlighted that with the development of opposing nationalist movements in Palestine, new public holidays were created to galvanise nationalist sentiments and mobilise the masses. These include a Palestinian Martyr's Day and Balfour Day, celebrated by the Zionists in remembrance of the Balfour Declaration on 2 November. Arab demonstrations against British support of Zionism on that day in Jerusalem in 1921 turned into a riot (Filastin, 5 November 1921: 3; TNA, CO 733/54723, 1921). Religious holidays in particular were of significance for the annual calendar and generated an annual rhythm to which violence synchronised. The riots of April 1920 took place during the Nabi Musa pilgrimage, a Muslim religious festival that overlaps with Orthodox Easter and Jewish Passover celebrations (for more details see Albrecht, 2022 and the chapter by Mazza in this volume). The official enquiry into the riots stated that it was anticipated that the week would bring 'inevitable religious disorders' because of the concurrence of the three religious festivities and the route of the pilgrimage through Jaffa Gate instead of Damascus Gate, thereby also traversing predominantly Jewish neighbourhoods (TNA, WO 32/9614, 1920: 57–9). Another new aspect was the politicisation of the religious procession by Arab nationalist speeches given by prominent Palestinian politicians and intellectuals at Jaffa Gate. This also contributed to the rhythm of linear repetition of the annual religious festival in that year being disrupted by violence. This difference was produced by several aspects related to that specific moment in history: the San Remo conference later that month that was to decide the future of the former territories of the Ottoman Empire; the proposal of British Jew Herbert Samuel for future High Commissioner; the declaration of Faisal as king over the self-proclaimed Arab Kingdom of Syria (including Palestine),[5] and the growing tensions owing to British support of Zionist immigration.

The Wailing Wall riots of 1929, too, were mainly triggered by two events that took place on annual religious holidays. On the Jewish fast day of Tisha B'Av, when the first and second destructions of the Temple are mourned, Jewish youth groups organised a provocative and militaristic political demonstration through Jerusalem, including Muslim neighbourhoods in the Old City, which Arab eyewitnesses described as particularly aggressive (Ṭannūs, 1982: 131–2). A day later, on a Friday, the Muslim celebrations for the Birthday of the Prophet (Mawlid an-Nabī) ended in a counterdemonstration after mid-day prayer during which the participants used religious banners and shouted assertive religious slogans (Report Palestine, 1930: 46, 51–6). In both cases, the religious celebrations were instrumentalised for political purposes and accompanied by symbolic appropriations of space. In the case of the Jewish demonstration, the difference to the usual rhythm of religious gatherings on those annual mourning days was the provocative expression of their nationalist aspirations that were focused on the contested sacralised space. In projecting their secular nationalist visions on the Wall, they also referred to a distant past, when the Temple Mount was in Jewish possession, and an imagined future, when it was to be returned to the Jews.

The impact of violence and memory on the reshaping of urban space-time

The potency of remembering ancient Jewish history at sacralised sites as an instrument to promote the national aspirations and the religious visions of the Yishuv (Jewish inhabitants of Palestine) and the Jewish diaspora were also a factor in the riots of 1920. Statements by rabbis concerning the belonging of the Temple Mount to the Jews and the envisioning of a time when the temple would be rebuilt upon it were a cause for grave concern by Muslims with regard to their centuries-old possession of the Haram area (TNA, WO 32/9614, 1920: 34–6). Moreover, there were several attempts to buy the Wall and its surrounding areas (Mazza, 2021; Wasserstein, 1991: 227), including one with the support of Ronald Storrs, the British governor of Jerusalem, as later criticised in a letter by Hajj Amin al-Husseini to *The Times* (TNA, CO 733/160/19, 1929). The political instrumentalisation of messianic religious imaginations by the Zionists as well as the Evangelical Protestant elements in the British government induced fears on part of the Muslims of losing ownership of the Haram compound. The commission report of 1920 shows that the British were acutely aware of the volatility of these initiatives:

> The Moslems, however, will be inclined to look to the practical activities of the Zionist Commission and to suspect that the less spiritually minded among them may be tempted to hasten the fulfilment of prophesy. In view of the sanctity of the Haram in the eyes of the Moslems, such a suspicion is enough to fire not only the Moslems of Palestine; but the whole of Islam. (TNA, WO 32/9614, 1920: 36)

In the run-up to the riots of 1929, Zionists and Palestinian Arabs formed societies for promoting their territorial claims on sacralised space and fought symbolic battles in local and international newspapers to garner support for their cause. One of the statements of the Zionist Pro-Wailing Wall Committee also refers to Jewish history, evoking memories of past violence and sacrifice and focusing them on the Wall:

> Ye Jews, and national Jews in all parts of the world! Wake up and unite! Do not keep silent or rest in peace until the entire Wall has been restored to us! [...] Those of us who are here will not rest until that relic which has always been ours which had been sealed with the blood of scores of thousands of our children through two millennia and which has absorbed the tears of Israel for two thousand years, has been restored to us. Come to our help by co-operating in this just struggle for the Wall and triumph is sure to come. (*Do'ar ha-yom*, 12 August 1929)

This and similar statements highlight the importance of affective attachments to sacralised space in the conflict for territorial dominance over Jerusalem. The reclaiming of urban space by relating it to an ancient or imagined past is a spatiotemporal practice of particular relevance in Jerusalem until today. Through archaeological excavations such as the 'City of David' in Silwan, Palestinian-owned space is claimed, expropriated and preserved for the Jewish community by transforming it into cultural heritage sites, thereby ousting the local residents (Pullan, 2013a: 76–101). Similar, though often less well-organised initiatives are undertaken by the Palestinian authorities, for example by renovating the Marwani Mosque (the subterranean chambers below the al-Aqsa Mosque) (Pullan, 2013a: 35–6). These archaeological activities not only have the effect of seizing contested space for a particular group, but they also contribute to a one-sided process of sacralisation of urban history, in which claims to the eternal are made and the urban present is connected to an ancient past.

Urban space-time is not only figuratively charged by religious imaginations, but practices of violence at particular locations and at specific times also inscribe it with symbolic meaning. Streets and public places as well as certain dates of the calendar relate to violent events and become a spatiotemporal repository of past violence where the combatants of today not only literally walk in the footsteps of their predecessors (Makdisi and Silverstein, 2006: 9) but also follow the same rhythm of violence. In commemoration rituals and performances, the violent past of the city is remembered at specific locations or along the routes of parades and processions. The huge military spectacles by the Israeli state on the Wailing Wall Plaza (Pullan, 2013b), the flag parades on Jerusalem Day, or the annual celebrations on the 'Twelfth' in Belfast are striking examples of spatiotemporal practices that remember past violence and intertwine it with the urban space and the rhythms of the city not only on the physical but also the symbolic level (Albrecht, 2021). In collective ritual performances, the participants link the past with the present and project it into the future, thereby permanently reshaping the urban space-time, which is overlapped and overshadowed by past violence.

However, violence is not only remembered in grand spectacles but also in spatiotemporal practices of everyday life and associated narratives that are handed down from one generation to the next. Marc Doyle describes the personal memories of a Protestant inhabitant of Shankill Road in the 1920s, who remembers the danger of accompanying a funeral procession to Milltown Cemetery, because one had to pass through the Falls area (Doyle, 2009: 224–6). This fear was not triggered by the remembrance of some historic battle but by his own memories of the riots in Belfast from 1920 to 1922, in which whole areas of the city became characterised as unsafe with 'shootings, burnings, raids or hold-ups [taking] place almost daily' (Public Record Office of Northern Ireland, CAB 6/37, 1922: 3). As violence was a regular feature of Belfast from the early nineteenth century until the mid-1930s, with large-scale riots every ten to twenty years and smaller ones nearly every other year, memories of violence persisted and were passed down in stories, ballads and poems.

Certainly, violence transforms urban space-time not only through memories, but also through permanent reconfigurations of the actual space and urban rhythms, e.g. in processes of residential segregation and by enforced measures of separation. As mentioned before, the division of Jerusalem's Old City into Armenian, Christian, Jewish and Muslim quarters in Ottoman times was a projection of 'Western' imaginations that did not represent the demographic reality. In the Mandate era, however, the residential segregation of the Old City and Jerusalem as a whole became reality, not least because of the imperial perceptions and urban planning of the British (Pullan, 2013a: 14; Hepburn, 2004: 199). The violence in Jerusalem played a significant role in accelerating this process, with inhabitants being driven from their houses or resettling in other areas. A particular turning point was the riots of 1929, in which long-time neighbours murdered each other, generating a severe lack of trust between the communities (Jacobsen and Naor, 2016: 153–5; Cohen, 2015; Winder, 2012). In Belfast, the process of residential segregation had already begun in the early nineteenth century and was amplified with each of the subsequent riots. A practice of forced removal was established that was sometimes enforced with violence. The commission report for the riots of 1857 states:

> The Pound district has for many years been chiefly inhabited by a Roman
> Catholic population while Sandy-row district has been chiefly inhabited by

a population of Orangemen and Protestants. Until lately, however, there was some intermixture, a few Catholics resided in the Sandy-row district, and a few Protestants in the Pound district. Since the commencement of the late riots, however, the districts have become exclusive, and by regular systematised movements on both sides, the few Catholic inhabitants of the Sandy-row district have been obliged to leave it, and the few Protestant inhabitants of the Pound district have been also obliged to leave that locality. These removals were often kindly enough effected on both sides: friendly notices to quit were often given; and the extreme penalty for non-compliance – namely, the wrecking of the house – was, in many instances, not resorted to until the lapse of some time after such notice. (Report Belfast, 1858: 2)

In later riots at the end of the nineteenth and beginning of the twentieth century, the practice of forced removal was also employed in other working-class areas of the city. Over time, this process of segregation, with the destruction of houses occupied by members of the 'other' group, became a regular feature of unrest in the city and part of Belfast's culture of violence. In the Troubles, this process of separation along sectarian lines culminated in the construction of the 'Peace Walls' that divide Catholic and Protestant neighbourhoods and whose gates open only during specific hours of the day, thereby imposing a strict time-regime and dominating urban rhythms. Although this served the purpose of security, it created a geography of division and fear that is still very palpable and characterises the fabric of the city by connecting its urban present with a violent past.

Conclusion: The urban pulse of violence in Belfast and Jerusalem

The configuration and transformation of the space-time of Belfast and Jerusalem was very dissimilar. Sacral space and its politicisation played an enormous role in the conflict in Jerusalem, especially its intertwinement with notions of the celestial and eternal as well as its connection to an imagined past derived from scripture. While the everyday rhythms of Jerusalem also underwent significant changes that were imposed by British rule, the fast-paced industrialisation of Belfast, an important impetus for the expansion of the British Empire, created very specific spatiotemporal conditions for collective violence, e.g. a housing shortage and overcrowding. Moreover, the experience of time in Belfast was subject to a process of acceleration and compression, in which the 'mechanical' rhythms of capitalist production dominated the rhythms of daily life, thus creating a new urban pulse. During the riots, the rhythms of violence were aligned with the daily rhythms of work shifts and connected to the routes of the workers within the city-space.

What is striking, however, is the number of similarities between Belfast and Jerusalem, which I argue is mainly because of the importance of religious rhythms in connection with 'sectarian' violence in contested cities. Religious practices of prayer in their weekly repetitions often had a substantial impact on the unfolding of riots in both cities. Violence in Jerusalem frequently began after Friday prayers in the Haram al-Sharif compound in close proximity to the Wailing Wall. In Belfast, incendiary sermons in the open air or in churches on Sundays were relevant for different riots. Furthermore, public and religious holidays with processions and parades traversing through the cities and especially through contested space played an important role in triggering and shaping violence. These holidays are part of a yearly rhythm of linear repetition that corresponds with the cyclical repetition of seasons, e.g. the 'marching season' in Belfast from spring to summer. While rhythms of violence were often synchronised with these yearly, weekly and daily urban rhythms, an element of difference had to be introduced into the urban pulse as a catalyst for violence. In both Belfast and Jerusalem, the riots themselves also disrupted the polyrhythmic character of the cities, created arrhythmic conditions in public life and profoundly changed the practices of the everyday.

Since the riots of the late nineteenth and early twentieth centuries, the space-time of Belfast and Jerusalem has been transformed time and again by further episodes of collective violence. However, I have shown that the spatial and temporal foundations for later episodes of violence were created in the time period covered here. Specific spatiotemporal patterns of violence emerged that became part of the respective cultures of violence in both cities. In this regard, the memories of past violence serve as a repository for the historical actors of later eras and provide a repertoire of violent practices that are characterised by the spatial characteristics and urban rhythms of each city. The transformation of the space-time in both contexts generated a new urban pulse to which collective violence became synchronised. Times of conflict also disrupted rhythms of public and everyday life and could initiate new spatiotemporal reconfigurations, e.g. processes of residential segregation or spatiotemporal divisions. The orientalist perceptions of the British Empire and their impact on urban policies played a major role in the formation of Belfast and Jerusalem as divided and contested cities. Thus, further research on urban planning, policing strategies and the assessment of urban violence by the British Empire will be expedient.

Acknowledgement

The work on this chapter was partly conducted during a fellowship at the Humanities Center for Advanced Studies 'Religion and Urbanity: Reciprocal Formations', funded by the Deutsche Forschungsgemeinschaft (DFG,

German Research Foundation) – FOR 2779. I wish to express my sincere thanks for the helpful comments to this chapter, especially by Konstantin Akinsha, Jens-Uwe Hartmann, Raminder Kaur, Asuman Lätzer-Laser, Harry Maier, Shail Mayaram, Kieran Patel, Susanne Rau, Corinna Riva, Jörg Rüpke, Thomas Schader, Emiliano Urciuoli and Christina Williamson. Special thanks also go to Sabine Schmolinsky, who commented on an earlier version of the chapter.

Notes

1 Eisenstadt has highlighted that the binary opposition of traditional v. modern societies is a Eurocentric construction that assumes the European cultural programme as the only natural way of development. Instead of one, there are 'multiple modernities' (Eisenstadt, 2000).

2 The Pound district and its western extensions later became known as the Catholic Falls area. While the Protestant Sandy Row district is located to the southeast of the Pound district, the Protestant Shankill neighbourhood is located north of the Pound/Falls area. Both the Shankill and the Falls neighbourhoods became the centre spots for violence in the late nineteenth century and figured prominently in the Troubles (1968–1998) as well.

3 On Belfast's Bloody Sunday (10 July 1921) alone, about 200 houses were destroyed, most of them belonging to Catholics, leaving more than 1,000 people without a home (Parkinson, 2004: 154).

4 To build the plaza, the centuries old Mughrabi Quarter was demolished within only a few days, expelling its approximately 650 residents.

5 In this context, it is noteworthy that the Nabi Musa riots coincided with a phase of surging Arab nationalist activities in Jerusalem and were preceded by violent political demonstrations in February and March 1920 (Jacobson, 2011: 172–3).

Bibliography

al-ʿAlamī, A. (2000). *Thawrat al-Burāq [The Buraq Revolt]* (Jerusalem (?): n.p.).

Albrecht, M. (2022). 'Open-air preaching and a Muslim festival: Religious rituals, violence, and urban space in mid-19th century Belfast and early-20th century Jerusalem', *Religion and Urbanity: Reciprocal Formations Blog*, 3 August 2022, https://urbrel.hypotheses.org/3130 (accessed 2 October 2022).

Albrecht, M. (2021). 'Ritual performances and collective violence in divided cities – The riots in Belfast (1886) and Jerusalem (1929)', *Political Geography*, 86, 1–13.

Anderson, B. (2009). 'Affective atmospheres', *Political Geography*, 2:2, 77–81.

al-ʿAref, A. (1951). *Tārīkh al-Quds [The History of Jerusalem]* (al-Qahira: Dar al-Maʿarif).

'Balfour Day', *Filastin* (5 November 1921), p. 3.

Barakat, R. (2007). *Thawrat al-Buraq in British Mandate Palestine: Jerusalem, mass mobilization and colonial politics, 1928–1930.* (PhD Dissertation, University of Chicago).

Belfast Riots Commission, 1886. Report of the Belfast Riots Commissioners; P.P. 1887 [C. 4925] xviii.

Boal, F. (2002). 'Belfast: walls within', *Political Geography*, 21:5, 687–94.

Boyd, A. (1987). *Holy War in Belfast*. 3rd ed. (Belfast: Pretani).

Budge, I. and O'Leary, C. (1973). *Belfast, Approach to Crisis: A study of Belfast politics, 1613–1970* (London: Macmillan).

Campos, M. (2011). *Ottoman Brothers. Muslims, Christians, and Jews in early twentieth-century Palestine* (Stanford, CA: Stanford University Press).

Cohen, H. (2015). *1929: Year Zero of the Arab-Israeli conflict* (Waltham, MA: Brandeis University Press).

Cunningham, N. and Gregory, I. (2014). 'Hard to miss, easy to blame? Peacelines, interfaces and political deaths in Belfast during the Troubles', *Political Geography*, 40, 64–78.

Doyle, M. (2016). *Communal Violence in the British Empire: Disturbing the Pax* (London: Bloomsbury).

Doyle, M. (2009). *Fighting like the Devil for the sake of God: Protestants, Catholics and the origins of violence in Victorian Belfast* (Manchester: Manchester University Press).

Eisenstadt, S. N. (2000). *Die Vielfalt der Moderne* (Weilerswist: Velbrück).

Farrell, S. (2000). *Rituals and Riots: Sectarian violence and political culture in Ulster, 1784–1886* (Lexington: The University Press of Kentucky).

Fregonese, S. (2017). 'Affective atmospheres, urban geopolitics and conflict (de)escalation in Beirut', *Political Geography*, 61, 1–10.

Fuccaro, N. (ed.) (2016). *Violence and the City in the Modern Middle East* (Stanford, CA: Stanford University Press).

Hepburn, A. C. (2004). *Contested Cities in the Modern West* (Basingstoke: Palgrave Macmillan).

Hepburn, A. C. (1996). *A Past Apart: Studies in the history of Catholic Belfast, 1850–1950* (Belfast: Ulster Historical Foundation).

Hirst, C. (2002). *Religion, Politics and Violence in Nineteenth-century Belfast: The Pound and Sandy Row* (Dublin: Four Courts).

Holmes, J. (2002). 'The role of open-air preaching in the Belfast riots of 1857', *Proceedings of the Royal Irish Academy*, 102C:3, 47–66.

Hughes, M. (2010). 'From law and order to pacification: Britain's suppression of the Arab Revolt in Palestine, 1936–39', *Journal of Palestine Studies*, 39:2, 6–22.

Jacobson, A. (2011). *From Empire to Empire: Jerusalem between Ottoman and British rule*, Syracuse (NY: Syracuse University Press).

Jacobson, A. and Naor, M. (2016). *Oriental Neighbors: Middle Eastern Jews and Arabs in mandatory Palestine* (Waltham: Brandeis University Press).

Kelly, M. K. (2015). 'The revolt of 1936: A revision', *Journal of Palestine Studies*, 44:2, 28–42.

Krämer, G. (2002). *Geschichte Palästinas. Von der osmanischen Eroberung bis zur Staatsgründung Israels.* (3rd ed.) (München: Beck).

Lefebvre, H. (1991a). *The Production of Space* (Oxford: Blackwell).

Lefebvre, H. (1991b). *Critique of Everyday Life: Foundations for a sociology of the everyday*, vol. 2 (London/New York: Verso).

Lefebvre, H. (2004). *Rhythmanalysis: Space, time and everyday life* (London: Continuum).

Lemire, V. (2013). *Jérusalem 1900. La Ville sainte à l'âge des possibles* (Paris: Armand Colin).

The Lincolnshire Regiment, Second Battalion, On Special Service in Malta and Palestine, 19 September 1935–20 December 1936, www.thelincolnshireregiment. org/malta+palestine.shtml (accessed 9 October 2021).

Lindenberger, T. and Lüdtke, A. (1995). 'Einleitung: Physische Gewalt – eine Kontinuität der Moderne', in Lindenberger, T. and Lüdtke, A. (eds) *Physische Gewalt. Studien zur Geschichte der Neuzeit* (Frankfurt a. M.: Suhrkamp), 7–38.

Makdisi, U. and Silverstein, P. (2006). 'Introduction' in Makdisi, U. and Silverstein, P. (eds) *Memory and Violence in the Middle East and North Africa* (Bloomington/ Indianapolis, IN: Indiana University Press), 1–24.

Malcolm, A. G. (1973 [1852]): 'The Sanitary State of Belfast', in Public Records Office of Northern Ireland (ed.), *Problems of a Growing City: Belfast, 1780– 1870* (Belfast: PRONI), 156–61.

Mazza, R. (2021). 'The deal of the century? The attempted sale of the Western Wall by Cemal Pasha in 1916', *Middle Eastern Studies,* 57:5, 696–711.

Mazza, R. (2018). ' "The preservation and safeguarding of the amenities of the holy city without favour or prejudice to race or creed": The Pro-Jerusalem Society and Ronald Storrs, 1917–1920', in Dalachanis, A. and Lemire, V. (eds) *Ordinary Jerusalem, 1840–1940. Opening New Archives, Revisiting a Global City* (Leiden/ Boston, MA: Brill), 403–22.

Mazza, R. (2015). 'Transforming the holy city: From communal clashes to urban violence, the Nebi Musa riots in 1920' in Freitag, U., Fuccaro, N., Ghrawi, C., and Lafi, N. (eds) *Urban violence in the Middle East: Changing cityscapes in the transition from empire to nation state* (New York/Oxford: Berghahn), 179–94.

Mazza, R. (2009). *Jerusalem: From the Ottomans to the British* (London: I.B. Tauris).

McDermott, J. (2001). *Northern Divisions: The old IRA and the Belfast pogroms, 1920–22* (Belfast: Beyond the Pale Publications).

Merrifield, A. (2006). *Henri Lefebvre: A critical introduction* (New York/ London: Routledge).

Minutes of Evidence and Appendix to the Report of the Commissioners of Inquiry, 1864, Respecting the Magisterial and Police Jurisdiction Arrangements and Establishment of the Borough of Belfast; P.P. 1865 [3466] xxviii.

Naïli (2018). 'The de-municipalization of urban governance: Post-Ottoman political space in Jerusalem', *Jerusalem Quarterly*, 76, 8–13.

National Archive of Ireland, CSORP/1857/6165, 'Roaring Hanna', *The Morning Post, Belfast* (13 October 1857).

Nicault, C. (2000). Diplomatie et violence politique: Autour des troubles palestiniens de 1929', *Revue d'histoire moderne et contemporaine,* 47:1, 159–76.

O'Dowd, L. and McKnight, M. (2013). 'Urban intersections: Religion and violence in Belfast', *Space and Polity,* 17:3, 357–76.

Palestine Commission on the Disturbances of August, 1929. Volume I. Evidence heard during the 1st to 29th Sitting, Colonial No. 48 (London: H.M. Stationery Office, 1930).

Palestine Royal Commission Report, Presented by the Secretary of State for the Colonies to Parliament by Command of His Majesty; P.P. 1937 [Cmd. 5479].

Parkinson, A. F. (2004). *Belfast's Unholy War: The Troubles of the 1920s* (Dublin: Four Courts).

Parkinson, A. F. (2010). 'Belfast's unholy war: The 1920s 'Troubles' in Parkinson, A. F. and Phoenix, É. (eds) *Conflicts in the North of Ireland, 1900–2000: Flashpoints and fracture zones* (Dublin: Four Courts Press), 70–85.

Popitz, H. (1986). *Phänomene der Macht* (Mohr: Tübingen).

Porath, Y. (1977). *The Palestinian Arab National Movement, 1929–1939: From riots to rebellion* (London/Totowa, NJ: Frank Cass).

Public Record Office of Northern Ireland, CAB 6/37, Transcript of a Meeting of the Prime Minister and the Minister of Home Affairs of Northern Ireland with a Delegation of Magistrates, Belfast, 16 May 1922.

Pullan, W., Sternberg, M., Kyriakou, L., Larkin, C., Dumper, M. (eds) (2013a). *The Struggle for Jerusalem's Holy Places* (London/New York: Routledge).

Pullan, W. (2013b). 'Bible and gun: Militarism in Jerusalem's holy places', *Space and Polity*, 17:3, 335–56.

Pullan, W. and Gwiazda, M. (2010). 'The development of modern sacred geography: Jerusalem's Holy Basin', *Conflict in Cities and the Contested State*. Working paper no. 19, Cambridge: Centre for Urban Conflict Research.

Rau, S. (2018). 'Rhythmusanalyse nach Lefebvre', in Stahl, H., Hitzke, D., and Schmolinsky, S. (eds) *Taktungen und Rhythmen. Raumzeitliche Perspektiven interdisziplinär* (Berlin/Boston, MA: De Gruyter Oldenbourg), 9–24.

Report of the Belfast Riots Commissioners. Minutes of Evidence and Appendices; P.P. 1887 [C. 4925-I] xviii.

Report of the Commission appointed by His Excellency the High Commissioner for Palestine by Notification No. 1561, *Palestine Gazette* (7 February 1934), 87–106.

Report of the Commissioners of Inquiry into the Origin and Character of the Riots in Belfast in July and September, 1857; together with Minutes of Evidence and Appendix; P.P. 1858 [2309] xxvi.

Report of the Commission on the Palestine Disturbances of August, 1929; P.P. 1930 [Cmd. 3530] xvi.

Report of the Commissioners of Inquiry, 1864, Respecting the Magisterial and Police Jurisdiction Arrangements and Establishment of the Borough of Belfast; P.P. 1865 [3466] xxviii.

Rokem, J., Weiss, C. M., and Miodownik, D. (2018). 'Geographies of violence in Jerusalem: The spatial logic of urban intergroup conflict', *Political Geography*, 66, 88–97.

Said, E. (1981). *Orientalismus* (Frankfurt/Main: Ullstein).

Segev, T. (2002). *One Palestine, Complete: Jews and Arabs under the British Mandate* (London: Abacus).

Sorek, T. (2013). 'Calendars, martyrs, and Palestinian particularism under British rule', *Journal of Palestine Studies*, 43:1, 6–23.

Springer, S. and Le Billon, P. (2016). 'Violence and space: An introduction to the geographies of violence', *Political Geography*, 52, 1–3.

Stahl, H., Hitzke, D., and Schmolinsky, S. (2018). 'Taktungen und Rhythmen. Einleitung', in Stahl, H., Hitzke, D., and Schmolinsky, S. (eds) *Taktungen und Rhythmen. Raumzeitliche Perspektiven interdisziplinär* (Berlin/Boston, MA: De Gruyter Oldenbourg), 1–8.

'Statement by Pro-Wailing Wall Committee', *Do'ar ha-yom* (12 August 1929).

Stewart, A. T. Q. (1977). *The Narrow Ground: Aspects of Ulster, 1609–1969* (London: Faber & Faber).

Swedenburg, T. (1995). *Memories of Revolt: The 1936–1939 rebellion and the Palestinian national past* (Minneapolis: University of Minnesota Press).

Tamari, S. (2000). 'Jerusalem's Ottoman modernity: The times and lives of Wasif Jawhariyyeh, *Jerusalem Quarterly*, 9, 5–27.

Ṭannūs, ʿI. (1982). *al-Filastīnīyūn: māḍin maǧīd wa-mustaqbal bāhir [The Palestinians: A noble past and a glorious future]* (Bairut: Markaz al-Abḥāṯ. Munaẓẓamat at-Taḥrir al-Filasṭīnīya).

TNA (The National Archives). London, WO 32/9614, Report of the Court of Enquiry into the Riots in Jerusalem during Last April, Jerusalem, 1920.

TNA (The National Archives). London, CO 733/54723, Report on Disturbance in Jerusalem, 3 November 1921.

TNA (The National Archives). London, CO 733/163/4, Telegram from The Zionist Organisation, Central Office, London to the Colonial Office, 19 August 1929.

TNA (The National Archives). London, CO/733/160/19, File Containing Documents Relating to Wailing Wall, 1928–29.

Thompson, E. P. (1967). 'Time, work-discipline and industrial capitalism', *Past & Present*, 38:1, 56–97.

Tilly, C. (2003). *The Politics of Collective Violence* (Cambridge: Cambridge University Press).

Wasserstein, B. (1991). *The British in Palestine: The mandatory government and the Arab-Jewish conflict 1917–1929* (2nd ed.). (Oxford: Blackwell).

Weinhauer, K. (2010). 'Youth crime, urban spaces, and security in Germany since the 19th Century', *Historical Social Research*, 35:4, 86–101.

Weinhauer, K. and Ellerbrock, D. (2013). 'Perspektiven auf Gewalt in europäischen Städten seit dem 19. Jahrhundert', *IMS*, 2, 5–20.

Winder, A. (2012). 'The "Western Wall" riots of 1929: Religious boundaries and communal violence', *Journal of Palestine Studies*, 42:1, 6–23.

Part III

Memories and (religious) imaginations:

Representations of urban violence

7

Beirut's violence palimpsest: Urban transformations, mnemonic spaces and socio-temporal practices

Christine Mady

Introduction

Beirut's geopolitical position and consociational government allowed external influences to affect its politics, at times resulting in violent conflicts, along with internal factors related to different sectarian perspectives. There are numerous recollections and histories narrating these violent events from multiple perspectives, or in other words, memories representing images of urban violence similar to other contexts. Forde (2022) for example refers to the interplay between violence and space and how one could lead to the other in Cape Town, and Ristic (2014) links between violence and social implications in Sarajevo. However, few references offer a mapping of temporal and spatial manifestations of violence and address the impact of these mnemonic spaces on everyday social practices. The systematic mapping of Beirut's violence in space-time would require a project including archival research and recording reminiscences (oral history). This chapter can only be a trigger, as it builds on the notion of the palimpsest as an investigative tool to reveal the spatiotemporal intertwining of emerging and disappearing traces of violence (Marshall et al. 2017; Berger and Seiffert, 2014; Huyssen, 2006 in Pirker et al. 2019: 2). The chapter presents Beirut's violence palimpsest, which serves to study the impact of mnemonic spaces and violence with its markers at various scales including Greater Beirut, administrative Beirut, its districts, sectors, streets and buildings. Implications for urban transformations and social practices are then examined. This approach to analysing violence in space-time lends itself to applications in other contexts and experiences in relation to crime, discrimination, segregation and exclusion.

The palimpsestic approach

The palimpsest refers to 'erasure and overlap in order to denominate practices of transforming cultural memory.' (Pirker et al., 2019: 2). It captures 'material traces of the past embedded in everyday surroundings', and is an urban exploration of memory layers that give significance to specific places (Marshall et al., 2017: 1164). The city palimpsest is an entanglement and disruption of different operations with a non-linear time reference (Dillon, 2005: 2, 37 in Marshall et al., 2017: 1165), which cannot be read on a single map or by comparing maps. It is a reading of spatial and morphological changes, their relation to social practices and their effect on one another, in the presence or absence of a place memory, especially as tied to unearthing 'memories of violence' (Marshall et al., 2017: 1163, 1164). 'Such processes of erasure and re-inscription' can be seen in acts of intentional urban destruction and the new layers of meaning inscribed upon post-conflict landscapes in the form of reconstruction and commemoration.' (Marshall et al., 2017: 1165). While reconstruction reinstates what was there, and if disconnected from the past, it could also delete or replace it, thus contributing to the erasure of a place's collective memory (Marshall et al., 2017). The urban fabric becomes a register of past traces, which are experienced today, sometimes surfacing to awaken memories for those who lived that past. The combination of traces and scars of violence, along with reconstruction, affects urban morphology and contributes to 'visualizing how new urban forms and ways of life are inscribed upon existing spaces and habits' (Marshall et al., 2017: 1164). Note that 'images of the past depend not only on the relationship between past and present but also on the accumulation of previous such relationships and their ongoing constitution and reconstitution' (Olick, 2007: 56 in Pirker et al., 2019: 3).

The mnemonic palimpsest

Memories result from activities that are registered as knowledge, which are dynamic and often represent conflicting voices of different groups (Larkin, 2012). Within a specific context and its socio-cultural, political, religious or other constructs, memories are transferred and 'displaced' with the conversion of a place, resulting in remembering and forgetting (Larkin, 2012: 14). These memory dynamics occur in time-space, turning space into a mnemonic tool (Hebbert, 2005). The operations behind these dynamics include demolition, renaming, adaptive reuse or annihilation of spaces, which impact collective remembering, and forgetting (Larkin, 2012), the latter being a tool to cope with negative events (Khalaf, 2006). In configuring and reconfiguring space, and specifically public spaces and streets, collective memories preserve a place's or even a city's history (Boyer, 1996). Memories are formed from the physical environment with its buildings, urban spaces and signs and from the collection of experiences associated and intertwined with these spaces (Hebbert, 2005: 592). Collective memories are 'narratives and commemorative practices' (Larkin 2012: 13), which include events and people and the perpetuation of their interaction in the present (Larkin, 2012). In the case of violent events which disrupt everyday life, a scar, as a latent layer in the urban fabric, is capable of impacting people collectively (Highmore, 2002), and affecting their spatial practices. This is expressed by Navaro-Yashin (2012) in reference to the affective impact of objects, places and memories on people's present-day behaviour in the context of the divided Cyprus. In cases of perpetual violence such as in wars, the impact is not only on those directly experiencing violence, but also on successive generations. While collective memories refer to past experiences of groups, Hirsch (2008) defines postmemory as an inherited form of memory, which represses connections with the present and strengthens those with the past (Larkin 2012: 2) to preserve an identity. For the post-war generation, inherited postmemory narratives tend to suppress lived experiences, and make room for the war-trapped ones, which resurface and affect their present everyday practices (Hirsch, 2008).

Methodology

To understand the violence palimpsest with spatiotemporal entanglements in mnemonic spaces, the starting point is a disaggregation, comprising a chronological tracing of violent events, their spatial mapping, and their reconnection to socio-cultural groups with the understanding of what constitutes their historical narratives (Pirker et al., 2019: 3). For the chronological tracing, various media and references provided the timeline indicating the year and event description, noting that the list of events could be incomplete and limited to the references used.[1] For the spatial mapping, the author superimposed spatial information from the chronological tracing with available violence mapping.[2] The reconnection to groups and their historical narratives is partly conducted through literature review and reference to websites that have directly addressed these groups. A more comprehensive representation would require narrative analysis of stories by residents and their descendants based on lived events in previously inflicted areas.

Violence is understood as intense sporadic or persistent activities leading to material, physical or psychological harm. Violence disrupts both the urban fabric and everyday social practices, which shifts the city from a polyrhythmic to an arrhythmic state (Lefebvre, 2004). In Lebanon it had many patterns and modes among which were artillery shooting, bomb shelling, sniping and explosions. The recurrence, duration and timing of combat all affect and are adapted to the urban context. Table 7.1 covers major violent events and forms the basis for Figures 7.1 and 7.2, which knit together in a non-linear manner the temporal accumulations, additions and erasures of violence in Beirut's recent history. Figure 7.1 presents an approximate

Table 7.1: A chronology of violent events in Beirut and its surroundings, and other events affecting Beirut.

Period	Location	Event
I. Ottoman	City centre	– Modernisation and demolition of the walled city, replacing the old souks – Killing of Martyrs demanding independence from the Ottoman Empire in 1916, and commemoration with statues in 1930 and 1960 at Martyrs Square
II. French	City centre	– The Plan Danger and the Haussmanian approach, constructing the star-shaped square
III. 1943–1974		
1950s	Administrative Beirut	– Highways construction: Ring, Istiqlal, Saeb Salam, Corniche Mazraa' in the 1950s
1951	Amman, Jordan	– Riadh Al Solh assassination on 17 July, Lebanon's first Prime Minister
1958	Administrative Beirut	– Civil conflict in 1958, with fighting excluding the centre, from Qantari, Moussaytbeh, Basta, Bashoura to Gemmayzeh, Muslim to Christian neighbourhoods, and American intervention to stop the conflict
IV. 1975–1989		
1975	Sidon Eastern suburb City centre Beirut Beirut Beirut suburbs	– Maarouf Saad assassination on 6 March, Sunni politician – Shooting at civilian bus with Palestinians in April in Ain Roumaneh – City centre demolition – Delineation of the Damascus Road demarcation line – Violence in Beirut port, Ashrafieh, Jnah, Ras Beirut, Hamra, Ramlet el Bayda – Violence in Bourj Hammoud, Naba', Nahr El Mott, Ras Dekwaneh-Tal El Zaatar, Ain Roumaneh, Chiyah, Haret Hreik, Mreijeh, Burj Al Barajneh, Hadath, Kfarshima, Choueifat, Khaldeh, Ouzai, Badaro, Furn El Chebback
	Lebanon	– Tripoli and Zgharta, Shouf including Barja, Ain al-Assad and Marj Barja, Sidon

Table 7.1: (Cont.)

Period	Location	Event
1976	Eastern suburbs	– Palestinian camp massacres: Jisr el Basha, Tal el Zaatar near Mkalles; Lebanese and Palestinian population displacement
	Beirut	– Violence in Arab el Maslakh, Quarantina, hotel district, Ras Beirut, Hamra – Violence in Qantari, Ain Mreisseh, Ashrafieh, Sioufi, Jeitawi, Ras El Naba', Beshra El Khoury
1977	Shouf area	– Kamal Jumblatt assassination on 16 March, Druze leader
1978	Ehden	– Tony Franjieh, assassination on 13 June, son of former president Suleiman Franjieh
1982	Beirut and suburbs	– President-elect Bashir Gemayel assassinated on 14 September, Sassine Square – Palestinian refugee camps massacres: Sabra and Shatila – Israeli invasion including Khaldeh, Aramoun, Bchamoun, Baabda, Jamhour, Aaleyh, Beit Merry, Mansourieh, Choueifat, Mreijeh, Laylaki, Bir Hassan, Chiyah, Burj Barajneh, Ouzai, Hay el Sellom, Sabra, Shatila, Sports City and Fakhani, Mazraa, Moussaitbeh, Aisha Bakkar, Ramlet el Bayda, UNESCO, Verdun, Ras Beirut, all of western Beirut, burning down of Pine Forest
1983	Beirut	– United States Embassy bombing on 18 April killing Lebanese and Americans, at Corniche near AUB, Jamia, Ain Mreisseh
	Beirut suburbs	– Beirut barracks bombing on 23 October killing American and French military personnel, near Beirut Airport
	Beirut and southern suburbs	– Ongoing armed fights between Shiite and Druze political parties in Hamra, Mazraa, Mar Elias and airport road until the war's end
1985	Southern suburbs	– Car bombing explosion on 8 March in Bir El Abed

(continued)

Table 7.1: (Cont.)

Period	Location	Event
1987	Helicopter flight	– Prime Minister Rashid Karami assassination on 1 June
1988	Eastern suburbs	– Fights between the Lebanese forces and army resulting in new divides in Ashrafieh, Furn El Chebback, Ain Roumaneh, Naba' and Dekwaneh, Sin El Fil and Fiat Bridge
1989	Beirut	– Head of the Sunni community Sheik Hassan Khaled assassination on 16 May in Malaab, Mazraa', behind Abdul Nasser Mosque – President René Mouawad assassination on 22 November near Sanayeh Garden
V. 1990–2005		
1990	Eastern suburb	– Leader of the National Liberal Party Dany Chamoun assassination on 21 October in Hazmieh
1992	Southern Lebanon Beirut and the suburbs	– Hezbollah leader Abbas al-Musawi assassination on 16 February in Jibsheet – Construction of the Tahwitta and Yerevan flyovers in the 1990s – The relocation of some embassies in and around Beirut: France along Damascus Road, USA to Awkar, northern suburbs, Germany in Rabiyeh then Dekwaneh, UK, Japan, Denmark and Australia in Wadi Abou Jmil, Bulgaria, from Australia street west Beirut near Corniche, to Hazmieh, Canada along Jal El Dib highway
2002	Eastern suburb	– Former Lebanese forces intelligence officer Elie Hobeika assassination on 24 January in Hazmieh
2004	Beirut	– Druze MP Marwan Hamadeh assassination attempt on 1 October along corniche Manara in Ras Beirut

Table 7.1: (Cont.)

Period	Location	Event
2005	Beirut	– Rafiq Hariri assassination on 14 February near the St. George Hotel along the Beirut Corniche, Minet El Hosn sector, in Minet El Hosn
	Eastern suburbs	– New Jdeideh on 19 March a car bomb exploded in a mixed commercial-residential area
		– Kaslik, Jounieh on 23 March a bomb exploded at the back entrance of the Kaslik shopping centre in Jounieh
		– Sad el-Bouchrieh on 26 March a car bomb exploded between two factories
		– Broummana on 1 April a bomb exploded the Rizk Plaza, 20 km east of Beirut
		– Jounieh on 7 May a car bomb exploded between the Christian Voice of Love radio station and the St. John Church
	Beirut	– Samir Kassir assassination on 2 June, an anti-Syrian journalist, at his home near Sassine
		– Former Lebanese Communist Party leader George Hawi assassination on 21 June, car explosion at Wata Moussaitbeh district
		– Elias Murr assassination attempt on 12 July with a car bomb in Antelias
	Eastern suburb	– Monnot Street on 22 July a car bomb exploded in front of a restaurant
	Beirut	
	Eastern suburbs	– Zalka on 22 August a bomb placed between a shopping centre and a hotel
	Beirut	
	Eastern suburbs	– Jeitawi on 17 September a car bomb explosion
		– May Chidiac assassination attempt on 25 September, journalist and critic of Syria in Jounieh
		– Journalist and lawmaker Gebran Tueni assassination on 12 December a car bomb in Mkalles
VI. 2006–2018		
2006	Southern suburbs	– The Israeli war and demolition of the southern suburbs and also bridges and infrastructure across the country
	Eastern suburbs	– Minister Pierre Gemayel assassination on 21 November in Jdeideh

(continued)

Table 7.1: (Cont.)

Period	Location	Event
2007	North of Beirut	– Bikfaya on 13 February bomb on a bus
	Beirut	– ABC mall in Mar Mitr, Ashrafieh on 20 May explosion near the mall, which is in a central mixed-use area
		– Verdun on 21 May explosion in a mixed-use area
	East of Beirut	– Aley explosion on 23 May
	Beirut	– Walid Eido assassination on 13 June, an anti-Syrian MP, in a car bomb explosion next to the Sporting Club at Corniche Beirut, Manara, Ras Beirut
	Eastern suburbs	– Antoine Ghanem assassination on 19 September, an anti-Syrian Lebanese MP, in a car bomb in Horsh Tabet, near Hayek roundabout
	South-east of Beirut	– Francois Elias Hajj assassination on 12 December, Brigadier General, in a car bomb in Baabda
2008	Beirut	– Wissam Eid assassination on 25 January, Lebanese Internal Security Forces senior terrorism investigator, explosion in Tahwitta-Aadliyeh area
	Tripoli	– Tripoli civilian bus bombing on 13 August
		– Tripoli on 29 September, a car bomb destroyed a bus with casualties
	Beirut and southern suburbs	– Clashes started on 11 May between Lebanese army and Hezbollah near the airport lasting a few days with airport closure, affecting various streets and neighbourhoods in the western part of Beirut; there were also conflicts among various politico-sectarian parties including Hezbollah, Progressive Socialist Party, Syrian Social Nationalist party
2012	Beirut	– Wissam al Hassan assassination on 19 October, head of the intelligence branch of the Internal Security Forces (ISF) in a massive car bomb in Ashrafieh near Sassine Square
		– New highways with Mathaf tunnel and Beshara El Khoury–Istiqlal tunnel between 2009 and 2014

Table 7.1: (Cont.)

Period	Location	Event
2013	Southern suburbs	– Roueiss neighbourhood bombing on 15 August, Haret Hreik – Tripoli dual bombings in August in two mosques – Bir Hassan on 19 November, a car explosion near the Iranian cultural centre
	City Centre	– Former Minister Mohamad Chatah assassination on 27 December, member of the Future Movement near STARCO, Bab Idriss, Minet El Hosn
2014	Southern suburbs	– Haret Hreik on 2 January an explosion in front of Hezbollah's political office, on Al-Arid Street
	Northern Lebanon	– Hermel suicide bombing on 16 January in a neighbourhood, 1 February at a petrol station – Van suicide bombing on 3 February in Choueifat
	Southern suburbs	– Iranian cultural centre suicide bombings on 19 February in Bir Hassan – Hermel suicide bombing on 22 February targeting an army post
	Northern Lebanon Beqaa	– Arsal on 29 March a suicide car bomb – Dahr al Baidar on 20 June a suicide bomb at a checkpoint – Beirut cafe on 24 June a suicide bomber driving near a cafe and a military checkpoint near Tayouneh
	Southern suburbs	– Duroy Hotel on 27 June a suicide bomber in Manara, Ras Beirut – Tripoli bomb on 6 August near an army checkpoint in Tripoli
	Beirut Tripoli Beqaa	– Arsal bombing on 19 September – Attack on Hezbollah on 20 September at a checkpoint – Arsal bombings on 14 November and 3 December targeting Lebanese Army soldiers

(*continued*)

Table 7.1: (Cont.)

Period	Location	Event
2015	Tripoli Northern Lebanon Beqaa Southern suburbs Northern Lebanon	– Jabal Mohsen cafe double-suicide bombing on 10 January – Ghassan Ajaj assassination on 26 January, an intelligence officer – Bader Eid assassination on 2 March, brother of Alawite leader Ali Eid – Arsal bombings on 5 and 6 with civilian and army casualties – Bourj el-Barajneh on 12 November, two suicide bombers in a mixed-use area – Deir Ammar on 5 December, a suicide bomber
2016	Beqaa Southern Lebanon Beirut Beqaa	– Arsal bombing on 24 March – Fathi Zaydan assassination on 12 April, a Fatah senior officer near Ain El Helweh Palestinian camp – Blom Bank bombing on 12 June, Dunant St. in Tallet El Druze, Moussaitbeh, opposite Concorde Building in Snoubra, Hamra – Qaa on 27 June, several suicide bombings – Arsal bombing on 15 August – Zahle bombing on 31 August – Al Ain explosion on 28 December killing its deputy mayor
VII. 2019–2020		
2019	Beirut	– Demonstrations and vandalism, leading to securitisation at: Riyadh Al Solh, Martyrs Square, Hamra Central Bank in Jounblat, Hamra, Ministry of Economy in Bashoura, Bashoura, Ministry of Water and Power in Corniche el Nahr, Ashrafieh, Ministry of Foreign Affairs in Hikmeh, Rmeil, Aazariyeh Building, Zalqa highway, Nahr el Kalb tunnel, Salome roundabout-Mirna Chalouhi St., Dbayeh highway
2020	Beirut	– Port explosion affecting the city centre, all sectors and neighbourhoods south and east of it, and the eastern suburbs of Bourj Hammoud, Sin El Fil, Dekwaneh, Jdeideh, Zalqa

location of these violent events at the scale of administrative Beirut, while Figure 7.2 presents locations in Greater Beirut including its north-eastern and southern suburbs.

Mapping violence in Beirut

Beirut witnessed episodes of violence before becoming Lebanon's capital after World War I and continues to perpetually do so. Since the Ottoman period and continuing to the present, its role as a nexus – a geopolitical crossroad of civilisations – led to the interplay of local, regional and international political powers. This resulted in episodes of conflicts and violence (cf. Hanf, 1993; El-Khazen, 2000; Khalaf, 2002; Salibi, 1988; Traboulsi, 2008), demonstrated in the arrival of Palestinian and other refugees, the civil war, Israeli invasions, the conflict with Syria, the arrival of Syrian refugees after 2011, the ISIS attacks on Lebanon, along with the struggles among the Lebanese politico-sectarian groups, particularly in the post-war period between 2005 and 2015. Being a manifestation of exogenous and endogenous causes, the long-lasting, intermittent violence took various forms, manifested at different scales in Beirut and beyond, and targeted different victims. In this chapter, these events are divided into seven periods further detailed in Table 7.1 and mapped in Figure 7.1.

Periods I and II briefly sum up events that happened before 1943, starting with the cycles of earthquakes resulting in seven archaeological layers of Beirut, which were excavated at the end of the civil war (Rabbat, 1998; Sader, 1998). Urban modernisation by the Ottomans led to the demolition of the walled city, and the replacement of the old souks (Tabet et al., 2001; Davie, 2001). Martyrs Square was established to commemorate the nationalistic struggle against the Ottomans (Farès and Tuéni, 2003; Kassir, 2003). The French mandate period continued with the medieval city's eradication in a Haussmanian approach, evident in the star-shaped central place symbolising the modernisation of the new Lebanese state with the Danger Plan in 1933 (Tabet et al. 2001; Tabet, 1996). This period also included the construction of the Parliament and the National Museum.

In Period III, after the constitution of the Republic, Lebanon adopted modernist French urban planning principles with activities including the construction of highways, which were considered a 'tool for nation-building' (Monroe, 2017: 193). The clashes in 1958 marked tensions between Christians and Muslims in some of Beirut's districts (Kassir, 2003).

Period IV marked the Lebanese civil war, which started in April 1975 and comprised several phases of internal and external violence including the destruction of the city centre, the East–West division and later the splintering

Figure 7.1: Violence in municipal Beirut.

VIOLENT EVENTS IN TABLE 1

I. Ottoman period
I.1 Walled Medieval city
I.2 Martyrs Square

II. French period
The star-shaped square

III. 1943–1974
<u>1950</u> III.1 Istiqlal, Ring, Saeb Salam, Corniche Mazraa'
<u>1958</u> III.2 Qantari, Moussaitbeh, Basta, Bashoura to Gemmayzeh

IV. 1975–1989
<u>1975</u>
IV.1 Ain Roumaneh
IV.2 Demolition of the centre
IV.3 Demarcation line, Damascus road
<u>1976</u>
IV.4 Arab al Maslakh, Quarantina, Ras Beirut, Hamra
IV.5 Qantari, Ain Mreisseh, Ashrafieh, Sioufi, Jeitawi, Ras El Naba', Beshara El Khoury
<u>1982</u>
IV.6 Sassine Street, near Sassine
IV.7 Sabra and Shatila Palestinian camps
IV.8 Chiyah, Mazraa', Sabra, Shatila, Moussaitbeh, Aisha Bakkar St, Ramlet El Bayda, UNESCO, Verdun, Ras Beirut, Sports City, Horsh Beirut
<u>1983</u>
IV.9 US Embassy, Corniche Beirut, near AUB
IV.10 Hamra, Mazraa', Mar Elias
<u>1988</u>
IV.11 Ashrafieh, Furn el Chebback, Ain Roumaneh, Nabaa', Sin El Fil, Fiat Bridge
<u>1989</u>
IV.12 Tariq l Jdideh, behind Abdel Nasser Mosque
IV.13 Near Sanayeh garden

V. 1990–2005
<u>1992</u>
V.1 Tahwitta and Yerevan flyovers
<u>2004</u>
V.2 Corniche el Manara, Ras Beirut
<u>2005</u>
V.3 Near the St. George Hotel, Minet El Hosn
V.4 Ashrafieh St, near Sassine
V.5 Wata Moussaitbeh
V.6 Monot Street
V.7 Jeitawi

VI. 2006–2018
<u>2007</u>
VI.1 ABC mall, Mar Mitr, Ashrafieh
VI.2 Verdun
VI.3 Next to Sporting Club, at Corniche Beirut
VI.4 Horsh Tabet, near Hayek roundabout
<u>2008</u>
VI.5 Tahwitta–Aadliyeh
<u>2012</u>
VI.6 Ibrahim el Mounzer St, Ashrafieh, near Sassine
VI.7 Mathaf and Beshara El Khoury tunnels
<u>2013</u>
VI.8 Near STARCO bldg, Bab Idriss, Minet El Hosn
<u>2014</u>
VI.9 Near Tayouneh
VI.10 Duroy Hotel, Manara, Ras Beirut
<u>2016</u>
VI.11 Blom Bank, opposite Concorde bldg in Hamra

VII. 2019-2020
<u>2019</u>
VII.1 Riadh Solh, Martyrs Square, Hamra Central Bank, Ministry of Economy in the Aazariyeh bldg, Bashoura, Ministry of Water and Power in Corniche el Naher, Ministry of Foreign Affairs in Hikmeh, Salome roundabout in Sin el Fil
<u>2020</u>
VII.2 Beirut Port, affecting the city centre, sectors east of it and eastern suburbs

BUILDINGS LEGEND

IV. 1975–1989
A. US Embassy, Jamia
B. Abdel Nasser Mosque, Malaab
C. Hotel Phoenicia, Minet El Hosn
D. Holiday Inn, Minet El Hosn
E. Bourj el Murr, Serail
F. Sports City, Malaab

V. 1990–2005
G. St. George Hotel, Minet El Hosn

VI. 2006–2018
H. ABC mall, Mar Mitr
I. Sporting Club, Manara
J. STARCO bldg, Bab Idriss
K. Duroy Hotel, Manara
L. Blom Bank, Verdun Dunant St, Tallet El Druze

VII. 2019–2020
M. Central Bank, Jounblat
N. Aazariyeh bldg, Bashoura, Ministry of Economy
O. Ministry of Water and Power, Corniche El Naher
P. Ministry of Foreign Affairs, Hikmeh

DISTRICTS LEGEND

⬚ Ashrafieh		⬚ Minet El Hosn
⬚ Ain Mreisseh		⬚ Moussaitbeh
⬚ Bashoura		⬚ Ras Beirut
⬚ Marfa'		⬚ Rmeil
⬚ Mazraa'		⬚ Saifi
⬚ Medawar		⬚ Zouqaq El Blatt

CHECKPOINTS

1. Port
2. Sodeco
3. Mathaf
4. Tayouneh-Kafa'at
5. Gallery Semaan – Mar Mikhael

NAMES LEGEND

Bold names in capital letters are districts.
Bold names in lower case letters are:
– Sectors or areas
– Rd: highways or main roads
– St: streets

Figure 7.1: (Cont.)

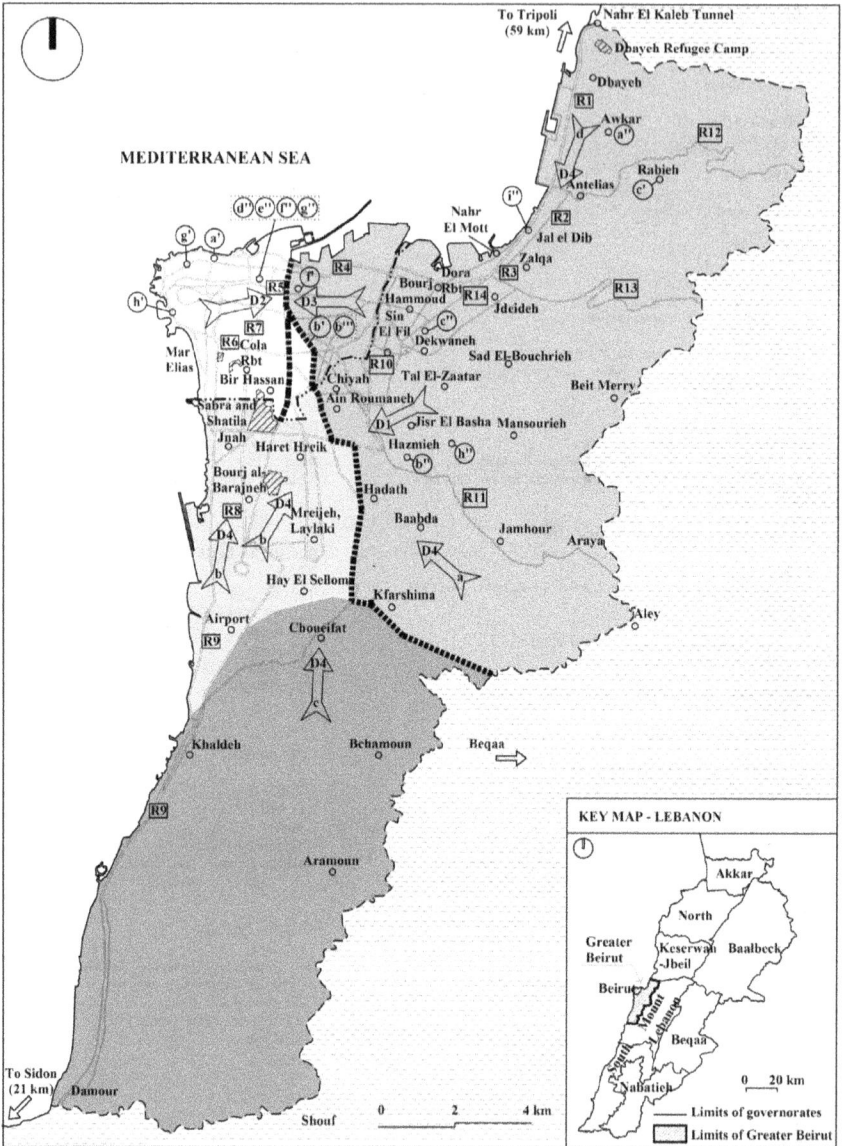

Figure 7.2: Violence in Greater Beirut.

▪▪▪	**Administrative Beirut**
▪▪▪	**Greater Beirut limits**
▦▦▦	**Demarcation line**
○	**Localised sites of violence**
▨▨▨	**Palestinian refugee camps**

Majority Sectarian Distribution

☐	**Christian**
☐	**Mixed**
☐	**Muslim Sunni**
☐	**Muslim Shiite**

▷ Displacement

D1. Palestinian refugees leaving Tal El-Zaatar to the camps in the southern suburbs

D2. Christians leaving West Beirut

D3. Muslims (Shiites) leaving East Beirut

D4. Displacement towards Beirut's suburbs
a. Muslims (Shiites) coming from Beqaa
b. Christians coming from the South
c. Christians coming from the Shouf
d. Christians coming from the North

ROAD LEGEND

Rd: Main road; St: Street
Rbt: Roundabout

R1. Dbayeh Rd	R8. Airport Rd
R2. Jal El Dib Rd	R9. Beirut-Saida Rd
R3. Zalqa Rd	R10. Emile Lahoud Rd
R4. Charles Helou Rd	R11. Beirut-Damascus Rd
R5. The Ring	R12. Antelias-Bikfaya Rd
R6. Saeb Salam Rd	R13. Matn Express Rd
R7. Salim Salam Rd	R14. Mirna Chalouhi St

EVENTS IN TABLE 1, OUTSIDE ADMINISTRATIVE BEIRUT

IV. 1975–1989
1975
IV.1'Ain Roumaneh
IV.2' Bourj Hammoud, Nabaa', Nahr El Mott,   Ras Dekwaneh-Tel El-Zaatar, Ain Roumaneh,Chiyah, Haret Hreik, Mreijeh, Bourj al-Barajneh, Hadath, Kfarshima, Choueifat, Khaldeh, Ouzai, Badaro, Furn   El Chebback
1976
IV.3'Jisr el Basha, Tal El-Zaatar near Mkalles, Lebanese and population displacement
1982
IV.4' Sabra and Shatila Palestinian camps
IV.5' Khaldeh, Aramoun, Bchamoun, Baabda, Jamhour, Aley, Beit Merry, Mansourieh, Choueifat, Mreijeh, Laylaki, Bir Hassan, Chiyah, Burj al-Barajneh, Hay El Sellom, Sabra, Shatila, Sports City
1983
IV.6' Near Beirut Airport
1985
IV.7' Bir El Abed, Haret Hreik
1988
IV.8' Furn el Chebback, Ain Roumaneh, Nabaa', Dekwaneh and Sin El Fil

V. 1990–2005
1990
V.1' Hazmieh
1992
V.2' Relocation of embassies, see detail V.2'
2002
V.3' Hazmieh
2005
V.4' New Jdeideh
V.5' Sad El-Bouchrieh
V.6' Antelias
V.7' Zalqa
V.8' Mkalles, Sin El Fil

VI. 2006–2018
2006
VI.1' Jdeideh
2007
VI.2' Horsh Tabet, near Hayek roundabout
VI.3' Baabda
2008
VI.4' Near Beirut Airport
2013
VI.5' Roueiss, Haret Hreik
VI.6' Bir Hassan
2014
VI.7' Al-Arid St, Haret Hreik
VI.8' Choueifat
VI.9' Near Tayyouneh
2015
VI.10' Bourj al-Barajneh

VII. 2019–2020
2019
VII.1' Zalqa Rd, Nahr el Kaleb Tunnel, Salome–Mirna Chalouhi St, Dbayeh Rd
VII.2'Bourj Hammoud, Sin El Fil, Dekwaneh, Jdeideh, Zalqa

Relocation of Embassies (Detail V.2')

Embassy	Old location (x')	New location (x")
a. USA	Corniche, Jamia	Awkar
b. France	Damascus Rd, Horsh Beirut	Hazmieh (b"), then, Horsh again (b"')
c. Germany	Rabieh	Dekwaneh
d. UK	-	Wadi Abou Jamil
e. Japan	-	Wadi Abou Jamil
f. Denmark	Tabariss	Wadi Abou Jamil
g. Australia	Bliss St, Hamra	Wadi Abou Jamil
h. Bulgaria	Raoushe	Hazmieh
i. Canada	-	Jal El Dib

Figure 7.2: (Cont.)

of the city and its suburbs. Divisions occurred, in relation to affiliations with politico-sectarian communities. Such territories became relative locations in terms of safety or danger, depending on whose perspective was considered (Pirker et al., 2019), while the centre and demarcations remained as neutral grounds, not controlled by either side of the conflict. Large-scale violent events including 'ethnic cleansing' (Davie, 1993) happened in 1975–1976 and in 1982 with the Israeli invasion (Tabet, 1996).

Period V was marked by the official ending of the civil war and the start of the reconstruction period, while violent events were ongoing. The most severe was the assassination of the former Prime Minister Rafic Hariri, an event followed by the withdrawal of the Syrian troops, the rise of civic activism and a series of assassinations disrupting everyday life.

Period VI was marked by the Israeli war in 2006 and the complete destruction of the southern suburbs, an armed conflict in 2008 causing the temporary closure of the international airport, a series of ISIS attacks, the construction of new highways, an uprising against the solid waste management crisis in 2015 and other civic activism movements including the full reopening of the Pine Forest in 2016 (Mady, 2018).

Period VII – this short but intensive period included nation-wide demonstrations, which started on 17 October 2019, the Beirut port blast on 4 August 2020, and on 14 October 2021 the clashes near the Pine Forest and former demarcation buffer, which resulted in several casualties.[3] The impact was the appearance of new congregation spaces for the protestors in and around administrative Beirut; the destruction of heritage buildings that had survived the civil war years, while the shock of this tremor continues as this chapter is being written, along with a revival of the war-time tensions among communities.

Unfolding Beirut's violence palimpsest

In reading the violence palimpsest, space becomes related to a different time layer, depending on processes of perceiving it for the first time, remembering its past, or replaying its narratives. I start with Beirut's changing divides, then explore urban transformations impacted by violence in and around Beirut at various scales. Subsequently, I identify tangible and intangible markers that emboss violence at present, to reveal the relation between urban transformations and socio-temporal processes and practices, especially when affected by memory and postmemory.

Divides and frontiers

Unlike the medieval city walls that were located at the city limits (Davie, 1991), divides generated by violence separated inherent city parts physically and mentally (Tabet, 1996). They reflected historical religious, ethnic, social and economic differences preceding the war, and resulted in a 'fragmented city' (Davie, 1991: 2). The distribution of population by religion, sect and ethnicity in specific quarters was the outcome of an expanding city, host-ing an incoming rural population who settled in quarters by affinity, while mixed areas emerged after the 1920s (Davie, 1991). Reference is made to three divide categories starting with those forming obdurate frontiers from cracks predating the civil war. The first, frontiers are differentiated from borders, as they are contested and could change over time, dividing what is 'safe' from the 'other' (Pullan, 2011). The second was the outcome of urban planning, particularly road infrastructure projects initiated in the 1950s–1960s. The third related to more recent violent events, and the definition of securitised urban pockets.

Streets as divides were used as corridors for fighting (Yahya, 1993). Divisions were designated by concrete blocks, barricades, barriers or barbed wire. Along streets, tall buildings and road junctions became strategic con-trol points, sometimes serving as checkpoints. In ceasefire, these checkpoints allowed for the exchange of goods, and the infiltration of civilians across the frontiers, especially for those living in one area but working in the other. Opening the checkpoints provided permeability and allowed everyday life to resurface, akin to peaceful times, while closing them signalled tension and forthcoming violence (Tabet, 1996).

Sparking the east–west divide, the Damascus Road demarcation line in 1975, the so-called green line (Sarkis, 1993), germinated from Martyrs Square (Khalaf, 2006) and splintered administrative Beirut and beyond including the southern suburbs; specifically in the east the predominantly Christian middle-income residential area Badaro and working-class Furn El Chebback from the Pine Forest included in the no-go buffer to the west, religiously mixed Chiyah from predominantly Christian Ain Roumaneh, and predominantly Lebanese Burj Barajneh from the Palestinian camps (Davie, 1993) (Figure 7.2). This line with its five checkpoints (Tabet, 1996) (Figure 7.1) turned the city centre and as far south as the Pine Forest into a no-man's land, annihilated from everyday life for at least fifteen years, causing this area to slowly fade away from collective memories (Tabet, 1996; Saliba, 1997). Moreover, Beirut's urban fabric was further restruc-tured through territorial demarcations by various militias, cracking the city along new divides with buffers around them. The 2008 events led to further formation of frontiers (Bou Akar, 2018) and new divisions. These new frontiers again appeared at the intersections of 'different politico-religious territories' (Fawaz et al., 2009: 181), indicating demographic changes and emerging tensions (Bou Akar 2012, 2018).

The second divide category sliced through the urban fabric rupturing and disconnecting its neighbourhoods, as manifested in the incisions of highway construction, bridges and tunnels, some executed before 1975 and some after 1990. The pre-war main roads exposed the severed urban fabric to the danger of new frontiers, and were cut off with various types of barriers (Tabet, 1996: 40) (Figure 7.1, III). Ironically, their closure enabled re-stitching neighbourhoods, and retrieving residents' memories (Tabet, 1996). Roads after 1975 had a similar rupturing effect (Figure 7.1, V.1, VI.7).

The third divide category was securitisation, which started in Beirut particularly after 2005 with explosions rattling in and around Beirut (Table 7.1, Figure 7.1). Securitisation applied to all governmental, political, religious and diplomatic presence and residences of political figures. Bombings resulted in long-lasting securitisation in these locations' immediate surroundings including blocking whole streets, complexes, buildings and residences (Fawaz et al., 2009). In Beirut 'securitisation may be the reflection of the fragmentation of a political system and society that are increasingly compartmentalising the respective city into territories, each securitised by its own system.' (Fawaz et al., 2009: 189).

Urban dynamics

For years, Beirut and its surroundings remained in flux, with changes to building and land uses in relation to violence but also meeting people's needs and securing some economic activity in the absence of the vital centre, thus signalling social disintegration (Davie, 1991; 1993; Tabet, 1996). Violence was a catalyst for urban transformations (Tabet, 1993). These ranged from destruction, demolition, the surge of informal urban development to post-war reconnection of the street network, reconstruction and the real estate boom. This patchwork of different urban shrinkage or growth resulted in an alarming contrast between contemporary, luxurious, real estate development of high-rise buildings and the neglected heritage ones (Marshall et al., 2017). Also, the city's collective memories were affected by a gradual eradication of historic urban places by different perpetrators and periods extending to the present. Add to this the development of a centre-less city with characterless polycentres (Tabet, 1996), and the gentrification of the divide buffers. For real estate entrepreneurs, what mattered was the availability of urban land for development, regardless of what should be preserved or not (Sarkis, 1993).

With population displacement from the divided city, other areas expanded, namely the north-eastern and southern suburbs (Figure 7.2). Polycentricity emerged from the destruction and sealing off of Beirut's centre (Khalaf, 1993). It led to the duplication of services and investment in the east and west, the development of housing projects and commercial centres each serving their own politico-sectarian community. Nevertheless, these centres, which are still present, could not overtake the capital's central role, neither in relation to identity nor transportation (Davie, 1993).

The centre's massive destruction included the old souks, which were a melting pot, and signified the erasure of the cultural and collective memory of the medieval city and its other layers (Tabet, 1996). As if the war damage was insufficient, reconstruction involved evictions of squatters, the selective and minimal preservation of some heritage buildings that would raise surrounding real estate value, real estate development of a new centre for selected users (Tabet, 1996), with the provision of controlled open urban spaces and the absence of a transportation hub. Another priority was the reconnection of divided war-time streets, with the construction of tunnels and bridges, which both connect and divide (Nucho, 2016).

To the north-east, expansion was due to the influx of mostly Christian population from Beirut, the Shouf and Sidon (Davie, 1993), and resulted in the emergence of several commercial strips and residential areas along the northern and eastern highways (Figure 7.2), with no place identity and no distinguishing features (Tabet, 1996). As these areas had access to the sea, several beach complexes were constructed 'to accommodate the well-off refugee population.' (Davie, 1993: 5). These suburbs continued to expand post-war, supported by investment from 'the new fortunes created during the war' (Davie, 1993: 3). As for the destroyed Palestinian refugee camps, they became urban voids, which, driven by the market economy, were repurposed and developed in later years with residential complexes.

The southern suburbs expanded due to the influx of mainly Shiite Lebanese coming from the south and the Beqaa (Davie, 1993), and Palestinian refugees from the north-eastern suburbs (Tabet, 1996) (Table 7.1). Densification and non-planned development occurred as the southern suburbs had to accommodate a population number higher than its housing and infrastructure capacities (Tabet, 1996). Vacant land in Chiyyah and near the airport was all built on, densifying the existing fabric, and leading to changes in land and building uses (Davie, 1993). This continued post-war in the originally predominantly Druze Choueifat as a struggle among sects, with increased Shiite presence (Bou Akar, 2018). The expansion of the refugee camps followed the massacres in 1976, and contributed to their growth as informal settlements on public and private land (Charafeddine, 1987; Clerc-Huybrechts, 2008). While administrative Beirut did not get affected by the 2006 war, the southern suburbs – predominantly populated by Hezbollah proponents – were completely demolished. With the Wa'ad project (Randall, 2014), these suburbs witnessed an unprecedented reconstruction scale supported by Hezbollah and completed by 2009.[4] In 2007–2017, and similar to the north-eastern suburbs, investment from war-time capital contributed to the rise of luxurious office and residential towers (Marshall et al., 2017; Davie, 1993).

As for the divide buffers, and right after the war's end, a preference for mixed areas was reflected in their high real estate value (Khalaf, 1993), and the entrepreneurial development of leisure activities serving all communities. Over time, these areas gentrified.

Displacement and social practices

Davie (1993: 3) highlights that 'during each round of fighting, transfers of population would take place, emptying areas or filling up others.' Bouts of displacement caused by recurrent violence during and after the war, accompanied by urban dynamics, occurred in some areas more than once, with more religions, sects and ethnicities being replaced (Davie, 1993). Displacement whether due to 'ethnic cleansing' (Davie, 1993: 2) or fleeing from danger led to the homogenisation of neighbourhoods formed in 'a series of enclosed territories founded upon the logic of exclusion and separation' (Yahya, 1993: 128). Their inhabitants shared their political leaders' ideologies (Yahya, 1993), and they attained some degree of perceived safety, while the few remaining mixed neighbourhoods became prone to instability, targeted by the majority groups surrounding them (Figure 7.2). The inhabitants in Beirut and its surroundings were reassembled in segregated politico-sectarian neighbourhoods/areas (Tabet, 1996; Davie, 1993).

With new frontiers being constantly and abruptly formed, reconfiguring relations between areas, 'the mental geography of the inhabitants required integrating new variables such as new perception of vulnerability, different movement circuits, new appreciations of geopolitical position of their quarter.' (Davie, 1993: 4). The need to cohabitate with violence even nowadays, resulted in some temporary and other permanent practices. The population established a new normalcy within their communities to cope with violence in a centre-less city, at the neighbourhood or building scale. Buildings constructed during the war provided all necessary aspects for sustenance under a siege including wells, generators and shelters (Davie, 1993). Older unequipped ones were reconfigured with stairwells and basements functioning as shelters (Sarkis, 1993). Along frontiers, building fronts turned their backs, when fighting occurred (Yahya, 1993). Under severe combat, complete evacuation of a building, or even of a street, could occur. This opened the possibility thereafter for squatting by other displaced people, which created tensions with the residents (Davie, 1993). When an urban location could no longer handle the instability, and fighters often took over – turning the building into their control point – relocating became a necessity. This meant that for security reasons, new building uses occurred in unexpected areas, such as embassies amidst residential neighbourhoods, as indicated in Figure 7.2 and Table 7.1.

At the neighbourhood scale, 'the means of sustenance have become increasingly sophisticated. They almost replace daily life's infrastructure … and have managed to transform the spaces of the city irreversibly' (Sarkis, 1993: 119) as we continue to observe reliance on community-provided services (Roy, 2009), upgrading of infrastructure for a community's autonomy, independently from the capital city (Davie, 1993). In addition to the east–west divide and its annihilated nodes (Yahya, 19993), all exposed spaces including terminals, shopping malls and public spaces were avoided (Khalaf, 2002: 248). At the city scale, 'familiar spaces of the city soon became strange and alienating' (Nucho, 2016: 23).

While places of residence changed and were mostly homogenised, business and leisure did not discriminate but rather shared the common interest of profit (Mady and Chettiparamb, 2016). Some facilities served only the east or west or opened in both, others remained in their places, for example hospitals and schools. This meant that daily commuting changed significantly for part of the population. Movement in Beirut was reconfigured rather than interrupted (Yahya, 1993; Davie, 1993). 'All urban mobility was under the control of various factions who defined their territorial boundaries' (Nucho, 2016: 23). A lasting consequence of these divides was that mobility was restricted by physical and mental barriers, generated by the fear of insecurity (Nucho, 2016). The city was not equally accessible to everyone or at any time, due to mental barriers – for instance to residents in suburban areas – which follow a ripple effect from the divide and consequent instabilities generating new divisions (Borell, 2008; Fawaz et al., 2009; Bou Akar, 2012). Add to this the impact of securitisation, which renders mobility unpredictable and compromised, with road closures and rerouting according to arising events (Monroe, 2011; Fawaz et al., 2009). One had to re-learn how to navigate the city depending on timing and one's positionality (Buhr and McGarriggle, 2017), reacting to safe and hazardous zones, checkpoints and road closures on a regular basis (Tabet, 1996). Navigating in east or west Beirut required the creation of new paths through gardens, patios, stairs, fences and walls, to enable people to reach their homes safely (Tabet, 1996: 71). Baaklini (NA) narrates his story as an eastern suburb resident, explaining how divides were masked by infrastructure and how easterners associated with Beirut only as a name. Despite the reconnections of the road network, these changes reflected in post-war mobility, which maintained the east–west divide, even for the shared taxis (Davie, 1993). With changes in places of residence, trips to work could take longer for those working in Beirut but residing in the suburbs, and commuting along the heavily congested highways. Congestion shifted from the historical centre towards the Ring Road and the entrances into Beirut.

The centre, which before the war had also been the transportation hub, with lines radiating to service all Beirut, remained absent from the post-war transportation network (Davie, 1993). The new hubs were now located to the east at Dora and to the west at Cola roundabouts (Figure 7.2), without direct connections between them, serving the home to work itineraries that persisted after the war, as evident in the map of the informal bus route system: busmap.me. Bus routes still service different communities rather than connect across the city. One exception is bus number 4, whose route retraces the green line and former divides, slicing through contested and contrasting city parts, exposing neighbourhoods that stood on opposite sides of the divide, and providing riders with a shared experience of the city at present (Pelgrim, n.d.).

Violence markers and memories

Tangible and intangible violence markers persist at various scales. Starting with the city scale, Martyrs Square and the Pine Forest are two public spaces disconnected from their urban fabric, still struggling to regain their position in everyday urban life, despite civic efforts. At a smaller scale, some buildings have become war symbols, for example the National Museum or Mathaf, the Holiday Inn, the Murr Tower and the Barakat building or Beit Beirut, currently the city museum. Scars of violence are evident on some buildings along or close to divides. There are also monuments commemorating violent events including Hariri's statue in place of the explosion (Figure 7.3), or shrines along roads and within neighbourhoods marking locations of killing such as in Furn el Chebback.

Intangible or soft markers (Davie, 1991) range from toponyms, posters, banners, flags, graffiti and signs marking territories, commemoration of violent events (Albrecht, 2017, 2020), to dormant divides across differentiated communities, which appear when tensions arise (Bou Akar, 2012, 2018); these could be physically absent but mentally very present, acquiring meaning and significance with time and memory. As Davie (1993: 8) stated, 'Even with the war effectively over, these sub-regions are still present and have their importance in moments of political tension.' The Damascus Road demarcation line, even if dissolved, generated persisting new names: East and West Beirut (Davie, 1993). Violence became synonymous with some area names: Qasqas, Cola, Tayouneh and others. As for national commemorations of violence, these include 13 April for the civil war's outbreak, 14 February for Hariri's assassination, while 6 May Martyrs Day was replaced by 25 May, liberation of the occupied security zone in southern Lebanon in the year 2000. Other events like the Black Saturday in 1976 where people were killed according to their sect, the massacres in the Palestinian camps, or victims of terrorist attacks are not commemorated on a national scale but in some cases by the respective political parties and their followers (Albrecht, 2017). The variation in scale, location and time of violent events and their markers formed multiple collective memories. The more localised the violent event, the lower the impact on everyday social practices and the less remembered beyond the boundaries of the homogenised community. The war 'desensitised' people and 'violence became morally indifferent', with the territorial boundaries marking 'the extent of human sympathy' beyond which it did not matter (Collins, 1974: 417 in Khalaf, 1993: 42).

As part of coping with violence, a defence mechanism of indifference, or even a 'collective amnesia' helped survivors to go on (Khalaf, 1993: 42). Nevertheless, collective memories and postmemories helped to preserve or erase identities over time, generating diverse urban experiences. For the insider with memories or narratives, the homogenised areas are normalised, so are military presence at frontiers and security checks in shopping centres, public spaces and transportation hubs. Some locations are frequented and others avoided (Saksouk-Sasso, 2015; Genberg, 2002; Tabet, 1996; Larkin, 2012; Monroe, 2011; Yahya, 2004) by being trained to read tangible and intangible territorial markers. The perspective changes depending on the community one comes from. Though the post-war generation has experienced less first-hand violent events, their social practices are impacted by postmemory narratives (Larkin, 2012; Marshal et al., 2017). This included confining their daily practices to public spaces within their communities and comfort zones (Deeb and Harb, 2013; Azmi et al. 2013 in Marshal et al., 2017: 1171). For example, Tariq el Jdideh is avoided by those who grew up with narratives of Lebanese and Palestinian conflicts (Marshal et al., 2017), or the city centre with its pubs and nightlife was avoided by some dwellers of the southern suburbs (Deeb and Harb, 2013).

Traces and possibilities for hope

In the absence of public spaces, a lively, popular city centre and formal public transport, possibilities for encounter and exposure to the other became meagre. As stated earlier, the impact was that some city parts remained unfamiliar to outsiders (Marshal et al., 2017) and the continuous expansion of homogeneous developments contributed to feeding the stubborn divides. This meant that discrimination, segregation and stigmatisation persisted, along with the need for conviviality and solidarity. The struggle among opposing politico-sectarian groups during the civil war happened in the absence of the state (Sarkis, 1993), whose reinstatement manifested through some projects with a national identity to support the healing and forgetting processes, for example the National Museum or the Sports City. Several

Figure 7.3: Violence markers: (a) political party monument in Ain Roumaneh, (b) Holiday Inn, (c & d) Hariri's memorial, and (e) traces near Badaro-Tayouneh.

attempts for emancipation from collective and postmemory addressed target groups or the public at large, to allow social practices to occur in present-time urban space. These ranged from narratives exposing contradictory viewpoints and experiences, to communication platforms strengthening a civic identity and rights to public spaces.

Mapping and narrative projects whose purpose was to break away from the past, give the post-war generation the opportunity to experience Beirut first-hand, have encounters, rub shoulders (Watson, 2006) and familiarise themselves with stigmatised neighbourhoods that were previously labelled as no-go areas (see http://youcitizen.org/maps/beirut-map/ presented in Marshal et al., 2017). In this manner, 'the spatial and palimpsestic nature of these stories helps us appreciate how memory, both the traumatic and mundane, can be passively transmitted through landscape, actively forgotten through erasure.' (Marshall et al., 2017: 117).

Beit Beirut, the city museum with its temporary and permanent exhibitions, is designed to reveal the city scars (Mollard, 2018) and initiate the healing process. Also, Martyrs Square, reminiscent of past nationalist achievements, became a congregation place in 2005, 2015 and 2019, where people gather, leaving their differences aside. Another case is the Pine Forest or Horsh (Mady, 2018), where by 2016, the NGO NAHNOO retrieved its nodal role in the present-time urban rhythm. Horsh, within the war-time buffer was reduced to ashes in 1982 (Davie, 1993) (Figure 7.1, IV.8). Until it reopened, Horsh became an embedded demarcation area, traced through the tools of confining with roads, enclosing with fences and nurturing post-memories. The challenge was to reinstate a socially 'neutral' space within Beirut's conflict-ridden context, and despite the politico-sectarian divides surrounding it (Figure 7.4).

Conclusion

This chapter unfolded Beirut's violence palimpsest and explored urban transformations and the impact on socio-temporal practices, which accumulated over the past century. Violence bit into the urban fabric, vacating and annihilating spaces and disembowelling buildings to make room for itself, while maintaining tangible and intangible markers. It radiated from the centre, reinforcing already existing fractures, forming new cracks and buffers, besieging some areas, marking secure hotspots and causing a polycentric urban augmentation around Beirut. It ruled by dividing, segregating and redirecting mobility. Simultaneously it impacted everyday life rhythms, caused population displacements, and generated coping mechanisms to live, work and navigate in a heartless city. The consequences were

Figure 7.4: Emancipation possibilities: (a) Martyrs Square, (b) National Museum, (c) Beit Beirut, and (d & e) the Pine Forest.

long-lasting changes in spatiotemporal social practices and differentiated urban experiences in present-day Beirut, which reflected the effects of collective memories and postmemories. These consequences indicate the failure of Beirut's artificial heart transplantation and its inability to reconnect with the social fabric that shaped and enlivened the surrounding urban tissue. Some attempts were made to emancipate from inherited memories and include sharing past stories, providing communication platforms, opportunities for dialogue and exchange across divides and resetting the zero hour of mnemonic urban spaces to facilitate everyday urban life and encounter in neutral, shared spaces. These approaches are valuable as violence remains immanent in Beirut.

Acknowledgements

The author thanks Jessica Lahoud for her tremendous support in preparing the maps for this chapter, and the book editors for their valuable comments.

Notes

1 The following references were used in compiling Table 7.1: Huybrechts, 1999; Faour, 1987; Tabet, 1996; Kassir, 2003; Sassine, and Tuéni, 2003; Civil Society website; Khalaf and Khoury, 1993; Davie, 1991, 1993.
2 The following references were used in constructing the maps along with Table 7.1: Charafeddine, 1987; www.pinterest.com/pin/188869778094816 002/; Daragahi, 2008; CRN News, 2008; Stel, 2008; Messenger, 2017; UNJLC, 2006; Randall, 2014; N/A, 2010; Bergman, 2015; Yassin, 2012; ACAPs, 2020; Hovsepian, 2017; Beirut Arab Institute.
3 www.aljazeera.com/gallery/2021/10/14/photos-armed-clashes-erupts-in-beirut-in-protest-against-blast-judge (accessed 26 August 2022).
4 www.waad.org.lb/pressinformation.asp?id=147&catid=28 (accessed 24 January 2021).

Bibliography

ACAPS (2020). *Analysis of Affected Areas in greater Beirut. Emergency Operations Centre* (Beirut: Assessment and Analysis Cell), https://reliefweb.int/sites/reliefweb.int/files/resources/20200825_acaps_situation_analysis_beirut_explosion.pdf (accessed 30 September 2020).
Albrecht, M. (2020). 'Clash of Memories: Commemorating the Civil War in Lebanon', *Public History Weekly* 8:6. https://doi.org/10.1515/phw-2020-16551
Albrecht, M. (2017). *Krieg der Symbole. Politische Parteien und Parteikultur im Libanon (1975–2015)* (Münster: Lit Verlag).

Azmi, F., Brun, C., and Lund, R. (2013). 'Young People's Everyday Politics in Post-conflict Sri Lanka', *Space and Polity*, 17:1, 106–22.

Baaklini, J. (n.d.). 'Geographies of Way', *Mashallah News*, https://mashallahnews.com/routes/geographies-of-war/ (accessed 30 September 2020).

Berger, S. and Seiffert, J. (2014). 'Erinnerungsorte – Ein Erfolgskonzept auf dem Prüfstand', in Berger, S. and Seiffert, J. (eds) *Erinnerungsorte: Chancen, Grenzen und Perspektiven eines Erfolgskonzeptes in den Kulturwissenschaften* (Essen: Klartext), 11–36.

Bergman, R. (2015). 'The Hezbollah Connection', *The New York Times Magazine* (10 February 2015), www.nytimes.com/2015/02/15/magazine/the-hezbollah-connection.html (accessed 30 September 2020).

Borell, K. (2008) 'Terrorism and Everyday Life in Beirut 2005: Mental Re-Constructions, Precautions and Normalization', *Acta Sociologica*, 51:1, 55–70.

Bou Akar, H. (2018). *For the War Yet to Come: Planning Beirut's Frontiers* (Stanford, CA: Stanford University Press).

Bou Akar, H. (2012). 'Contesting Beirut's Frontiers', *City and Society*, 24:2, 150–72.

Boyer, C. (1996). *The City of Collective Memory: Its Historical Imagery and Architectural Entertainments* (Cambridge, London: MIT Press).

Buhr, F. and McGarrigle, J. (2017). 'Navigating Urban Life in Lisbon: A Study of Migrants' Mobilities and Use of Space', *Social Inclusion*, 5:4, 226–34.

Civil Society Centre (n.d.). 'Fighting broke out in several areas in Beirut', https://civilsociety-centre.org/sir/fighting-broke-out-several-areas-beirut (accessed 30 September 2020).

Civil Society Centre (n.d.). 'Sieges', https://civilsociety-centre.org/sir/sieges-set-clashes-other-areas (accessed 30 September 2020).

Civil Society Centre (n.d.). 'Fall of Tal el-Zaatar and Jisr el-Basha', https://civilsociety-centre.org/sir/fall-tal-el-zaatar-and-jisr-el-basha (accessed 30 September 2020).

Charafeddine, W. (1987). 'L'Illégalité dans une Ville en Guerre: Le Cas des Quartiers 'Illégaux' de la Banlieu Sud de Beyrouth', in Nasr, S. and Hanf, T. (eds) *Urban Crisis and Social Movements: Arab and European Perspectives* (Beirut: The Euro-Arab Social Research Group), 175–92.

Clerc-Huybrechts, V. (2008). *Les Quartiers Irréguliers de Beyrouth: Une Histoire des Enjeux Fonciers et Urbanistiques la Banlieu Sud* (Beyrouth: Institut Français du Proche-Orient (IFPO)).

Collins, R. (1974). 'The Three Faces of Cruelty: Towards a Comparative Study of Violence', *Theory and Society*, 1, 415–40.

CRN News, Naharnet (2008). 'Iranian, Syrian, Hizbollah Terror War: Day 4', *Naharnet* (10 May 2008), https://cedarsrevolution.net/jtphp/index.php?option=com_content &task=view&id=1589&Itemid=35 (accessed 30 September 2020).

Daragahi, B. (2008). 'Both Sides Pull Back in Lebanon Civil Conflict', *Seattle Times* (11 May 2008), www.seattletimes.com/nation-world/both-sides-pull-back-in-lebanon-civil-conflict/ (accessed 30 September 2020).

Davie, M. (2001). *Beyrouth 1825–1975: Un Siècle et Demi d'Urbanisme* (Beyrouth: L'Ordre des Ingénieurs et Architectes).

Davie, M. F. (1993). 'A Post-War Geography of Beirut', European Association for Middle East Studies (EURAMES), British Institute for Middle Eastern Studies (BRISMES), Association Français pour l'Etude du Monde Arabe et Musulman (AFEMAM), *EARAMES Conference*, Warwick, July.

Davie, M. F. (1991). 'Demarcation Lines in Contemporary Beirut', *Second International Boundaries Research Unit Conference,* University of Durham, Durham, 18–21 July.

Deeb, L. and Harb, M. (2013). *Leisurely Islam: Negotiating Geography and Morality in Shi'ite South Beirut* (Princeton/Oxford: Princeton University Press).

Dillon, S. (2005). 'Re-inscribing De Quincey's Palimpsest: The Significance of the Palimpsest in Contemporary Literary and Cultural Practice', *Textual Practice,* 19:3, 243–63.

El-Khazen, F. (2000). *The Breakdown of the State in Lebanon* (Cambridge: Harvard University Press).

Faour, A. (1987). 'The Displacement Crisis and Forced Migration in Beirut in 1984', in Nasr, S. and Hanf, T. (eds) *Urban Crisis and Social Movements: Arab and European Perspectives* (Beirut: The Euro-Arab Social Research Group), 165–74.

Fawaz, M., Harb, M., and Gharbiyeh, A. (eds) (2009). *Beirut: Mapping Security* (Stuttgart: Diwan).

Forde, S. (2022). 'The Violence of Space and Spaces of Violence: Peace as Violence in Unequal and Divided Spaces' *Political Geography,* 93, 102529, https://doi.org/10.1016/j.polgeo.2021.102529

Genberg, D. (2002). 'Borders and Boundaries in Post-War Beirut', in Erdentug, A. and Colombijn, F. (eds) *Urban Ethnic Encounters: The Spatial Consequences* (London: Routledge), 81–96.

Hanf, T. (1993). *Coexistence in Wartime Lebanon: Decline of a State and Rise of a Nation* (London: Centre for Lebanese Studies/I.B. Tauris).

Hebbert, M. (2005). 'The Street as Locus of Collective Memory', *Environment and Planning D* 23:4, 581–96.

Highmore, B. (ed.) (2002). *The Everyday Life Reader* (London/New York: Routledge).

Hirsch, M. (2008). 'The Generation of Postmemory' *Poetics Today,* 29:1, 103–28.

Hovsepian, G. (2017). 'Kesrwan and Jbeil to be Merged into A Governorate', *The961* (18 August 2017), www.the961.com/keserwan-and-jbeil-merged-into-a-governorate/ (accessed 30 September 2020).

Huybrechts, E. (1999). 'L'Oubli de la Ligne', in Huybrechts, E., Douayhi, C. (eds) *Reconstruction et Réconciliation au Liban: Négociations, Lieux publics, renouement du lien social* (Beyrouth: Le Cahier du CERMOC Centre d'Étude et de Recherches sur le Moyen-Orient Contemporain 23), 209–20.

Huyssen, A. (2006). *Present pasts. Urban palimpsests and the politics of memory* (Stanford: Stanford University Press).

Kassir, S. (2003). *Histoire de Beyrouth* (Paris: Fayard).

Khalaf, S. (2006). *Heart of Beirut: Reclaiming the Bourj* (London: SAQI).

Khalaf, S. (2002). *Civil and Uncivil Violence in Lebanon: A History of Internationalization of Communal Conflict* (New York: Columbia University Press).

Khalaf, S. (1993). 'Urban Design and the Recovery of Beirut', in Khalaf, S. and Khoury, P. (eds) *Recovering Beirut: Urban Design and post War Reconstruction* (Leiden, New York: Brill Academic Publishers), 11–62.

Khalaf, S. and Khoury, P. (1993). *Recovering Beirut: Urban Design and post War Reconstruction* (Leiden, New York: Brill Academic Publishers).

Larkin, C. (2012). *Memory and Conflict in Lebanon: Remembering and Forgetting the Past* (Oxford, New York: Routledge).

Lebanese Arabic Institute (n.d.). 'Administrative Divisions of Lebanon', www.lebanesearabicinstitute.com/administrative-divisions-lebanon/#Governorates_of_Lebanon (accessed 30 September 2020).

Lefebvre, H. (2004). *Rhythmanalysis: Space, Time and Everyday Life* (London and New York: Continuum).

Mady, C. (2018). 'Public Space Activism in Unstable Contexts: Emancipation from Beirut's Postmemory', in Knierbein, S. and Viderman, T. (eds) *Public Space Unbound Urban Emancipation and the Post-Political Condition* (New York, Oxford: Routledge), 189–206.

Mady, C. and Chettiparamb, A. (2016). 'Planning in the face of 'deep divisions': A view from Beirut, Lebanon', *Planning Theory*, 16:3, 296–317.

Marshall, D. J., Staeheli, L., Smaira, D., and Kastrissianakis, K. (2017). 'Narrating Palimpsestic Spaces', *Environment and Planning A*, 49:5, 1163–1180.

Messenger (2017). 'The Lebanese Civil War in Beirut: The Invisible Green Line', *Foreign Service Messages* (25 September 2017), https://foreignservicemessages.com/2017/09/25/the-lebanese-civil-war-in-beirut-the-invisible-green-line/ (accessed 30 September 2020).

Mollard, M. (2018). 'Spent shell: Museum of Beit Beirut, Lebanon, renovated by Youssef Haidar', *The Architectural Review* (25 June 2018), https//architectural-review.com /buildings/spent-shell-museum-of-beit-beirut-lebanon-renovated-by-youssef-haidar (accessed 12 October 2020).

Monroe, K. V. (2017). 'Circulation, Modernity, and Urban Space in 1960s Beirut', *History and Anthropology, 28*:2, 188–201.

Monroe, K.V. (2011). 'Being Mobile in Beirut', *City and Society* 23:1, 91–111.

N/A (2010). 'Beirut: Mapping Security', *Social Design Notes* (30 September 2010), https://backspace.com/notes/2010/09/beirut-mapping-security.php (accessed 30 September 2020).

N/A (n.d.). 'Beirut Relgions Divides Map', www.mappery.com/Beirut-Relgions-Divides-Map (accessed 30 September 2020).

Navaro-Yashin, Y. (2012). *The Make-Belief Space: Affective Geography in a Post-war Polity.* Durham, NC: Duke University Press.

Nucho, J. R. (2016). *Everyday Sectarianism in Urban Lebanon: Infrastructures, Public Services and Power* (Princeton: Princeton University Press).

Olick, J. (2007). *The Politics of Regret: On Collective Memory and Historical Responsibility* (London: Routledge).

Pelgrim, R. (n.d.). 'Bus 4', *Mashallah News,* https://mashallahnews.com/routes/bus-4/ (accessed 30 September 2020).

Pirker, P., Rode, P., and Lichtenwagner, M. (2019). 'From palimpsest to memoire: Exploring urban memorial landscapes of political violence', *Political Geography*, 74, 1–19. https://doi.org/10.1016/j.polgeo.2019.102057

Pullan, W. (2011). 'Frontier urbanism: the periphery at the centre of contested cities', *The Journal of Architecture,* 16:1, 15–35. https://doi.org/10.1080/13602365.2011.546999

Rabbat, N. (1998). 'The Interplay of History and Archaeology in Beirut', in Rowe, P. and Sarkis, H. (eds) *Projecting Beirut: Episodes in the Construction and Reconstruction of a Modern City* (Munich, London and New York: Prestel), 19–22.

Ristic, M. (2014). '"Sniper Alley": The Politics of Urban Violence in the Besieged Sarajevo', *Built Environment,* 40:3, 342–56.

Sader, H. (1998). 'Ancient Beirut: Urban Growth in the Light of Recent Excavations', in Rowe, P. and Sarkis, H. (eds) *Projecting Beirut: Episodes in the Construction and Reconstruction of a Modern City* (Munich, London and New York: Prestel), 23–40.

Randall, E. (2014). 'Divided Cities, Contested States', in *Conflict in Cities and the Contested State.* Working paper no. 29. www.urbanconflicts.arct.cam.ac.uk/working-paper-29-edward-randall (accessed 30 September 2020).

Roy, A. (2009). 'Civic Governmentality: The Politics of Inclusion in Beirut and Mumbai', *Antipode,* 41:1, 159–79.

Saksouk-Sasso, A. (2015). 'Making Spaces for Communal Sovereignty: The Story of Beirut's Dalieh', *Arab Studies Journal,* 23:1, 296–318.

Saliba, R. (1997). 'The Mental Image of Downtown Beirut, 1990: A case Study in Cognitive Mapping and Urban Form', in Davie, M. F. (ed.) *Beyrouth Regards Croisés. Collection Villes du Monde Arabe* (vol. 2), UMR 6592-CNRS (Tours: Université de Tours), 305–49.

Salibi, K. (1988). *A House of Many Mansions: The History of Lebanon Reconsidered* (London: I.B. Tauris Publishers).

Sarkis, H. (1993). 'Territorial Claims: Architecture and Post-War Attitudes towards the Built Environment', in Khalaf, S. and Khoury, P. (eds) *Recovering Beirut: Urban Design and post War Reconstruction* (Leiden, New York: Brill Academic Publishers), 101–27.

Sassine, F. and Tuéni, G. (eds) (2003). *El-Bourj. Place de la Liberté et Porte du Levant* (Beyrouth: Editions Dar an-Nahar).

Stel, N. (2008). *Beirut under Siege* (M.A. Thesis, Utrecht University), www.researchgate.net/figure/Map-of-Beirut-NowLebanon-wwwnowlebanoncom-accessed-4-July-2009_fig5_37807645 (accessed 30 September 2020).

Tabet, J. (1996). *Al-I'maar Wal-Masslaha Al-A'amah [Reconstruction and the Public Good]* (Beirut: Dar Al-Jadid).

Tabet, J. (1993). 'Towards a Master Plan for Post-War Lebanon', in Khalaf, S. and Khoury, P. (eds) *Recovering Beirut: Urban Design and post War Reconstruction* (Leiden, New York: Brill Academic Publishers), 81–100.

Tabet, J. (1987). 'Images de Beyrouth', in Nasr, S. and Hanf, T. (eds) *Urban Crisis and Social Movements: Arab and European Perspectives* (Beirut: The Euro-Arab Social Research Group), 129–40.

Tabet, J., Ghorayeb, M., Huybrechts, E., and Verdeil, E. (2001). *Beyrouth: Portrait de Ville* (Paris: Institut Français d'Architecture, Supplément à Archiscopie 17).

Traboulsi, F. (2008). *A History of Modern Lebanon from the Imarah to the Taef Accords* (Beirut: Riad El-Rayyes Books [Arabic Version]).

UNJLC (2006). 'Unsafe Areas: Beirut Southern Suburbs, as of 17 August', *Relief Web* (22 August) https://reliefweb.int/map/lebanon/unsafe-areas-beirut-southern-suburbs-17-aug-2006 (accessed 30 September 2020).

Watson, S. (2006). *City Publics: The (Dis)enchantments of Urban Encounters* (Oxford: Routledge).

Yahya, M. (2004). *Let the Dead Be Dead: Memory, Urban Narratives and the Post-Civil War Reconstitution of Beirut* (Centre of Contemporary Culture of Barcelona (CCCB) Conference: Urban Traumas. The City and Disasters, Barcelona: CCCB, 7–11 July).

Yahya, M. (1993). 'Reconstituting Space: The Aberration of the Urban in Beirut', in Khalaf, S. and Khoury, P. (eds) *Recovering Beirut: Urban Design and post War Reconstruction* (Leiden, New York: Brill Academic Publishers), 128–66.

Yassin, N. (2012). 'City Profile: Beirut', *Cities,* 29:1, 64–73. https://doi.org/10.1016/j.cities.2011.02.001

8

'Humiliation Days': Remembering, repeating and expecting urban violence in British Malaya and the Dutch East Indies

Andreas Bolte

On 2 June 1928 the streets of Ipoh were lined with Chinese flags, flying from windows and flagpoles, the banners on the latter having been set to half-mast – signifying the sadness of the occasion. The Chinese government had declared the day to be a *guochi jinianri*, a 'Day of National Humiliation', dedicated to the remembrance of the so-called 'Jinan Incident', a clash between Chinese and Japanese troops in May of that year, which had resulted in thousands of civilian casualties. Accordingly, the second day in June was treated as a day of mourning in Ipoh. Most shops were closed, and the Chinese living in the city did not go to work on this particular day, following the precise instructions of the Chinese government (*Straits Times*, 6 August 1928).

The city of Ipoh, however, is (and was) not in China, but lies on the west coast of Malaysia, in Perak. At the beginning of the twentieth century, Perak was part of British Malaya, a group of British colonies consisting of present-day peninsular Malaysia and Singapore. Only its large Chinese population accounted for the fact that this urban space outside of China would commemorate this particular event. In fact, this was not the first time a Day of National Humiliation had been observed by the local Chinese population, nor was the practice restricted to Ipoh. Most urban areas in Malaya had significant enough Chinese populations to render such com-memorations observable, but while shops were shuttered and Chinese flags hoisted also in Penang and Singapore, Ipoh was the only place in which this particular remembrance of past violence also led to new violence. Around midday, small groups of Chinese rioters started roaming the streets, pressur-ing the owners of any open shops to close, thus forcing them into compli-ance with the Humiliation Day rules. Witnesses later described the groups as 'marching like an army' through the streets, before attacking the patrons of theatres and cinemas that had remained open. In the commotion, a small number of people were injured. Most of the rioters were eventually tried and send to jail (*Straits Times*, 14 August 1928).

The incident only furthered the concerns of the British colonial government about the practice of Humiliation Days – because this was not the first time one such observance had led to conflict in the colony. For many British officials, events such as these confirmed their suspicions of the Chinese state as a potential threat to peace, or even to European rule in Southeast Asia as a whole (The National Archive, London [hereafter TNA], CO 273/561/ 13; Png Poh Seng, 1961: 22). Similarly, the colonial government of the neighbouring Dutch East Indies (present-day Indonesia), also a colony with a large Chinese population, debated banning the practice of Humiliation Days (Nationaal Archief, den Haag [hereafter NA], 2.05.90.567).

The problem grew to an international incident in 1928, when the Chinese government published a calendar of National Humiliation Days. Each of these 26 days commemorated an event of imperialist violence, at which the British, French, Germans, Russians or Japanese had – in the language of the government at Nanjing – 'humiliated' the Chinese. The resulting calendar was to be observed by all Chinese citizens, no matter their country of residence, and as such was addressed also to the Chinese living in British Malaya and the Dutch East Indies. This meant that for 26 days of the year, the Humiliation Days lifted events of past violence from history as far back as the mid-nineteenth century to the present of the 1920s and 1930s, while simultaneously spreading the commemoration of these events to any place inhabited by a sufficiently large Chinese population. In this way, the days were inserted into the larger framework of temporal and spatial connections already in place in the respective locations, a process that was often accompanied by conflict. At the same time, the schedule of constant repetition endemic to any calendar furthered an interdependency between the Humiliation Days and other rhythms and schedules of the urban areas. As we will see, this meant that more and more temporal layers were being constantly added to the phenomenon, because every recurrence of a Humiliation Day brought with it the repetition of every preceding act of the day's insertion into the specific space-time of a given city.

While past research on the Humiliation Days has focused primarily on their role in Chinese history and their function in government policy, this chapter aims to cast a light on their place in the history of British Malaya and the Dutch East Indies (Luo, 1993; Cohen, 2002; Sun Xiangmei, 2007; Callahan, 2012; Wang, 2014). Additionally, the analysis is focused not only on the aspects of the Humiliation Days related to time but acknowledges the connection between the temporal and spatial dimensions inherent in cases such as this. Only in treating both the Humiliation Days and the environment of the colonial cities in which they took place as space-times, an amalgamation of constantly shifting temporalities and spatialities influenced by the constant bargaining for imperial rule, can the entire extent of the topic be understood.

The aim of this chapter is to investigate how the commemoration of urban violence was practiced in an environment that was temporally and spatially removed from the original event. Following the idea that cities often seem bound to dynamics from distant places (Robinson, 2016), the question becomes how this double displacement, in both time and space, influenced the practice of remembering violence. Acts of violence have been described as following certain sequential patterns on shorter timescales (Collins, 2009). Were there other patterns connected to longer timeframes? How did the remembrance itself add to the space-time of the cities? What can the case of the Humiliation Days teach us about the spatial and temporal roots of urban violence? And how did the practice change in the interplay with other aspects of urban space-time in the colonial cities of Southeast Asia?

In dealing with the history of temporally and spatially highly entangled subjects such as the Humiliation Days, the question of how to depict the resulting complexity can be a difficult one. One could follow the temporal strand and narrate the topic like a story, chronologically from beginning to end.

A different approach would be to arrange the topic along spatial lines and focus on the different locations, one after another. While these approaches are valid options for most subjects, in a case like the Humiliation Days it seems opportune to choose a different path, one that can reveal the entanglement of the topic without burying it in a mess of complexity. With this aim in mind, this analysis of the Humiliation Days will be split up along the lines of the three temporal dimensions, focusing first on the aspects connected primarily to the past, then the aspects connected to the present, and lastly those connected to the future. While this approach allows for most of the interconnections of space and time to become visible, there is the risk of severing the connections and neglecting the interferences between the three dimensions themselves. Since space-time is as subject to the flow of time as anything else, not accounting for the relationship between its past-, present- and future-oriented aspects would mean to deny space-time its own historicity. To preclude this risk, inter-temporal connections will be covered step-by-step as the chapter proceeds through the dimensions, showing how elements connected to the past influenced those connected to the present (and vice versa) in the second section, with interferences among all three dimensions covered in the section on the future-related elements of the Humiliation Days.

Remembering violence

The notion of National Humiliation has occupied a key position in Chinese nationalism since at least the beginning of the twentieth century. It evokes the treatment of China by the imperial powers of Europe and Japan from the 1840s onward as constituting the main formative experience of the Chinese nation. In the years of the Chinese Empire until the Xinhai Revolution of 1911, Chinese intellectuals advocated the establishment of National Humiliation Days to commemorate the influence of the imperial powers on the Chinese (Cohen, 2003: 148). But it was not until 1915 that the first National Humiliation Day was proclaimed. During the First World War, Japan pressured the Chinese government into making several concessions, called the '21 Demands', effectively accepting Japanese imperial influence in China. After the signing of these demands by the Chinese government on 9 May 1915 a group of political activists, centred around a Beijing teachers' union, called for the yearly commemoration of the event as the *wujiu guochi jinianri*, literally the 'Five-Nine National Humiliation Day' (Callahan, 2012: 63–8). When the date recurred in 1916, it was marked by protests and strikes in larger cities throughout China, with some stores and offices closing for the day.

More Humiliation Days were added after the end of the war. The protests that broke out in Beijing on 4 May 1919, directed against the disregard of China's claims in the Treaty of Versailles, were remembered as a second day of National Humiliation, again appealing to both anti-Japanese and anti-Western feelings in the Chinese population. The third event added to the calendar of National Humiliation occurred on 30 May 1925, when British soldiers shot and killed Chinese students demonstrating in Shanghai. With this third case, we can already see how the space-time of the Humiliation Days began to become layered: it had been the ten-year anniversary of the '21 Demands' that furthered the protests and strikes in Shanghai and eventually led to the escalation inside the International Settlement (Osterhammel, 1997: 12). The violence connected to the Humiliation Days seems to have catalysed new events of violence. These first Humiliation Days have many of the spatial and temporal attributes we can also observe with later examples: the act of remembrance lifted the event from history, anchored it in the present, and spread it over a larger space. Although the protests were mainly directed against Japan (and the acceptance of the Japanese demands by the Chinese government), a profound sense of betrayal by the 'Western powers' meant that over the years, the first National Humiliation Day was also connected to a broadly anti-imperial, and sometimes even distinctly anti-British narrative (Osterhammel, 1989: 239; Zhao, 2005: 50; Wang, 2014: 68).

The Humiliation Days were also mainly an urban phenomenon. In the larger cities, with their high number of students and merchants, the narrative of National Humiliation fitted neatly into the anti-government and anti-imperial agitation fuelling the protest movements known as the *wusi yundong* (4th of May Movement) and *wusa yundong* (30th of May Movement) (Luo, 1993: 301). This only changed when the Guomindang under Chiang Kai-shek took over large parts of China in 1927, reuniting many of the areas that had come under the control of warlords and rival governments after 1911. The Guomindang introduced a calendar of 26 National Humiliation Days, each one with precise information on the historical events (nations involved, number of Chinese casualties) and instructions for commemoration, which could include the singing of anthems, bowing before the flag and/or a portrait of Sun Yat-Sen, and some sort of lecture on the historical event being commemorated (Liang Xinbian, 1931; Huang Shaoxu et al., 1934). The relatively large number of 26 came about because the Guomindang was attempting to unify the commemorations across China by including a number of older events, going back as far as the mid-nineteenth century.

As in China, the Chinese of British Malaya and of the Dutch East Indies did not follow a fixed protocol for Humiliation Days until 1927, although some generalisations can be made. In British Malaya, observation of the Humiliation Days started in the early 1920s and became more frequent over the following years. In the Dutch East Indies, publicly visible commemorations did not occur until the mid-1920s, which was probably due to the composition of the Chinese population in the Dutch colony. While both colonies were (at least periodically) home to large numbers of seasonal workers on the plantations outside of the larger cities, both also had a long tradition of Chinese merchants and students living in urban areas (Lockard, 2013). In the Dutch East Indies, the number of students was still increasing in the 1920s. It seems that this growth of the generally more politically active parts of the Chinese population also increased the likelihood of publicly visible celebrations of the Humiliation Days.

Even though the Guomindang had officially raised the number of Humiliation Days to 26 in 1928, commemorations did not noticeably increase in any of the colonies. Looking more closely at those days that aroused the Chinese population to express their national feelings, it becomes clear that one group of days was mainly ignored: those added to the 1928 calendar that commemorated events from before 1911. It seems that this double distance of both time and space took its toll. The Guomindang government at Nanjing had selected the events for the calendar with the intention to include most parts of China, but even in China itself it seemed difficult to communicate exactly why these long-gone days were now to be commemorated (TNA, CO 273/573/12). Outside of China, and outside of any of the spaces represented in the calendar, the space-time of the more obscure Humiliation Days seems to have been too far removed to prompt any commemoration activities.

To understand the further implications of this double distance, we must turn our attention to the ways in which the commemorations took place. By far the most common demonstration of remembrance among the Chinese of British Malaya and the Dutch East Indies was by the use of flags. On many of the Humiliation Days the Chinese republican flag was hung from private or company houses and hoisted in front of newspaper buildings, chambers of commerce, or the Chinese embassies and consulates. Since this practice was also common on other Chinese holidays, such as the New Year, it did not attract much attention on its own. Only when the flags were set at half-mast to mark the negative connotation of the occasion, which seems to have happened increasingly throughout the 1920s, did the European populations of cities like Batavia (now Jakarta) and Singapore start to wonder about the implications of this practice. Was this not an affront? Where these flags not directed against the nations of other inhabitants of the colonies, such as the Japanese and the British? Furthermore, if these were anti-imperial com-memoration days, was this not a rejection of the whole concept of a colony? In setting their flags to half-mast, the Chinese made the connection to the violence of the Humiliation Days visible to outsiders, thus forcibly add-ing it to the specific space-time of these urban areas. They transported the urban violence of the original events from their (temporal and spatial) place in history to 1920s Batavia, Singapore, or any of the other cities in British Malaya and the Dutch East Indies. Rendering imperialist violence visible to the imperialists did not fail to raise tensions. A comment in the Singaporean newspaper *The Straits Times* speculated about the loyalties of anyone who would follow this practice, and warned the Chinese population: 'We think that the Chinese in Malaya would be well-advised not to observe any "day of mourning" at all' (*Straits Times*, 26 May 1928). The governments of both British Malaya and the Dutch East Indies made several attempts to ban the half-masting of flags on the Humiliation Days, although it turned out that this was harder to police than originally anticipated. Both also tried to impose pressure on the Chinese consuls not to display flags at half-mast, which they argued was even worse than when private persons did it, since this was now an official act of the Nanjing government (TNA, CO 273/573/ 12; TNA, CO 273/561/13; NA, 2.05.90.567).

At the root of this conflict around the remembrance of urban vio-lence lay a particular aspect of the specific space-time of the Humiliation Days. The spatial distance from the original events commemorated by the Humiliation Days meant that while there were certainly enough Chinese in the cities of British Malaya and the Dutch East Indies to reach the critical mass necessary for visible commemoration, these people were still living under the roof of a state that was not Chinese, and in fact that was ruled by one of the perceived oppressors of China. This was even more true for British Malaya than for the Dutch East Indies, since Britain was one of the nations directly responsible for some of the violence commemorated by the Humiliation Days.

Among the other practices used to publicly commemorate the violence of the Humiliation Days were different forms of protest marches and the closure of shops and businesses for the day. These practices were less common than the hoisting (or half-masting) of flags, presumably because protests required more time and organisation, and closing down shops was in the end still not very good for business. Protest marches were quite common during the second half on the 1920s in both British Malaya and the Dutch East Indies, but became less frequent in the 1930s, for reasons we will turn our attention to later. The closing of shops seems to have been more common over the whole time frame, which may be because it took the actions of only a handful of merchants to close down enough shops to raise the attention of the non-Chinese inhabitants of a city, while it required a larger number of people and more of an organisational effort to arrange even a small protest march. Often, protests were subject to city guidelines and had to be approved beforehand, or could otherwise be subject to police intervention, a case that will be dealt with in the next section. Shop closures, on the other hand, were often announced in the run-up to the Humiliation Days, to inform customers, but were crucially not subject to government scrutiny. On top of that, shop-owners tended to arrange things with their colleagues so that no one had to suffer financial losses if one of them did not partake in the Humiliation Day.

Crucially, such agreements only worked among Chinese businesses, which might also explain why it was much more common for a shop owner to put up a Chinese flag on a Humiliation Day than to close for the day. The Humiliation Days in British Malaya and the Dutch East Indies were part of the different space-times of multi-ethnic colonial cities, with their rhythms and temporal and spatial relations. While all shops closed on those days designated public holidays in the respective colonies, every national group also had a number of calendars to follow, religious and secular ones, and the Humiliation Day calendar was only one among many – so merchants had to calculate the financial risk of closing one more day a year, or of closing on a day on which many of their (non-Chinese) colleagues remained open. This was a problem that was not faced by their counterparts in China, where the Humiliation Days did not have to compete with the other temporal and spatial features of urban space-time.

The flags, protests and shop-closures were not only inserted into the urban space-time of the colonial cities of British Malaya and the Dutch East Indies – they also added to the space-time of the Humiliation Days. The remembrance was more than just an image of past violence conjured up from nowhere; it also became a practice in itself that added a layer to the specific space-time of the Humiliation Days outside of China. Every protest and every flag always had a part in the procedure that repeated the next year, and the year after that. This is even more striking in those cases that went beyond remembering violence and included the expression of new violence, to which we will now turn our attention.

Repeating violence

On a spatiotemporal level, the new violence on Humiliation Days went beyond the commemoration of past violence. Even though time had moved on, and the places at which the violence occurred were mostly different from those of the original events, both the 'new' violence and the original outbreaks of violence were connected through the space-time of the Humiliation Days. This formed a continuity that is best described as a repetition of violence. This explicitly does *not* mean that history repeated itself. While some contemporaries actually made such observations, in this case the term repetition is used in an analytical sense, and is directed more towards the calendrical recurrence of any kind of violence than the exact replication of a past event, something that would in any case be impossible. For every case of urban violence on a Humiliation Day, the degree of repetition must be assessed, judging how similar the new violence was to the old one, and additionally explaining why it was similar. For even if time, place, situation, participants and other circumstances seem different to us at first glance, there might be a connection hidden amongst the multiplicity of complex temporal and spatial references.

To illustrate this point, it might be best to turn our attention once again to China and take a look at how violence played out on the Humiliation Days there. Before 1927, most larger Humiliation Day protests had featured some form of violent clash with the police, because of the protests' anti-government messages. The two most prominent protest movements even took their names from Humiliation Day events, the '4th of May Movement' and the '30th of May Movement'. While the original events at the root of the commemorations were connected much more to violence among nations – Japan's imposition of the 21 Demands, with its more-or-less obvious military threat, and the decision at Versailles to grant to Japan those parts of China that it had already occupied – the violence that erupted as an immediate reaction to the events in 1915 and 1919, respectively, was strikingly similar to the protests in the years that followed. On both occasions similar groups – anti-government protesters comprised of teachers, students and merchants – clashed with the police in the streets of the bigger cities like Beijing. This also meant that the repetition of violence inscribed itself into the space-time of the Humiliation Days. In China, these days were not only reminiscent of violence – they were an occasion of violence. This is still a problem for the PRC government today, 4 May 1989 being only one example from recent Chinese history (Wasserstrom, 2005: 60).

Only after 1927, when the Guomindang had taken over large parts of China, did this practice stop. Even as the new calendar added many new Humiliation Days to the established ones, the Ministry of the Interior published accompanying schedules that minutely described the protocol for the respective days. For most days, in the morning there were to be short commemorative speeches at every workplace, with flags flying, and sometimes large festivities in the evening. Under no circumstances were there to be any protests on any of the Humiliation Days (Huang Shaoxu et al., 1934). The Guomindang strategy meant a complete reformulation of the spatiotemporal implications of the Humiliation Days, excising every mention of intra-Chinese violence and focusing instead on instances of imperialist violence against China. While this certainly had the desired effect in terms of stifling anti-government protests, it also led, after a few years, to a lack of enthusiasm for the practice as a whole, as fewer and fewer people seemed to follow the protocols at all. Contemporary explanations for this trend argued that the number of days was simply too large (as was reasoned by the Chinese government) or that the Guomindang had gravely misjudged the historic preferences of its subjects (which was the prevailing hypothesis among British officials) (TNA, CO 273/573/12). The sources do not allow a definitive answer in this case, but it seems feasible that at least some Chinese lost interest in the practice as a rejection of what could be construed as over-regulation. The Guomindang government eventually tried to amend the calendar, to counteract this trend, but the Humiliation Days did not return to their previous popularity until after the end of Guomindang rule in mainland China (Cohen, 2002). In essence, the only thing the Guomindang's version of the Humiliation Days had in common with the Humiliation Days popular in China before 1927 was that they referred to the same original events. The temporal and spatial references embedded in the phenomenon were otherwise completely different, because the Guomindang had changed the interpretations of the original events to fit their political agenda. This led to the end of the repetition of violence, but also ultimately ended the practice for the time being.

In both British Malaya and the Dutch East Indies, the overwhelming majority of Humiliation Day commemorations were non-violent, in the sense that while they certainly drew attention to the events of violence that had occurred on those days in the past, temporally, this was the extent of it. From time to time, however, violence occurred in the colonies as well, as we have seen in the example of Ipoh at the beginning of this chapter. Rather than examining all instances of violence on Humiliation Days in the two colonies, we will take a look at some general features they shared, before analysing a few paradigmatic cases in more detail.

The first observation we can make is that 1927 does not seem to have been a turning point among the overseas Chinese as it was in China. The repetition of violence on Humiliation Days occurred before as well as after 1927, even though the number of incidents decreased after 1930, which might be related to the practice's decreasing importance in China. Generally, the introduction of the calendar changed little in terms of the occurrence of violence. The newly added Humiliation Days, which did not lead to a significant number of protests or other remembrance activities, were also no occasion for repeated violence. The other days, however, those that had been established during the1920s, sometimes did lead to recurrences of violence. No particular day seemed more prone to such events than any other. This is also true for those days that commemorated events that had originally involved violence in British Malaya or the Dutch East Indies, such as 4 May, which had led to protests in Singapore (Kenley, 2013). New violence occurred on different Humiliation Days in May just as frequently as on the other previously established days of the calendar. Spatially, there is one observable pattern that coincides with the occurrence of remembered violence: as well as being an urban phenomenon in general, violence tended to break out in those cities with large Chinese populations, simply because there were more potential participants. At the same time, such outbreaks rarely took place in different cities at the same time, which suggests that the phenomenon was a very localised one and that the configuration of space-time in the various cities influenced the violence on Humiliation Days in different ways.

The kind of violence evident during the Humiliation Days in the cities of British Malaya and the Dutch East Indies shared some of the characteristics of the violence observable in China. Aside from the urban setting in which the events took place, parts of the violence centred around a mixture of anti-imperial and anti-governmental protests as well – although anti-governmental in this case meant against the colonial governments of the colonies. As in China we can observe a number of clashes between Humiliation Day protesters and the police. The largest of such events connected to the Humiliation Days occurred in Singapore's Kreta Ayer neighbourhood in 1927.

On 12 March 1927, the Humiliation Day commemorations devoted to the death of Guomindang-founder Sun Yat-sen two years previously took place in Singapore's Happy Valley Amusement Park in Tanjong Pagar. Contemporary reports speak of about 20,000 Chinese participants. After the celebrations, a group of about 1,000 (supposedly Guomindang-loyal) Chinese started a protest march through the streets of Singapore, waving Chinese national flags and distributing anti-imperialist pamphlets. After a confrontation with a trolley bus, the driver of which then tried to escape the protesters by steering his vehicle towards the nearest police station, the crowd ultimately arrived at the Kreta Ayer police station, where violent confrontations ensued. Feeling overrun, the police finally resorted to the use of firearms, killing six protesters and injuring fourteen others (Hung-Ting Ku, 1976). The case is especially interesting, because this particular Humiliation Day did not commemorate a single violent event, but rather served as a reminder of imperialist violence in China in general, through the remembrance of the founder of the Guomindang, who had also been the first president of the Republic in 1911. From this perspective, the violence that occurred in 1927 was only a repetition in the sense that it repeated the violence of the general constellation of 'China v. Imperialism', which the Chinese protesters felt had harmed their nation in the past. It was a bitter irony of history, that the confrontation of armed and trained policemen against unarmed protesters, and its tragic outcome, was similar to the many historical incidences of imperialist violence in China.

The Dutch East Indies did not suffer any incidents of this magnitude on Humiliation Days, although clashes between police and protesters were not uncommon. On 7 May 1928, one of the Humiliation Days connected to the 21 Demands, a group of Chinese protesters in Batavia got into a skirmish with local police. It later transpired that the group had been handing out anti-imperialist and anti-Japanese flyers, which the police interpreted as threatening the peace of the colony, for which they arrested the group after a brief struggle (Sumatra-Bode, 8 May 1928). A similar event occurred in Medan on 14 October 1931, a Humiliation Day dedicated to the Japanese occupation of Manchuria, when a group of Chinese students calling themselves the *Comité van Actie tegen Japan* (Committee for Action against Japan) was arrested for protesting and, again, handing out anti-Japanese pamphlets (De Indische Courant, 14 October 1931). At the same time, a number of similar events took place in some cities of British Malaya (Malaya Tribune, 10 August 1932). In these cases, the degree of repetition was limited to the vague alignments of the involved parties, again being a clash between Chinese and what they conceived as imperialists, personified by colonial policemen.

The dates of this small selection of cases already illustrate one of the major differences to the Chinese cases: 1927 did not institute a similar change in the repetition of violence. As with the remembrance of past violence, these events took place on Humiliation Days already established before 1927, or on those dedicated to the contemporary difficulties between China and Japan – there were no incidents on those new Humiliation Days that had been introduced with the Guomindang calendar. But while these events involved violence between protesters and the police, as in the Chinese cases, there were also cases of Humiliation Day violence in the colonies that had no equivalent in China, that were connected less to protests, and more to Humiliation Day discipline. At the beginning of this chapter, the case was recounted of a group of Chinese rioters pressuring other Chinese into acting in accordance with the Humiliation Day procedures in Ipoh in 1928. Similar cases can be found throughout British Malaya and the Dutch East Indies. One example took place in Surabaya on 12 November 1926, again one of the Humiliation Days devoted to Sun Yat-sen. Here, a number of Chinese merchants were similarly pressured into closing their shops for the day, although violence did not erupt in a similar manner to the case in Ipoh (Bataviaasch Nieuwsblad, 22 October 1926).

This kind of disciplinary violence amongst the Chinese community did not have an equivalent in China. The reason for this new form of repeated violence probably lies in the context of other urban space-times, into which the Humiliation Days had to be integrated. Since the areas of British Malaya and the Dutch East Indies had for centuries been the destination of Chinese merchants, many Chinese had settled there long before the founding of the Chinese Republic. Even after 1911, it can be presumed that many of the Chinese emigrating to the colonial cities did not affiliate themselves with the Republic, and hence took less of an interest in the Humiliation Days. Their spatial connections to China had been severed long ago, and their individual temporal rhythms were often still those of the old Chinese Empire, with many still following the lunar calendar instead of the republican solar calendar (*Singapore Free Press and Mercantile Advertiser*, 24 October 1929). This set them apart from those who retained an interest in current Chinese politics and were thus much more involved in the commemoration of the Humiliation Days, a contrast that could result in events of disciplinary violence.

In any case, both kinds of repeating violence in the British Malaya and the Dutch East Indies were, in the overwhelming majority of cases, restricted to urban areas. More specifically, to the Chinese quarter of such cities, if there was one. The cinemas attacked in Ipoh were all in an area mainly inhabited by Chinese, while Kreta Ayer Road lies in the heart of Singapore's China Town. These temporal and spatial patterns of violence did not escape the notice of the governments of British Malaya and the Dutch East Indies and their colonial police forces, to whom we will now turn our attention.

Expecting violence

Most of the Europeans living in British Malaya and the Dutch East Indies had an impression of the Humiliation Days that ranged from neutral surprise to aggressive rejection. The reaction to Chinese flags flying on certain days of the year in the Dutch East Indies was not automatically negative, but revealed a certain sense of bewilderment, especially if Chinese shops were also closed on the respective days (De Sumatra Post, 11 October 1920; De Indische Courant, 31 May 1926). In British Malaya, even these forms of commemoration activities evoked negative feedback, with newspaper commentators arguing that this practice should have no place in a British colony (*Straits Times*, 26 May 1928). Whenever the remembered violence escalated into repeated violence, all European newspapers and the governments at Batavia and Singapore naturally condemned the Humiliation Days in the strongest terms. The problem was twofold: being colonial governments themselves, the local officials of British Malaya and the Dutch East Indies found it problematic that the Humiliation Days were devoted to the remembrance of imperialist violence. This was the case in the Dutch as well as in the British colony, even though the former was one of the few European powers not directly connected to any of the original Humiliation Day events. Therefore, the European population did not agree with the fact of the Humiliation Days focusing on the past in the first place.

Even less accepted were those aspects that focused on the present. From the point of view of the colonial governments, the European merchants and private persons living in the cities, the repetition of violence was unacceptable, as it not only caused trouble in general, but also seemed to draw the anti-imperialist message to its logical conclusion: colonial society was inherently violent and unjust. It did not help that most European officials in the colonies already viewed the Chinese state with a great deal of suspicion, with many believing China to be striving for a Southeast Asian empire of its own. Cecil Clementi, the Resident General of British Malaya, was already speaking of a Chinese '*Imperium in Imperio*' in the late 1920s and warned against much of the area being viewed as Chinese '*terra irredenta*' (TNA, CO 273/561/13).

For the leaders of the colonies, the Humiliation Days did not seem to be focused on history; they saw them as a threat to their present power in Southeast Asia. For them, the space-time of the Humiliation Days had far fewer temporal connections to the past, and far fewer spatial connections to

China, at least to the locations of the original events. When Clementi and his Dutch counterpart Dirk de Graeff heard the words 'Humiliation Days', the term elicited associations with 'Soerabaya 1926' and 'Kreta Ayer 1927'. These emerging temporal and spatial patterns created a situation in which the colonial governments came to expect urban violence on these occasions, which added a third temporal dimension to the space-time of Humiliation Days. The fear among the European officials that events like the Kreta Ayer incident could repeat themselves, raised the question of how the future of the Humiliation Days could be appropriately influenced.

While both colonial governments had realised relatively early the potential problem that Humiliation Days could pose to the integrity of imperial rule, no official steps were taken against the practice until the late 1920s. Only after a number of violent Humiliation Days, and after the Guomindang had raised the official number of Humiliation Days to 26, did the two colonial governments make attempts to ban the commemorations (NA, 2.05.90.567; TNA, CO 273/573/12). As a first step, the officials looked into the possibility of banning the raising of flags on the specific days, with one Dutch official arguing that 'since the National Government declared some days officially as Humiliation Days ..., it is in my opinion correct to speak of an in this country undesirable influence on the Chinese population' (NA, 2.05.90.567). It turned out that a full-blown ban on raising flags was too difficult to enforce, so the legal action taken against the practice only prohibited the half-masting of flags on certain days.

The second step taken by the colonial governments concerned police tactics. In the late 1920s, the Humiliation Day calendar became something of a schedule for the policing of Chinese-dominated urban areas. It seems that the observable pattern of the Humiliation Days' space-time formed an important part of the successful strategies employed by the Special Branch of the Straits Settlements' Crime Investigation Department, giving them and their Malayan equivalent an upper hand in the policing of the Chinese community (Ban Kah Choon, 2001: 140). Similarly, the *Algemeene Recherche Dienst*, the Dutch colonial political police, seems to have paid close attention to the possibility of violence taking place in the Chinese quarters during Humiliation Days (Shiraishi, 2003: 69; Bloembergen 2006: 83–8). The two units also worked together, exchanging knowledge and techniques, while also informing one another of potential upcoming moments of unrest. In a way, this was a successful method of policing – at least in terms of statistics. Arrest numbers in both colonies tended to coincide with Humiliation Days. This points towards a system that made heavy use of future-oriented policing techniques (Poeze, 1988; Poeze, 1994; TNA CO 273/616/8).

Even on the occasions of repeated violence that we have looked at, there were usually already some members of the police on the ground, because the anticipation of violence had become a mainstay of police work. During the Kreta Ayer incident, five constables had been escorting the protest march throughout Chinatown, but ultimately failed to prevent the escalation that followed (Yong and MacKenna, 1990: 88). In the cases in the Dutch East Indies, the police had been on the lookout for potential protesters. This expectation of violence became another layer of the space-time of the Humiliation Days, one that had a number of repercussions for the remembrance and repetition of violence.

We have already covered the most obvious effect of the policework on the Humiliation Days: it probably reduced the number of violent outbreaks, although it is hard to assess to what extent. From the police reports we can gather that there would have been more events of repeated violence had there not already been policemen present at the scene. In this interpretation, Kreta Ayer and other instances were exceptions that proved the rule. A less flattering interpretation would be that in cases of smaller scuffles between police and protesters, violence would not have occurred at all, had the police not been expecting it. In those instances of small groups of Chinese students getting into trouble with a larger number of police officers, the expectation of violence might have acted like a self-fulfilling prophecy. In any case, it is reasonable to assume that, after a few instances of repeated violence, similar occurrences might also have been anticipated by those Chinese potentially interested in the Humiliation Day remembrances. The layering of the Humiliation Days with repeated and expected violence probably deterred a large number of Chinese from joining in the commemoration of the original events, for fear of getting caught up in such violence.

The layered space-time of the Humiliation Days

Looking at the space-time of the Humiliation Days in British Malaya and the Dutch East Indies has enabled us to examine how urban violence was commemorated in a temporally and spatially distant environment. Whereas in China, the main obstacle to overcome was the temporal distance, in the colonies there was a double displacement, which influenced the practice of remembering in several ways. The most obvious result was the fact that the anti-imperial Humiliation Days were to be commemorated in a space that was not only imperial itself, but also run by imperialists, who tended not to take lightly the fact that the commemoration days questioned the very basis of their rule. While this applied to both the Dutch and the British, the latter had even more reason to work against the Humiliation Days, since some of the original violence was committed by British forces in China.

A second effect of the double displacement seems to have been that it was harder to add new Humiliation Days to the list. When the Guomindang raised the number of days to 26 in 1928, most of the newly added days commemorated events that had happened before 1911. While this had the potential to at least include more parts of China in the historical narrative, the Chinese of British Malaya and the Dutch East Indies seem to have been less receptive to the new additions. This was also true to an even greater extent for those Chinese who had left China before 1911 or were integrated into family and business networks that had been established before the end of the Chinese Empire. Being generally less invested in the daily politics of the Chinese republic, they were focused on other temporal and spatial connections to their Chinese heritage, such as the lunar calendar, which had been abolished in China in 1912. Here we can clearly see how the space-times of the British Malayan and Dutch East Indian cities already contained spatiotemporal patterns that hindered the success of the Humiliation Days. This was also true in a more general sense: the Humiliation Days were not only competing against other Chinese space-times; each of the colonial cities followed its own rhythms, into which the Humiliation Days had to be integrated. Space-times were still subject to historic change, but it can be argued that it was quicker to simply declare new Humiliation Days in China than to gradually integrate them into the lives of Chinese overseas.

The space-time of the Humiliation Days changed not only because it clashed with the space-times already in place in the larger cities. The different temporal dimensions also had a reciprocal effect upon each other. In some cases, the repetition of violence had the potential to overshadow the remembrance of violence. Those viewing the Humiliation Days in a more critical way generally tended to focus on this aspect. For the colonial governments of British Malaya and the Dutch East Indies, the Humiliation Days were clearly much more strongly connected to the violent events taking place in those colonies during commemorations, than to the original events in China. This eventually led to the expectation of violence, not only on the part of Europeans, but from the Chinese as well, which had a negative effect on the remembrance, since fewer people were inclined to take part in Humiliation Day festivities, fearing potential clashes with the police. It is unclear whether the repetition of violence was actually increased by this expectation. While the colonial officials certainly argued that occasions of violence could be prevented through proper policing, it might also have been the case that the expectation of violence led police officers to seek out confrontations with the Chinese on Humiliation Days.

On a more general level, we have seen how sequential patterns of urban violence (Collins, 2009) can also be found on a different timescale of months or years through the constant repetition of remembering and expecting violence. These longer timeframes mirror the spatial dimension of a city bound up and connected to dynamics and processes from a distant 'elsewhere' (Robinson, 2016). In the creation of these connections, the role of public rituals of remembering is especially striking with the Humiliation Days, where commemoration and violence seem to have formed an inseparable connection, as in the case of other examples of urban violence recently raised in historical research (Albrecht, 2021).

We can observe a layering of the space-time of the Humiliation Days, not only from the interactions with spatiotemporal connections already established in the urban areas of the colonies, but also from the interdependence between the different temporal dimensions of the Humiliation Days. What was originally an occasion to remember the past violence of imperial powers in China came to involve the events of remembrance themselves, the different kinds of repeating violence, and eventually even the expectation of violence. Thus, the temporal and spatial roots of urban violence became embedded not only in history, but in all temporal dimensions, in addition to the urban space and its interactions with these dimensions. All these connections formed a complex amalgamation, which made it easier for anyone encountering the phenomenon to reduce this complexity by focusing on single elements, such as certain temporal connections over others. This in turn led to the addition of new layers of remembrance, repetition and expectancy to the space-time of urban violence in British Malaya and the Dutch East Indies, layers that were added each year anew.

Bibliography

Albrecht, M. (2021). 'Ritual Performances and Collective Violence in Divided Cities – The Riots in Belfast (1886) and Jerusalem (1929)', *Political Geography*, 86. https://doi.org/10.1016/j.polgeo.2021.102341

Ban Kah Choon (2001). *Absent History. The untold story of Special Branch Operations in Singapore, 1915–1942* (Singapore: Raffles).

Bataviaasch Nieuwsblad (1926). 'De Chineesche Relletjes te Soerabaia', *Bataviaasch Nieuwsblad* (22 October 1926).

Bloembergen, M. (2006). 'Koloniale staat, politiestaat?: Politieke politie en het rode fantoom in Nederlands-Indië', *Leidschrift*, 21, 69–90.

Callahan, W. A. (2012). *China. The Pessoptimist Nation* (Oxford: Oxford University Press).

Cohen, P. A. (2002). 'Remembering and Forgetting National Humiliation in Twentieth-Century China', *Twentieth-Century China*, 27:2, 1–39.

Cohen, P. A. (2003). *China Unbound. Evolving perspectives on the Chinese past* (New York: Routledge).

Collins, R. (2009). *Violence. A Micro-sociological Theory* (Princeton, NJ: Princeton University Press).

De Indische Courant (1926). 'Chineesche Herdenkingsdag', *De Indische Courant* (31 May 1926).

De Indische Courant (1931). 'Arrestatie Chineesche Jongelieden', *De Indische Courant* (14 October 1931).

De Sumatra Post (1920). 'Een Herdenkingsdag', *De Sumatra Post* (11 October 1920).

Huang Shaoxu et al. (1934). *Chongbian riyong baike quanshu.* [*New edition of encyclopaedia for everyday use*] (Shanghai: Publisher unknown).

Hung-Ting Ku (1976). *Kuomintang's Mass Movement and the Kreta Ayer Incident (1927) in Malaya* (Singapore: Institute of Humanities and Social Sciences, College of Graduate Studies, Nanyang University).

Kenley, D. L. (2013). *New Culture in a New World. The May Fourth movement and the Chinese diaspora in Singapore, 1919–1932* (New York: Routledge).

Liang Xinbian (1931). *Guochi Shiyao* [*History of national humiliation*] (Taipei: Publisher unknown).

Lockard, C. A. (2013). 'Chinese Migration and Settlement in Southeast Asia Before 1850: Making Fields From the Sea', *History Compass,* 11:9, 765–81.

Luo (1993). 'National Humiliation and National Assertion: The Chinese Response to the Twenty-one Demands', *Modern Asian Studies,* 27:2, 297–319.

Malaya Tribune (1932). 'Racial and Communal Disturbances', *Malaya Tribune* (10 August 1932).

Nationaal Archief, den Haag, *2.05.90.567, Nederlandse Gezantschap in China, Stukken betreffende het halfstok vlaggen door de Chinese consuls in Nederlands-Indië op zgn. Chinese vernederdagen* (Nederlandse Gezantschap in China).

Osterhammel, J. (1989). *China und die Weltgesellschaft. Vom 18. Jahrhundert bis in unsere Zeit* (München: Beck-Verlag).

Osterhammel, J. (1997). *Shanghai, 30. Mai 1925. Die chinesische Revolution* (München: dtv).

Png Poh Seng (1961). 'The Kuomintang in Malaya, 1912–1941', *Journal of Southeast Asian History,* 2:1, 1–32.

Poeze, H. A. (1988). *Politiek-politioneele overzichten van Nederlandsch-Indië. Bronnenpublikatie, Deel III, 1931–1934* (The Hague: Nijhoff).

Poeze, H. A. (1994). *Politiek-politioneele overzichten van Nederlandsch-Indië. Bronnenpublikatie, Deel IV, 1935–1941* (Dordrecht: Foris).

Robinson, J. (2016). 'Thinking Cities through Elsewhere', *Progress in Human Geography* 40:1, 3–29.

Shiraishi, T. (2003). 'A New Regime of Order: The Origin of Modern Surveillance Politics in Indonesia', in Kahin, A. and Siegel, J. T. (eds) *Southeast Asia over Three Generations* (Ithaca: Cornell University Press), 47–74.

Singapore Free Press and Mercantile Advertiser (1929). 'Matters Chinese', *Singapore Free Press and Mercantile Advertiser* (24 October 1929).

Straits Times (1928). 'Day of Mourning', *Straits Times* (26 May 1928).

Straits Times (1928). 'Rowdyism in Ipoh', *Straits Times* (6 August 1928).

Straits Times (1928). 'Gaol for Ipoh Extremists', *Straits Times* (14 August 1928).

Straits Times (1928). 'Ipoh Politics', *Straits Times* (14 August 1928).

Sumatra-Bode (1928). 'Anti-Japansche Propaganda', *Sumatra-Bode* (8 May 1928).

Sun Xiangmei (2007). 'Minguo shiqi de guochi jinianri', *Zhongshan Fengyu* 4, 16–19.

The National Archives. London, CO 273/616/8, Annual Police Reports, 1934 and 1935: confidential appendices and reports of Special Branch.

The National Archives. London, CO 273/573/12, Chinese Consul at Penang.

The National Archives. London, CO 273/561/13, Kuo Min Tang organization and activities in Malaya and Hong Kong.

Wang, Z. (2014). *Never Forget National Humiliation. Historical Memory in Chinese Politics and Foreign Relations* (New York: Columbia University Press).

Wasserstrom, J. N. (2005). 'Chinese Students and Anti-Japanese Protests, Past and Present', *World Policy Journal,* 22:2, 59–65.

Yong, C. and MacKenna, R. B. (1990). *The Kuomintang Movement in British Malaya. 1912–1949* (Singapore: Singapore University Press).

Zhao, S. (2005). *A nation-state by construction. Dynamics of modern Chinese nationalism* (Stanford: Stanford University Press).

9

Counter-mapping the divided city: Topographies of violence and the religious imagination in urban Brazil

Christian Laheij

Introduction

On 31 March 2005, a group of 12 off-duty police officers, driving down the streets of Nova Iguaçu and Queimados in Rio de Janeiro's sprawling zone of suburbs called the Baixada Fluminense, randomly shot and killed twenty-nine pedestrians. It was later claimed that they were protesting against their new commander's zero-tolerance approach towards corruption and misconduct; a couple of weeks earlier, the group had already expressed its dismay by throwing a human head over the fence of a police station.[1] The massacre is but one instance of the continuing tragedy of urban violence that haunts the periphery of Rio de Janeiro. Ever since the 1960s and 1970s, when vigilante groups such as Mão Branca (White Hand) roamed the region, the Baixada Fluminense has been a notorious hotbed for death squads, extra-judicial killings, impunity, poverty and political clientelism (Alves, 2003; Sousa, 1997; Souza, 1980).

In the wake of the massacre, an intriguing misconception surfaced. While attending a burial service for six of the victims in the centre of Nova Iguaçu on behalf of his well-known anti-violence organisation Viva Rio, anthropologist Rubem César Fendes noted that Catholic leaders remained conspicuously absent from the proceedings. 'Have the churches succumbed to fear?' he pointedly asked journalists (UERJ Notícias, 2005). Fernandes expressed surprise because many politicians and representatives of civil society had turned up, and the Catholic Church of the Baixada Fluminense has long been at the forefront of protests against violence in the region; following the liberationist doctrine that the poor should be freed from oppression through socio-political engagement in this world, the Church ranked among the most fervent denouncers of violence during Brazil's 1964–85 military dictatorship.

Fernandes' observation was considered to be so significant that a local university organised a debate two weeks later, in which a panel of experts discussed whether the perceived non-attendance of the Church could be interpreted as a sign of surrender to the ever-increasing power of vigilante groups and drug gangs in Brazil. The panellists agreed that this was probably the case. Apparently, they were unaware that at the very moment Fernandes posed his question, Catholic priests and laypeople were actively attending as many funerals of victims of the massacre as they could. They had deliberately chosen to be present at the funerals far from the city centre, because they anticipated that relatives of victims at the central ceremony would receive abundant support and attention from the notables and media there.

This misunderstanding is suggestive of the implication of temporal assumptions in understandings of urban violence. Liberationist Catholicism was a widely studied religious phenomenon in the 1980s. Attracted by glowing commentaries from theologians who hailed liberationism for its revolutionary potential, social scientists were curious to see how it worked in practice, their conclusions often being much more moderate (Burdick, 1993; Casanova, 1994; Mainwaring, 1986; Mariz, 1994; De Theije, 1999; Vásquez, 1998). Interest quickly faded, however, after Brazil democratised in the late 1980s and early 1990s. The fall of the Berlin Wall, the Catholic Church's conservative turn, a decline in the numbers of Catholics in Brazil, and the growth of new religious movements such as Pentecostalism and the Catholic Charismatic Renewal made liberationist Catholicism and its preoccupation with social justice appear increasingly outdated – the expectation was that it would soon be history. While this expectation has been unwarranted, and surveys (Lesbaupin et al., 2004; Oliveira, 2009) indicate that liberation theology continues to be a force in many Brazilian dioceses, little empirical data has been collected on its situation since its heyday; any continued involvement of Catholic communities in opposition to violence is easily overlooked.

Importantly, Fernandes' question and the subsequent panel debate are also informative in another respect, relating to spatialised conceptions of violence. The assumption that violence-ridden communities are paralysed with fear matches the default position in studies of urban violence that presume that the resistance manifested by Catholic communities during Brazil's dictatorship would not be possible today. Patrícia Birman and Márcia Leite (2000) claim in this regard that many Brazilians find the commitment of liberationist Catholicism toward fighting all forms of injustice to be ill-considered and dangerous in the face of contemporary violence; they therefore abandon the Catholic Church for other churches (Stoll, 1990). Robert Gay observes:

> Fifteen years ago, my friends in various *favelas* talked enthusiastically about
> organising and attending meetings and asserting their newly established

democratic rights. Now all they talk about – in hushed voices and behind closed doors – is their reluctance to participate in public life and their strategies for surviving the undeclared civil war between increasingly violent drug gangs and the police. (Gay, 2005: 6)

The reason for this changed outlook is the radical transformation of urban violence during the 1990s. Whereas it used to be a largely deterritorialised affair, enacted upon localities from the outside by the police, vigilantes and criminals, violence has become localised; drugs have entered the scene, raising the stakes of crime and vigilantism to such an extent that those involved have sought to establish defendable bases in low-income neighbourhoods from which to operate their businesses, keep out or collaborate with others and conquer adjacent territory. The result has been entrenched residential segregation and the emergence of what journalist Zuenir Ventura (1994) has termed 'the divided city': while wealthy residents of Rio de Janeiro's walled enclaves and centrally located upper-class neighbourhoods enjoy the full benefits of citizenship, the urban poor live in slums and the periphery where they are subject to the whims, regulations and brutality of both state and non-state actors. According to Luke Dowdney (2003: 55), factions employ 'a double tactic of mutual support and tyrannical enforcement ... of a punitive system of violence for non-collaboration' in which even the slightest hint at transgression is severely punished (see also Alves, 2018; Denyer Willis, 2015; Hume and Wilding, 2020; Müller, 2016). Inhabitants of low-income neighbourhoods have no choice, in other words, but to look away, retreat inside and hush their voices, making it incumbent upon those living in the city centre to speak out and condemn violence on their behalf.

Yet the fact was that Catholic priests and laypeople did not look away in response to the massacre in the Baixada Fluminense. To the contrary, while public attention was trained on Nova Iguaçu's city centre, Catholic communities opted to express their solidarity and concern at remote gatherings where they lacked the protection afforded by publicity. Their focus on the margins, together with people's failure to notice these efforts, reveals the paradoxical effects of spatiotemporal notions of marginality encapsulated in discourses of the 'divided' city. On the one hand, premised on past–present and centre–periphery dichotomies, such binary conceptions of city-space disregard the capacity of peripheral communities to effect change, meaning that their efforts to contest violence go unregistered (Oosterbaan, 2017). On the other hand, even if the concept of the 'divided' city does not accurately capture people's agency in coping with violence, the different loci of the official and Catholic responses suggest it does structure their coping strategies. The concept serves as a map or mental image, directing city-dwellers towards some sites rather than others, enabling or restricting particular forms of political action and informing religious practice in actual and concrete ways.

In this chapter, I reflect on this paradox by venturing the notion of counter-mapping. My analysis is grounded in the so-called 'spatial turn' in urban studies, which emphasises the mutual implication of spatial narratives and configurations of power (de Certeau, 1984; Lefebvre, 1991; Harvey, 2003; Susser, 1996). Against an earlier tendency in the research literature to juxtapose urban 'brown areas', where the state has little presence, with 'green' and 'blue' areas, where the rule of law operates (O'Donnell, 1993; see also Arias, 2006), recent studies of urban violence have fruitfully elaborated upon the spatial turn to document how segregation is not only a function of state presence, but also shaped by 'talk of crime' (Caldeira, 2000), fear (Falzon, 2008), mobility patterns (Monroe, 2016) and other practices of confinement (Rodgers, 2019), including violent state intervention itself (Appadurai, 2000). Similarly, to the degree that these studies show that urban ecologies need to be understood in relational terms, others have demonstrated that spatialised understandings of violence are not static, but can give rise to new modes of 'street politics' (Bayat, 2012) and 'insurgent citizenship' (Holston, 2008), as well as strategies of anticipation (Zeiderman, 2016) and improvisation (Simone, 2018). As I will show, such dynamics apply to the context of the Baixada Fluminense, too, where discourses of urban segregation both underpin existing conjunctures of social and spatial marginalisation and facilitate their contestation. However, against a tendency to locate struggles for the city primarily from within spatialised logics and contradictions, I argue for a spatiotemporal reading of discourses and counter-discourses of urban violence. Not only can collective memories and imaginations of justice be inflected by religion to furnish alternative mappings of city-space and unsettle topographies of violence along temporal lines, but the relationship between conceptions of space and time is also dynamic, as religious practitioners adapt to violence-driven processes of spatialised segregation through evolving practices of hope and remembrance.

Below, I develop these points with reference to a case study of a Catholic community called Nossa Senhora dos Mártires da Baixada Fluminense (NS dos Mártires).[2] This community was established in 1989 in Amapá, a peri-urban neighbourhood near Nova Iguaçu, with the specific aim to 'respond to every sign of death with expressions of life' (NS dos Mártires, 2004). In analysing the community's trajectory leading up to the 2005 massacre, I describe the encouragement its members drew from liberation theology, and the unexpected alliances they formed locally as well as trans-locally as they sought to enact their vision of justice.

The account is based on a historical ethnography consisting of seven months of fieldwork conducted in 2005, complemented by follow-up conversations and archival research at a documentation centre of the Catholic Diocese of Nova Iguaçu, which holds newspaper clippings and Church records of incidents of violence in the region. A limitation of these methods is that they privilege the points of view of Catholic activists. Other actors, such as vigilantes, drug gangs, the police and politicians are described as they were narrated to me by members of NS dos Mártires and in archival documents, meaning that their presentation is frozen in time and essentialised. Furthermore, several of the violent events described in this chapter are based on rumours and hearsay – research participants did not always directly bear witness, even if they were personally affected. As Peter Shirlow and Brendan Murtagh (2006) point out in their study of sectarian violence in Belfast, guesswork, knowing, not-knowing and stereotypes are intrinsic features of urban life in violent cities, for people's survival often depends on their ability to quickly make sense of their surroundings and work with these images; and as I will highlight, choosing what to believe and disregard is also an essential part of people's agency in navigating and counter-mapping urban violence. But this does mean that the following is neither an objective, nor a comprehensive account of violence in the Baixada Fluminense. Rather, my aim is to uncover how members of a remote Catholic community experienced life under these conditions, and sought to counter violence through discourse and practice as urban segregation took hold of Rio de Janeiro's periphery.

I present the community's trajectory in four stages; the first discussing the Fluminense's history of violence; the second, Catholic opposition; and the third and fourth sections analysing people's tactics as they adapted to changes in the region's spectre of urban violence. The chapter concludes with a discussion of the implications of these findings for theories of urban violence, as well as for understandings of contemporary political developments in Brazil.

A good thug is a dead thug

Before turning to NS dos Mártires and its foundation in 1989, it is necessary to analyse the historical context of urban violence in the Baixada Fluminense. As I will show in this section, the final years of the 1980s marked a turning point in the region, as vigilante groups – the main perpetrators of violence in the periphery of Rio de Janeiro – increasingly defined their modus operandi in spatial terms. The resulting territorialisation meant that violence was inscribed into the landscape and became constitutive of a distinct normative order wrapped around ideas of urban segregation. It also meant that forward-looking temporal orientations, characteristic of regional vigilantism, gained in salience for inhabitants who abandoned 'bad' neighbourhoods in anticipation of future violence.

The presence of vigilantes in the Baixada Fluminense dates back to Brazil's first wave of urban migration to the region in the 1930s when an economic crisis and severe droughts resulted in an exodus from rural areas to Brazil's southern cities. Many migrants settled in urban peripheries. In response, seeking to protect their material assets and political influence, local landlords, businessmen and politicians hired the services of vigilante groups consisting of off-duty police officers who were eager to supplement their meagre salaries (Grynszpan, 1990).

Activities of vigilante groups ranged at the time from security provision, criminal extortion, gold smuggling and theft, to intimidation, abduction and assassination. They received institutional backing from the political establishment and the authoritarian police administration. In 1969, five years after the army had ousted Brazil's then-President João Goulart in a military coup, Rio de Janeiro's State Secretary for Security assembled 11 police officers known as Os Homens de Ouro (The Men of Gold). Stating that 'Bandido bom é bandido morto' (A good thug is a dead thug), he gave the officers licence to fight crime as they saw fit. Soon, dozens of dead bodies appeared in the Baixada Fluminense with signs of torture and postcards saying 'Will never steal again' or 'You will be next' (Tribuna de Imprensa, 1987; Jornal de Hoje, 1987). The group was dismantled a few years later when it became evident that many of its victims were political opponents of the regime. Other death squads, such as Mão Branca, however, readily stepped in to take its place. The region suffered a high incidence of violence. With its estimated homicide rate of 70 per 100,000 inhabitants, one commenter in 1980 ranked the Baixada Fluminense as the most violent place on Earth (Souza, 1980).

The neighbourhood of Amapá, home of NS dos Mártires, expanded against this backdrop. Scattered across the woodlands between Nova Iguaçu and the neighbouring suburb of Duque de Caxias lived approximately 500 people in the late 1980s, occupying zinc houses built at a distance from one another. Most had migrated to the area only years before; they had come from the northeast and the interior of Brazil in the hope of finding work and better lives in Rio de Janeiro (cf. Perlman, 1976: 67–9).

There were several Protestant churches in Amapá, as well as two liberationist Catholic base communities (CEBs): small groups of Catholic lay people who regularly meet in order to read and discuss the Bible and apply their reflections to their daily lives (De Theije, 1999: 19–22). Apart from the activities organised by these religious groups, social life was limited in the neighbourhood. During the day, men left for their odd jobs in Duque de Caxias and Nova Iguaçu, or worked as groundskeepers for Rio de Janeiro's landed gentry, who owned vast tracts of land in the Baixada Fluminense (de Oliveira et al., 1999: 1). At night, people kept to themselves, and it was dark and quiet; although Amapá had a bus connection and electricity, there were no asphalted roads or street lights. Some families lived in extreme poverty. One of the founding members of NS dos Mártires remembered how one day a mother came up to her with the deceased bodies of a young boy and his brothers. They had died from hunger: 'He had been given so little to eat that even with his one year and eight months of age he fitted in the palm of my hand'.[3]

The neighbourhood became a target of violence in 1989. Regional homicide rates had by that point risen to nearly 96 per 100,000 inhabitants, and residents were accustomed to the sight of mutilated bodies washing up on the banks of the nearby river.[4] But little could prepare them for the shock of waking up one morning to discover that an entire family had been murdered in their vicinity. According to a reconstruction of events, the home of a man called Sebastião, his pregnant wife Maria das Neves and their three daughters was invaded in the night by a group of approximately five men. The men engaged in a series of gruesome acts of torture and sexual violence before killing their victims (Jornal de Hoje, 1988; Época, 1999).

Many residents decided to leave the neighbourhood after the murders. For some, it was the sheer horror of what had happened. For the majority, however, the main reason for moving was their fear of what would happen next. Unconfirmed rumours maintained that drug gangs were implicated in the violence; the family had reportedly paid the price for a conflict between Sebastião and traffickers over revenues for drugs sold from his bar in a nearby town.

Drug trafficking was a relatively new phenomenon in the Baixada Fluminense in those years. People had heard of drug gangs using shantytowns near Rio de Janeiro's city centre to sell marijuana and cocaine to middle-class youth from the surrounding areas, but the trade had not yet reached the periphery (cf. Zaluar, 2000). Still, the possibility that drug gangs might one day enter the suburbs was certainly on people's minds; ever since gang leader Luís Carlos dos Reis Encina had escaped by helicopter from a maximum-security prison in 1985 and drugs became a central issue in the 1986 elections for the post of Governor of Rio de Janeiro, vigilantes had increasingly positioned themselves against drug traffickers, vowing to protect the Baixada Fluminense from the threat (CDJP Nova Iguaçu, 1990; see also Vásquez, 1998: 146–9). The expectation was that vigilantes would soon arrive, now that Amapá had been exposed as harbouring potential drug criminals. There is a popular saying in the region, which maintains: *Quem com porcos se mistura, farelo come* ('He who plays with pigs eats pig feed'). Signifying that someone who goes about in bad company is either like them or will soon become so, it is invoked to legitimise indiscriminate violence against people from neighbourhoods where drug gangs are present. Residents wanted to avoid getting caught up in these dynamics by moving elsewhere (CDJP Nova Iguaçu, 1989).

Their decision to move out of Amapá is indicative of the processes of segregation and territorialisation set in motion by the expansion of Rio de Janeiro's drug trade. Discourse analysis of newspaper clippings of the time suggests that even prior to this expansion vigilantism was characterised by the conceptual division of society into distinct spheres (Jornal do Brasil, 1987a, 1987b; Tribuna de Imprensa, 1987a, 1987b; Última Hora, 1988b; see also Almeida, 1998; Huggins, 1997; de Sousa, 1997). 'Good people' were located on the inside: they were the hardworking, law-abiding citizens who sustained society, and to whom state law applied. Outside were 'bad people' seeking to overturn the social system, such as political dissidents and drug gangs, who were perceived to have forfeited their rights to be treated according to the law. Following a consequentialist conception of justice, in which considerations of the future beneficial effects for society applied, vigilantes pursued the 'bad people' with unrestrained terror and violence, as well as a wilful disregard for their victims' potential innocence (cf. Lacey, 1988). Another proverb, describing the murdering of criminals as a necessary evil, is telling in this respect: 'The rotten apple needs to be destroyed before it spoils all the other apples' (Chiera, 1996: 22).

Yet, before vigilantes began to define themselves in opposition to drug traffickers, the line separating inside and outside had been primarily normatively oriented, whereas now it was mapped onto space. Places where 'good people' lived were seen to fall within the bounds of state law; the rest became a legal no man's land. The spatialisation of moral boundaries had the effect of directing vigilante justice towards the frontiers and concentrating it on the borders. Violence acquired a pivotal role in sustaining the limits separating 'good' from 'bad'; it became simultaneously constitutive of 'good places', set apart by being non-violent and thus requiring protection, and 'bad places', where violence merited more violence. Furthermore, as the abandonment of Amapá by its residents suggests, the effects of spatialisation were reinforced by the temporal dimensions of urban violence: the orientation of vigilante groups towards the future was reflected in the anticipation by residents of future violence, and their decision to move away reinforced the impression of Amapá as a 'bad place'.

One can see why, under these conditions, populations of low-income neighbourhoods would appear at the mercy of violent perpetrators. To whom could the residents of Amapá have turned for support? As mentioned, the Brazilian state provided cover for vigilantes. Even though by 1989 officials no longer openly encouraged vigilantism, many continued to exploit their privileged access to the state in order to facilitate it. Officers used information obtained through police investigations to track targets after work, while their superiors and colleagues guaranteed near total impunity by ensuring that witnesses were intimidated, incriminating evidence was lost, or cases were delayed to forestall prosecution. Society at large, meanwhile, upheld vigilantism by using vigilante boundaries as a framework for social interaction. Employers refused to hire staff from certain neighbourhoods, reasoning that whoever lived there must be a criminal. Likewise, politicians were commonly elected into office on the basis of their image as 'tough guys', an image derived from their connections with vigilantes (CDJP Nova Iguaçu, 1989).

As argued in the introduction to this chapter, the apparent hegemony of vigilantes and their supporters should not blind us, however, to the opposition that did take place. In one example, bishop Dom Adriano Hipólito from the Catholic Diocese of Nova Iguaçu issued a series of public denunciations of vigilantism in 1983 with the help of a private detective and Catholic lay leaders. These efforts prompted Rio de Janeiro's then-Governor Leonel Brizola to order an official enquiry into vigilantism, which saw several vigilantes tried in court. Similarly, as we shall see in the next section, the Catholic community of Amapá did not accept the inevitability of the murder and its consequences, but rallied against violence through its own spatiotemporal rendering of the event.

A place of hope in this violent region

Not everyone felt disposed to leave Amapá. One Catholic lay leader commented to the media:

> The people are scared, they are moving out. It is a crime to see them sell their houses, which they have bought with so much sacrifice. I am not in favour of leaving. It is better to organise ourselves and ask for measures. (Última Hora, 1988a)

Under the direction of the local Catholic Church, religious groups of the neighbourhood mounted an ecumenical mass to draw attention to their plight and demand action from the government: Clamor dos Mártires (Plea of the Martyrs). Hundreds of members from surrounding religious communities joined, and the event would later feature in the press as an example of people refusing to submit to violence, instead chasing the aggressors away (O Globo, 1988).

Yet, despite the public attention, the government did not respond to this religious call for action. When the police investigation of the murders was closed the following year without result, the Catholic Diocese of Duque de Caxias took the additional step of buying the house where Sebastião, Maria das Neves and their daughters had lived. Sealed off by the police, the house had stood in Amapá as a daily reminder of their gruesome killing. The idea was to turn the house into a chapel, or as bishop Dom Mauro Morelli of the Diocese of Duque de Caxias put it: 'A place of hope in this violent region.' The task of administering the chapel was given to the CEB located nearest to the house, which until then had been operating without a permanent place of worship. The CEB was renamed Nossa Senhora dos Mártires da Baixada Fluminense (Our Lady of the Martyrs of the Baixada Fluminense) for the purpose.

The inspiration for both the protest mass and the acquisition of the house derived from a distinct Catholic vision of justice. Its groundwork had been laid by Pope John XXIII in his encyclicals *Mater e Magistra* and *Pacem in Terris*, in which he emphasised justice, love and respect for human dignity and human rights as fundamental Christian values (Walsh and Davies, 1985). After the 1962–65 Second Vatican Council, where *Mater e Magistra* and *Pacem in Terris* constituted the basis for the new pastoral constitution *Gaudium et Spes*, a group of theologians further reworked the encyclicals into what would become the central principles of liberation theology. One: religion cannot be separated from its socio-economic context. Two: God loves both the rich and the poor, but supports the poor in their struggle for liberation from oppression. Three: instead of waiting for salvation after life, Christians have a duty to try to construct the Kingdom of God on Earth (De Theije, 1999: 6–9).

Implementation of these principles varied across Brazil. In many places, the emphasis was on the extension of experiments with CEBs and other forms of lay organisations to counter the prospect of secularisation and the growth of evangelical Protestantism (Mariz, 1994: 15). The Church leadership in the Baixada Fluminense, in contrast, favoured a socio-political interpretation: under the guidance of bishops Dom Adriano Hipólito, Dom Valdir Calheiros and later also Dom Mauro Morelli, priests supported CEBs in creating residents' associations and trade unions that lobbied politicians and employers for better living conditions. Their approach gained traction in the 1970s when Brazil's military dictatorship grew more repressive and the clergy increasingly became a target of state brutality. By 1976, when Dom Adriano was kidnapped, molested, stripped of his clothes and left covered in red paint along the roadside near Nova Iguaçu by a local vigilante group called Aliança Anticomunista Brasileira (Brazilian Anti-Communist Alliance), the National Conference of Brazilian Bishops advocated outright opposition to the regime. State–church relations gradually improved with the country's return to democracy in the second half of the 1980s, but clergy and CEBs in the Baixada Fluminense continued their political engagement (Mainwaring, 1986; Serbin, 2000).

Why did members of NS dos Mártires feel they could follow this vision of justice and ignore the imperatives that drove their neighbours away? To begin with, they classified the murders differently. They had known Maria das Neves personally and concluded that the violence had not resulted from Sebastião's alleged involvement in the drug trade. Quite the opposite was held to be true: the family was murdered because Sebastião had refused to let traffickers sell drugs from his bar, a refusal of which he had notified the police. Going to the police was a dangerous move, given the potential repercussions of being perceived by gangs as a police informer. Officers had therefore advised Sebastião to leave his bar and go into hiding in his house in Amapá. Although Sebastião had heeded their advice, gang members had tracked him down and murdered him and his family, members of the CEB claimed. With this account, NS dos Mártires steered away from the framework of the imminent spread of drug trafficking and vigilante justice. Instead, the massacre was placed firmly within the bounds of state law and the normative order of liberation theology, which centred on the rights of the poor and the duty of the government to protect them.

Secondly, several Catholic symbols and images were invoked to give the profane acts of the murders and the founding of NS dos Mártires sacred meaning. First, the daughters of Sebastião and Maria das Neves were unofficially proclaimed martyrs. Then, a rose was found when the community first entered the house of the family. As the assaulters had gone to some lengths to destroy all vegetation around the house, and the flower did not survive exposure to daylight, members of NS dos Mártires interpreted the discovery to be a message: 'The rose was simply waiting there to hand over to us the responsibility of continuing to construct signs of life' (NS dos Mártires, 2004). Finally, Our Lady of Guadalupe was elected patron saint of the CEB. She simultaneously embodies notions of motherly love and resistance, and the legend of her incarnation bears a striking resemblance with the foundational story of the community; roses play a major part in both narratives, and images show Our Lady of Guadalupe to be pregnant, just like the mother of the family (cf. Wolf, 1958). The result of each of these elements was to strengthen members of NS dos Mártires in their conviction of the righteousness of their approach. Moreover, sacralisation worked to offer protection: any harm done to members of NS dos Mártires would be an attack on the Catholic Church, as well as on Brazilian society as a whole. In fact, as their martyrdom indicates, the murdering of the children was already taken as such, and it was upon Catholics to respond and to ensure that their death would not be in vain.[5]

Thirdly, Amapá's Catholic community had at its disposal the network of the Catholic Church, which transcended the connections of vigilantes and local politicians in the Baixada Fluminense and could be mobilised to exert pressure. 1988 was the year of the 25th anniversary of Dom Adriano's ordination as bishop, and in honour of his socio-political commitment the General Assembly of the Diocese of Nova Iguaçu had launched a campaign against violence. A letter sent by the Assembly to CEBs read: 'We cannot act as if we do not know, we cannot wait any longer, we need to do something together' (Diocese de Nova Iguaçu, 1988a). The protest mass in Amapá was a direct outcome of the campaign's insistence that communities support each other in organising vigils in reaction to violence in their surroundings. Other activities included the disclosure of information relating to the root causes of violence in the Baixada Fluminense, and the creation of a forum where clergy, religious laymen, residents' associations, other social movements and academic researchers could jointly discuss solutions to violence and petition the government (Diocese de Nova Iguaçu, 1988b).

Liberationist Catholicism, then, provided members of NS dos Mártires with the inspiration, reference points and means for an alternate framing of the 1989 events. Their religious imagination not only facilitated a recalibration of public understandings of the murdering of Sebastião's family. It also enabled them to contest the emergent topography of violence instituted by vigilantes and drug gangs in the Baixada Fluminense through their own temporal orientation. Instead of focusing on the future of society and its derivative logic that 'good' places must be protected from 'bad' places and that present violence predicts future violence, they drew the public gaze towards the past and invoked religious forms of collective memory to ask: Had Sebastião's family, in fact, been blameless victims of violent oppression, and if so, which religious antecedents could provide meaning and direction for appropriate next steps?

This is not to suggest that there were no limitations on the CEB's actions. The initiative for the protest mass and other manifestations against violence largely came from bishops, parish priests and others in the ecclesiastic hierarchy. Their views of justice and the role of the Church in the Baixada Fluminense were geared towards a categorical denunciation of vigilantism, as well as based on idealist conceptions of the law, the role of the state and the obligation of the Church to contest violence. Catholic lay people, including members of NS dos Mártires, conversely, were careful to observe the boundaries maintained by vigilantes; they might dispute on which side victims were to be placed and thereby question the use of violence, but the line itself was not contested.

Consider, for instance, the following: whereas the title of the protest mass, Plea of the Martyrs, had referred to the family in its entirety, the notion of martyrdom applied exclusively to the children. The parish priest of NS dos Mártires, an Italian missionary, told me he would have liked to include the parents, but was persuaded by members of the CEB that the interpretation of the murders that had driven residents out of Amapá could not be disregarded: 'Everyone was convinced of the innocence of the children. As for the parents... the people always carry a certain amount of suspicion. If we had mentioned the whole family, many would have turned up their noses.'[6]

A further indication of the influence of the boundaries instituted by vigilantes came in 1991, when another murder befell Amapá: a local barkeeper and his girlfriend were found dead inside their house, killed by numerous gunshots. Although the girlfriend was expecting her first child at the time of the murders and she was eight months pregnant, no one planned to move or organise a protest this time around. NS dos Mártires even purchased the bar of the victims a few years later to build a church in honour of the children of Sebastião's family, yet without referencing the more recent murders. When I asked community members about this discrepancy, they explained that the barkeeper and his girlfriend had been known for their criminal involvement, which had rendered them vulnerable to violence. The barkeeper was also the one who had tipped off drug gangs in 1988 about the whereabouts of Sebastião, these members of the CEB maintained. Their grisly evidence for this allegation was that the perpetrators had waited for the barkeeper's girlfriend to be in the same month of her pregnancy as Maria das Neves before they killed her.

Such negotiated understandings of urban violence reveal the potential of religious discourses to oppose violence-driven processes of urban segregation. As the examples of the protest mass and the founding of NS dos Mártires show, religion constitutes a powerful source of moral authority, remembrance, social support and hope in the face of aggression and intimidation, and gives residents of low-income neighbourhoods access to ulterior visions of justice, which can neither be reduced to notions of dominance, nor controlled by violent actors. At the same time, for these ulterior visions to be effective, their articulation must be fitted to existing norms and boundaries of control. Religion's power in contesting socio-spatial patterns of violence lies not in the rejection of the latter, it emerges, but in its capacity to afford alternative mappings of urban space and time. These religious counter-maps may not replace prevalent understandings. But they can generate sufficient doubt for these not to be acted upon.

If we want to get something done, we need to reach out

During the first years of its existence, NS dos Mártires continued to rally its past-oriented imagination of justice against vigilante conceptions of space and time by endeavouring to anchor its practices of remembrance in the landscape and share its experience with others. Together with neighbouring CEBs, an annual *Via Sacra* was set up, leading along sites in the parish that had previously been targets of violence. According to an announcement in the parochial newsletter, the objective of this pilgrimage was to draw areas that had been declared out-of-bounds by vigilantes and other violent actors back into society by reinscribing their associated memories and representations with religious meaning, seeking to 'bring the power of God among the people, especially in those places that are most desolate and most marked by violence and neglect' (Paróquia São Simão, 2005: 4–5).

Members of NS dos Mártires were also active participants in the Amapá residents' association. Established by the neighbourhood's Catholic community in the mid-1980s, this association had achieved an initial measure of success in 1987 by lobbying for Amapá's bus connection with Duque de Caxias. CEB members hoped to build on this success, following the killing of Sebastião and his family, by campaigning for better services such as a police station, asphalted roads and streetlights to improve the neighbourhood's security situation. Yet their hopes were quickly dashed in 1990 when, for the association's first elections, local politicians put forward one of their henchmen with a reputation for violence. After winning the presidency through ballot rigging and voter harassment, the new president sold the association's inventory and stalled any plans for further activities, including future elections.

Many residents' associations suffered the same fate in the first decade of Brazil's transition to democracy. A survey conducted among 3,500 community leaders of shantytowns in Rio de Janeiro suggests that at least 350 presidents of residents' associations were murdered between 1992 and 2001, 450 were forced to flee their neighbourhoods, 400 actively collaborated with gangs and vigilantes, and the councils of an unknown number of associations were appropriated (O Globo, 2005). These numbers reveal the extent to which public life in the city's peripheral neighbourhoods came to be controlled by violent actors during the 1990s, as well as of the latter's resolve in establishing and maintaining patterns of violence and segregation (cf. Leeds, 1996: 70–6; Mafra, 1998; Zaluar, 1985: 235–56).

NS dos Mártires responded to this setback by prioritising the organisation of devotional tasks: various bible groups were instituted, the community began to offer sacramental preparation courses, and in 1994 a spiritual centre for religious retreat was built next to the chapel. This shift in priorities came against the backdrop of the so-called 'restoration' drive in the Catholic Church, starting with the ascension of Pope John Paul II to the papacy in 1978 and reaching the Baixada Fluminense in 1993 when Dom Adriano retired. His replacement with the conservative Dom Werner Siebenbrock represented a shift in the Church's regional affairs: Catholics who had long felt that socio-political activism ought to be left to others now felt emboldened to argue that the Church should exclusively concentrate on religious matters, such as countering the exponential rise of Pentecostal churches, a position soon accepted by the General Assembly of the Diocese of Nova Iguaçu as its official line (Diocese de Nova Iguaçu, n.d.: 194). Brazil's economic crisis of the early 1990s also played a role. This crisis, a legacy of the military regime's excessive borrowing, left Catholic lay people with little spare time for engagements other than basic religious concerns (cf. Kingstone, 2000).

It took until the end of the 1990s before the impact of Dom Adriano's retirement had waned. By that point it had become clear that competition with Pentecostal churches was not as impactful as initially feared: in the case of NS dos Mártires, several members converted, but these losses were eclipsed by an increase in the community's membership resulting from the neighbourhood's expansion. Amapá grew rapidly in the 1990s because of the economic crisis; looking to offset the negative effects of hyper-inflation, people traded their rented apartments in the city centres of Duque de Caxias and Nova Iguaçu for the relative security of investing money in construction materials and a plot of land in Amapá, which caused the size of its population to soar to 4,569 residents by the year 2000 (IBGE, 2000).

The majority of new members hailed from lower middle-class backgrounds. Manuel Vásquez (1998: 153–61) has described how a CEB elsewhere in the Baixada Fluminense cut back on social activism once middle-class Catholics joined; they were allegedly more interested in constructing a beautiful church building than in fighting for socio-economic change. In Amapá, however, the inclusion of middle-class members had the opposite effect. Newcomers quickly took to contesting the living conditions they found themselves in. In 1998, when the local bus company cancelled Amapá's bus connection to Duque de Caxias due to the poor state of the roads, they compiled a report detailing their grievances, and asked residents to sign a petition calling on the Municipality of Duque de Caxias to make funds available for neighbourhood improvements. Councillor José Clemente Zumba, with whom the Catholic Church maintained close ties, scheduled a vote, but it was blocked by the party in power, that of Mayor José Camilo Zito dos Santos Filho (NS dos Mártires, 1999). Subsequently, NS dos Mártires approached the Governor of Rio de Janeiro, Anthony Garotinho, and State Deputy Geraldo Moreira da Silva, whose party competed in the Baixada Fluminense with Mayor Zito's. These two politicians put the CEB in touch with the state-owned companies tasked with providing services in the Baixada Fluminense. In 2000, Amapá's main road was asphalted as a result of NS dos Mártires' entreaties to these companies. In 2001, the neighbourhood was provided with water and sewage connections, as well as streetlights, telephone connections and a direct bus line to Rio de Janeiro.

The president of Amapá's residents' association reacted with anger to NS dos Mártires' initiative. In 1999, he announced that he would kill people if the CEB continued its campaign for neighbourhood improvements, claiming that he alone had the authority to speak for residents. He was confident no one would complain to the police, as the municipal administration was in the hands of his fellow political party member Zito, known for his links to vigilantes. Yet his leverage was not as strong as it had been in the past: when members of the CEB approached another vigilante in the area to complain about what they regarded as the president's criminal behaviour, the threats stopped. The vigilante in question, who was reportedly associated with State Deputy Moreira, swore that he would 'take out' the president if anything were to happen to the CEB. CEB members were pragmatic about this step, commenting to me: '…if we want to get something done, we need to reach out'.[7]

The CEB's troubled relationship with the corrupt president of Amapá's residents' association further demonstrates the limitations of its earlier counter-mapping efforts. By and large, members appeared successful in averting violence after the murders of 1988. But they were unable to stop the incorporation of their neighbourhood into the advancing web of territorial alliances between politicians and vigilantes, which fanned out across the Baixada Fluminense and restricted citizens' access to their newly established rights. Incorporation into this web prompted a reversal in strategy on the part of the CEB's membership. As detailed in the previous section, the sacralisation of the murdering of Sebastião's family had reduced the threat of violence by placing Amapá at the centre of a religiously defined landscape, thus challenging its marginal status based on prevalent spatiotemporal imaginaries and subverting a process of segregation by which moral boundaries of vigilantism were mapped onto urban space. However, while the pilgrimage set up in the early 1990s was still organised around these aims, by the late 1990s the CEB no longer seemed as invested in contesting spatialisation through its own temporal mappings. Instead, efforts were dedicated towards counter-mapping the emplacement of Amapá within these established parameters of city-space: NS dos Mártires' political lobbying for neighbourhood improvements continued to defy preconceived notions of marginality and political apathy to lessen the impact of violence, but did so in actual terms, as the CEB sought to centre Amapá both in a material sense and with a focus on the present.

With this implicit acquiescence to processes of spatialisation came a certain willingness to work with actors responsible for its upkeep. Existing patterns of segregation were not absolute, as the CEB's dealings with rival politicians and their associates reveal. Following the consolidation of democracy, the political arena in Brazil became more pluralised in the 1990s, which made it easier for community representatives to enlist politicians for their cause. The position of vigilantes in the Baixada Fluminense had also changed during this time. After Governor Brizola's official inquiry into vigilantism in 1983, the links of vigilantes with the regional state apparatus had gradually weakened, and they began to include non-police officers in their ranks, leading to a proliferation in the number of vigilantes, as well as to competition among them (Alves, 2002). As their political dependence grew, control over populations within their territories dwindled; in cases of discontent, they were now vulnerable to people threatening to withdraw support from their political patrons, or to call in other vigilantes. The result was a shift in the temporal moorings of vigilantism: instead of relying on broad-based appeals to the future beneficial effects of violence for society, they were forced to consider for each violent act whether it was justified by its intended target's past behaviour and would therefore be legitimate, lest they themselves be classified as criminals.

These developments provide an indication as to how discourses of the 'divided city' were internalised in peripheral neighbourhoods of Rio de Janeiro. To the extent that members of NS dos Mártires had initially sought to prevent this discourse from becoming reality by holding on to their own vision of justice, highlighting God's partiality towards the poor, they adapted once segregation could no longer be circumvented. Marginality was appropriated, both as a description of reality, an explanation of suffering and as a problem to be battled in order to fulfil God's assignment to 'construct signs of life'. In pivoting away from sacralisation towards social mobilisation for urban services as a means of contesting violence, liberationist understandings of justice were redirected: they became channelled through the language and practices of urban segregation.

To defend life

This evolving relationship between spatialisation and people's temporal orientations – leading vigilantes to adapt their focus on the future while members of NS dos Mártires redirected their invocations of the past towards the present – was reinforced in 2004 when the organised drug trade reached Amapá. In the interim, drug trafficking had become a common sight in the Baixada Fluminense, with gangs steadily moving into increasingly remote low-income neighbourhoods, sometimes after reaching agreements with vigilantes, who received a share of their profits for keeping out competitors (Alves, 2003; Sousa, 2001).

Ironically, what attracted drug traffickers to Amapá was precisely the neighbourhood's reduced marginality, described above. The specific event to facilitate their arrival was the construction by the municipal government of a public square with a children's playground at the heart of the neighbourhood. Surrounded by asphalted roads and easily accessible via Amapá's main street, the square represented an opportunity for the drug traffickers' preferential mode of operation in the perimeters of the Baixada Fluminense: instead of permanently manning sale points with heavily armed gunmen, they drove by at night and waited for customers before they proceeded to their next point of sale. Some clients travelled from the neighbouring suburbs to buy drugs under the cover of anonymity, but the square also attracted foot traffic from the neighbourhood's youths. Soon, they could be seen gathering in small groups around the square, filling the air with the smell of marijuana. A series of assaults on shops in the area was subsequently blamed on this group, and local vigilantes reacted by beating up two of the youths involved and forcing their families to relocate elsewhere. NS dos Mártires had several youth projects that had been operating since 2002, when the CEB enrolled in a programme of the Diocese of Duque de Caxias that supported communities in organising out-of-school instruction for children from poor families, based on 'the principles of justice, solidarity and Christian theology' (ASPAS, 2001). The programme was funded by telecom provider Telemar, which, like other Brazilian companies, had become increasingly involved with topics of corporate social responsibility; with the Brazilian economy's return to growth in the late 1990s, these companies also had the financial means to do so (cf. Cardoso Sousa, 2006). NS dos Mártires' second project originated in Lula da Silva's 2002 presidential election campaign, during which he promised to eradicate hunger in Brazil. After Lula was sworn in as the country's president, bishop Dom Mauro of Duque de Caxias persuaded the federal government to co-finance the construction of five integrated health centres in the region, which would provide pre-schoolers with supplementary food and health care services.[8] The sites for these centres were to be selected according to need, and CEBs of the diocese went house-to-house in their respective localities to weigh all pre-schoolers. With 8.2 percent of Amapá's children below five years of age critically undernourished, malnutrition was well above the regional average, and one of the health centres was therefore built in the neighbourhood (NS dos Mártires, 2002).

Finally, the third project consisted of dance classes for teenagers. These were taught by instructors from a shantytown elsewhere in Duque de Caxias, who were part of a dance troupe called Projeto Luar de Dança (Dance Project Moon) that aimed to increase the self-confidence of children from low-income neighbourhoods. Appropriately, the first dance this group performed when it was founded in 1990 was a depiction of a tale of a rose, which had been inspired by the history of NS dos Mártires.

NS dos Mártires began to frame these projects more explicitly in terms of violence prevention now that drug traffickers had arrived in the neighbourhood. Thus, extra instruction and nutritional care were claimed to offer youth an alternative to drug trafficking by improving their school performance and chances in the formal job market, while dance classes shielded youngsters from the lures of the drug trade by keeping them off the street. The expression members of the CEB used in this regard was 'to defend life'. As a Catholic notion, this was generally intended to mean the safeguarding of human rights, but it was also an objective that vigilantes could approve of: a member of NS dos Mártires recounted to me how one day a local vigilante approached her to commend her for the work the CEB was doing with youth.

The project-based approach and emphasis on youth work reflect a broader trend in Brazilian society to combat violence through prevention. Several NGOs, such as Viva Rio in Rio de Janeiro and Instituto Sou da Paz in São Paulo, were founded in the early 1990s to encourage mobilisation on issues of violence. Media-savvy, run by middle-class professionals operating from central city offices, and representing a diverse mix of public and private interests, they defined violence less in terms of socio-economic oppression, as liberation theologists would have it, but rather as a matter of personal choice; the focus was on small-scale interventions to equip residents of gang-dominated areas with the moral fibre and means to make the 'right' choice (cf. Leite, 2001; Moraes da Silva, 2001). For example, Viva Rio promoted the project Luta pela Paz (Fight for Peace) in shantytowns to encourage children to gain confidence and resilience through sports, so that they were more likely to say 'no' to drug gangs. The actual differences with the CEBs may seem trivial, as NGOs also paid attention to larger factors that enabled or constrained people's choices in relation to violence, but a vital distinction between the two approaches was that liberationist Catholicism was grounded in a deterministic world view, focusing on structural effects, whereas NGOs held a voluntarist perspective, privileging free will.

Partly, the incentive for adopting a youth-oriented perspective on urban violence also came from within the Catholic Church. Although as indicated in the previous section, local manifestations of a Church-wide turn to conservatism did not stop CEBs from campaigning on socio-political questions, this did prompt a number of prayer groups associated with the Catholic Charismatic Renewal to operate alongside CEBs in the Baixada Fluminense.

Charismatic Catholicism resembles evangelical Pentecostalism in terms of its experiential form of spirituality, healing rituals and emphasis on a direct relationship with Jesus Christ (Machado, 1996). Liberationist sectors of the Church have regularly voiced concern that the movement might lead Catholics away from activism (cf. Oro, 1996), but, at least in the Baixada Fluminense, it primarily meant that social commitments were expressed differently. Like the aforementioned NGOs, charismatic Catholics focused on individualised effects and solutions to suffering, which translated into outreach activities such as self-help groups for alcohol and drug addicts (cf. Machado and Mariz, 1997). Amapá's first Charismatic group was organised in 2004, the same year drug traffickers established their presence in the neighbourhood. Not long after its founding, convenors of the group approached NS dos Mártires about contributing to their activities, which had the effect of reinforcing the community's drive towards protecting vulnerable groups.

The Catholic Church's response to the massacre of March 2005, detailed in this chapter's introduction, illustrates the significance of these changes. As soon as news broke, NS dos Mártires and CEBs from across the region mobilised to visit the affected areas and show their solidarity, including by attending the funerals of the victims. It was the same support NS dos Mártires had once received when Amapá was targeted. However, following the murders of Sebastião's family in 1988 the self-stated aim of mobilisation had been to call attention to the situation of the neighbourhood's residents, amplify their claims of abandonment and worthiness, and demand action from the government. Now, community members explained to me, they went to 'pray for peace' for those caught in the crossfire between drug gangs, the police and vigilantes. Bishop Dom Luciano Bergamin, who had replaced Dom Werner Siebenbrock at the helm of the Diocese of Nova Iguaçu in 2002 and led the response to the massacre, formulated the rationale in a media interview as follows:

> We are going to protect life. Laypeople, religious actors, authorities, and the people need to unite to defend life, increase the number of jobs available, so that children and youth can lead worthy lives... We must fight greed, individualism, corruption, trafficking in arms and drugs, prostitution, and impunity. (Diocese de Nova Iguaçu 2005)

As this quote suggests, key aspects of the Catholic reaction were a focus on youth and children, as well as the transformation of individually held socio-cultural values that the Church associated with violence. A difference with the era of the founding of NS dos Mártires was also that those involved did not seek government intervention, but, as the prayers indicate, directed their plea towards God, aiming at divine intercession. In terms of socio-spatial demarcations, what stands out from the above is the community members' explanation that their support was directed at those caught 'in the crossfire' between violent actors. The objective was no longer to contest distinctions between 'good' and 'bad' neighbourhoods, nor to redraw boundaries between non-violent 'centres' and violent 'margins', but to help residents navigate the perils of marginal life. This speaks to a further internalisation of discourses of urban segregation, with members of NS dos Mártires seemingly adopting as a frame of reference the markers that perpetrators of violence asserted to separate their respective territories in Rio de Janeiro and its surroundings from those of their competitors. Using these markers, the role of liberationist communities was reduced to 'defending life' and minimising the impact of violence on innocent bystanders.

Finally, the CEB's changing discourse about young people reflects the evolution of its temporal outlook in response to processes of urban segregation. In declaring the murdered children of Sebastião and Maria das Neves to be martyrs, in the late 1980s, NS dos Mártires had opposed the insistence of vigilantes that the future of society depended on their violent intervention: by drawing the public gaze backwards, the CEB had asked who pays the price for a world ruled by dynamics of violence and counter-violence. During the 1990s, as the community campaigned to obtain urban services for the neighbourhood, the focus shifted to the present; then, in the early 2000s, children and youth reappeared in the CEB's avowed stance against violence when its members became concerned with the near-future: from beneficiaries of the CEB's work, young people were reimagined as principal objects and agents of transformation. A possible interpretation of this finding is that as segregation became more entrenched in the Baixada Fluminense, opportunities for action moved to the temporal plane, where they were increasingly detached from space to be invested, instead, in people. The counter-mapping of topographies of violence became once more an exercise in imagining times different from the present, but hope was no longer a reminder of a sacred past or 'a place', as Dom Mauro had once described the founding of NS dos Mártires, but a prospect of a better future.

Conclusion

By way of conclusion, the history of NS dos Mártires suggests that it is unwarranted to assume that Catholic communities in peripheral neighbourhoods of Rio de Janeiro have become too fearful or unwilling to contest violence in their surroundings. It is certainly the case that vigilantes and other violent actors seek to thwart resistance to their rule by imposing their own sets of norms over neighbourhood populations, which prohibit residents from interfering with their business, or from turning to outsiders for support. These attempts are often successful; the self-censorship of those who moved elsewhere after the murder of the family in Amapá is one example. More generally, it also seems true that opportunities for opposition have become more restricted as city-spaces in Brazil become increasingly segregated and inhabitants of low-income areas have, to a degree, internalised conceptions of the city as 'divided'. Yet, this does not mean that agency itself has become suppressed; instead, it has been reconfigured. The material presented in this chapter shows the fundamental importance of people's religious imagination to the possibility of such reconfiguration: it redirects memory, mobilises, protects, counteracts, remaps and offers hope. In the face of violence, religiously inspired struggles for the city promise justice, in a vision radically different from the sort of justice perpetrators of violence claim to uphold.

These findings have implications for theories of urban violence, for they point to the significance of discourses and practices that operate from outside existing configurations of power. As mentioned in this chapter's introduction, there is a tendency in urban studies to understand contestations of violence in relation to the internal workings of dominant discourses. One example is Daniel Goldstein's (2012) research on the plight of suburban shantytown dwellers in Bolivia, who get caught in a vicious circle: lacking access to the right to safety, they turn to self-help forms of justice, which in turn increases their insecurity as the state outlaws and pursues vigilantes. There is evidence in this chapter of similar dynamics: the episode in the history of NS dos Mártires when community members turned the tables on the president of the local residents' association reveals a potential to challenge vigilantism from within. However, an exclusive focus on this potential would ignore the evolving role of liberationist Catholicism in structuring the community's actions. CEB members exploited tensions within socio-spatial instantiations of vigilantism in order to realise their own vision of justice. When the spectre of violence in Amapá changed, they adapted, looking to achieve the same goals through different means.

A key insight to emerge from this analysis concerns the dynamic relationship between conceptions of space and time in structuring experiences of urban violence. Religion's capacity for hope and remembrance reveals temporality to be a crucial axis of opposition to violence-driven processes of urban segregation, yet temporality itself is not static but co-evolves as violence becomes more entrenched. Future research may further uncover how notions of time impinge upon topographies of violence, and vice versa. This is especially urgent in light of contemporary political developments in Brazil, which saw Jair Bolsonaro elected to the country's presidential office in 2018. In what could be seen as an extension of the theme identified in this chapter of vigilantism's increasing gaze towards the past, Bolsonaro ran on a ticket expressing his explicit admiration for Brazil's 1964–1985 military dictatorship and vigilantism, reintroducing the slogan 'Bandido bom é bandido morto' (A good bandit is a dead bandit) to the public. Long before his election, he had made the following statement in a 2003 address to Rio de Janeiro's Chamber of Deputies as he spoke about news reports of vigilante violence in the state of Bahia:

> As long as the state does not have the courage to adopt the death penalty, these extermination groups, in my understanding, are welcome. And if there is no space in Bahia, they can come to Rio de Janeiro. If it depended on me, they have complete support, because in Rio de Janeiro only innocent people are decimated. In Bahia, according to the information that I have – logically these groups are illegal, but [I give] my congratulations – marginality has decreased. (Reist, 2018)

As Brazil's president, Bolsonaro acquired a platform giving vigilantes his 'complete support'. Following his election, his government pushed through an anti-crime bill that extended the latitude for police killings without facing criminal prosecution (Durão, 2020).

Bolsonaro also claimed significant support from Brazil's religious quarters, including sectors within the Catholic Church, whom he skilfully pitted against the Church's liberationist tendencies, just as he claimed to represent the poor against 'left-wing elites', or the interests of those living on the margins against 'globalists' (cf. de Almeida, 2020). Opposition to the state's corruption by his politics of division could, on bleak days, seem futile. Yet, it is important to remember that these divisions were never objective facts, but discursive constructs designed to achieve specific political ends. Anthropology, itself embattled under Bolsonaro (cf. Neiburg and Thomaz, 2020), can help to analyse these divisions and undo their effects. Not only can it expose the manipulation of these divisions by politicians and others in power, but it can shine a spotlight on the creativity and tenacity of those fighting for change, thus recovering hopeful narratives. This chapter has offered a tentative step in this direction by scrutinising the spatiotemporal underpinnings of discourses of the 'divided city', as well as foregrounding the significance of religion in furnishing alternative imaginations of possibility and action.

Notes

1 Random killing sprees have been a regular method of police officers for obstructing anti-corruption efforts since the 1980s. Their logic is that superiors invariably replace reformist commanders if the number of homicides in a district rises too sharply (Moreira, 1999).

2 The community, locations and persons who are not directly involved in the community are identified by their real names in this chapter at the request of NS dos Mártires; the community would like its story to be told. Individual community members have been anonymised for reasons of confidentiality.

3　Interview with Oliviane, Amapá, 24 May 2005.
4　These rates are based on police records. Given that many murders were not documented by the police or were registered with 'cause of death unknown', it is probable that homicide rates were in reality much higher (cf. Alves, 2003: 123).
5　Donna Goldstein (2003: 19) has expressed a somewhat similar analysis of the functionality of the sacred for Pentecostal churches in shantytowns in Rio de Janeiro. She describes how Pentecostal preachers are able to publicly condemn drug gangs by framing their condemnations in terms of demoniacal possession.
6　Interview, Duque de Caxias, 8 August 2005.
7　Interview, Sara, Amapá, 4 June 2005.
8　Dom Mauro Morelli has a longstanding record of raising awareness of malnutrition, and he was an advisor for President Lula's trademark anti-hunger programme entitled Fome Zero (Hunger Zero).

Bibliography

Almeida, M.F. (1998). *Extermínio Seletivo e Limpeza Social em Duque de Caxias: A Sociedade Brasileira e os Indesejáveis* (Campinas. PhD thesis, Universidade Estatual de Campinas).

Alves, J.A. (2018). *The Anti-Black City: Police Terror and Black Urban Life in Brazil* (Minneapolis: University of Minnesota Press).

Alves, J.C.S. (2002). 'Violência e Religião na Baixada Fluminense: Uma Proposta Teórico Metodológica', *Revista Rio de Janeiro*, 8, 59–80.

Alves, J.C.S. (2003). *Dos Barões ao Extermínio. Uma História da Violência na Baixada Fluminense* (Duque de Caxias: APPH-CLIO).

Alves, J.C.S. (2004). 'Religião, Violência e Poder Político numa Favela da Baixada Fluminense', *Ciências Sociais e Religião*, 6:6, 153–78.

Appadurai, A. (2000). 'Spectral Housing and Urban Cleansing: Notes on Millennial Mumbai', *Public Culture*, 12:3, 627–51.

Arias, E.D. (2006). 'The Dynamics of Criminal Governance: Networks and Social Order in Rio de Janeiro', *Journal of Latin American Studies*, 38:2, 293–325.

Ação Social Paulo VI (ASPAS) (2001). *Relatório Anual das Atividades Desenvolvidas durante o Ano de 2001* (Duque de Caxias: Diocese de Duque de Caxias).

Bayat, A. (2012). 'Politics in the City-Inside-Out', *City & Society*, 24:2, 110–28.

Birman, P. and M.P. Leite (2000). 'Whatever Happened to What Used to Be the Largest Catholic Country in the World?', *Daedalus*, 192:2, 271–90.

Burdick, J. (1993). *Looking for God in Brazil. The Progressive Catholic Church in Urban Brazil's Religious Arena* (Berkeley: University of California Press).

Caldeira, T. (2000). *City of Walls: Crime, Segregation and Citizenship in São Paulo* (Berkeley: University of California Press).

Casanova, J. (1994). *Public Religions in the Modern World* (Chicago: University of Chicago Press).

Cardoso Sousa, A.C. (2006). *Responsabilidade Social e Desenvolvimento Sustenável: A Incorporação dos Conceitos à Estratégia Empresarial* (PhD thesis, Universidade Federal do Rio de Janeiro).

Certeau, M. de (1984). *The Practice of Everyday Life* (Berkeley: University of California Press).

Chiera, R. (1996). *Filhos do Brasil. Um Caminho de Solidariedade na Baixada Fluminense* (São Paulo: Editora Cidade Nova).

Comissão de Justiça e Paz de Nova Iguaçu (CDJP Nova Iguaçu) (1984). *Relatório de Atividades 1984* (Nova Iguaçu: Diocese de Nova Iguaçu).

Comissão de Justiça e Paz de Nova Iguaçu (CDJP Nova Iguaçu) (1985). *Relatório de Atividades 1985* (Nova Iguaçu: Diocese de Nova Iguaçu).

Comissão de Justiça e Paz de Nova Iguaçu (CDJP Nova Iguaçu) (1989). *Seminário sobre Violência na Baixada* (Nova Iguaçu: Diocese de Nova Iguaçu).

Comissão de Justiça e Paz de Nova Iguaçu (CDJP Nova Iguaçu) (1990). *Relatório de Atividades 1990* (Nova Iguaçu: Diocese de Nova Iguaçu).

De Almeida, R. (2020). 'Bolsonaro, Evangelicals, and the Brazilian Crisis', *Hot Spots, Fieldsights* (28 January 2020), https://culanth.org/fieldsights/bolsonaro-the-evangelicals-and-the-brazilian-crisis (accessed 26 November 2020).

Denyer Willis, G. (2015). *The Killing Consensus: Police, Organized Crime and the Regulation of Life and Death in Urban Brazil* (Berkeley: University of California Press).

de Oliveira, F.L.P., Santos Silva, R. dos, Souza, G.R.A. de and M.S. dos Santos (1999). *Origem e a História do Bairro Amapá*. Unpublished manuscript.

Diocese de Nova Iguaçu (n.d.). *A Diocese de Nova Iguaçu e a Questão dos Movimentos Sociais em Relação à Educação e Saúde* (Nova Iguaçu: Diocese de Nova Iguaçu).

Diocese de Nova Iguaçu (1988a). *Nossa Diocese e a Violência na BF* (Nova Iguaçu: Diocese de Nova Iguaçu).

Diocese de Nova Iguaçu (1988b). *Nossas Propostas Diocesanas. Contra a violência em defesa da Vida* (Nova Iguaçu: Diocese de Nova Iguaçu).

Diocese de Nova Iguaçu (2005). *Reage Baixada*, www.novaiguacu.rj.gov.br/ver_noticia.php?codNoticia=566 (accessed 3 May 2005).

Dowdney, L. (2003). *Children of the Drug Trade. A Case Study of Children in Organised Armed Violence in Rio de Janeiro* (Rio de Janeiro: 7Letras).

Durão, S. (2020). 'Bolsonaro's Brazil and the Police Fetish', *Hot Spots, Fieldsights* (28 January 2020), https://culanth.org/fieldsights/bolsonaros-brazil-and-the-police-fetish (accessed 26 November 2020).

Época (1999). 'A Violência como Rotina. Moradores da Baixada convivem com mais Mortes do que em uma Guerra', *Época* (30 August 1999).

Falzon, M. (2008). 'Paragons of Lifestyle: Gated Communities and the Politics of Space in Bombay', *City & Society*, 16:2, 145–67.

Gay, R. (2005). *Lucia. Testimonies of a Brazilian Drug Dealer's Woman* (Philadelphia: Temple University Press).

Goldstein, D. (2012). *Outlawed: Between Security and Rights in a Bolivian City* (Duke: Duke University Press).

Goldstein, D.M. (2003). *Laughter Out of Place: Race, Class, Violence, and Sexuality in a Rio Shantytown* (Berkeley: University of California Press).

Grynszpan, M. (1990). 'Açao Política e Atores Sociais: Posseiros, Grileiros e a Luta pela Terra na Baixada', *Dados*, 33:2, 285–310.

Harvey, D. (2003). 'The Right to the City', *International Journal of Urban and Regional Research*, 27:4, 939–41.

Holston, J. (2008). *Insurgent Citizenship: Disjunctions of Democracy and Modernity in Brazil* (Princeton: Princeton University Press).

Hume, M. and P. Wilding (2020). 'Beyond Agency and Passivity: Situating a Gendered Articulation of Urban Violence in Brazil and El Salvador', *Urban Studies*, 57:2, 249–66.

Huggins, M. (1997). 'From Bureaucratic Consolidation to Structural Devolution: Police Death Squads in Brazil', *Policing and Society*, 7, 207–34.

Instituto Brasileiro de Geografia e Estatística (IBGE) (2000). *Censo Demográfico 2000* (Rio de Janeiro: IBGE).

Jornal do Brasil (1987a). 'Baixada Vive Pavor e Mortes Há 100 Noites', *Jornal do Brasil* (26 June 1987), 4.

Jornal do Brasil (1987b). 'Um Holandês na Baixada', *Jornal do Brasil* (12 July 1987), 22–5.

Jornal de Hoje (1987). 'População Apavorada com Onda de Violência', *Jornal de Hoje* (6 June 1987), 1–6.

Jornal de Hoje (1988). 'Nova Chacina na Baixada', *Jornal de Hoje* (11 May 1988), 6.

Kingstone, P. (2000). 'Muddling Through Gridlock: Economic Policy Performance, Business Responses, and Democratic Sustainability', in Kingstone, P.R. and Power, T.J. (eds), *Democratic Brazil. Actors, Institutions, and Processes* (Pittsburgh: University of Pittsburgh Press), 185–203.

Lacey, N. (1988). *State Punishment: Political Principles and Community Values* (London and New York: Routledge & Kegan Paul).

Leeds, E. (1996). 'Cocaine and Parallel Polities in the Brazilian Urban Periphery: Constraints on Locallevel Democratization', *Latin American Research Review*, 3, 47–83.

Lefebvre, H. (1991). *The Production of Space* (Oxford: Blackwell).

Leite, M.S.P. (2001). *Para Além da Metafora da Guerra. Percepções sobre Cidadania, Violência e Paz no Grajaú, Um Bairro Carioca* (PhD thesis, Universidade Federal do Rio de Janeiro).

Lesbaupin, I., Fiorin, N., Ribeiro, L. and S. Rodrigues (2004). *As CEBs Hoje. Síntese de uma Pesquisa em Minas Gerais e Rio de Janeiro* (Rio de Janeiro: ISER/Assessoria).

Low, S.M. (2001). 'The Edge and the Center: Gated Communities and the Discourse of Urban Fear', *American Anthropologist*, 103:1, 45–58.

Machado, M.C. (1996). *Carismáticos e Pentecostais. Adesão Religiosa na Esfera Familiar* (Campinas: Editora Autores Associados/ANPOCS).

Machado, M.C. and C. Mariz (1997). 'Mulheres e Prática Religiosa nas Classes Populares: Uma Comparação entre as Igrejas Pentecostais, as Comunidades Eclesiaís de Base e os Grupos Carismáticos', *Revista Brasileira de Ciências Sociais*, 12:34, 71–81.

Mafra, C. (1998). 'Drogas e Símbolos: Redes de Solidariedade em Contextos de Violência', in Zaluar, A. and Alvito, M. (eds) *Um Século de Favela* (Rio de Janeiro: Editora FGV).

Mainwaring, S. (1986). *The Catholic Church and Politics in Brazil, 1916–1985* (Stanford: Stanford University Press).

Mariz, C.L. (1994). *Coping with Poverty. Pentecostals and Christian Base Communities in Brazil* (Philadelphia: Temple University Press).

Monroe, K. (2016). *The Insecure City: Space, Power, and Mobility in Beirut* (New Brunswick: Rutgers University Press).

Moraes, A.S. (2001). *'Rio Abaixe Essa Arma': Um Estudo sobre a Forma de Fazer 'Política' da 'Sociedade Civil'* (PhD thesis, Universidade Federal do Rio de Janeiro).

Moreira, T.M.S. (1999). *Chacinas e Falcatruas* (Rio de Janeiro: Lúmem Juris).

Müller, M.-M. (2016). 'Entangled Pacifications: Peacekeeping, Counterinsurgency and Policing in Port-au-Prince and Rio de Janeiro' in Hönke, J. and Müller, M.-M. (eds) *The Global Making of Policing: Postcolonial Perspectives* (London: Routledge), 77–95.

Neiburg, F. and Thomaz, O.R. (2020). 'Ethnographic Views of Brazil's (New) Authoritarian Turn', *HAU: Journal of Ethnographic Theory*, 10:1, 7–11.

Nossa Senhora dos Mártires da Baixada Fluminense (NS dos Mártires) (1999). *Revindicações* (Amapá: Nossa Senhora dos Mártires da Baixada).

Nossa Senhora dos Mártires da Baixada Fluminense (NS dos Mártires) (2002). *Dados do Mutirão: Amapá Geral* (Amapá: Nossa Senhora dos Mártires da Baixada).

Nossa Senhora dos Mártires da Baixada Fluminense (NS dos Mártires) (2004). *Nossa Senhora dos Mártires da Baixada Fluminense* (Amapá: Nossa Senhora dos Mártires da Baixada Fluminense).

O'Donnell, G. (1993). 'On the State, Democratization, and Some Conceptual Problems: A Latin American View with Glances at Some Postcommunist Countries', *World Development*, 21:8, 1355–69.

O Globo (1988). 'Medo Frustra a Organização Popular', *O Globo* (2 October 1988), 20.

O Globo (2005). 'Assassinados, Expulsos ou Vooptados no Rio', *O Globo* (20 March 2005), 17.

Oliveira, P.A.R. de (2009). 'Lideranças de CEBs no Brasil. Um Estudo Cómparativo: 1981–2000–2005', *Interações – Cultura e Comunidade*, 5:6, 165–81.

Oosterbaan, M. (2017). *Transmitting the Spirit: Religious Conversion, Media and Urban Violence in Brazil* (University Park: Penn State University Press).

Oro, A.P. (1996). *Avanço Pentecostal e Reação Católica* (Petrópolis: Vozes).

Paróquia São Simão (2005). *Jornal Comunidade* (Lote XV: Paróquia São Simão).

Perlman, J.E. (1976). *The Myth of Marginality. Urban Poverty and Politics in Rio de Janeiro* (Berkeley: University of California Press).

Reist, S. (2018). 'The Deadly Genealogy of Bolsonaro's Favorite Slogan', *Jacobin Magazine* (30 November 2018), https://jacobinmag.com/2018/11/brazil-bolsonarosecurity-guns-sivuca-militias (accessed 6 December 2018).

Rodgers, D. (2019). 'Urban Anti-Politics and the Enigma of Revolt: Confinement, Segregation, and (the Lack of) Political Action in Contemporary Nicaragua', *Ethnos*, 84:1, 56–73.

Serbin, K. (2000) 'The Catholic Church, Religious Pluralism, and Democracy in Brazil', in Peter Kingstone and Timothy Power (eds), *Democratic Brazil. Actors, Institutions, and Processes*. (Pittsburgh), 144–67.

Shirlow, P. and Murtagh, B. (2006). *Belfast: Segregation, Violence and the City* (London: Pluto Press).

Simone, A. (2018). *Improvised Lives: Rhythms of Endurance in an Urban South*. (New York: Polity).

Sousa, J.A. de (1997). *Os Grupos de Extermínio em Duque de Caxias – Baixada Fluminense* (MA thesis, Universidade Federal do Rio de Janeiro).

Sousa, J.A. de (2001). *Sociabilidades Emergentes. Implicações da Dominação de Matadores na Periferia e Traficantes nas Favelas* (PhD thesis, Universidade Federal do Rio de Janeiro).

Souza, P. de (1980). *O Maior Violência do Mundo: Baixada Fluminense* (São Paulo: Traço).

Stoll, D. (1990). *Is Latin America Turning Protestant? The Politics of Evangelical Growth* (Berkeley: University of California Press).

Susser, I. (1996). 'The Construction of Poverty and Homelessness in US Cities', *Annual Review of Anthropology*, 25, 411–35.

Theije, M.E.M. de (1999). *All That is God's is Good. An Anthropology of Liberationist Catholicism in Garahuns, Brazil* (Utrecht: CERES).

Tribuna de Imprensa (1987a). 'Esquadrões Voltam a Matar por Atacado na Baixada Fluminense', *Tribuna de Imprensa* (21 March 1987), 4.

Tribuna de Imprensa (1987b). 'Baixada, 850 Mortes em 4 Meses', *Tribuna de Imprensa* (25 May 1987), 9.

Universidade do Estado do Rio de Janeiro (UERJ) (2005). 'Quando a Violência Intimada a Fé', *UERJ Notícias* (19 April 2005).

Última Hora (1988). 'Nova Iguaçu Vai Protestar contra Morte de Família', *Última Hora* (31 May 1988), 4.

Última Hora (1988). 'Força Policial se Defronta Novamente com as Chacinas', *Última Hora* (30 August 1988), 3.

Vásquez, M.A. (1998). *The Brazilian Popular Church and the Crisis of Modernity* (Cambridge: Cambridge University Press).

Ventura, Z.A. (1994). *Cidade Partida* (São Paulo: Compania das Letras).

Walsh, M. and Davies, B. (1985). *Proclaiming Justice & Peace: Documents from John XXIII to John Paul II* (Mystic: Twenty-Third Publications).

Wolf, E. (1958). 'The Virgin of Guadalupe. A Mexican National Symbol', *Journal of American Folklore*, 71:1, 34–9.

Zaluar, A. (1983). 'Condomínio do Diabo: As Classes Populares Urbanas e a Lógica do 'Ferro' e do Fumo', in Pinheiro, P.S. (ed.) *Crime, Violência e Poder* (São Paulo: Editora Brasiliense).

Zaluar, A. (1985). *A Máquina e a Revolta: As Organizações Populares e o Significado da Pobreza.* (São Paulo: Editora Brasiliense).

Zaluar, A. (2000). 'Perverse Integration: Drug Trafficking and Youth in the Favelas of Rio de Janeiro', *Journal of International Affairs*, 53: 2, 653–72.

Zeiderman, A. (2016). *Endangered City: The Politics of Security and Risk in Bogotá.* (Durham: Duke University Press).

Epilogue: Rhythms and space-time of violence in and of the city

Jutta Bakonyi

The chapters in this edited volume explore the spatiotemporal features of violence in and of the city. They delve into the rhythms that relations and acts of (urban) violence generate, investigate urban transformations and how they are linked to the space-time of violence, and explore the spatial and temporal effects of violence which are often felt over generations. The authors have selected different approaches and lenses for this endeavour. Rather than attempting to critically comment on the chapters, I will draw on some observations and thoughts that I developed while reading the book and participating in the workshop on space-time that was jointly organised by the Universities of Erfurt and Durham. First, however, I would like to compliment the editors and authors on their contributions to our understanding of violence. While attending conceptually and empirically to the times, rhythms and spaces of violence in and of the city, the authors are also moving beyond binary concepts such as city and countryside, structure and agency, stasis and mobility, material and discursive. Herein lies, in my view, one of the core strengths of this volume and the benefit of looking at violence and the urban through the lens of time and space. The authors also contribute to a research agenda that aims to bring time and temporality back on to the horizon of world affairs, moving beyond Foucault's (1986) famous and powerful contention that the epoch we live in is characterised by a shift in thinking from time to space. However, Foucault also immediately added that the present 'epoch of space' is also an 'epoch of simultaneity', characterised by a 'fatal intersection of time with space' (Foucault, 1986: 22). A much broader number of social scientists have explored the spatial relations of urban violence while less attention has been paid to the aspect of time or its 'fatal intersection' with space. It is the latter which the volume and its authors have courageously taken up in exploring the space-time of violence and the city.

The chapters contribute to an empirically detailed investigation of forms and logics of violence, yet they also demonstrate the difficulties of

conceptually unpacking both the city and violence, let alone the relationship between them. They each engage with aspects of the space-time of the
urban and of violence, but it seems that while these aspects are described
and analysed, both the urban and violence continue to resist attempts to
render them legible. The question of what violence is and how to define
or delineate the city (or the urban) are highly debated, and if answers are
provided, they are speedily contested. Of course, this applies to most concepts. After all, Adorno and Horkheimer (1992) identified early on the non-
identity between a concept and the substance or 'thing' it claims to represent
(*Begriff und Sache*) as key to an understanding of the dialectic of enlightenment, and described the arbitrariness of definitions as among the aporia that
enlightenment is both embedded in and generates. They also analysed the
differentiation of concept and substance as both cause and effect of violence
and domination, which reaches its peak in capitalist mass-consumer culture
and its promotion of quantifiable, easily digestible but meaningless concepts. Therefore, instead of carving out definitions, Adorno recommended
engaging with conceptual meaning from a historical-theoretical perspective
(Adorno, 1995: 11). The rich historical and empirical case studies in this
volume provide the building blocks for a theorisation of the space-time of
cities and violence. In this epilogue, I will try to identify some of these building blocks, engaging further with the literature and adding some additional
thoughts on violence and the city.

About rhythms and temporalities of violence

The works presented in this volume fall roughly into what von Trotha
(1997) called a theoretical ethnography of violence. The authors base their
analyses on thick descriptions of violent phenomena, but also interpret
their findings from an emotionally, and in most cases also spatially, more
distanced theoretical perspective. What the authors also have in common
is that they primarily, although not exclusively, attend to violence in its
physical forms: violence that intentionally and deliberately inflicts pain and
harms others. Violence, in its direct physical form, has immediately visible
and feelable effects, which the authors describe at times in disturbing detail.
Violence mutilates and damages bodies, leads to suffering, and ends lives.
Physical violence is very intimate. It targets and penetrates bodies, often
quite literally leaving holes in the body. Violence can even, as for example
Jenss shows in this volume, make whole bodies disappear.

Physical violence, of course, can also be directed against things. It can
be used, for example, to challenge regulations of property, and with it, the
socio-spatial enclosures and relations of in- and exclusion that property

demarcates (Blomley, 2003; Bakonyi et al., 2019). In this respect, some of the authors have explored how urban rioters damage things they perceive as causing harm, banks or government buildings, for example, as Weinhauer's chapter shows, or at levelling social hierarchies and compensate for differences in status and wealth (Hobsbawm, 1959). Jenss' chapter also analyses how protestors interrupt the accelerated mobility of supply chains to protest material deprivation but also against the violence that accompanied the expansion of the port and the aligned acceleration of global trade. Violence against supply chains can of course also become an ordinary weapon of war, used to deprive social groups of access to necessities, at times with life-threatening consequences, when for example humanitarian supplies are disrupted.

Direct physical violence has a specific temporality (detailed in Sofsky, 1997a). From the perspective of its victims, violence is experienced as sudden and fast. Even if it is expected, as is so often the case in domestic violence for example, it continues to take the victim by surprise, it weighs down on her with an unprecedented abruptness. Violence damages bodies and impedes the human ability to express and to remember. Victims of physical violence often lack the voice and words to express experiences of pain, except for the cries and moans that are exclaimed when violence hits, utterances that often continue to accompany the memories of violence. The lack of language and the suddenness of violence may explain the regular use of metaphorical language that, for example, likens violence to forces of nature – violence that 'breaks out', 'bursts out' or 'erupts' like volcanoes or diseases that spread unstopped. These metaphorical depictions do not allow for the identification of actors, and neither do they account for the preparation necessary to organise violence. They do, however, emphasise a further temporal feature of violence: its ability to set people into motion and to accelerate movement (also see Albrecht in this volume). The speed with which violence hits the victim is only matched by the speed of victims' attempts to flee. Violence can set masses into motion, as the steady stream of displaced people and refugees in violent conflicts and wars attests to. The Russian invasion of Ukraine and, as of March 2022, the approximately two million refugees that the war has set in motion, is just one among many recent examples.

Physical violence can be so repeatedly used by perpetrators that it loses its sensationalism and becomes part of the monotonous, boring repetitions and routines that characterise the everyday (Felski, 1999). However, violence can never be fully routinised by the victim, and this may differentiate physical violence from all other social activities (Bakonyi, 2022a). Even if violence hits regularly, every stroke is experienced as a single event, constitutes a spectacular moment of pain that, as Scarry (1985) described it, 'unmakes the world'. Violence thus creates its own times (in plural). The time of the victim's violence differs from the times of the perpetrators. The perpetrators' times of violence display enormous variation: acts of violence can be conducted suddenly, born out of affect and accompanied by strong emotions – anger and rage spring to mind. Violence can, however, also be conducted with a cold, instrumental and systematic rationality that cautiously weighs means and ends and may even consider unintended (side-) effects. The peak of this can be found in the instrumental rationality and bureaucratic performances of violence in the Nazi concentration camps (Bauman, 1989; Sofsky, 1997b).

Again, while affects and emotions on the side of the perpetrator often differ, the experience of violence itself is more homogeneous. Violence produces extreme and powerful emotions on the side of the victim, among them, fear, horror, guilt. Beyond the 'making and unmaking of the world' (Scarry, 1985), violence is also making and unmaking subjects, as Frantz Fanon (1963) or Veena Das (2000) have powerfully shown from decolonial and feminist perspectives. Once it hits, violence terminates options to act, and forces people to succumb to the power of others. For Tyrell (1980), the termination of the ability to act differentiates violence from coercion. Coercion can significantly limit actions but does not aim at terminating all options to act as it prefers voluntary subordination (even if the voluntariness is caused by the anticipation of violence). In the context of coercive relationships, violence can also have a liberating effect if people use it to overcome the violence that is inscribed in their submission, to break the chains that bind them to their masters or to a society that promotes their submission (prominently again Fanon, 1963).

In any case, violence marks the body and mind, and if regularly repeated and socially reproduced, it contributes to and normalises relations of submission and dominance. Violence has, therefore, generative effects, as it creates and shapes social relations and forms social hierarchies. As I will discuss later, it is also generative of space and time. Due to the productive characteristics of violence, authors such as Max Weber or Norbert Elias identified it as the basis of power and domination. They were referring to a change in the form of violence, a sublimation[1] in which the mere physical force and sheer display of power are transformed to more subtle relations of domination. This social transformation, however, requires that violence and other constituting factors of domination are concealed, disguised and eventually misrecognised and euphemised in moral concepts (honour, loyalty, kinship, law). In the process of sublimation, violence becomes something else. It does not disappear but takes on a new form as it is institutionalised, embedded in hierarchies, enshrined in rules and laws and inscribed in the habitus of people.

To account for this transformation, authors have argued against the delimitation of violence to physical and intentional acts. Influential among these authors are Scheper-Hughes et al. (2003), who have identified a continuum of violence, ranging from direct physical acts to indirect, more hidden or even invisible forms. Multiple agents are involved in producing these more invisible forms of violence through their interactions and practices, but not necessarily intentionally. Here, violence is inscribed in social relations and transported through structures (Galtung, 1969), institutions (Bauman, 1989), cultures (Galtung, 1969), symbols (Bourdieu, 1977), language (hate-speech, Butler, 1997), epistemologies (Spivak, 1988), norms (Chambers, 2007; Butler, 2004) and infrastructures (Rodgers and O'Neill, 2012). For the sake of the argument, I will group these more indirect and often less visible forms of violence together under the label of 'structural violence' to which they are closely related and interlinked (see Davies, 2019). What these structural forms of violence have in common is that they are not easily perceived as violence, as they can mainly be identified through their harmful effects.

I agree with critics who have challenged the analytical usefulness of the expansion of violence to an ever wider array of harmful phenomena and practices (for example Wacquant, 1996). Structural violence focuses more on outcomes than processes, which is not sufficient for a deeper understanding of violence. Moves to expand concepts are usually politically motivated, here they aim to scandalise practices that are causing harm and thus draw attention to serious social problems (Koloma Beck and Schlichte, 2014: 37–8).[2] However, a narrow definition does not avoid the general problems of definition or the politics imbued in them. Even if narrowly defined as an intentional physical act directed towards others, violence includes a wide array of social actions, actors and aims. What is considered as physical violence and which forms of violence are socially and morally discouraged or even outlawed is time- and place-bound, embedded in culture and potentially contested (Blok, 2000). Violence is, for example, not only used with the intention to harm (and it always does harm) but it can also aim towards betterment, improvement and development, for example, when children are disciplined by adults who indeed believe it to be in the best interest of their children; when parents decide to circumcise their girls to allow them to maintain decency and to increase their chances of being married; when colonialists use violence to missionise unbelievers, civilise savages and develop backward people; or when violence is used in counterinsurgencies for 'the betterment of the population in whose midst it is exercised' (Bell, 2012). These forms of violence are often described through medical and therapeutic metaphors as they emphasise an 'interconnection between biology and politics' and, maybe, more importantly, identify war and violence as a 'politics of life' that takes place amidst suffering or even death (Bell, 2012: 225, 226).

Instead of continuing the debate on what should be called violence and what not, the volume looks at the different phenomena of bodily harm and lethality through the lens of time and space. Such a view can reveal marked differences between actions and structures that cause harm. Both display a different if not radically opposed temporality. The temporal characteristics of physical violence are its speed, immediacy and suddenness, while structural violence is slow, indirect and gradual. Nixon was using the example of toxification when he coined the concept of 'slow violence' (Nixon, 2011; Davies, 2019), a type of structural violence that is neither immediate nor spectacular and often hidden from the public gaze. Tyner (2016), in a similar vein, used the example of the death of a leukaemia patient who could not receive life-saving medicines due to budget cuts in the US health system to point to the structural violence imbued in the commercialisation of health care and, by extension, the commodified distribution of values of life. These authors emphasise the 'agonizingly slow death' (Tyner, 2016: 6) that is attributable to, for example, hunger, lack of labour safety standards and preventable diseases. Here, the perpetrators do not intend to harm others, but decide not to take action to prevent suffering and deaths that could and should have been prevented. Physical violence is conducted by actors; structural violence is embedded in social relations that promote inaction and acts of omission with the result that people are left to suffer and left to die (Tyner, 2016). Structural violence demonstrates the differential recognition and distribution of values of life (Butler, 2009a). It is imbued in politically generated conditions that expose some populations to 'injury, violence, and death' (Butler, 2009b, II). These conditions also generate social indifference towards the suffering of lives constituted as abject, disposable (Bauman, 2004; Tyler, 2013) and 'socially dead' (Mbembé, 2003: 24, 21; Wilcox, 2019: 310–11).

Violence as the making and unmaking of places and times

Violence displays different temporalities. It also always takes place somewhere, while it unfolds through and is shaped by the specific materiality of places. However, it simultaneously transforms this materiality and thus makes places. The spatial features of violence have garnered considerable academic attention in the past few decades (Springer, 2011; Springer and Le Billon, 2016; Fuccaro, 2016; Laliberté, 2016; Elfversson et al., 2019). The authors in this volume provide additional examples of the way violence makes places: violence accompanies evictions and dispossessions (Kapoor;

Jenss) and contributes to urban segregation (Kapoor; Laheij; Mady; Mazza); it can be routinised in riots and massacres that emphasise claims to urban space or protest against spatial injustices (Albrecht; Kapoor; Mazza); violence can accompany strikes, demonstrations and counter-protests (Jenss; Weinhauer); and it can be used to accelerate or disrupt mobilities and the social orders which these mobilities generate and represent (Jenss; Weinhauer).

All authors in the volume foreground that space is produced by movement (see Thrift, 2006). Physical violence tends to accelerate movements and thus necessarily also contributes to the making of spaces. Within the acceleration it generates, violence can also enforce standstill, entrap and contain people (Lubkemann, 2008; Bakonyi, 2022a). The transformation of violence into more subtle forms of authority manifests itself in the ability to shape, direct and control such mobilities. Political technologies often attempt to make spaces appear static and stable, most pronounced through the establishment of barriers, roadblocks and walls (Weinhauer in this volume). As crude spatial materialisations of power, barriers can be considered a first step in the transformation of physical violence into more subtle forms of domination. While physical violence is experienced as acceleration, the barrier does the opposite: it interrupts mobility and slows down movement, often enforcing queuing and waiting. Stationary barriers and roadblocks, therefore, are often the first sign of an initial institutionalisation of violence, a form of violence that stems from the ability to slow down the movement of others (Bakonyi, 2011: 323–4). Barriers can, of course, also be established as an expression of counter-power or resistance. Jenss' chapter shows how Columbian port dwellers used barriers and developed disruptive agencies. If only for a short moment, the protestors displayed their joint power to slow down and interrupt the accelerated circulation of goods, drawing attention to the socio-spatial conditions and structural inequalities that determine their lives. In a similar vein, Weinhauer and Albrecht show how strikes, boycotts and demonstrations disrupt or even suspend the rhythms of everyday life in the city. Thus, while violence is both physical and direct, it is also externalised in the physical fabric of a city, where it is attached with meaning, and thereby becomes indirect and develops its own symbolic qualities while shaping and transforming rhythms and temporalities.

Violence, therefore, is imbued into the morphology of cities. This was most pronounced in colonial cities, where the unmixing, separation and ghettoisation of residential areas along racial, ethnic or religious lines (Albrecht, Mady, and Mazza's chapters) were facilitated by physical barriers and pass-laws, differentiating the attachments of urban residents to places, their lifestyles and life changes. Violence materialises in the physical fabric of cities across the globe where it contributes, for example, to the segregation of places and the territorialisation of status and stigma (Wacquant et al., 2014), and continues to be further differentiated within stigmatised neighbourhoods (Kapoor in this volume). And while physical segregations co-constitute relations of class, race and gender (Wacquant, 2008), they also delineate, as Laheij's contribution shows, distinct normative orders that determine the lifeworlds and life chances of residents. The transformation of violence into domination is perfected when these differences are normalised, and relations of power and social hierarchies inscribed in places are essentialised. Residents then no longer require physical barriers but instead develop mental maps that direct their movement and shape their (political) interactions and practices accordingly – as Laheij emphasised.

When violence inscribes itself in spaces, it also always inscribes itself in times (again in plural) as both are indivisible and produce each other. For example, the colonially imposed urban divisions were aligned to 'orientalist infused imaginations of time' (Albrecht in this volume; also Neep, 2012: 151–2). After violent conflicts and wars end, physical violence can still be seen in damaged buildings, ruins, rubble and voids left by bombs, mortars and looters. Physical violence produces material traces that continue to evoke meaning while becoming memory (Edensor, 2005; Mady in this volume). These traces provide links to the past that can be used for the mobilisation of violence in the present or as a reminder of the necessity to foster reconciliation and keep the peace.

The material scaffolding of cities seemingly reflects layers of time. However, the material traces of 'epochs' as well as the material traces of violence are not just out there but are actively produced by those who are deciphering and rendering these traces legible. Mady attempts in her chapter to sketch the material layers and traces of violence that characterise Beirut's history. Her insight that these layers can be used, forgotten or erased in processes of narration and memorialisation, directly feeds into Warnecke's chapter, who emphasises the making of time. Building on the work of Norbert Elias, Warnecke shows that time is made by linking past and present events while constructing histories and life stories. Violence is, in different forms, part of this making. The traces that violence leaves behind can be detected, remembered, forgotten or erased. Revenge, from this perspective, becomes an activity that lays bare certain traces of violence, thus is violently making time. Other traces of violence are constructed when children murdered by gangs (or the police) are declared as martyrs (Laheij's chapter). While this declaration points towards eternity, it also becomes a method for renegotiating the boundaries drawn by urban segregation and gang violence. Both examples – revenge and martyrdom – show how urban residents combine time and space in unique ways while they are (violently or not) re-negotiating the norms and relations in which their everyday is embedded. Another example of the intertwined production of time and space can be seen when memorials and monuments are established to remember violent events, or when archaeological excavations are organised to strengthen the property claims of contesting groups (Albrecht in this volume). Both produce a particular understanding of the past. While monuments and memorials aim at 'freezing the past' (Björkdahl and Kappler, 2017: 67) they are producing time and constituting the past, drawing particular connections between events and people, making memory and aligning it with meaning and emotions.

The making of time remains contested, as the many destructions, defacements and demolitions of monuments attest to. Laheij shows in his chapter how interpretations of violence, the discourses and counter-discourses that accompany violence (as justification, contestation or explanation of violence) are fostering, challenging and re-shaping existing violence–space–time figurations. The material urban fabric, as Mady in her chapter outlines, becomes a dense 'register of past traces' as ongoing constructions, destructions and reconstructions produce the scaffolded and layered morphology of urban forms. In as much as wars speed-up movements, they also accelerate processes of destruction and reconstruction. The narrative and material creation of links to the past can be officialised in national calendars and continue to shape the memorialisation practices of people even when they migrate (see Bolte in this volume). Memories can also be enacted violently, as Albrecht, Bolte and Mazza show in their contributions. Violence then aims at routinisation, aligning present experiences with the past while mitigating expected or feared erasure and forgetting in the future. Routinisation through the repetition of violence displayed in riots around commemoration days is an attempt to keep one interpretation of the past alive.

The fear of erasure of memory already shows that violence can be directed towards the future, for example, when it is enacted as self-defence, as a first strike aimed at preventing the expected violence of others. Governments may anticipate violence and prepare for it at denoted times or days of the year (see Bolte) or the fear of strikes and revolutions can initiate governmental and/or paramilitary actions (see Weinhauer). In this respect, security and risk analysis create temporal links between past, present and future. They project past experiences (of violence, crime, etc.) into the future, constructing what Koselleck (2004) termed 'horizons of expectation'. Koselleck described the de-linkage of experiences from expectations as a core feature of modern life. Accordingly, the future is increasingly interpreted as open, to be moulded by social practices. The delinking of experiences from expectations and the mutual unfolding of time and space can also be seen in the increasing use of notions such as emergence or contingency across the social sciences (Palonen, 1997: 61). Security and risk analysis are then used to compensate for the general loss of certainty as they aim at taming contingencies and thus at what has not yet happened. Such analyses operate through scenarios that outline probabilities derived from past experiences while monitoring the unfolding of events to adapt, correct and identify new probabilities. Risk assessments thus aim to control events that have not yet happened and 'might never happen but are always possible' (Wichum, 2013: 165). These analyses then give rise to risk mitigation measures, notably insurance provisions that further divide the 'insured' – those living in welfare states and/or are able to participate in mass consumer cultures – from the 'uninsured' who have to build on self-reliance, receive community support or, and this reveals once more the violence that underlies these practices, are contained and prevented from moving to try their luck elsewhere (Duffield, 2007).

Mitigation measures work through and with time and space. The identification of risks of violence has, for example, given rise to an 'architecture of fear' (Ellin, 1997) that increasingly shapes contemporary cities across the globe (Calderia, 1996; Blakely and Snyder, 1997; Lemanski, 2004) contributing further to the territorialisation of difference. Such differences also structure international attempts to mitigate human suffering. Humanitarian and military interventions increasingly rely on modular designs that allow for a speedy adaptation of security provisions, but also point to the temporal and liminal character of the intervention. Zonal arrangements provide a spatial template that seems to replace the archipelago of fortified aid compounds that usually structure interventions in unruly environments (Duffield, 2012: 477). These zones shield humanitarian and international aid workers from potential risks, enabling the circulation of some people and goods, while limiting the circulations of others (see Bakonyi, 2022b).

These are only a few examples of how violence generates space through time and time through space. As physical violence, it enacts space and shapes rhythms in the here and now; as memory of violence, it links the past in meaningful ways to the present; as anticipation of violence (risk) and preparation for it (insurance, wall, zonation, etc.), it projects the past-present into the future. While generating spaces and times, violence also inscribes itself in the habitus of urban residents, constituting and differentiating subject positions and options for action, and thus continues to contribute to the emergence of new socio-spatial-temporal formations characterised by speedy and slow forms of violence. Violence, to summarise, is taking place in space and time and can be strategically used to mould place and time while simultaneously producing both.

Space-time, violence and the city

Violence unfolds an enormous dynamic. I use dynamic here in the same sense as Barad (2001: 90) who argues against the conceptualisation of dynamics as mere transformation unfolding in space and through time. Instead of taking space and time as both given and external to human action, Barad contends that dynamics produce and reconfigure temporality and spatiality. Barad's work aims at overcoming the 'Euclidian geometric imaginary' that projects 'space as container/context for matter in motion' and time as incremental sequences that mark progression (Barad, 2001: 76). The authors of this volume have explored and shown the dynamic production of time and space through violence. They have used the city as the vantage point. Most have interrogated the space-time of urban violence in applaudable detail but have avoided further discussions of the city and how it is distinct from other socio-material figurations. Cities are notoriously difficult to grasp. Early urban sociologists elaborated that the size, density and heterogeneity of cities are its characteristic features leading to a distinctly urban lifestyle (Wirth, 1938). Other authors have emphasised the central function of cities as economic hubs, facilitators and mediators of global flows (Sassen, 1991; Jessop, 2002; Brenner et al., 2010) and as both drivers and manifestations of industrial capitalism and important centres of political regulation that provide important coordinates of territorial power. Global cities may even enter in competition to the state (Brenner, 2004; Tilly, 2010; Acuto, 2011; Scott, 2011). These features show that cities are above all the 'site of multiple, transversal, and reflexive circulations' that are, however, stabilised through practices 'that seek to objectify the city as totality' (LiPuma and Koelble, 2005: 154).

Like all other spaces, cities are constituted through mobility, movement and circulation – although the speed, density, heterogeneity, extension and volatility of circulations likely increase in cities. Political technologies, some of them violent or based on violence, contribute to these processes of spatial objectification that constitute the city as a bounded, integrated, enclosed, cohesive entity rather than as an ever unfinished and continuously evolving spatiotemporal formation. Urban planning, policies, maps, gates, roadblocks, pass-controls, surveillance, memorials and monuments make spaces appear static as they enframe and territorialise cities while narrating their past and carving out potentials for their future. Once established, the material fabric of cities, among them 'buildings, parks, highways, neighbourhoods, shopping malls' are (re)aligned with 'the dispositions, desires, and sensibilities of circulating subjects' in daily practices that mould and shape the urban imaginary that reifies the city as a bounded entity (LiPuma and Koelble, 2005: 157). However, cities are comprised of multiple, overlapping circulations, temporalities, spaces and scales, and could better be described as a 'mosaic of "cities"' and urbanising spaces (LiPuma and Koelble, 2005: 162). Such mosaics become particularly pronounced in the fragmented spaces and lifestyles of segregated and highly securitised neighbourhoods to which the authors in this volume attest.

The chapters have provided multiple examples of how the temporal modes and spatial forms are contributing to the insertion of boundaries and the promotion of (urban) ideologies that shape gendered, ethnicised and racialised subject positions. The question of whether there is something explicitly urban in the way that violence is organised and conducted, and thus in how far violence is of the city (Fuccaro, 2016), however, remains. Mazza uses Jerusalem as an example in his chapter to argue that violence is 'contingent on the rhythms of urban life, dictated by space, time and religion'. While the colonial segregation of neighbourhoods may not have caused violence, Mazza shows how it shaped the way violence unfolded, as contesting groups made use of the built environment to (violently) articulate their claims, foster alignments to urban places. Urban segregation intensified the violence of such claims. Albrecht and Mady demonstrate how the built environment facilitated violence: streets provided corridors for fighting, concrete blocks were used as barriers, road junctions were transformed into checkpoints and buildings into control points of fighting groups. The congestion of residential neighbourhoods facilitated violent interactions while specific temporalities, among them arrangements and sequences of religious events and holidays, commemorations or other political events, facilitated violence and defined the actor groups involved. Competing groups built upon the rhythms of their neighbourhoods and synchronised violence with the annual calendar of their city to execute government or to protest and resist. Violence also adhered to the rhythms of work schedules and religious arrangements.

Official knowledge about the city is created as topographical and cartographical data, in surveys, maps, planning documents, registries and calendars. However, knowledge is also produced in everyday practices that make use of and form urban spaces, rhythms and times, while facilitating violence or adapting daily mobilities in attempts to escape (anticipated) violence. Important for the study of counter-knowledge are micro-spatial and micro-historical studies that move beyond a homogenising narrative. In particular Weinhauer, but also Albrecht and Kapoor, attend to the spatiotemporal transformations that accompanied industrialisation, and emphasise how the everyday resistance of workers was often directed against the disciplinary rhythm and tight time regime of capitalism, displayed in factories, shipyards or mills. These examples underscore that violence is not of the city, but of multiple city spaces and of material–time–space formations that are assembled in different rhythms and speeds while constituting the urban imaginary.

Notes

1 Thanks to Shrey Kapoor, who alerted me to the concept of sublimation.
2 Another concept that was widened in this way is security, as captured in the notion of human security which has overlaps with structural violence.

Bibliography

Acuto, M. (2011). 'Finding the Global City: An Analytical Journey through the "Invisible College"', *Urban Studies* 48:14, 2953–73.
Adorno, T.W. (1995). 'Gesellschaft', in Tiedemann, R. (ed.) *Theodor W. Adorno Soziologische Schriften I* (Frankfurt a.M.: Suhrkamp), 9–19.
Adorno, T.W. and J. Horkheimer (1992). *Dialektik der Aufklärung. Philosophische Fragmente* (Frankfurt a.M.: Fisher).
Bakonyi, J. (2022a). 'War's Everyday: Normalising Violence and Legitimizing Power', *Partecipazione e Conflitto*, 15:1, 121–38.
Bakonyi, J. (2022b). 'Modular Sovereignty and Infrastructural Power: The Elusive Materiality of International Statebuilding', *Security Dialogue*, https://doi.org/10.1177/09670106211051943
Bakonyi, J., P. Chonka and K. Stuvoy (2019). 'War and City-making in Somalia: Property, Power and Disposable Lives', *Political Geography* 73, 82–91.
Bakonyi, Jutta. (2011). *Land ohne Staat. Wirtschaft und Gesellschaft im Krieg am Beispiel Somalias* (Frankfurt am Main: Campus).
Barad, K. (2001). 'Re(con)figuring space, time, and matter', in Dekoven, M. (ed.) *Feminist Locations: Global and local, theory and practice* (New Brunswick, New Jersey and London: Rutgers University Press), 75–109.
Bauman, Z. (2004). *Wasted Lives: Modernity and its Outcasts* (Cambridge: Polity).
Bauman, Z. (1989). *Modernity and the Holocaust* (Ithaca: Cornell University Press).
Bell, C. (2012). 'Hybrid Warfare and Its Metaphors', *Humanity: An International Journal of Human Rights, Humanitarianism, and Development* 3:2, 225–47.
Björkdahl, A. and S. Kappler (2017). *Peacebuilding and Spatial Transformation: Peace, Space and Place* (Abingdon: Routledge).
Blakely, E.J. and M.G. Snyder (1997). 'Devided we Fall. Gated and Walled Communities in the United States', in Ellin, N. (ed.) *Architecture of Fear* (New York: Princeton Architectural Press), 85–99.
Blok, A. (2000). 'The Enigma of Senseless Violence', in Ajimer, G. and Abbink, J. (eds) *Meanings of Violence. A Cross Cultural Perspective* (New York: Berg), 23–38.
Blomley, N. (2003). 'Law, Property, and the Geography of Violence: The Frontier, the Survey, and the Grid', *Annals of the Association of American Geographers* 93:1, 121–41.
Bourdieu, P. (1977). *Outline of a Theory of Practice* (Cambridge: Cambridge University Press).

Brenner, N. (2004). *Urban Governance and New State Space in Western Europe* (Oxford: Oxford University Press).

Brenner, N., J. Peck and N. Theodore (2010). 'Variegated neoliberalization: geographies, modalities, pathways', *Global Networks: A Journal of Transnational Affairs* 10:2, 182–222.

Butler, J. (1997). *Excitable Speech. A Politics of the Performative* (New York and London: Routledge).

Butler, J. (2009a). *Frames of War: When is Life Grievable?* (New York: Verso).

Butler, J. (2009b). 'Performativity, Precarity and Sexual Politics', *AIBR. Revista de Antropología Iberoamericana* 4:3, I–XIII.

Butler, J. (2004). *Precarious Life: The Powers of Mourning and Violence* (New York: Verso).

Calderia, T. (1996). 'Fortified enclaves: the new urban segregation', *Public Culture* 8:2, 303–28.

Chambers, S. (2007). 'Normative Violence after 9/11: Rereading the Politics of Gender Trouble', *New Political Science* 29, 43–60.

Das, V. (2000). 'The Act of Witnessing. Violence, Poisonous Knowledge, and Subjectivity' in Das, V., Kleinman, A., Ramphele, A. and Reynolds, P. (eds) *Violence and Subjectivity* (Berkeley and London: University of California Press), 205–25.

Davies, T. (2019). 'Slow violence and toxic geographies: "Out of sight" to whom?', *Environment and Planning C: Politics and Space*, https://doi.org/10.1177/2399654419841063

Duffield, M. (2007). *Development, Security and Unending War. Governing the World of Peoples* (Cambridge: Polity Press).

Duffield, M. (2012). 'Challenging environments: Danger, resilience and the aid industry', *Security Dialogue* 43:5, 475–92.

Edensor, T. (2005). *Industrial Ruins: Spaces, Aesthetics, and Materiality* (Oxford; New York: Berg).

Elfversson, E., I. Gusic and K. Höglund (2019). 'The spatiality of violence in postwar cities', *Third World Thematics: A TWQ Journal* 4:2–3, 81–93.

Ellin, N. (ed.) (1997). *Architecture of Fear* (New York: Princeton Architectural Press).

Fanon, F. (1963). *The Wretched of the Earth* (London: Penguin).

Felski, R. (1999). 'The invention of everyday life', *New Formations* 39, 13–31.

Foucault, M. (1986). 'Of other Spaces', *Diacritics* 16:1, 22–7.

Fuccaro, N. (2016). 'Urban Life and Questions of Violence', in Nelida Fuccaro (ed.) *Violence and the City in the Modern Middle East* (Stanford: Stanford University Press), 3–22.

Fuccaro, N. (ed.) (2016). *Violence and the City in the Modern Middle East* (Stanford: Stanford University Press).

Galtung, J. (1969). 'Violence, Peace, and Peace Research', *Journal of Peace Research* 6:3, 167–91.

Hobsbawm, E. (1959). *Primitive Rebels* (New York: W.W. Norton).

Jessop, B. (2002). *The Future of the Capitalist State* (Cambridge: Polity).

Koloma Beck, T. and K. Schlichte (2014). *Theorien der Gewalt. Zur Einfuehrung* (Hamburg: Junius).

Koselleck, R. (2004). *Futures Past: On the Semantics of Historical Time* (New York: Columbia University Press).

Laliberté, N. (2016). ' "Peace begins at home": Geographic imaginaries of violence and peacebuilding in northern Uganda', *Political Geography* 52, 24–33.

Lemanski, C. (2004). ' A new apartheid? The spatial implications of fear of crime in Cape Town, South Africa', *Environment and Urbanization* 16, 101–12.

LiPuma, E and T. Koelble (2005). 'Cultures of Circulation and the Urban Imaginary: Miami as Example and Exemplar', *Public Culture* 17:1, 153–80.

Lubkemann, S.C. (2008). 'Involuntary Immobility: On a Theoretical Invisibility in Forced Migration Studies', *Journal of Refugee Studies* 21:4, 454–75.

Mbembé, A. (2003). 'Necropolitics', *Public Culture* 15:1, 11–40.

Neep, D. (2012). *Occupying Syria under the French Mandate. Insurgency, Space and State Formation* (Cambridge: Cambridge University Press).

Nixon, R. (2011). *Slow Violence and the Environmentalism of the Poor* (London: Harvard University Press).

Palonen, K. (1997). 'An Application of Conceptual History to Itself: From Method to Theory in Reinhart Koselleck's Begriffsgeschichte', *Finnish Yearbook of Political Thought* 1:1, 39–69.

Rodgers, D. and B. O'Neill (2012). 'Infrastructural violence: Introduction to the special issue', *Ethnography* 13:4, 401–12.

Sassen, S. (1991). *The Global City: New York, London, Tokyo* (Princeton: Princeton University Press).

Scarry, E. (1985). *The Body in Pain: The Making and Unmaking of the World* (Oxford: Oxford University Press).

Scheper-Hughes, N. and P. Bourgois (2003). 'Introduction: Making sense of violence' in Scheper-Hughes, N. and Bourgois, P. (eds) *Violence in War and Peace: An Anthology* (Oxford: Wiley-Blackwell), 1–31.

Scott, A. J. (2011). 'Emerging cities of the third wave', *City* 15:3–4, 289–321.

Sofsky, W. (1997a). 'Gewaltzeiten' in von Trotha, T. (ed.) *Soziologie der Gewalt*, 102–21.

Sofsky, W. (1997b). Die Ordnung des Terrors: Das Konzentrationslager (Frankfurt a.M.: Fischer).

Spivak, G.C. (1988). 'Can the Subaltern Speak?' in C. Nelson and L. Grossberg (eds) *Marxism and the Interpretation of Culture* (London: Macmillan), 271–313.

Springer, S. (2011). 'Violence sits in places? Cultural practice, neoliberal rationalism, and virulent imaginative geographies', *Political Geography* 30:2, 90–8.

Springer, S. and P. Le Billon (2016). 'Violence and space: An introduction to the geographies of violence', *Political Geography* 52, 1–3.

Thrift, N. (2006). 'Space', *Theory, Culture & Society* 23:2–3, 139–46.

Tilly, C. (2010). 'Cities, states, and trust networks: chapter 1 of cities and states in world history', *Theory and Society* 39:3, 265–80.

Tyler, I. (2013). *Revolting Subjects: Social Abjection and Resistance in Neoliberal Britain* (London: Zed Books).

Tyner, J. (2016). *Violence in Capitalism: Devaluing Life in an Age of Responsibility* (Lincoln: University of Nebraska Press).

Tyrell, H. (1980). 'Gewalt, Zwang und die Institutionalisierung von Herrschaft: Versuch einer Neuinterpretation von Max Webers Herrschaftsbegriff', in Pohlmann, R. (ed.) *Person und Institution. Helmut Schelsky gewidmet* (Würzburg: Verlag Dr. Johannes Königshausen and Dr. Thomas Neumann), 59–93.

von Trotha, T. (1997). 'Zur Soziologie der Gewalt' in von Trotha, T. (ed.) *Soziologie der Gewalt* (Opladen, Wiesbaden: Westdeutscher Verlag), 9–58.

Wacquant, L. (1996). 'Answer to Paul Farmer's "An Anthropology of Structural Violence"', *Current Anthropology* 45:3, 322.

Wacquant, L. (2008). *Urban Outcasts. A Comparative Sociology of Advanced Marginality* (Cambridge: Polity Press).

Wacquant, L., T. Slater and V. B. Pereira (2014). 'Territorial Stigmatization in Action', *Environment and Planning A: Economy and Space* 46:6, 1270–80.

Wichum, R. (2013). 'Security as Dispositif: Michel Foucault in the Field of Security', *Foucault Studies* 15, 164–71.

Wilcox, L. (2019). 'Bodies and embodiment in IR' in Edkins, J. (ed.) *Routledge Handbook of Critical International Relations* (London: Routledge).

Wirth, L. (1938). 'Urbanism as a way of life', *American Journal of Sociology* 44:1, 1–24.

Index

Index

EU authorised representative for GPSR:
Easy Access System Europe, Mustamäe tee 50,
10621 Tallinn, Estonia
gpsr.requests@easproject.com

www.ingramcontent.com/pod-product-compliance
Lightning Source LLC
Chambersburg PA
CBHW050630280326
41932CB00015B/2588